Close Relationships

Close Relationships

Incest and Inbreeding in Classical Arabic Literature

GEERT JAN VAN GELDER

I.B. TAURIS
LONDON · NEW YORK

Published in 2005 by I.B. Tauris & Co. Ltd.
6 Salem Road, London W2 4BU
175 Fifth Avenue, New York NY 10010
www.ibtauris.com

In the United States of America and in Canada distributed by St Martins Press,
175 Fifth Avenue, New York NY 10010

Library of Middle East History 9

ISBN: 1 85043 855 2
EAN: 978 1 85043 855 7

A full CIP record for this book is available from the British Library
A full CIP record for this book is available from the Library of Congress

Library of Congress catalog card: available

Printed and bound in Great Britain by TJ International Ltd, Padstow, Cornwall from camera-ready copy edited and supplied by the author

CONTENTS

Abbreviations and Conventions vii

Transliteration vii

Acknowledgements ix

Introduction 1

Chapter One: Stunted Nobility 7
Ancient Ignorance? 7
Arab Awareness: The Root ḌWY 11
A Paradox 14
Seeking a Sperm-Donor in Pre-Islamic Arabia 19
Seeking Explanations 22
Verses on Horses, Camels, and People 28
The Silence of the Doctors 34

Chapter Two: Magian Marriages 36
Zoroastrian Close-Kin Marriages 36
Arabs v. Persians: A Key Text by Abū Ḥayyān al-Tawḥīdī 39
Some Comments on al-Tawḥīdī's Text 44
Pre-Islamic Arabs with Magian Leanings 52
Arabic Historiography on the Majūs 55
Zoroastrian Marriage as an Arabic Invective Motif 60
A Digression: Muslim Anti-Jewish Polemics 62
Magian Marriage in Lampoons, Love Poetry, and Literary Riddles 66
Muslim Heresiography on the Zoroastrians 72
Incest in Sects 75

Chapter Three: Islamic Incest Regulations 78
Pre-Islamic Ignorance 78
Forbidden Degrees in the Qur'an 81
Stepmothers 84
Mothers, Daughters, Sisters, Aunts, Nieces et aliae 89
Milk-Relationship 93
Mothers-in-Law 96
Stepdaughters and Daughters-in-Law 96
Two Sisters 98
Foundlings 102
Punishments 103
Islamic Law and Zoroastrian Marriage 109

Justifications 112
Mother's Back 118
Revealing One's Adornment 119
An Early Case of Necessary Incest 120

Chapter Four: Incest in Legend and Literature 122
An Early Case of Necessary Incest (Continued) 122
Canaan/Kanᶜān and Nimrod/Namrūd 125
Stories of Prophets 126
Sisterly Love 128
Lampoons and Insults 129
Metaphorical Incest 136
Genealogical Puzzles 138
More Stories and Legends 143
Taᵓabbaṭa Sharran 143
Luqmān 144
A Bed-Trick with Compounded Incest in Baghdad 146
The Lovers of Fatḥ Alley, Baghdad 154
ᶜArūs al-ᶜArāᵓis 159
The Cohabiting Bedouin Siblings 160
Burning Love Between Siblings 162
Blood that Yearns for Blood 164
Father's Wives Again 166
Popular Epics 168
Dreams 172
Dreams Denoting Incest 173
Dreams About Incest 176

Epilogue 181

Notes 187

Bibliography 237

Index 269

Abbreviations and Conventions

AH	*Anno Hegirae*
b.	ibn ('son of'), when used between names
bt	bint or ibnat ('daughter of'), when used between names
EI^2	*The Encyclopaedia of Islam, New [= Second] Edition*
pl.	plural
Q	The Qur'an (followed by number of sura and number of 'verse').
reg.	*regnavit* ('reigned')
sg.	singular
s.v.	*sub voce* ('under the/that heading')
tr.	translation/translated by

Full bibliographical details are normally given in the Bibliography only; titles are usually shortened in notes by giving only the beginning or omitting the article. Dates are often given according to both the Islamic Era and the Christian Era (or 'Common Era', according to the rather silly oecumenically correct diction) as in 700/1300. If only one of these is given, it is the Christian Era, unless it is marked with AH. All translations are mine, unless indicated otherwise. Translations from the Qur'an are marked by guillemets (French quotation marks), to indicate the special status of the Qur'an in Islamic discourse. Medieval Arabic poets and writers are often extremely scurrilous and foul-mouthed; I have not tried to mask this by using Latin or by euphemistically softening the register. Note that an Arabic poet (one who produces Arabic poetry) is not necessarily an Arab poet, in the multi-ethnic civilization of medieval Islam. The usefulness of the Hodgsonian distinction between 'Islamicate' (society and culture) and 'Islamic' (religion), however, could not override my sense of euphony.

Transliteration

Although it is hoped that this book will be read or consulted by non-Arabists, I am enough of a philologist to abhor improperly transliterated Arabic in any work with scholarly pretension. Non-specialists should therefore ignore the many dots, dashes and other unfamiliar signs that clutter these pages. Arabic (as well as the occasional Persian) is transliterated according to the system employed in *The Encyclopaedia of Islam, New Edition*, with the following changes: *j* for *d̲j̲*, *q* for *ḳ*, no underlining of digraphs, an apostrophe to separate letters that might otherwise be taken as digraphs (e.g. *qālat'hu*), no apostrophe if *alif al-waṣl* is elided (*fī l-bayt, wa-khtartu* instead of *fi 'l-bayt, wa-'khtartu* or *wa-ikhtartu*), and no shortening of long vowels before two consonants (Abū l-Ḥasan, not Abu 'l-Ḥasan). A dot is used occasionally for an uncertain vowel. *Iʿrāb* (final short vowels expressing desinential inflection) is given sparingly, wherever helpful, in prose quotations, and fully in quotations from the Qur'an and poetry, observing the customary rules for words in pausal forms or rhyme. As a consequence, the feminine ending normally rendered as *-a* occasionally appears as *-ah*, when it forms a rhyme. In accordance with customary practice the final ending *-iyy* is rendered as *-ī* in *nisbas* such as al-Baghdādī and names such as ʿAlī; however, in ordinary nouns *-iyy* (e.g. *ḍāwiyy*) is distinguished from *-ī* (e.g. *ḍāwī*). Names and terms common in English are not transliterated according to this system (Qur'an, Mecca, Abbasids rather than Qurʾān, Makka, ʿAbbāsids).

The transliteration of pre-Islamic forms of Persian, including Pahlavi, languages I do not master, seems utterly chaotic to me. I have followed whichever authority I happened to quote.

Acknowledgements

Some close relations and colleagues have been exposed to smaller or larger parts of this book, in written or oral form. I have benefited from their comments, especially since I have ventured into territories that were unfamiliar to me. If my inexperience is still visible there, it is not their fault. I am indebted for helpful remarks and corrections to Christoph Melchert, Chase Robinson, Donald Richards, Marlé Hammond, Fritz Zimmermann, Emilie Savage-Smith, Gerald Hawting, Robert Gleave, Charles Burnett, Matthew Caswell, Paul Dresch, and especially Ulrich Marzolph, Everett Rowson and Edmund Bosworth. My indebtedness to my former student Irma van der Post is explained in the Introduction. Finally, my closest relationship (of affinity, not consanguinity) has been, as always, with Sheila Ottway, who as always has polished my English.

Introduction

Large claims have been and are being made for the importance of incest. According to the blurb of a recent work on incest and the early English novel, 'incest lies at the discursive center of modern normative conceptions of gender, sexuality, desire, and power.'[1] If the reader agrees with this, or likes the way it is put, the present book is probably not for him or her. Even if incest were really such a central concept in European society and literature—and reading Otto Rank's *Das Inzest-Motif in Dichtung und Sage* (*The Incest Theme in Literature and Legend*), published in 1912, would almost convince one of this if one accepted his premises—I believe that the same is not true in medieval Arab and Islamic society, where it was a marginal concept (which is one of the reasons why I was attracted to the subject). If am wrong, then I hope that this book will at least serve as a useful first attempt to bring together material from widely different sources, with Arabic textual facts and opinions on the related topics of incest and inbreeding. To my knowledge, no comprehensive monograph on these subjects in medieval Arab and Islamic culture has ever been written, even though some important studies of a more limited scope have appeared, particularly by specialists in Islamic law or anthropology.

Inbreeding and incest are two very different things. The former is above all a biological concept. The rate of inbreeding in a population can be measured objectively and descriptive methods can be applied irrespective of species, race or society, animal or human. It is a process, for it refers not to one particular relationship but to a series and a pattern of relationships. It is a gradual thing: there is no exact point where it ends or begins. Incest, on the other hand, is a cultural concept, the meaning of which depends on criteria that differ from society to society. It is, usually, very precisely defined, and efforts are made to lay down exactly where it begins and where it ends. It is found only in human society. It is not a process but an occurrence.

The two concepts, however, are obviously closely related. Both have to do with kinship, the former with kinship in absolute, biological terms, the latter with kinship as perceived by human societies (in biological terms, there are no unrelated people if one goes back sufficiently far). In human society both are linked with norms and values; what would count as incest in one society may be a normal and accepted form of intermarriage in another. As a result the term incest is often used improperly or subjectively, as when one speaks of 'incestuous' marriages in ancient Iran or Roman Egypt, where next-of-kin marriage was legal and therefore no incest. Germaine Tillion, provocatively and wrongly, argues that 'throughout the Mediterranean world "incestuous marriage" is held to be the ideal marriage.'[2] She can only say this because she defines 'incest' as 'marriage with a very close relative belonging to your own lineage' and thus the system of cousin-marriage (that great male Mediterranean complot, according to her) is 'incest'. This will not do, of course.

The nature of the relationship between incest and inbreeding is among the objects of research in what is called sociobiology, or evolutionary biology, or evolutionary anthropology. Being neither a sociobiologist nor an anthropologist, but an Arabist with an interest in medieval literature, I shall steer away from making bold claims on inbreeding and incest in Arabic society, but mainly confine myself to what is found in medieval Arabic literature, letting the texts speak for themselves in numerous translated quotations. Yet I am sure that some sociologists and anthropologists will find that I am trespassing on their territory. Literature is here taken in a broad sense, including not only belles-lettres but historical, religious and legal texts. Of course I do not wish to imply that these texts, when they discuss incest or inbreeding, do not refer to realities in the life of the medieval Arabs or those who wrote in Arabic; but this study is mainly concerned with ideas and not with facts. To do full justice to the subjects of inbreeding and incest in Islam and Arabic literature it is not enough to be an Arabist specializing in literature: one ought to be a biologist, an anthropologist, a sociologist, a historian, an expert on Islamic doctrine and law, a literary critic or even, some will argue, a psychoanalyst. Specialists in literature, however, have rarely been daunted by such requirements; since literature may deal with any conceivable subject, they imagine that this is enough justification for venturing into all kinds of strange territory with only a minimum of trepidation. I am one of these. Although writing as an Arabist for fellow Arabists and Islamologists, I am aware (and hope) that anthropologists, students of comparative literature and others may be interested; therefore I have added some qualifications ('the well-known poet X') and explanations that will seem superfluous to some readers, for which I ask their indulgence.

With 'classical Arabic literature' I refer to pre-modern Arabic literature in general, not to texts written in Classical Arabic only, for vernacular or semi-vernacular texts are not in principle excluded. It is sometimes called 'medieval Arabic literature', because it conveniently includes what is conventionally considered medieval in Europe. Its beginning is not too difficult to define, since with very few (and sometimes questionable) exceptions the most ancient Arabic texts are not older than the sixth century AD. The end is harder to determine but is generally placed somewhere in the nineteenth century, although locally and in some milieus the pre-modern period persisted considerably longer.

Since the Zoroastrian custom of next-of-kin marriage is a recurrent topic in Islamic discussions of incest, I should not have limited myself to Arabic texts but ought to have included Persian literature. If I venture into this field only very occasionally, it is because of a lack of competence and not because it is unimportant. Yet I am under the impression that the topic is not a popular one in Persian literature, which is perhaps understandable. A notable exception is the romance of Wīs and Rāmīn (on which see the Epilogue), but I do not believe that one can use this example to show that next-of-kin marriage 'has symbolically been the obsession of Muslim Iran'.[3]

The germ of this study was sown many years ago, in the late 'eighties, when a student of mine at the University of Groningen in the Netherlands, Irma van der Post, wrote an undergraduate dissertation[4] on incest and inbreeding in the Arab world, a topic chosen by her. Collecting material, especially on incest, was understandably not without problems. Having helped her with references found in the classical heritage, I have subsequently jotted down any relevant bit that I came across. After lying dormant for years the scattered material has been fashioned into some kind of shape; here I acknowledge my debt to her for inspiring this book.

The difficulty encountered by Ms van der Post was unevenly distributed. As is very well known, a form of inbreeding that is common in traditional Middle Eastern societies (though not as common as is often assumed) is the pervasive custom of the *bint ʿamm* marriage, or marriage of a man with his father's brother's daughter; an anthropologist might speak of patrilateral parallel cousin marriage. Anthropological and sociological studies of this phenomenon are rife. On the other hand, it is perhaps not surprising that data on the occurrence of incest and studies of this delicate subject are extremely scanty. It is often ignored or dismissed as not existing in the modern Middle East. Malek Chebel, in his erratic and sloppy but rich *Encyclopédie de l'amour en Islam*, cannot be called a prude, yet he tells us that 'Condemned by the Qur'an, the crime of incest is banned from the local customs of Arabs and Muslims',[5] thus falling victim, perhaps even willingly and consciously, to the fallacy that because the Qur'an (or 'Islam', whatever that may be) says something, it must therefore be the case. In a separate and equally brief entry that follows, on 'sisterly incest' (*inceste sororal*), Chebel remarks that folklore is rather silent or even mute on this topic, and goes on to quote from a French translation from *The Thousand and One Nights* in which a mildly sensual relationship between Shahrazād and her sister is suggested; it is not even erotic, let alone sexual, and one feels that Malek Chebel has been carried away by his imagination when he calls this incest. One could argue that the term incest in a strict sense implies sexual intercourse, in which case same-sex incest would be impossible. Chebel obviously takes it in a broader sense that includes forms of forbidden physical contact with sexual connotations. The adjective 'incestuous' is often used metaphorically, not in the biological sense, indicating a measure of intimacy that is unhealthy in the writer's view. The same word is abused when, for instance, a recent work on Saddam Hussein claims that it is 'difficult to imagine a more incestuous arrangement dominating the ruling elite of a modern republic',[6] referring to a form of intermarrying that is, by Middle Eastern standards, by no means unusual and certainly not incestuous.[7]

Precise definitions and descriptions of sexual matters are difficult enough in English, and may be more difficult in Arabic, which does not seem to have words for either incest or inbreeding. An authoritative modern English-Arabic dictionary ponderously renders 'incest' as *irtikāb al-zinā bayn al-maḥārim (mathalan bayn al-akh wa-l-ukht); ghashayān al-maḥārim*, 'committing fornication between unmarriageable members of family (e.g. between brother and sister); sexual intercourse with unmarriageable members of family' and 'inbreeding' as *tazāwuj al-aqārib*, 'intermarriage of relatives'; 'inbred' is circumscribed as *salīl al-tazāwuj bayn al-aqārib li-ʿiddat al-ajyāl*, 'offspring of intermarriage between relatives during a number of generations'.[8] Having said that Arabic has no term for incest, I must admit that a modern lexicographer, in addition to some circumlocutions, gives *rahaq* as the equivalent of 'incest' in a couple of English-Arabic dictionaries.[9] This looks like a conscious attempt to reintroduce a 'heritage' word into modern Arabic. It is true that some old dictionaries define *rahaq* as 'copulation with non-marriageable relations, as a result of drinking wine or something like it'.[10] The problem is that these same dictionaries attach a plethora of meanings to the word *rahaq*, including stupidity, lying, troublemaking, injustice, pride, sin, error, precipitance, weakness, perdition, and that to my knowledge the word has never been used in a context that unambiguously refers to incest. The few verses quoted in support by the lexicographers certainly are not convincing: Ibn Aḥmar praises the governor al-Nuʿmān ibn Bashīr (d. 65/684) as 'a bright star splitting the darkness; no *rahaq* is in him, nor miserliness'. Here the word *rahaq* obviously means something like 'injustice': it would be odd indeed if the governor was praised for not copulating with his mother or daughter.[11]

Incest, literally or at least etymologically 'unchaste', is by no means the same as a union that is unchaste. Neither does it always imply sexual intercourse between two people who are too closely related biologically. The three cases discussed most often in Islamic texts on unmarriageable members of family are, first, marriage to one's stepmother; second, marriage to two sisters simultaneously; and third, marriage between partners that have been suckled together. In none of these cases are the sexual partners necessarily related genetically: the first two concern affinity (*ṣihr*) rather than consanguinity (*nasab*). Both kinds may be called incest.

The lack of precise equivalents of incest and inbreeding in both pre-modern and contemporary Arabic does not mean, of course, that the concepts were unknown or suppressed. The ancient Greeks, too, seem to have lacked a word for incest, and surely nobody would maintain that they were unaware of or uninterested in the topic. In the case of incest, the key word in Arabic is *maḥram*, the plural of which, *maḥārim*, I have translated above, clumsily in turn, as 'unmarriageable members of family'. The word is derived from the well-known root *ḤRM* (familiar in English in the word harem), which is associated, in Arabic and in other Semitic languages such as Hebrew, with the notions of taboo, inviolability, or sacrosanctity. The root has a much wider denotation than incest or sexual relations. Anything forbidden in Islam is called *ḥarām* or *muḥarram*, and not every woman who is forbidden, *muḥarrama*, to a man is a *maḥram*, for any woman married to someone else is also forbidden, of course, as is any other woman if one is already married to the maximum number of four women. When applied to a person, *maḥram* means 'person being in a degree of consanguinity precluding marriage', to quote another dictionary,[12] although this definition is too narrow because it leaves out the matters of milk-relationship and affinity. Of course, the relationship is reciprocal: if a certain woman is a man's *maḥram*, the man is the woman's *maḥram*. If the word is usually applied to females, this is because Islamic discourse is traditionally male-oriented. The implied readers of the Qur'an and the legal books are men, if not exclusively, then at least primarily, and it is they who are addressed or taken as the norm. Incest regulations specify the categories that are marriageable and unmarriageable to a man; the female corollary rules are easily deduced but rarely made explicit.

The oldest Arabic prose text, the Qur'an, already has rules about incest, and throughout the centuries specialists in Islamic law have interpreted and defined the Qur'anic rules, discussing the finer points and difficult cases, real or imaginary, in detail. This will be discussed in Chapter Three. Marriage rules help to define a religion and a culture; the alleged practices of the Zoroastrians are a recurrent motif in Arabic literature, used to distinguish between 'us' and 'them',[13] and heretical sects are not rarely credited with a sexual free-for-all or holding women as communal sex objects, with all the implications of possible incest. Chapter Two will deal with this in some detail. Incest, moreover, is a not uncommon motif in stories, legends and tales, found universally on earth. Arabic literature is no exception; it is the topic of Chapter Four. Since literature may deal with any topic including those that form the principal subjects of the other chapters, the division into chapters cannot be neat. Rather than as a defect, I should like to see the occasional overlap between them and the lack of clear boundaries as a necessary corollary and even desirable evidence of the interdependence of the several fields of discussion. In some treatments of incest in literature the material is organized by the kind of incest (mothers and sons, fathers and daughters, brother and sister, etc.).[14] I have not done so, being less concerned with precise genetic relationships than with motivations and attitudes. Lot's daughters slept with their father as did Ovid's Myrrha, but they had very different motives: Lot's daughters were pragmatic and wanted offspring, Myrrha was passionately in love. Incest committed unknowingly is very different from conscious incest, in terms of Islamic law, morality, and narrative structure. However, a classification on the basis of motivation turned out to be impractical, since motives are not always provided, and therefore the chapter is organized largely by genre.

As for inbreeding, which forms the subject of Chapter One, in this book I am again not so much interested in describing facts as in attitudes towards it and its results. Much has been written by anthropologists on the marriage patterns and habits in the Arab, or Muslim, world, especially on marrying one's father's brother's daughter, traditionally the preferred marriage amongst Arabs, and I do not intend to add to this. Instead, I shall discuss the awareness of the conflict between cultural and biological considerations connected with marrying close relatives. The advantages are economic and social, in tightening bonds between members of a group, the disadvantages are physical, and each society finds its own solution to reconcile the conflicting tendencies that pull in opposite directions.

Chapter One: Stunted Nobility

Ancient Ignorance?

A Dutch scholar, B. H. Stricker, published in 1975 a short but richly documented monograph in Dutch on the incestuous practices ascribed to the ancient Egyptians, the Zoroastrian Persians, and other cultures.[1] Speaking about the Persians, he makes the following remarks:

> The ethical motive for incest was that of endogamy, the desire to banish foreign influence from one's family ... Incest exposes offspring of the first degree to the danger of congenital defects. This danger, however, can be demonstrated only with statistical means and it must be deemed out of the question that it could have been recognized in antiquity, in view of the social hygiene prevailing at the time.[2]
>
> Even though the genetic danger was not recognized, nevertheless incest was banned from society in antiquity. It is a still unresolved question why its reputation became so bad. Today it is thought that incestuous intercourse formed an impediment to a harmonious relationship in the family and the hierarchy of authority pursued in it, and thus was suppressed when family relationships became stronger. It is possible.[3]

The suggestion that the taboo on incest is not related to hereditary, congenital defects that may result, because these defects were not recognized, is surprising for two reasons.

Firstly, it shows a lack of understanding of how evolution, as explained by Darwinism and neo-Darwinism, works. Surely, it is by no means necessary that a population is aware of the reasons why a certain pattern of behaviour is beneficial or harmful. Populations that persist in practices unfavourable to their own survival simply succumb in the competition with other populations; successful populations do not necessarily survive because they know consciously that they are doing the right thing. It is evident to me that incest taboos in human cultures are above all the result of natural selection, and to a far lesser degree determined by ethical, moral, psychological, ritual, religious, social, or economical motives, which, if present, are largely secondary, and have arisen either unconsciously in a society as a result of the biological basis, or consciously among scholars and lawgivers, used as support or justification of existing tendencies. This does not mean necessarily that humans are biologically designed and genetically programmed to shun sexual relations with close relatives, but merely that groups with incest taboos have a better chance of survival. There are certainly indications that children growing up together in the same household, especially in the first two or three years of one's life, tend to avoid each other as sexual partners, a form of 'familiarity breeds contempt'. This was Westermarck's explanation of the origin of incest taboos, and his thesis has been confirmed by subsequent studies; only some diehards among Freudianists and stubborn opposers of the theory of evolutionary biology will reject it.[4] I do not maintain that *all* incest avoidance has the ultimate purpose of avoiding physical and mental degeneration: anthropologists have given several good reasons for out-marrying and exogamy other than the avoidance of the effects of inbreeding. Some forms of marriage forbidden in Islamic law, and thus often called incestuous, are not based on consanguinity (e.g. marriage with mother-in-law, or being married to two sisters simultaneously) and therefore cannot be explained simply by the 'Westermarck effect'. Nor do I maintain that all consanguineous incest avoidance has a genetic basis: this has not yet been proved conclusively, although the available evidence strongly suggests that it is largely so. The traditional opposition between nature and culture as being considered mainly responsible for human behaviour is in the process of being bridged in any case: the terms epigenetics and coevolution have been coined to denote the interdependence of nature and culture. Humans are the only species that has the ability, and sometimes the moral duty, to resist consciously its genetic make-up. Incest avoidance presents a particularly interesting case, which is why it is singled out for special attention in some recent works on evolutionary biology and enlightened anthropology.[5]

The detrimental consequences of inbreeding ('inbreeding depression') have often been played down in the past, but more recently biologists have demonstrated conclusively that this was wrong. Morbidity and mortality among offspring of uncle-niece unions in human society have been shown to be significantly higher than among non-inbred children, and the effect is clearly noticeable even in inbreeding between first cousins.[6] Persistent inbreeding on a large scale is harmful, even though in some cultures, in some periods, extreme forms of inbreeding were customary. Once it was thought that this could only have occurred on a limited scale, in certain privileged classes, such as among Pharaohs, Magians, or, on a more fictional level, Greek gods. It has been shown that, exceptionally, close marriages were not confined to a ruling elite but were more widespread through a population, such as happened in Egypt during the Graeco-Roman period.[7] There, brother—sister marriages were common, not among the indigenous Egyptians, but among the Greek or Roman colonizers of all classes. As a group, however, they can be considered a ruling elite who took to extremes their *apartheid* from the natives. Something similar happened in Roman Mesopotamia and Osrhoene, where parent—child marriages as well as sibling marriages seem to have occurred until the reign of Justinian.[8] It happens sometimes that particular features arise in a culture that run counter to the Darwinian concept of fitness, but such features do not last long. If incest avoidance is not strictly a universal of culture, then it is at least a near-universal.[9]

One ought to make a distinction between couplings of the first and second degree (parent with child or brother with sister) and those further apart, such as between first cousins: the former is far more dangerous from a genetic point of view, whereas the chance of a bad recessive gene appearing in the latter case is much smaller, and may be outweighed by economic and social advantages; inbreeding depression as a result of unions between second cousins are negligible. This explains why cousin marriage is very common in many societies, including the Arabs, who prefer unions with parallel cousins.[10] However, it is an exaggeration to say that 'there is nothing much wrong with marriage between cousins':[11] this may be true for individual cases, but if 'cousins' is interpreted as 'first cousins' and such marriages happen systematically and protractedly in a group, the effects are not negligible. As fig. 1 shows, it is theoretically possible for one person to have only four ancestors at any one level, going up an indefinite or even infinite number of generations, instead of the possible maximum of 2^n (two parents, four grandparents, eight great-grandparents, and so on). This case would be perfectly legal and incest-free according to Islamic regulations. All it needs is, in each generation, a pair of full brothers marrying a pair of first cousins who are full sisters (instead of parallel marriages of two brothers and two sisters in this example, crossed marriages between two pairs of siblings of opposite sex are also possible). As a result, Ego and his wife have the same grandparents, great-grandparents, great-great-grandparents, and so on.

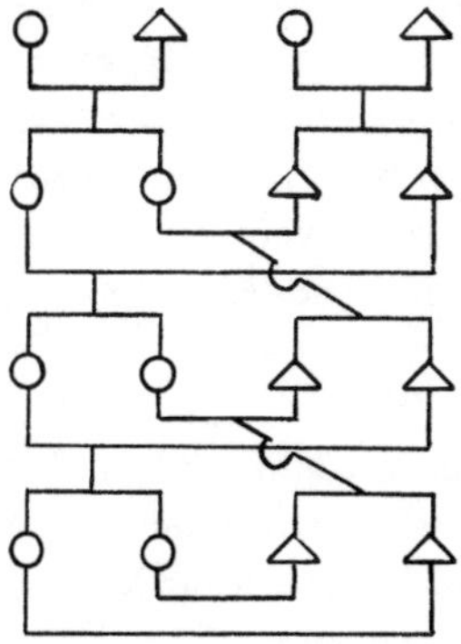

Fig. 1: extreme non-incestuous inbreeding

It is of course extremely unlikely that such a genealogical pattern would persist for more than two or three generations, yet the principle makes it obvious that Muslim religious law in itself does not offer full protection against inbreeding. As we shall see, Islamic law and Muslim customs are supplemented by wise advice, given religious sanction by putting it in the mouth of the Prophet or influential Muslims.

Anthropologists used to be wary of sociobiological explanations;[12] as for the fascinating but wholly misguided explanation offered by Freud and his followers, which was based on a series of unjustified assumptions that were both unprovable and unfalsifiable, the less said the better. Stricker was under the spell of influential anthropologists such as Durkheim, who sought the origins of the incest taboo in the ritual and religious role of blood, and who declared that it is 'very improbable that the Australians and the American Indians had a sort of anticipation of this theory [*viz.*, that close unions "weaken the race"] which did not see the light of day until much later.[13] In an article published in 1963, which is willing to admit inbreeding as lying behind the incest taboo, it was nevertheless argued that it is 'difficult to see, however, how primitive man would come to understand the connection between familial inbreeding and low net reproduction rate or the production of monstrosities'.[14]

The second reason why Stricker's opinions quoted above are surprising is that it can be shown that the allegedly benighted people in antiquity and other pre-modern cultures were not always unconscious of the relationship between physical degeneration and inbreeding or incest. It is true that monstrous births were often merely seen as the result of sexual irregularity in general, without a direct link to incest, as in the popular manual of sexual conduct entitled *Aristotle's Masterpiece.*[15] In medieval Europe, 'among all the contemporary explanations of these complex laws [on incest], conspicuous by its absence is any mention of the dangers of inbreeding'.[16] However, Robert Burton, writing in the early seventeenth century as a representative of traditional wisdom rather than modern science, said, speaking of congenital defects:

> For these reasons, belike, the Church and commonwealth, human and divine laws, have conspired to avoid hereditary diseases, forbidding such marriages as are any whit allied; and as Mercatus adviseth all families to take such, *si fieri possit, quae maxime distant natura* [if possible, as are most distant in nature], and to make choice of those that are most differing in complexion from them, if they love their own, and respect the common good.[17]

The Persian archbishop Īshōᶜbokht wrote his book on Christian law around AD 775-779 (the original Pahlavi Persian, now lost, was soon translated into

Syriac). Attacking Zoroastrian customs, he refers to the abnormalities often witnessed in offspring of marriages with mother or sister, such as weak limbs and eyes or peculiar skin colour.[18] In a study of sixty societies, chosen at random around the world, it turned out that twenty, or one third, showed awareness of some sort of the consequences of incest.[19] Most of the twenty cultures in question would have been called primitive by Stricker. If cultures from the past had been included, the ancient Greeks, in spite of the high intellectual level of their culture and their science, would not have counted among the enlightened cultures in this respect, although even they seem to have had an inkling of the connection between incest and bad offspring.[20] I shall now turn to another early society that was not included in the sample: that of the Arabs.

Arab Awareness: The Root ḌWY

The Arabs, even before the arrival of Islam, still in their 'ignorance'[21] as uncouth, illiterate, irreligious and uncivilized nomads and semi-nomads, were equally aware of the effects of inbreeding.[22] Perhaps it is not surprising in a people that excelled in breeding camels and horses. They knew (as did Aristotle[23]) that inbreeding may produce good results in generating good animals. If things go wrong and serious defects appear, this is no disaster, since the animals die or are slaughtered. Obviously, in human and humane society these breeding techniques cannot be applied unchanged, hence the restrictive rules of consanguinity. The Qur'anic incest regulations, on which more below in Chapter Three, are not given any justification related to eugenics, nor are clear biological explanations and justifications to be found in the vast exegetical and legal literature. Nevertheless, there are unequivocal texts that demonstrate an awareness of the matter.

These pre-Islamic or early Islamic texts, in verse and prose, are often difficult to date precisely. Somewhat arbitrarily, therefore, my starting-point is a maxim chosen not only because it is admirably short (one of these elegant conditional structures in Arabic that require a multiple of words in translation), but also because it is very common, and, moreover, frequently put in the mouth of the Prophet Muḥammad, although more often it is given anonymously, attributed to 'the Arabs', which usually refers to the Bedouin Arabs of the pre-Islamic and early Islamic periods: *Ightaribū lā tuḍwū* (Take strangers, then you will not produce stunted offspring!)[24]

The masculine plural imperative urges men to take 'strangers', that is wives from outside their own families (*gharāʾib*), rather than spouses from among their relatives (*qarāʾib*). It is a clear recommendation of out-marrying.[25] More interestingly, the remainder of the maxim provides a justification. It employs form IV of the root *ḌWY*, a root that is rare in Arabic. However, when it does occur, it is found so often in contexts similar to that of the quoted saying that one is practically forced to conclude that the pre-Islamic Bedouins, in spite of what Stricker would no doubt call their inferior 'social hygiene', apparently had a verb meaning 'to be stunted as a result of inbreeding'. This, at least, is how some early lexicographers defined it: '*ḍāwī*, that is someone born from a brother and sister, or from unmarriageable relations (*bayna dhawī l-maḥārim*)';[26] '*ḍawiya*: to be weak as a result of closeness of lineage (*taqārub al-nasab*)';[27] '*ḍawā* means smallness of the body of someone born, because of closeness of lineage of his parents (*taqārub nasab abawayhi*)'.[28] Only rarely does one come across the root in the pre- or early Islamic periods without a clear reference, explicit or implicit, to genetic disposition. Among the exceptions is an anonymous line on food 'that fills out the flesh of scrawny man'.[29] Ruʾba ibn al-ʿAjjāj (d. *c.* 145/762) says, eulogizing his patron, 'I am no weakling (*lastu aḍwā*) now that Bilāl is on my side'.[30] Al-Jāḥiẓ says mockingly, 'If only I were shorter than you, or scrawnier (*aḍwā*), or punier or weaker'.[31] The verb is sometimes used metaphorically: the dictionaries give the idiom *aḍwaytu l-amr*, 'I have bungled the matter';[32] Bahāʾ al-Dīn al-ʿĀmilī (d. 1030/1621) says in a poem, 'My heart is weakened (*wa-inniya ḍāwiya l-qalbi*)'.[33] There seem to be a few wholly unrelated senses to the root that will not concern us here. But clearly there is a very close connection between the verb and the concept of being congenitally stunted, and a digression on the root and its derivatives is in order.[34]

The causative form IV, used in the quoted saying on taking strangers as wives, is also found in a very similar saying attributed to the second caliph, ʿUmar ibn al-Khaṭṭāb (*reg.* 13-23/634-644): *Qad aḍwaytum fa-nkiḥū fī l-nazāʾiʿ* ('You have produced stunted offspring, therefore marry women from outside your tribe!')[35] The word *nazāʾiʿ*, plural of *nazīʿa*, literally means '(women) taken, or "plucked" away', which obviously refers to the old practice of forcibly procuring spouses by taking captives, often mentioned in poetry, as e.g. in the lines by Ḥātim al-Ṭāʾī:

> They did not [willingly] give us Taites their daughters in marriage;
> but we wooed them against their will with our swords.
> And with us captivity brought no abasement to them;
> and they neither toiled in making bread nor boiled the pot.
> But we commingled them with our noblest women, and they bore us
> fine sons, white of face [*i.e.* of pure descent].[36]

However, in the mouth of ʿUmar the word *nazāʾiʿ* is presumably to be taken figuratively. With these words the caliph addressed the Banū l-Sāʾib, 'the sons of al-Sāʾib'; unfortunately, the sources do not specify which family or clan is intended, nor do they inform us on the background and the consequences of ᶜUmar's words. In what looks like an elaboration of the same anecdote, ᶜUmar is more explicit:

> ᶜUmar (may God be pleased with him) once looked at some small-bodied (*ṣighār al-ajsām*) people of the tribe of Quraysh and said to them,
> —Why are you so small?
> They answered,
> —Our mothers were close relatives of our fathers.
> [ᶜUmar] said,
> —You have spoken the truth! Get yourself strangers (*ightaribū*) and marry among distant people (*buᶜadāʾ*), then produce children![37]

The root *ḌWY* also appears in form I (*ḍawiya*), as in the following verse, which is almost always quoted anonymously:

> A young man not born from a close cousin, father's brother's daughter,
> and thus not stunted (*yaḍwā*)—the issue (*radīd*) of close relatives is often stunted.[38]

Adjectival forms of the root *ḌWY* appear either as a participle, *ḍāwī* (indefinite *ḍāwⁱⁿ*), or, more frequently, in the form *ḍāwiyy*, of the rather uncommon adjectival morphological pattern *fāᶜūl*. The latter is found in a variant of the saying quoted above, attributed to Muḥammad: *Lā tankiḥū l-qarābata l-qarības fa-inna al-walada yukhlaqu ḍāwiyyan*, 'Do not marry close relatives, for the children will be created stunted.'[39]

Or an anonymous line of verse:

> Your efforts are all the more ridiculous since you are a stupid man,
> from stunted stock (*ḍāwiyyati l-aᶜrāq*) that breeds stupid sons.[40]

It is said that the very early poet ᶜAbīd ibn al-Abraṣ (first half of the sixth century) began making verse after he was unjustly derided by a man who mocked him in a few lines of *rajaz* when he saw ᶜAbīd sleeping under a tree, side by side with his sister Māwiyya (shortened to Mayya in the poem):

> There is ᶜAbīd, who has banged Mayya!
> I wish he had knocked her up with a baby boy;
> Then she would be pregnant and give birth to a runt (*ḍāwiyy*).[41]

The word applies to people and animals alike, including birds. Al-Jāḥiẓ (d. 255/868-9) notes that pigeon breeders keep a close eye on their mating 'and are apprehensive of the stuntedness (*ḍawā*) that might result from their pedigrees' being too close'.[42] In a book devoted to camels, or rather to Arabic words related to camels, and attributed to the philologian al-Aṣmaʿī (d. 216/831), we read,

> When a she-camel is closely related to the stallion and its offspring turns out to be stunted (*ḍāwiyyan*) as a result, one says *qad aḍwat ... iḍwāʾan qabīḥan*, 'she has produced a bad runt' (...). One says, 'he is badly stunted (*yaḍwā ḍawan shadīdan*)' when one is weak as a result of having closely related parents. It has been said, 'Seek strangers, then you will not produce stunted offspring', meaning 'Marry those that are only distantly related, so that the bones of your children will not be small'.[43]

The basic meaning of the root is also variously given as having thin bones or a puny body or being skinny (*huzāl, naḥāfa*). *Ḍāwiyy* is also explained as weak and no-good (*ḍāʿif fāsid*), which seems to involve moral as well as physical debility.[44] As near-synonyms some other, rather rare words are given, such as *ḥāriḍ*, which in turn is glossed as 'as good as dead (*alladhī qad qāraba l-halāk*)' and 'no good at all' (*alladhī lā khayr fīh*); or *mawdūn/mūdan*, the root of which (given either as *WDN* or as *ʾDN*) combines the ideas of shortening and being wet or moist; the verbal form *awdanat* is said to mean 'she gave birth to a child with a short neck and hands and narrow shoulders'. One authority equates *ḍawā* with 'weakness in body and judgement', adding that 'if *ḍawā* encompasses a child from all sides he will be *ḥāriḍ*, without intelligence (*lā ʿaql lahu*)', thus adding an intellectual aspect to the physical and moral aspects.[45] The anonymous verse quoted above, on the 'stupid man from stunted stock', makes the same connection. A certain Abū l-Ḥasan al-Anṣārī (late 4th/10th century) confirms that the Bedouin Arabs 'knew intuitively (*shaʿarū*) that the degeneration (*ḍawā*) that affects the body will spread to the mind (*sārⁱⁿ fī l-ʿuqūl*)'.[46]

In spite of the general association of the root *ḌWY* with inbreeding depression in early Arabic, it seems that in subsequent centuries the connection was often lost from sight by those, admittedly not many, who used words derived from the root, which came to denote being thin and puny in general. Apart from the few examples given above, one may consider a line of verse in one of the *Maqāmāt* of Badīʿ al-Zamān al-Hamadhānī (d. 398/1008), in a riddling description of a comb: 'Sweet, nicely shaped, scrawny (*ḍāwī*), abstemious'.[47] Obviously, there is no hint at inbreeding here.

A Paradox

In the light of all the negative connotations of the root *ḌWY* it seems at first sight odd to find a horse named Ḍāwiyy 'Runt', said to have belonged to the tribe Ghanī,[48] and another called Mawdūn, property of Mismaᶜ (or Shaybān) b. Shihāb.[49] It is easily explained in two ways, even though it is impossible to decide which of the two was the more important. It could be imagined that a negative name was given for apotropaic reasons, to ward off the evil eye. On the other hand, the name could be a proud token of the nobility of the horses in question. This sounds paradoxical, but similar boasts are made by people, not about their horses but about themselves. A relevant passage is found in a work by al-Jāḥiẓ, devoted to physical defects[50] and full of paradoxes, whereby an ailment or deformity is turned into an occasion for pride or praise.[51]

> It happens that a Bedouin is puny (*shakht*), skinny (*mahzūl*), scrawny (*muqarqam*), and slight (*ḍaʾīl*), but turns this into an indication of his noble origin and birth. Al-Aṣmaᶜī once said to a Bedouin boy, 'Why are you so weak and thin, with a small body, little, and skinny?' The boy replied, 'Glory has made me scrawny (*al-ᶜizzu qarqamanī*)'. The following lines of poetry have been quoted:
>
> She knew that we two were strangers,
> Two stunted ones (*ḍāwiyyān*) because of our noble descent.
>
> and
>
> Glory has made him scrawny and nobility has stunted him
> (*Qarqamahū l-ᶜizzu wa-aḍwāhu l-karam*[52]).
>
> The strange thing is not that one says that one's descent can make one stunted, but that one can say that glory can make one scrawny, since an early poet has said,
>
> A young man not born from a close cousin, father's brother's daughter,
> and thus not stunted (the issue of close relatives is often stunted).[53]
>
> And a poet of the tribe of Asad has said,
>
> I am no runt (*ḍāwiyy*) whose bones are shaky,[54]
> born from a line of Khālid after Khālid,[55]
> Whose mothers were nearer to his fathers,
> in one line of kinship, than a single span,
> Sons of sisters whom they made to mate with brothers,
> in a mutual marriage arrangement (*mushāghara*),
> so that the whole tribe is father to itself.[56]

> There is much of this. Being stunted is more commonly found among domestic animals (*bahā'im*) than among people. It is not strange that they speak about being stunted when offspring is repeatedly born within close relationships. But what is strange is that one could say 'Glory makes one scrawny', because when a Bedouin is afflicted with an ugly appearance or a defect, he is loath to confess to being lowly and weak. Therefore he uses it as an argument, to make people aware of what they cannot grasp from observation. This is an example of their cleverness and cunning.[57]

As one might expect, in normal circumstances a tall stature is considered a sign of nobility, as in an anonymous line in Abū Tammām's famous anthology entitled *al-Ḥamāsa*:

> She gave birth to him as a boy with straight bones [and he grew up]
> with his turban among the men like a banner.[58]

Or as in a line by Muslim ibn al-Walīd (d. 208/823):

> He stands as tall as a Rudaynī lance;
> all sword-straps are too short for him.[59]

It is a clear example of the paradox, of which al-Jāḥiẓ is so fond, that one may boast of physical defects on the ground that it is an indication of nobility. The word translated as 'glory' in the passage from al-Jāḥiẓ's *Burṣān* reinforces the paradox, because it could also mean 'power, strength'. The 'Bedouin boy' in this passage is identified in another work by al-Jāḥiẓ as a certain Abū l-Dhayyāl Shuways, who proudly identified himself as a true Arab by saying, among other things, that he cannot swim ('I sink faster than a stone'), and that his puniness is a sign of good breeding: 'Nothing but nobility has made me scrawny (*mā qarqamanī illā l-karam*).[60] The verb *qarqama* and its passive participle *muqarqam* are extremely rare; the latter is found in a *rajaz* couplet by an unknown poet:

> I complain to God of puny children (*ʿiyālan dardaqā*),
> scrawny ones (*muqarqamīn*), and an old evil-tempered wife.[61]

The word *muqarqam* is glossed in the sources as 'slow to grow up' or 'ill-fed', and a few times more precisely as 'what the Persians call *shīr-zada*', meaning a sucking child that does not accept the milk, and hence weak.[62] The latter would point to an acquired rather than congenital debility, but the line itself leaves the matter open. The paradox of stuntedness as a sign of nobility is felt in a remark in Ibn Manẓūr's great dictionary: 'The (Bedouin) Arabs maintain that a child of a man begot from his close relative will be stunted and skinny (*ḍāwiyyan naḥīfan*), but noble, stamped with the characteristics of his tribe'.[63] However, such boasts about one's own inbred physique are rare, and it is no coincidence that the translated passage contains more quotations in which the poet clearly recommends out-marrying than those in which the poet boasts of extreme in-marrying.[64] More examples are found in other sources:

> Our (grand)sons are the sons of our sons; but our daughters,
> their sons are the sons of unrelated men (*al-rijāl al-abāʿid*).[65]

> A lofty family has empowered me, and courage,
> and a maternal uncle like a naked star, from outside the tribe (*nazīʿ*).[66]

Ibn Qutayba (d. 276/889), quoting this line, explains: 'He means that his maternal uncle is no relative of his father, which could have made him stunted'. The poet Jarīr (d. 111/729) said on his son,

> Bilāl's mother has not disgraced him,
> his maternal and paternal uncles are unrelated.[67]

The verbal phrase 'has not disgraced him' (*lam tashinhū*) could also be translated as 'has not disfigured him': as so often, the aesthetic and the moral are difficult to distinguish from each other. The two brothers called 'the two Khālidīs' (al-Khālidiyyān, late 4th/10th century), who quote these lines in a passage on out-marrying in their poetic anthology *al-Ashbāh wa-l-naẓāʾir* ('Likes and Parallels'), find it necessary to explain that the second line is meant to have a positive sense, and add the following comment:

> He boasts that (the boy's) maternal and paternal uncles are not related, for the (Bedouin) Arabs maintain that strangers produce better offspring (*al-gharāʾib anjab*), and that the son of closely related parents may be stunted.[68]

The word *anjab* is the comparative of *najīb*, which is usually translated as 'high-born, of noble breed, aristocratic', said of people and horses or camels alike, or more generally as 'excellent, superior': physically and in terms of behaviour and character. It is in fact a fairly precise antonym of *ḍāwiyy*: the quality of being *najīb* is genetically innate and cannot be acquired by education, training or treatment: thus there is no verb **najjaba* 'to make noble', just as there is no verb **ḍawwā* 'to make stunted'; the fourth verbal form *anjaba* means 'to produce noble offspring', parallel with *aḍwā* 'to produce stunted, or degenerate, offspring'.

Aristocracy and physical excellence were of course thought to be closely linked. Excessive intermarriage could enhance one's aristocratic status in spite of the physical degeneration that may accompany it. The Bedouin who paradoxically boasted of his puny physique used the word *ʿizz*, 'glory' or 'high rank'; it is unlikely that he could have described himself as *najīb*.

Jarīr, who proudly mentioned his son Bilāl in the line quoted above, made a similar line on himself:

> A mother from outside the tribe (*ummun nazīʿatun*), from Shaybān, raised me:
> such is the kind made by women from outside, who have good offspring.[69]

An unknown Bedouin, quoted in Abū Tammām's *al-Ḥamāsa* said,

> O for a young man who attained the heights through his zeal,
> Whose father is not his mother's father's brother's son.[70]

That is, a man whose father and mother are not first cousins. Another nameless poet of the tribe Kināna said,

> I chose her in order to have noble offspring; she was a stranger. Then she brought him (i.e. a son) forth like a full moon, noble, a chief.[71]

Among the anonymous lines that explicitly condemn marrying cousins for eugenic reasons is the following:

> I avoided my paternal cousin, for she is a close relative,
> fearing that my son would turn out to be stunted.[72]

Al-Māwardī (d. 450/1058), who quotes this verse, comments: 'The Arabs used to prefer marriage with those distantly related, with strangers, because they thought that this would produce better children, with a more splendid constitution, and they avoided marrying in one's own family and relatives, thinking that this would harm the child's constitution'.[73] Another anonymous poet said,

> I warn everyone with far-reaching ambition:
> Do not let children marry their paternal cousins,
> For one will not escape stuntedness and sickliness;
> If you feed them they will not grow.[74]

We hear of a particularly bad example, unfortunately without details such as names, of a certain family that 'intermarried for four generations until they had become so weak that they had to crawl, unable to stand up'.[75] A great-grandson of the Prophet, Ḥasan b. Ḥasan b. ᶜAlī, said to his maternal grandfather Manẓūr b. Zabbān, 'I married the daughter of my paternal uncle al-Ḥusayn b. ᶜAlī.' Far from applauding this auspicious match, Manẓūr exclaims, 'A bad thing! Don't you know that if bloodlines meet they produce runts! (*idhā ltaqati l-arḥāmu aḍwat*). You ought to have married a stranger!'. Fortunately, a son, ᶜAbd Allāh, is living proof of the fact that the laws of heredity are by no means as rigid as the old man had feared, and he is pleased.[76] Interestingly, Manẓūr himself had married Mulayka bt Sinān who had been his father's wife—a forbidden union in Islam, which caused a little scandal; their daughter Khawla was Ḥasan ibn Ḥasan's mother.[77]

Seeking a Sperm Donor in Pre-Islamic Arabia

An often-discussed report on the forms of marriage in pre-Islamic Arabia is preserved in Tradition literature, on the sayings and deeds of the Prophet Muḥammad, but in this case going back to ᶜĀᵓisha, the Prophet's wife. In al-Bukhārī's near-canonical compilation *al-Ṣaḥīḥ* she is quoted as listing four types of *nikāḥ*. One of these corresponds with what became the Islamic standard form; in the three remaining forms a woman is involved with more than one man. One of them is described as follows:

> A man says to his wife, as soon as she is ritually clean after her menstruation, 'Send for So-and-So and ask him to copulate with you (*fa-stabḍiᶜī minhu*).'[78] Then her husband abstains from contact with her and does not touch her at all, until it is clear that she is pregnant from that man whom she asked to mate with. When her pregnancy is obvious, her husband may touch her again if he wishes. He only does this from a desire for noble offspring. This *nikāḥ* is called *nikāḥ al-istibḍāᶜ*.[79]

Since the woman remains married to her husband and the husband becomes the legal father of the child, one cannot properly speak of a form of 'marriage' between the woman and the stranger here: *nikāḥ* has its old meaning of 'sexual intercourse'. It is impossible to say how widespread this custom was; there is very little evidence apart from the quoted description. A pre-Islamic Sabaic votive text from South Arabia seems to speak of a childless woman's temporary union with a passing stranger, and R. B. Serjeant has connected this with the *istibḍāᶜ* 'marriage' of al-Bukhārī. 'No social anthropologist will find it surprising that a childless woman should seek to get offspring by a temporary mating with such a person', the advantage being that a passing stranger will not claim the rights of paternity.[80] Wilken, when discussing *istibḍāᶜ*, also takes it for granted that the woman is childless.[81] There seems to be a difference, however, in that al-Bukhārī does not speak of a childless couple taking desperate measures, but merely of the wish to produce good stock. Al-Bukhārī's passage has been used as evidence for matrilineal tendencies in early Arabia.[82] W. M. Watt thinks that in this passage 'the precautions to make sure that the child was procreated by the stranger sound like an Islamic rewriting of an old custom', in accordance with the principle that is also accepted in Islam: *al-walad li-l-firāsh*, 'the child belongs to the (marriage-)bed', meaning that legally a child is recognized as the husband's, irrespective of whether he is or is not the biological parent.[83] To traditional Muslim ears, this early version of procuring a sperm-donor surely sounds shocking, and it is true that it would only be accepted in a society where the status of the male and his virility was less important than traditional Islam will have it, and where paternity implied dominance and possession rather than biological parenthood, *pater* being distinguished from *genitor*. Nevertheless, the custom fits in with the general awareness of the early Arabs of the importance of genetic diversification. Watt is wrong in thinking that the insistence on ascertaining the stranger's biological paternity is a later rewriting, for therein lies precisely the point. The purpose of the custom is *najābat al-walad*, good quality offspring, and one may imagine that some care was taken in selecting a suitable sperm-donor. Ibn Ḥajar (d. 852/1449), in his commentary on al-Bukhārī, explains:

> That is, in order to acquire the qualities of that 'stud's' sperm (*iktisāban min māʾ al-faḥl*), because they asked this from their leaders and chiefs, excelling in bravery, generosity/nobility (*karam*), etc.[84]

However, *najāba* is not the same as bravery and generosity, as some modern commentators too, writing on this passage, will have it;[85] it denotes a general soundness of body and mind, the opposite of *ḍawā*. Those who took recourse to this form of 'marriage' would have known that any unrelated stranger would have been better than a kinsman, however brave or generous. The justification given in the report shows that good quality offspring is sought and does not suggest that it is the last recourse of an infertile or impotent husband in order to get any offspring at all. Moreover, it is done openly and the story of the sister of the legendary Luqmān, who tricked him into her bed to get clever sons,[86] cannot be used as an example of *istibḍāʿ* in the sense it has in ʿĀʾisha's report, as does al-Tarmānīnī in his study of early Arab marriage.[87]

The Bedouin Arabs were not alone in being aware of the biological advantages of out-marrying, if we are to believe what the great traveller and encyclopedist al-Masʿūdī (d. 345/956) says of the Chinese, whom he describes generally very positively:

> A man traces his lineage back to fifty generations, more or less, until he reaches the ancestor of his clan.[88] A member of a clan (*fakhidh*) will not marry anyone belonging to it. This is equivalent to someone from Muḍar marrying someone from Rabīʿa or *vice versa*, or from Kahlān marrying from Ḥimyar or *vice versa*.[89] They maintain that therein lies the health of the offspring and a good constitution, and that it is healthier for the sake of survival and a long life.[90]

The extreme lineage-consciousness of traditional Chinese society is well-known. Al-Masʿūdī does not connect these views attributed to the Chinese with the Bedouin ideas on *ḍawā*. He seems to be somewhat sceptical ('they maintain') but this concerns probably not the principle itself but the excessive form of exogamy it takes here. Customs such as *istibḍāʿ* are found among various peoples[91] and some of these were known to the Muslim Arabs, to whom such practices must have been more distasteful than the excessive Chinese strictness. The earliest Arabic dictionary, attributed to al-Khalīl ibn Aḥmad (d. 175/791), mentions that 'when the pagans (*ʿulūj*) of Kabul see a stout and handsome (*jasīm jamīl*) Arab they leave him alone with their women, hoping that a child like him will be born among them.' This practice he calls *istifḥāl*, literally 'procuring a stallion, or stud'.[92] A similar (or perhaps the very same) practice among the Central Asian Kharlukh or Qarluq Turks was reported by the tenth-century traveller Abū Dulaf Misʿar ibn Muhalhil, who witnessed women coming to meet an arriving caravan: a married woman would take home any man who pleased her, while her menfolk would look after him well and her husband would temporarily abstain from approaching her.[93] Exceptionally, such customs are found in the lands of Islam. Ibn al-Mujāwir (d. 690/1291), geographer and anthropologist of Southern Arabia with a distinct taste for the salacious, describes similar hospitality towards strangers in the area between Mecca and Yemen among one particular tribe (called al-Bahīmiyya, a name that would translate as 'the Bestial Ones', which may not be a coincidence): 'A husband would say to his wife, "Come, honour our guest!", upon which she would go and sleep in the guest's lap until morning, without any fear or caution. The following morning everybody would get up and do business as usual.'[94] Naturally, the Muslim travellers and geographers ascribe such deplorable foreign customs to the depravity of the women and the lack of honour on the part of the men. Only in the case of the pre-Islamic Arabs do they recognize a noble intention: the procuring of good progeny.

Seeking Explanations

The biological explanation of the laws of genetic heredity was of course unknown until recent times. The Bedouin Arabs, from early on, knew the observable facts but did not even try to explain them, in spite of the countless fanciful 'scientific' explanations one finds in pre-modern cultures, Arab and non-Arab alike. It should be noted here that one strange and misguided non-genetic explanation of the saying 'Nothing but nobility has made me scrawny' is given in Ibn Manẓūr's great dictionary: 'It means: I am stunted only because of the nobility of my parents, and their generosity with food to others'.[95] It is true that generosity is hyperbolically praised in Arab lore and literature, but this would be driving it to excess. I have found only a few serious attempts at explaining the biological facts. One of the most revered theologians of Islam, al-Ghazālī (d. 505/1111) says, enumerating the conditions of a good marriage,

> Eighth, the girl should not stand in too close a relationship, for that gives few offspring.[96] The Prophet (God bless and preserve him) said, 'Do not marry close relatives, for the children will be created stunted (*ḍāwiyyan*)', i.e. scrawny (*naḥīfan*). That is because of its effect on the weakening of sexual desire, for this is aroused according to the strength of feeling and touching, and this feeling is stronger in the case of something strange and novel. Whatever is familiar and has been seen for a long period will weaken feeling, so that it cannot reach full perfection and one is not under its influence, nor is sexual desire aroused.[97]

Al-Ghazālī, in this passage, gives a glum picture of marriage, which according to his reasoning would necessarily deteriorate sexually over the years; but perhaps this is not what the author intends. It is worth noting that he is not talking about incest regulations here. His 18th-century commentator, Murtaḍā al-Zabīdī, even interprets the words *al-qarāba al-qarība*, which I have rendered as 'too close a relationship', not in the genealogical but in the plainly local sense: 'raised in a place close to the other, where they can see each other'. The Arabic root QRB is ambiguous, implying nearness of any kind, although normally the word *qarāba* refers to kinship. Al-Zabīdī, who unwittingly anticipates Westermarck in suggesting proximity rather than kinship as lying at the basis of incest avoidance, adds that the diminishing of sexual drive in such cases 'is well known among the Arabs; indeed, everybody knows this'.[98] A popular encyclopedia from the twelfth century gives a summary of al-Ghazālī's words, but adds one phrase not found in al-Ghazālī: 'It is said that the reason is shame (or modesty, *al-ḥayāʾ*), for near-relatives are ashamed of each other, and sexual desire is therefore weak. God knows best'.[99] Al-Tijānī (d. after 709/1309), in his work on erotics, also brings in the element of shame: a close relative cannot please as much as a stranger, because a relative has been seen too often, and

> bashfulness and embarrassment may occur, to the extent that libido is weakened; and it is only when libido is complete that the child is formed perfectly, and its strength is complete. That is why they say 'He who is ashamed of his wife will not produce good children'.[100]

A popular saying recorded in the large anthology of prose by al-Ābī (d. 421/1030) states that 'He who is ashamed of his cousin (father's brother's daughter) will have children in the Hereafter',[101] which sounds like a sweetened version of the matter-of-fact form the saying has in the well-known compilation of proverbs by al-Maydānī (d. 518/1124): 'He who is ashamed of his cousin will have no children born to him'.[102] This saying is no recommendation of out-marrying; it takes it almost for granted that one's spouse is one's *bint ʿamm* (and it happens that this phrase is used as a synonym of 'spouse' even when it does not literally refer to a father's brother's daughter). It is striking, in any case, that a saying about shame for one's wife uses precisely this phrase, rather than *zawj* or other words for 'spouse'.

The famous preacher and theologian Ibn al-Jawzī (d. 579/1200) also says that libido is weakened if the partner is too familiar. Sexual pleasure was created to urge people to make sure of engendering children, he explains. Procreation is optimal when all the semen is ejaculated; it is bad to store it or to excrete it only partly, which happens when the libido is not strong enough. 'Therefore', he adds,

> it is bad to marry relatives, for this prevents the soul from being relaxed[103], so that one imagines that one is marrying part of oneself;[104] and marrying strangers is applauded. In this manner these harmful excretions[105] are expelled as much as possible, by marrying someone novel.[106]

Together, these passages provide an interesting psychological explanation which, even though mistaken in positing a direct link between affects and genetic laws of procreation, contains a grain of truth, for it has been demonstrated that growing up together—being potty-trained together, one might say—in some intimacy and physical interaction, in a nuclear family, kibbutz or commune, normally forms some kind of impediment to sexual attraction after puberty. The critical period for this 'negative imprinting' seems to be the first thirty months of one's life, according to the persuasive research of Arthur P. Wolf.[107] The relationship between growing up together in early childhood and later lack of sexual attraction had already been posited by Edward Westermarck in his important study of marriage.[108] The mechanism of this 'Westermarck effect' is not yet clear; there may be unrecognized stimuli that trigger it, but whether these are visual or olfactory, or based on common experiences and habits, is unknown. Freud and his followers realized, of course, that Westermarck's thesis, if true, would be lethal to the Freudian explanation of incest and its taboo. The popularity, among scholars and laymen in the West, of the theory behind what is called the 'Oedipus complex' is among the more astonishing aberrations of the twentieth century.[109]

Those who were unaware of the biological cause and effects of the incest taboo, or were unwilling to consider them, have put forward various psychological explanations for the incest taboo, among them the fact that the sexual act is regularly thought of as an aggressive and inimical act on the part of the male, as is abundantly clear from the vocabulary and imagery of sex in any language, Arabic being no exception. This aggression ought not be directed at those with whom one has developed friendly relationships during childhood.[110] One might consider this a rather bleak view of sex, which one hopes has been outgrown in modern times, but it might offer some insight into the origins of the incest taboos. Some have been tempted to conclude that 'true' love and sexual desire are two different things, and the equation of chaste love with true love is a commonplace in the so-called ᶜUdhrite love stories and poems, in which love is chaste and consummation not hoped for, or even spurned when the opportunity offers itself.

The opposite opinion has been expressed by others, such as the theologian Ibn Ḥazm (d. 456/1064), not in his famous book on love *Ṭawq al-ḥamāma* (*The Ring of the Dove*) but in his ethical treatise *Fī mudāwāt al-nufūs wa-tahdhīb al-akhlāq* ('On Curing the Soul and Refining the Character'). There he argues that love in all its forms is of one kind (*jins wāḥid*), and the various gradations of love are proportionate to one aspiration (*ṭamaᶜ*), which may be weaker or stronger according to the customs of one's community:

> We find that those who allow marrying strange women are not content with what will satisfy those who forbid outmarrying. The love of the former will not stop there, whereas the love of those who do not desire it (viz. outmarrying) will stop there. Similarly, we find that those who allow marrying one's daughter or one's niece, such as the Zoroastrians and the Jews, will have no qualms about loving them, unlike Muslims. Rather, we find that these two groups fall passionately in love with a daughter or a niece, just as a Muslim falls passionately in love with those he wishes to commingle with in copulation. But we do not find a Muslim who goes that far with either daughter or niece, even if they were fairer than the sun and if he were the most lecherous and amorous person on earth. In the rare cases that this is found to happen, it invariably concerns someone whose religion has become corrupt so that his inhibition (*rādiᶜ*) has been

> removed, his hopes have become extended and the door of his desire has been opened wide. However, in the case of a first cousin (father's brother's daughter) there is nothing that prevents a Muslim from becoming extremely fond of her, to the point of falling passionately in love and loving her more than his daughter or his niece, even if these are more beautiful than she. That is because he aspires to be united with his cousin, whereas he does not aspire to be united with either his daughter or his niece. We find that a Christian is not in danger of falling in love with his cousin, because he does not aspire to this, while nothing prevents him from loving his milk-sister,[111] because he may legally aspire to have her.[112]

This passage is an interesting analysis of how nurture may determine nature, of how biological drives are regulated by cultural institutions, be they imposed by religion or custom. Ibn Ḥazm, one of the great polemicists of Islam, is remarkably neutral here; while it goes without saying that he condemns Jewish, Zoroastrian and Christian marriage customs (as will be apparent below), in this passage he does not give any arguments, religious, ethical, social, or biological, why the Islamic rules are superior. The passage is unique in the extensive Arabic literature on the theory of love. Many authors discuss the various kinds of love, taking pains to distinguish between the numerous words for love, lust and longing and their gradations, such as *ḥubb, mawadda, hawā, ᶜishq, shaghaf, gharām, shahwa*, and dozens more. In the course of this they may mention the difference between love between parents and children or siblings on the one hand and love between true lovers on the other. 'A man may love (*yuḥibbu*) his father or his son', says Ibn al-Jawzī, contrasting the general *ḥubb* with the specific *ᶜishq*, 'but this will not induce him to self-destruction, unlike the passionate lover (*al-ᶜāshiq*).'[113] However, to my knowledge Ibn Ḥazm is the only one to offer some kind of explanation why these kinds of love are different, and how this may vary between different cultures. The collective authors of the *Epistles of the Sincere Brethren*, writing in the tenth century, also discuss the various kinds of love and passion. They offer an interesting explanation of the pederastic love that was so common in medieval Arab society. Whereas al-Jāḥiẓ had attributed it to the habit of the Persian armies, mainstay of the early Abbasids, of campaigning without their women (unlike the Arabs) and getting used to the proximity of male servants,[114] the Sincere Brethren argue that among civilized nations, such as the Persians, Greeks, Iraqis and Syrians, young boys, after being brought up by their fathers and mothers, are taught by teachers and tutors, who often conceive a strong attachment that may become sexual. 'Among peoples that are not concerned with the sciences, arts, and humaniora (*adab*), such as the Kurds, the (Bedouin) Arabs, the Negroes, and the Turks, this is rarely found and it is not in their nature to desire copulation with young men and to be in love with beardless boys.'[115] Passion and proximity are closely related, as they argue. However, this does not explain why the love between parents and children remains, with very few exceptions, non-sexual; incestuous passion is passed over in silence by the Sincere Brethren.

Notwithstanding the indications that Westermarck's thesis is correct, in Arabic literature one finds many romantic stories that seem to contradict the thesis of prepubescent love being incompatible with love at a later age. Laylā and her Fool, Majnūn, are merely the most famous of numerous couples. The stories are underpinned by many verses. Here is a small selection:

(1) I became attached to Laylā when she was a young innocent girl,
The shape of her breasts not yet visible to her playmates.

(2) I became attached to Salmā long ago,
A girl of eight years old, her breasts not yet formed.

(3) We got used to passion, and love became strong between us,
as infants, not yet two years old.

(4) I became attached to her as an infant,
and until today my love for her has been growing.

(5) He fell in love with Salmā when growing up,
with a love that dwelt in the heart and did not cease.

(6) I fell in love with you when growing up,
until I saw that my hair had become white.

(7) That is because I fell in love with you ardently
as an infant, which increased as I increased in age.[116]

Many more examples could be given. It is clear that this is a literary topos of love, not necessarily reflecting what happens in ordinary life. Moreover, all these lines of verse (with the possible exception of the one by al-Mukhtār ibn Wahb about whom nothing is known) are part of love-lyrics precisely in the ᶜUdhrite style, mentioned above. Love may be extreme, but it is like a love between brother and sister. The idea that the love between brother and sister, though not sexual, may exceed (or indeed usually exceeds) love between sexual partners is expressed by the words of ᶜAlī ibn Hishām (3rd/9th-century) on his slave-girl, the singer Mutayyam: 'She used to love me very much, with a love surpassing that of a sister for her brother'.[117] Thus these ᶜUdhrite verses and the stories spun around them could serve as confirmation of the Westermarck thesis, rather than as literary exceptions. A study of child-marriage in Kerala reports that boys and girls that are married as children happily play together, but around fourteen become 'shy and aloof',[118] and there seems to be some evidence that child marriages are less fertile.[119] The Taiwanese women raised as young children together with their future husbands, studied by Wolf, produced 40% fewer children and committed adultery far more frequently than those married without having grown up with their partners.[120] A study of Lebanese patrilateral parallel cousin marriage (the culturally preferred union with father's brother's daughter) showed a divorce rate that was four times as high as, and a fertility that was 20% lower than, non-FBD marriages.[121]

Against the stories of loving cousins, one also finds examples of unsuccessful couplings, especially those made for economic reasons. Ibn al-Jawzī tells a story of a man who married his father's brother's daughter because she was rich, even though he did not love her at all, and who secretly married 'a pretty young girl agreeable to my nature';[122] similar domestic troubles must have occurred frequently. An anonymous Arabic verse seems to confirm that true love is to be sought outside one's group:

> I abandoned my father's brother's daughters, for love led me
> to the daughter of a renowned man of the Persians.[123]

Out-marrying may have advantages other than purely genetic, and the Arabs were well aware of the domestic, social and political benefits. The famous pre-Islamic poet ᶜAmr ibn Kulthūm is said to have admonished his children on his death-bed in a prose 'testament', which ends with 'Do not marry in your tribe, for it leads to nasty hatred',[124] even though in another version he advocates the opposite: 'Marry the daughters of fathers' brothers to the sons of fathers' brothers, for if you pass them over and marry them to strangers, you will never find them a suitable match'.[125] Al-Māwardī, who as we saw mentions the physiological aspect, also gives a social justification of out-marrying: 'The Arabs always drew in strangers and reconciled enemies through marriage relationships (*muṣāhara*, implying drawing in women from outside), so that people's aversion would turn into familiarity and an enemy would become an ally. A relation by marriage (*ṣihr*) could develop into intimacy between two tribes, or an alliance between two clans.'[126] Social and genetic benefits could be combined since it was believed that physical resemblance is inherited especially through the maternal side. ᶜAbd al-Karīm al-Nahshalī (early 5th/11th century), after quoting some lines to that effect, adds that 'Kings are therefore desirous to enter into a marriage relationship with noble Arabs, since children often take after the mother's brother (*al-shabah yanzaᶜu ilā l-khāl kathīran*).'[127] Al-Thaᶜālibī discusses a saying expressing this idea, *ᶜirq al-khāl lā yanām*, 'the stock of the mother's brother does not sleep',[128] and quotes al-Jāḥiẓ as saying that 'Many scholars maintain that offspring take more after the stock of the mother's brother than after the father's brother (*ᶜirq al-khāl anzaᶜ min ᶜirq al-ᶜamm*)'. Whatever the benefits of in-marrying, popular wisdom provided some counterweight to the in-marrying trend. A standard collection of Arabic proverbs includes a brief saying, 'Strange women, not related women! (*al-nazāʾiᶜ* [var. *al-gharāʾib*] *lā l-qarāʾib*)'.[129] One is at liberty to provide one's own justification, domestic, genetic, or otherwise. Various interpretations, too, may be given to a saying attributed to the Prophet (on weak authority, it seems): 'He who marries in his own people is like someone who grows (or gathers?) herbage in his house (*al-nākiḥ fī qawmihi ka-l-muᶜashshib fī dārihi*).'[130] The *tertium comparationis* may not be wholly clear, but obviously it is something to avoid.

All these recommendations of out-marrying cannot hide the fact that in-marrying has always been popular among the Arabs, who generally like their marriages to be close for comfort and convenience, just as the rural English traditionally thought it 'better to wed over the mixen than over the moor'. The very frequency of the advice to marry outside one's group is an indication that the advice was often ignored. There are, after all, many obvious social and economic advantages of in-marrying. When Qays ibn Dharīḥ (d. 70/689), poet and famous early Arab lover, wanted to marry his beloved Lubnā, his father objected: 'Son, you should marry one of your paternal cousins, for they are more entitled to be yours.' The narrator adds: 'Dharīḥ possessed great wealth and was rich, so he did not want his son to move out to a strange woman'.[131]

Verses on Horses, Camels, and People

Precisely because marrying outside one's group was not quite the norm, the subject was recognized by some anthologists and critics as a distinct topic. In their verse anthology which loosely arranges poems and fragments thematically, the two al-Khālidī brothers, Abū Bakr Muḥammad (d. 380/990) and Abū ᶜUthmān Saᶜīd al-Khālidī (d. *c.* 390/1000), devote a passage to it, and similar passages are found in other anthologies such as al-Rāghib al-Iṣbahānī's *Muḥāḍarāt al-udabāʾ* ('Colloquies of the Cultured').[132] In general in Arabic literature, when human society and procreation are discussed, recommendations of out-marrying outnumber those that are in favour of in-marrying, no doubt because the latter was so common that no encouragement was needed. At the same time, strict regulations against incest, about which more in Chapter Three, prevented the most serious forms of degeneration that may result from excessive inbreeding. It is rather different in the case of breeding animals, where incest laws do not exist and where one can freely exploit the successful results of inbreeding while discarding the failures. Even here, we find hints that inbreeding is to be avoided, as in the lines on his camel by ᶜUmar ibn Lajaʾ (1st/7th century):

> When you feared two lineages (that would cause her) to produce runts (*nasabay iḍwāʾihā*),
> From the side of the mother and of her male ancestors,
> You looked with an examining eye, choosing
> An ash-coloured (male) built the way she was built.[133]

Against this, there are several instances where inbreeding is proudly flaunted. A line from one of the most famous poems in Arabic literature, the ode made on the Prophet Muḥammad by Kaᶜb b. Zuhayr, describes the poet's she-camel:

> A sturdy/lean one,[134] her brother being her father, of good breed,
> her paternal uncle being her maternal uncle
> (*Ḥarfun akhūhā abūhā min muhajjanatin*
> *wa-ᶜammuhā khāluhā ...)*[135]

This is one of the several genealogical puzzles that we shall encounter. The various solutions are discussed in a much later commentary.[136] The simplest one involves two matings between first-degree relatives:

> This happens, for instance, when a stallion (3) mates with his mother (2), so that she gives birth to a son (5) and a daughter (4); then the stallion (3) mates with the daughter (4), who gives birth to a son (6). Then the son (6) mates with his mother (4), who gives birth to a daughter (7), which is the she-camel [in Kaᶜb's line].

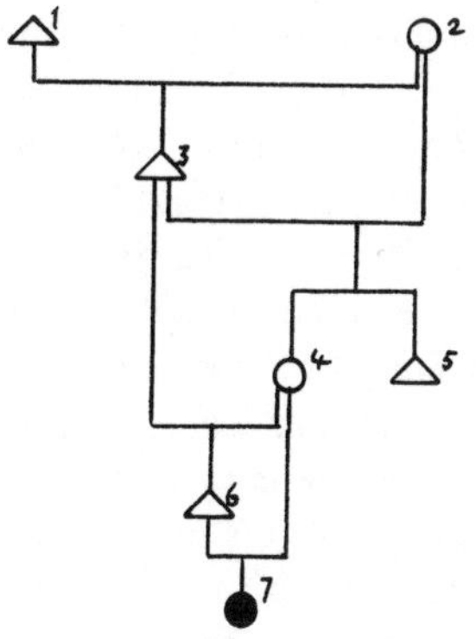

Fig. 2: Kaᶜb's noble camel (1)

Here (5) is the *khāl* of (7), being the brother of her mother, and also her *ʿamm*, because (3) is father of both (6) and of (5) and therefore (5) is a brother of her father (6). Another explanation, attributed to ʿUmāra ibn ʿAqīl (d. between 232/847 and 247/861), goes:

> This is when a male camel (1) mates with a she-camel (2), who gives birth to a son (4) and a daughter (3). Then this male camel (1) mates with his daughter (3), who gives birth to a male (5). The latter (5), when he has grown up, mates with its mother (3), who gives birth to a she-camel (6, i.e. Kaʿb's camel). Then he (5) is father and brother, and his brother (4) from the old stallion (1) is the maternal uncle of the younger female (6) and also her paternal uncle, because he is a brother of the father [since (4) and (5) have the same father (1) though different mothers] and a brother of the mother.[137]

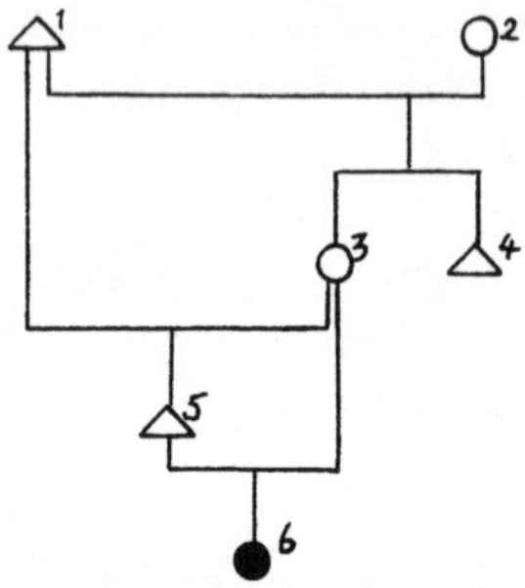

Fig. 3: Kaʿb's noble camel (2)

All this is an interesting exercise, but the assumption that the line is to be taken literally may be too rash. Al-Aṣmaʿī, correctly I think, explained the line as describing 'a noble she-camel, inbred because of her noble descent'.[138] For this he is criticized by a certain Abū l-Makārim, who sneered: 'Doesn't al-Aṣmaʿī know then ... that inbreeding (*tadākhul al-nasab wa-muqārabatuhu*) weakens a camel?'[139] Al-Suhaylī (d. 581/1285), in his commentary on the Ibn Hishām's biography of the Prophet, also denied inbreeding, saying that 'her father is her brother' is to be taken metaphorically, meaning that she as well as her father and brother are all of the same noble kind.[140] I believe that al-Aṣmaʿī was right, in assuming some degree of inbreeding. However, this does not necessarily mean that the line is to be taken at face value and that Kaʿb b. Zuhayr gives an exact picture of his mount's pedigree. What he did was in fact to lift almost the whole line, with the exception of the rhyme-word, from an older poet, Aws b. Ḥajar, who died shortly before the Hijra.[141] Kaʿb's father, the famous poet Zuhayr, was the *rāwī* (transmitter) of Aws b. Ḥajar, so the borrowing is easily explained.

In other words, the motif of 'inbreeding equals nobility' is something of a literary topos, admittedly rarely found, but nevertheless attested elsewhere. An anonymous line quoted in a ninth-century work describes a horse:

When they saw what the signs showed them,
  they called to each other: This is the noble steed we hoped for!
Its sire is a son of Zād al-Rakb ('Travellers' Provision'), and it is
  its sister's son: yes, with paternal and maternal uncles among noble horses.[142]

It is vain to try and reconstruct an exact pedigree, for Zād al-Rakb is a legendary horse that Solomon, son of David, according to the storytellers, once gave to the tribe of Azd;[143] Solomon's association with horses goes back to the Qur'an.[144] Al-Ushnāndānī (d. 288/901), who quotes these lines, veers between a literal and a freer interpretation, because after explaining 'it is its sister's son' literally as 'he means that its sister is its mother', and quoting the line by Aws (anonymously) in support, he then adds, '(the poet) says: the paternal and maternal uncles of this horse are descended from noble horses'. The same idea is found in a line by a certain ᶜUbayda ibn Rabīᶜa of the Banū Tamīm, on his mare:

The offspring of two winners who have begot him together;
  both, if their pedigree is traced, found in the strain of al-Kurāᶜ.[145]

The motif has survived in nineteenth-century Arabian poetry, which, though not in Classical Arabic, has preserved much of the old Bedouin diction and motifs. A certain Ibn Ḥuṣn says, describing his camel:

Its legs moving smoothly to suit a desert crosser's desire,
  Spaced at the axillae to avoid friction, sired by her mother's stud (*ibūha khālha*, literally, 'her father is her maternal uncle').[146]

In their innumerable verses on camels and horses, the Arabs were far more concerned with describing the outward appearance and the achievements of their own mount than with its pedigree. A treatise by Hishām ibn Muḥammad ibn al-Kalbī (d. *c.* 204/819) is promisingly entitled *Nasab al-khayl*, 'The Genealogy, or Pedigree, of Horses', but it cannot be compared with the great work on human Arabs and their genealogies by the same writer, *Jamharat ansāb al-ᶜArab*. The main purpose of this and similar works, it seems, is not to provide exact pedigrees but to record names of famous horses and their owners, the knowledge of which belonged to the repertory of lore about the early Arabs indispensable for erudite and literate people; it is for this reason that Ibn Rashīq incorporates two chapters, on human and equine names, in his work on poetry and poetics.[147] Yet it is likely that the Bedouin Arabs, who were obsessed with their own genealogies, also kept a mental record of their thoroughbred horses and camels, even though poetry offers little concrete evidence of this. In the early monograph on horses by Abū ᶜUbayda (d. 210/835), we read:

> A horse is preferably of noble and ancient stock, huge, and with known male and female ancestors, with a sound lineage that is free from base admixtures, descended from full-blood Arabs.[148]

He goes on to quote some lines of verse, such as one by the pre-Islamic poet ᶜAlqama who speaks of a horse 'with a pedigree known in the tribe',[149] and remarks that a good horse of unknown pedigree is called an 'outsider', *khārijī*.[150] In spite of all this, and in contrast to the elaborate genealogies of human Arabs, we do not possess such pedigrees for equine or camelid Arabs, only names of legendary mounts. If these really existed, they must have lived in the remote past; it is no coincidence that some common words meaning 'noble' also mean 'ancient' or 'deep-rooted': *ᶜatīq*, *ᶜarīq*, both found in the quotation from Abū ᶜUbayda given above. Matings between first- or second-degree relatives certainly are recorded, even though they are said to have occurred in the legendary past. Thus Dāḥis and al-Ghabrāᵓ, the famous horse and mare that are linked with the pre-Islamic war between the tribes of ᶜAbs and Dhubyān, were closely related: 'al-Ghabrāᵓ was the sister of Dāḥis's mother, and his sister from his father', meaning that Dāḥis's father (called Dhū l-ᶜUqqāl) had two daughters, al-Ghabrāᵓ and Jalwā, and impregnated the latter, begetting Dāḥis.[151] However, many seemingly precise indications of close-kin mating may be explained away if the words for paternal and maternal uncle, *ᶜamm* and *khāl*, are interpreted as paternal and maternal ancestor ('vertically' remote) or any relative ('horizontally' remote). Similarly, *ab(ū)* and *umm*, 'father (of)' and 'mother', are very often used in the sense of forefather or ancestor, and *ᶜamm* and *akh* 'brother' are customarily used to address any male in one's group, the former for someone older and the latter for someone of one's own generation. When the Umayyad Bedouin poet al-Ṣimma al-Qushayrī is said to have fallen in love with 'a woman of his clan, one of his father's brother's daughters, closely related'; the emphatic statement suggests that they were first cousins, but in fact their common ancestor was not a grandfather but a great-grandfather.[152] Relationships are not always as close as they seem.

Given that the extreme inbreeding suggested by Kaᶜb's famous line may be no more than a literary topos, the at first sight startling line by the famous Meccan poet ᶜUmar ibn Abī Rabīᶜa (d. 93/712 or 103/721) becomes less strange:

Her paternal uncle is her maternal uncle; if one day he is considered
he is her maternal uncle, when (also) considered her paternal uncle.[153]

What is startling is not so much the atrociously clumsy diction, unworthy of our poet (and making the poem somewhat suspect), as the fact that he is not speaking of a camel or horse, but of one of his numerous lady friends, who has left him. As the poem tells us, she is called Qurayba, 'a noble woman of the clan ᶜAbd Manāf', and her name seems to hint at the 'closeness' of the genealogy imputed to her.[154] It is obvious that the translation given above should be adapted: the poet only says that her parents are related, and 'noble from each side' as al-Baghdādī explains, not that she is the product of marriages that were clearly incestuous by Islamic standards. It is the same motif used in vaunting poetry, such as when a pre-Islamic poet of Hudhayl, Sāᶜida ibn Juᵓayya, says of his own tribe,

Close to each other are their lineages (*mutaqāribun ansābuhum*), glorious men ...[155]

The extreme opposite of 'incestuous' inbreeding is the mating of different species, producing hybrids. Although in popular lore and mythology the coupling of man or woman and animal or demon is a not uncommon theme (marriages between man and *jinniyya* or woman and *jinnī* are discussed by serious Islamic scholars), no hard facts exist about such semi-human hybrids. It is different in the animal world. Al-Jāḥiẓ, particularly interested in hybrids of all kinds, points out that such extreme forms of out-breeding may have positive as well as negative effects. It is true that a mule is infertile, yet its penis is bigger than that of a horse or donkey (al-Jāḥiẓ does not specify what advantage this may offer), and the *rāᶜibī* pigeon, a cross between a turtle-dove (*warashān*) and an ordinary pigeon (*ḥamāma*), is bigger than either. On the other hand, it inherits neither the homing instinct of its mother, nor the longevity of its father.[156] Crossing Bactrian (two-humped) camels with Arab dromedaries may result in offspring combining all the good qualities of both parents.[157] A hybrid kind of chicken called *khilāsī* ('bastard, mulatto'), explained as a cross between *muwallad* ('half-breed', in fact the origin of the word 'mulatto') and 'Indian' fowl, is said to have more flesh and fat.[158]

Naturally, al-Jāḥiẓ also discusses human 'bastards'. He reports the opinion of a certain Abū l-ᶜAbbās on the good qualities of women; the context leaves no doubt that their sexual habits and abilities are meant. The secret, we are told, lies in the product of two racially distant partners, such as coupling an Indian woman with a Khurāsānī man: 'Their offspring is pure gold!'[159] A cross, also called *khilāsī*, between an Abyssinian man (*ḥabashī*) and a white woman, says al-Jāḥiẓ, is usually bigger and stronger than his parents, whereas a cross between whites and Indians, called *baysarī*,[160] is smaller and weaker, but more handsome and elegant than the parents.[161] Thus there may be physical advantages of such unions, even though these are generally outweighed by the social disadvantages.[162]

The Silence of the Doctors

As far as I have been able to ascertain, medical treatises do not discuss inbreeding and its results, and rarely mention hereditary diseases as such.[163] ᶜAlī al-Ṭabarī (d. after 241/855) says that heredity (*warātha*) may be responsible for a disposition towards some diseases, such as *judhām* (a kind of leprosy) or hemorrhoids.[164] Following Galen, Abū Bakr al-Rāzī (d. 313/925 or 323/935) is aware that some diseases tend to run in a particular tribe or race (*qabīla wa-jins*); they are termed *amrāḍ jinsiyya*, 'congenital diseases', where 'congenital' does not so much mean 'acquired from birth' as 'shared among a *gens/jins*'.[165] Among diseases acquired through heredity he mentions *sabal* (an eye disease), leprosy (*baraṣ*), epilepsy (*ṣarᶜ*), and gout (*niqris*).[166] It is true that stunted growth is not properly a disease, and it is perhaps not strange that such a vague concept as *ḍawā* is not found in these medical handbooks, which cannot be expected to deal with incurable debilities. Stuntedness cannot be treated, it can only be masked to some extent, as an anonymous poet said, no doubt jokingly and hyperbolically, when he described a beaker with milk 'that would bring out the flesh of a stunted man (*al-rajul al-ḍawiyy*) / until you could see him with firm breasts (*nāhid al-thudiyy*)'.[167] It is striking, however, that when ᶜAlī al-Ṭabarī, for instance, speaks of the various defects found in newborn infants, he does not even consider the possibility of inbreeding: a short body is due either to the narrowness of the womb (for comparison he refers to fruit grown in a narrow bottle, or trees growing between rocks) or to the fact that the foetus was ill-fed in the womb.[168] Mostly, the physical characteristics of a newborn child are explained by processes in the womb, in addition to astrological influences, for those who believe in them. The poet Ibn al-Rūmī (d. 283/896) brings together the root *ḌWY* and the idea, common in Graeco-Islamic medicine, that an embryo is 'cooked' in the womb: 'People say: You are stunted (*ḍawīta*) badly; women's wombs have not cooked you well (*lam tunḍijka*)', but his epigram does not refer explicitly to inbreeding.[169] Even those texts that seem to have been composed to give Graeco-Islamic medicine a grounding in pre-Islamic medical wisdom do not, to my knowledge, yield anything relevant: I refer to the body of texts known as 'Prophetic medicine', *al-ṭibb al-nabawī*, which bases itself on sayings and deeds attributed to the Prophet Muḥammad, and the discussion of the pre-Islamic Arab al-Ḥārith ibn Kalada, who allegedly studied in Gondeshapur/Jundīshāpūr, the famous Sasanian centre of learning, and who convinced the initially contemptuous Sasanian emperor of his medical wisdom in a famous conversation.[170] The latter text looks like a promising occasion for finding allusions to Magian marriage customs, which are the subject of the following chapter. Such hopes, however, are quickly dashed. Both the 'Prophetic medicine' and al-Ḥārith give a good deal of attention to matters of sexual intercourse and marriage, but only with regard to the possible good and harmful effects this may have on the male (al-Ḥārith is particularly concerned with the bad effects of marrying an older woman); a bias that remains present in much of Arabo-Islamic medical texts.

Apparently, the Bedouins' knowledge of the effects of inbreeding was inherited by the lexicographers and all others who kept the pre-Islamic heritage alive, but was ignored by those who practised the modern science that was Graeco-Islamic medicine. A theory of inbreeding was never developed by the Arabs. It would have demanded a different outlook. The Arabs were wont to consider lineages, from top to bottom as it were, beginning with a forefather down to oneself and only taking into account a paternal line. In order to determine the degree of kinship, however, one ought to look at kindred rather than lineage, that is, from the bottom ('Ego') up, including all ancestors male and female for a number of generations. But this concept was of very limited practical relevance in Arab or Muslim society.

Chapter Two: Magian Marriages

Zoroastrian Close-Kin Marriages

The Graeco-Roman close-kin marriages in Egypt may well be the only well-documented example of its kind in the Near and Middle East, but it did not enter the collective memory of subsequent Middle Eastern cultures. In Arabic sources, at least, virtually nothing is recorded on this episode. The only, somewhat dubious, reference known to me[1] is the translation by Ḥunayn ibn Isḥāq (d. 260/873) of Ptolemy's *Tetrabiblos*, Book II, ch. 3, where he discusses the influences of the stars and planets on Egypt and neighbouring regions (including Arabia): 'Their men take many wives, and their women likewise take numerous men. They are obsessed with copulation and they cohabit with their sisters'.[2] The Egyptian physician Ibn Riḍwān (d. 453/1061), in his commentary on this text, remarks that intercourse with sisters is found among 'ancient customs, or religions (*madhāhib qadīma*)', but offers no further comments on the habits of his countrymen in the remote past.[3] It is different with the Persians. The Persian heritage in Islam is immense, even though few pre-Islamic books were translated into Arabic. The Zoroastrian next-of-kin marriages became a frequent polemical topos in Arabic.

To the pre-Islamic Sasanid king Artaxerxes, son of Papak, in Arabic sources called Ardashīr or Azdashīr ibn Bābak, is ascribed a 'testament' addressed to his subjects, in which he recommends in-marrying: 'Marry close kin, for that is closer to kinship (*amass li-l-raḥim*) and a stronger affirmation of relationship (*athbat li-l-nasab*).[4] Whatever its Iranian origin (if it has one), the Arabic wording seems to emphasize both the maternal and paternal sides, since the literal meaning of *raḥim* is 'womb' and *nasab* usually implies lineage through the male line. The saying is the precise opposite of ᶜAmr ibn Kulthūm's testament to his children, quoted in the preceding chapter, even though both use socio-political or domestic arguments. It is also the opposite of the maxim ascribed to the Prophet, 'Marry strangers, then you will not produce stunted offspring', which unequivocally uses the physiological, genetic argument.

The Arabs were aware of the existence, among the Zoroastrians (Majūs in Arabic, which from Old Persian through Greek reached English as 'Magus' and 'Magians'), of a custom called *khvaētvadatha* in the Avesta (in later stages such as Pahlavi *khētokdas*, *khwētōdas*, *khwētūdās*, or *khwēdōdah*, not forgetting *khwētūkdas* and *khwētukdādh*[5]), next-of-kin marriage, which was 'approved as a means of preserving the social exclusiveness, solidarity, and purity of descent of the upper classes'.[6] The principal Pahlavi texts are available in the English translation by Edward William West, in the series *The Sacred Books of the*

East.[7] Thus we find that 'the most perfectly righteous of the righteous is he who remains in the good religion of the Mazdayasnians, and continues the religious practice of next-of-kin marriage';[8] the custom 'will extirpate mortal sins';[9] 'the greatest good is liberality, and the second is truth and next-of-kin marriage';[10] the fourth most heinous sin is to break off a next-of-kin marriage;[11] to practise next-of-kin marriage is a means of 'deprecating' demons, the greatest kinds being 'the most intimate of them, those of father and daughter, son and she who bore him, and brother and sister';[12] the third of three customs which Zarathustra prescribed as the best is next-of-kin marriage, which, 'for the sake of the pure progress of your race, is the best of the actions of the living, which are provided for the proper begetting of children.'[13] A long defence is offered by ch. 88 of *Dēnkard (Dīnkard)*, Book III.[14] The relentless recommendation, together with strong hints that the practice is 'perplexing' and that people have turned away from it,[15] suggest that next-of-kin marriage never had strong popular support.

Stricker, taking the reports from classical, non-Persian sources at face value, remarks that they all concern royalty or the upper classes, and concludes that it must have been more frequent among the lower classes, asking rhetorically: 'If things were thus in court circles, what would the situation have been like among the populace?',[16] which seems to express a remarkable belief in the superior morals of the upper classes. It seems more likely that the custom was restricted to the privileged elites, the aristocracy and above all the ruling dynasty and the priestly caste of the Magi. Spooner suggests that, rather than being a very common practice, it had a sacramental value in the state religion, and that with the disappearance of the Sasanian state 'there was no longer any reason to continue a practice which was never an integral part of the social structure but simply a vehicle to a type of "grace" which was now no longer valid'.[17] Sidler, rejecting a monocausal explanation of the custom as either a cultic-Magian doctrine or a tendency towards extreme endogamy, believes that a combination of these may have given rise to next-of-kin marriage, possibly helped (as in Egypt) by Hellenistic influence and the example of the Seleucid kings.[18]

Since in the Islamic period the term *majūs* was used indiscriminately for all adherents of Zoroastrianism, the custom was seen by the Arabs as an abomination of the Persians in general. The custom was, in a sense, central in Zoroastrianism, for it is mentioned as a righteous act in a text that serves as a Creed, the *Fravarānē*. However, its odd placement there could mean that it is a later interpolation. The first evidence in the history of the Zoroastrian Persians is offered by Cambyses (*reg.* 530-522 B.C.), who married two of his full sisters, as Herodotus tells us (III.31). It is questionable to what extent this may be taken as an example of *khwētōdas*; Herodotus was keen to show that Cambyses breached existing norms.[19] According to Plutarch, Artaxerxes II married his daughters Atossa and Amestris. Again, the accusation is somewhat suspect.[20] Consanguineous marriages, if only sporadically, were also known from other peoples in the ancient Near East, and the Zoroastrians may have adopted the custom from them. In any case, the practice has been attested from the sixth century B.C., during the Achaemenids, Arsacids, and Sasanians, although it was only during the last-mentioned dynasty that it was more or less common; it disappeared under Muslim rule, surviving as first-cousin marriage.[21] What survived, too, was the memory of something deemed scandalous. In many stories next-of-kin marriage is associated with murder, such as the story of the fifth-century Sasanian king Yezdegird II, who supposedly married his own daughter and then had her killed.[22] Or it is fabulously compounded, as in the fantasy of an Iranian father who, attempting to produce a son, sires a granddaughter by his daughter, then a great-granddaughter by his granddaughter, and so on for nine or ten generations until he finally succeeds as the last daughter bears him a son:[23] a story that sounds like a faint echo of the activities ascribed to the Sumerian god Enki.[24]

The precise origins of the custom or its history in pre-Islamic times need not concern us here; data on its occurrence in Islamic times are extremely scanty. In polemics, numbers do not always matter much. Many an Arab tribe was derided collectively and tainted in perpetuity on the basis of one incident that took place, or was thought to have taken place, in the legendary past; tribes have been branded as farters, penis-eaters or cannibals because of one unfortunate incident that happened to one of their members. Although the custom is well-attested, it has not always been a central issue in Zoroastrian belief and practice. The passages referring to next-of-kin marriage in the oldest texts are either vague or may not be authentic.

Regardless of how widespread or how central an issue close-kin marriage may have been among the Persians, among other nations at least they had a bad reputation on this account. Catullus lampoons a certain Gellius, whose alleged incest with his mother, Persian-style, will produce a Magian (*magus*).[25] The statement by Antisthenes (a friend of Socrates) that 'Alcibiades lay with his mother, his daughter, and his sister, as Persians do' is quoted by Athenaeus (d. *c.* 230 AD), who wrote his Greek *Deipnosophists* ('The Gastronomers') in Rome but was born in Naucratis in Egypt, where marriages of full siblings were widespread at the time.[26] The Persian custom was an important point in Christian polemic against Zoroastrianism.[27] After the coming of Islam, the Melkite bishop of Ḥarrān, Theodore Abū Qurra (d. *c.* 820), writing in Arabic, mentions the Persian marriage with mothers, sisters and daughters, linking it with cosmological ideas about the creation of the universe: children born from next-of-kin unions are hoped to be as beautiful as the sun and the moon, both of which also resulted from incestuous couplings.[28] Among the Muslims, too, it is a recurrent topos, exploited by the pro-Arab participants in their debates and polemics with the so-called Shuʿūbiyya, those who protest the cultural superiority of the non-Arabs, particularly the Persians.[29] In polemics against the Other, few issues are as eagerly pounced upon as sexual matters, and Islamic polemics against other religions is no exception.

It ought to be mentioned that the term Majūs was also applied, confusingly, to the Vikings,[30] apparently because their religion, involving fire-worship, reminded the Muslims of the Zoroastrians. To my knowledge the Vikings did not practise close-kin marriage, but it is not surprising that, at least in one Arabic source, this is alleged, obviously because of the Muslim association of Majūs with immoral marriage. The Andalusian poet and scholar Ibn Diḥya (d. 633/1235) remarks that the Vikings are now Christians, having given up fire-worship,

> except the inhabitants of some isolated islands of theirs, who still practise their original religion, worshipping fire and marrying mothers and sisters, and such scandalous things.[31]

Not surprisingly, the Vikings do not loom large in Arabic literature. In all other instances in this study of the word Majūs, the reader can be certain that the Zoroastrians are intended.

Arabs v. Persians: A Key Text by Abū Ḥayyān al-Tawḥīdī

Striking throughout the polemics between, on the one hand, Arabs or Arabophiles, and Persians or Iranophiles on the other hand, is the obsession with pre-Islamic past: almost all the virtues and vices that are marshalled to prove one's excellence and the other's depravity relate to pre-Islamic Arabs and the Sasanid Persians. A relatively lengthy text that is particularly relevant to our purpose is a debate of the late 4th/10th century, recorded—and judging from its stylistic qualities probably extensively edited—by the great prose writer Abū Ḥayyān al-Tawḥīdī, in his *al-Imtāᶜ wa-l-muʾānasa* ('Enjoyment and Geniality'), which purports to be a record of a series of nightly sessions with a vizier in Baghdad. At the beginning of the sixth session[32] the vizier, Ibn Saᶜdān (in function from 373/982 to 375/985) suggests the night's topic: Do you think the Arabs (*al-ᶜArab*, i.e. the Bedouins in particular) are superior to the non-Arabs (*al-ᶜAjam*, the Persians in particular), or *vice versa*? Al-Tawḥīdī begins by quoting a famous Persian, Ibn al-Muqaffaᶜ (d. *c.* 139/756), who, contrary to what might be expected from him, had argued that the Arabs are superior to other peoples, including the Byzantines, Chinese, Turks, Indians, Negroes (Zanj), and Persians.[33] Al-Tawḥīdī adds to this some thoughts of his own. The first part of the discussion focuses on the diverse virtues of the peoples, but after quoting some anti-Arab invective by a certain al-Jayhānī,[34] he counter-attacks with a lengthy quotation attributed to Abū Ḥāmid al-Marwarrūdhī al-qāḍī (d. 362/973).[35]

Reading the text one may be forgiven for supposing that this person was actually present, but in view of his year of death this is ruled out: al-Tawḥīdī is quoting him. Although this cadi shows himself an ardent partisan of the Arab cause, it seems that ethnically he was a Persian himself: al-Tawḥīdī, who praised him highly,[36] also says that he spoke with 'a strong Khurāsānī accent and the uncouthness of the Persians, being from Marw al-Rūdh'.[37] His descent may not have mattered to him, for he believed that one should not be praised or blamed for one's descent, just as one should not be praised or blamed for physical characteristics; a view that, if practised, would have radically changed Arabic poetry in general.[38] In any case, it is by no means exceptional that a non-Arab should espouse the pro-Arab cause: Abū Ḥāmid had illustrious predecessors in al-Jāḥiẓ and Ibn Qutayba. It is, however, entirely possible that Abū Ḥāmid is wholly innocent of the fierce opinions ascribed to him. A later writer, Ibn Abī l-Ḥadīd (d. 656/1258), has argued that al-Tawḥīdī (whose own ethnicity is somewhat uncertain but probably Persian[39]) used this cadi, one of his teachers, as a foil for some of his own more controversial opinions.[40] I quote al-Marwarrūdhī's speech almost in full, as well as the words of another speaker, Abū l-Ḥasan al-Anṣārī, who is explicitly said to have been present.

Abū Ḥāmid al-Marwarrūdhī, the cadi, said:

—Suppose that all virtues, strung as a necklace or unstrung, were combined in the Persians, invested round their necks, hanging from their ears, or showing on their foreheads, then it would still be more befitting to them not to mention them and to keep silent[41] about all the small and great of these virtues, what with all their fucking their mothers, sisters and daughters! For this is a thing that is naturally abhorred, loathsome to hear,[42] rejected by everyone with a sound innate disposition, found repugnant by everybody with a well-balanced nature. To complete their insolence and their gross perversion, they have alleged that this happened with the permission of God, and through a Law coming from God. God has forbidden the eating of offensive food; so how could He have allowed offensive marriages?

[i, 91] These people have lied: Zoroaster [or Zarathustra; Arabic Zarādusht] was no prophet. If he had been a prophet, God would have mentioned him among the prophets that He mentions by name, and mentions repeatedly, in His Book. It is therefore that the Prophet—God bless and preserve him—said, 'Deal with them as with the People of the Book',[43] for they do not have a book coming from God, revealed to a messenger. It is no more than a fable, by which Zoroaster has deceived them, through the power of the king who accepted this from him and

who made the people act in this way, willingly or unwillingly, either enticing them or intimidating them. But how could God ever have sent a prophet who would preach belief in two gods? This is rationally absurd, and God has created reason only so that it could testify to the truth when someone speaks the truth, and to the falsehood of someone who speaks falsehood. If this practice were revealed law, it would be widely known among the people of the Two Books, I mean the Jews and the Christians, and similarly among the Sabians,[44] for of all people they used to be most interested in religions and studying them, to arrive at the knowledge of the truths of them, so that they could have faith in their own religion. So how is it possible that the Christians know Jesus, and the Jews know Moses, while Muḥammad—God bless and preserve him—mentions both of them as well as others, such as David, Solomon, John [the Baptist] and Zacharias, but does not mention Zoroaster as a prophet, or that he brought a truthful and true message from God, like Moses and Jesus [and Muḥammad, who said,][45] 'I have been sent to abrogate every revealed law, and to renew a revealed law by which God has singled me out among the Arabs'?!

This is a useful exposé of their lies. But 'they found a little tear and ripped it apart'[46], they found something forbidden by reason and declared it lawful, a practice naturally deemed offensive which they committed, a foul custom which they approved. We have found in animals that a stallion, if incited to mount his mother, is unwilling; if he is forced by means of deception and then becomes aware of the truth he gets angry with its owners and either runs away or is vicious to them. What, therefore, do you say about a practice that even a beast rejects because it goes against its nature, and is scorned by its feelings, however weakly developed, [i, 92] its lust cooling down after having flared up—while these people, who are so proud of their intelligence and conceited about themselves, accept it gladly?

Even if Zoroaster had shown to them all kinds of miracles and proofs in support of this base conduct and this ugly practice, if he had scattered on them the stars of the sky or made the sun rise in the west for them, or had crumbled the mountains, or had dried up the oceans, or shown them Orion walking on earth in the streets and testifying to the truth of what he said, then it would still have been their duty, on the basis of reason, honour,[47] zeal, proud disdain, loathing and self-respect, to reject his command, to doubt every miracle he showed them, to kill him, and make an example of him ...[48]

The (Bedouin) Arabs would have a better excuse if they had had this ugly character and had practised this base deed, for their libido and excitability are stronger than those of others, they are more capable of coition and more inclined to copulate with women, as is demonstrated in their love poetry and their passionate love, expressed in verse and prose, in their leisure[49] and their lust. In spite of all these urges and drives, you will find that they do neither approve of this deed nor practise it. If someone were to force them to do it, if someone urged them to do it, they would not obey. It is therefore that it has never happened that someone stood up among them to trick them [i, 93] into this: if there had been someone like that, he would have been the first to have his head bashed in with a cudgel or his belly ripped by a dagger. It is only their noble souls that restrain them (from incestuous relationships), and their balanced nature, strong pride, disdainful spirit, agreeable habits, and good natural disposition. Burying girls was to them a better way to avoid shame or to ward off evil things than what Zoroaster approved and what the Persians adopted from him,[50] whereas they lay claim to wisdom, knowledge, prudence and firm resolution. But because of their boundless ignorance and overcome by their lust they were unaware of what God might have made permissible or forbidden to them, either giving them a free hand or restraining them, making it licit or taboo. No, they wouldn't! But God does not impose on people endowed with intelligence a religion and a search for truth except in order to ennoble them in this world and to hold them to account for it in the world to come.

Abū l-Ḥasan al-Anṣārī,[51] who was also present, said,

—The Indians would have a better excuse in this matter, for they practise it as a pious act in their temples, thus attaining their desire by means of this (self-)deceit; at least they do not ascribe anything of this to God, they do not consider it permissible to utter lies about Him, nor do they attribute it to some prophet who had it from God. Rather, they believe that it is the right thing to do by common consensus, and by the force of habit and custom they have come to like it. In any case, they are mentally disordered, there are few intelligent people among them, they have an inclination towards lying, delusion and magic, and they are proficient in these things.

Abū l-Ḥasan continued,

—Look at Zoroaster's ignorance in this matter, and the feeble minds of the Persians who adopted this [i, 94] practice from him! Now compare this with the intelligence of the Arabs, who said, 'Take strangers, then you will not produce stunted offspring'. This was a common saying among them, to the extent that the Lawgiver[52]—God bless and preserve him—has been heard to say it too. The reason is that stuntedness (*al-ḍawā*) is abhorred. The Arabs knew this intuitively, through their pure instincts and bright minds, their noble nature, their high-born lineages, and their sound customs. They realized that the degeneration that affects the body will spread to the mind. The Persians, on the other hand, remained unaware of this truth. Only brilliant and sagacious minds will grasp this and similar facts. Al-Aṣmaʿī quotes a line by an unknown Arab, praising a patron:

A young man not born from a close cousin, father's brother's daughter,
and thus not stunted (the issue of close relatives is often stunted).[53]

The Arabs also use the expression 'to stunt someone's right (*aḍwāhu ḥaqqahu*)', meaning 'to impair someone's right'. Another said to his son, 'By God, I have protected you from stuntedness and have chosen (your mother) for you from among my maternal uncles' family. The Arabs also said, 'No-one is more stunted than (children from) close relatives, nobody gives birth to better children than strange women (*laysa aḍwā mina l-qarāʾib, wa-lā anjabu mina l-gharāʾib*)'. A poet said,

I warn everyone with far-reaching ambition:
Do not let children marry their paternal cousins,
For one will not escape stuntedness and sickliness;
If you feed them they will not grow.[54]

A man from (the tribe of) Asad boasted:

I am no runt (*ḍāwiyy*) whose bones are shaky,
born from a line of Khālid after Khālid,
Repeatedly, until his paternal uncle is his mother's maternal uncle,
in one line of kinship closer than a single span.[55]

What the Arabs mean is in fact only the debility of the mind and the intelligence, for if they meant physical defects, they would be wrong, since they mean plumpness of body, together with being sound and firm. It is the same with the nature of soil. Thus, it is said, when it is much overturned by strong winds the earth becomes fertile, because when it is exposed to winds from various sides they move the soil of the earth from one place to another. Now if 'strange' soil affects other soil, all the more so will humans influence other humans by mingling with strangers (*bi-l-ightirāb*), for man is made of soil.

Abū Ḥāmid said,

—So what do you think of people who are ignorant both of the effects of nature and the secrets of revealed law! It is not for nothing that God has humbled them, and He was not wrongful when He robbed them of their rule. He struck them with ignominy and degradation only as a punishment for their wicked behaviour and their insolent and arrogant lying about God. God does not wrong His servants.[56]

At this stage, the vizier interrupts and remarks that it has been a lengthy discussion indeed, even though he enjoyed it. He asks al-Tawḥīdī to put it down in writing, which the latter promises to do.

Some Comments on al-Tawḥīdī's Text

As said before, in the quoted text no reference is made to contemporary practices, even though at the time of the discussion there were still many Zoroastrians in Iran.[57] It has been said that the extreme forms of *khwētōdas* marriages persisted until the tenth century, after which it survived only as the marriage of first cousins, wholly compatible with Islamic law and customs.[58] Spuler, in his study of Iran in the first four Islamic centuries, says that the stamping out of close-kin marriage in Iran during the ninth and tenth centuries was a difficult process, but the evidence he gives is meagre, limited to two not very convincing reports.[59] First, there is a report by al-Muqaddasī, whose geography was written in 375/985 (almost exactly when al-Tawḥīdī was writing his *al-Imtāᶜ wa-l-muʾānasa*), according to which strict endogamy was observed among what Spuler calls the primitive tribes of Daylam, south of the Caspian Sea; transgression was punished with death, as al-Muqaddasī was told when he saw a girl being pursued by a man brandishing a sword.[60] The second case that Spuler mentions as indicating the survival of Sasanian marriage practices is a story, given by Ibn Khallikān, on Abū Saᶜīd al-Ḥasan ibn Aḥmad al-Iṣṭakhrī (d. 328/940), who was appointed *qāḍī* under al-Muqtadir (reg. 295-320/908-32) in Sijistān. There he was shocked to find that marriages were arranged without a *waliyy*, the 'guardian' of the bride who gives her away in marriage according to Islamic law; and he abolished that custom.[61] It is obvious that neither of these reports can serve as evidence for close-kin marriage of the un-Islamic kind. I have not found much firmer evidence myself, if we disregard some invective poems that should not be taken at face value, or reports on people altogether outside the pale of either Islam or Zoroastrianism, such as the Turks in 'the land of Chigil', 'where a man may marry his daughter or sister and other close kin, who are not Zoroastrians',[62] or the Khuṭlukh Turks 'who marry their sisters'.[63] A certain Ḥamza ibn ᶜUmāra al-Barbarī who is said to have married his daughter and to hold marriage with all the forbidden degrees as lawful is mentioned by al-Nawbakhtī (d. between 300 and 310/912-22).[64] This Ḥamza was a sectarian, a Shīᶜite with some followers in Medina and Kufa, who believed that 'Whoever knows the Imam may do whatever he wishes, without sinning'. There is nothing here that suggests Zoroastrian vestiges, even though Watt refers to him as '[o]ne man [who] is said to have allowed the Persian practice of marriage to daughters', and speaks of 'a Persian element' among the *mawālī* (non-Arab Muslims) of southern Iraq.[65] Some reports are too vague to be taken into consideration, such as when al-Muqaddasī says of Fārs (southwest Iran) that 'the practices of the Magians are in the open there', or that in Shiraz 'the practices of the Magians are common':[66] he may be referring to the Nayrūz (New Year's) celebrations, for instance.[67] Arab writers in the Middle Ages, including al-Tawḥīdī, were by no means prudish, least so when engaged in polemics. It is difficult to imagine that, if they had been able to give hard proof of the survival of the close-kin marriage customs in their own day, they would not have described it with some relish, giving details of place, time, and names. One authority even believed that the custom was abolished already in Sasanian times:

> Al-Suddī said: After Bukhtnaṣṣar (Nebuchadnezzar) came a king from the Tyrants (*al-Jabābira*) called Bardādas[68], in the town of Ādharbayjān. He was of the Zoroastrian persuasion and allowed people to marry their mothers and sisters, and to worship fire. This situation remained in practice among the Persians until the time of Kisrā Anūsharwān [*reg.* AD 531-579], who abolished it during his reign.[69]

Although Islamic jurisprudence deals with the matter of Zoroastrianism on various occasions, its marriage customs are very rarely discussed. As will be shown in Chapter Three, the Muslim legal authorities generally let the Zoroastrians carry on with their own customs as long as they did not interfere with Muslim life. Further evidence that, at least in the eleventh century, virtually all Zoroastrians had abandoned next-of-kin marriages, are verses of the poet Abū l-ᶜAlāᵓ al-Maᶜarrī (d. 449/1058). He is always prepared to believe the worst of mankind in general:

> Are there pure persons anywhere among mankind,
> or are all people filth?
> Paternal cousins are spurned by Christians
> and Magians wedded sisters.[70]

The implication is that to forbid what should be permissible is perhaps as bad as to permit what is forbidden. However, it may not be just for metrical reasons that the poet uses a present tense (*taᵓbā*) for the Christians but a past tense verb (*aᶜrasat*) for the Majūs. Elsewhere, accusing a heretical Islamic sect, the Carmathians, of incestuous practices,[71] he contrasts them with the Zoroastrians, who allegedly had given up their habits:

> Even the brute beasts did not approve the crimes
> committed by you on your mothers and mothers-in-law.
> We questioned some Magians as to the real nature of their religion.
> They replied, 'Yes: we do not wed our sisters.

That, indeed, was originally permitted in Magianism,
 but we count it an error.
We reject abominable things ...'[72]

*

The only Persian mentioned by name in al-Tawḥīdī's text is Zoroaster, Zarādusht in Arabic, who lived in the remote past.[73] Similarly, all references to the 'Arabs' employ the past tense. They are attacked, in the passages preceding the above translation, for their uncouth Bedouin past, and subsequently defended because, for all their 'ignorance' in the time of the pre-Islamic Ignorance (*al-Jāhiliyya*), they nevertheless instinctively knew or cleverly learnt many essential things that remained hidden from the Persians with all their refined culture and civilization in pre-Islamic times.

The counter-attack is not merely directed at one particular practice of the Zoroastrians but, through it, against their entire religion. Zoroaster, here considered the initiator of the close-kin marriage practice, is denied the status of a true prophet sent by God. The very fact that he recommended close-kin marriage, it is argued, would be enough to refute his status as a prophet, but further corroboration is found in the fact that Zoroaster is mentioned as such neither by any revealed scripture nor by the pagan but knowledgeable Ḥarrānians.

So strong, according to al-Marwarrūdhī the cadi—and obviously to al-Tawḥīdī as well—is the case against close-kin marriage that not even the most fantastic miracles could possibly have rocked the Arabs' opinion. It is a well-known point of doctrine in Islam that miracles may occur to corroborate a truth, and must in fact do so in the case of those sent by God as His messengers and apostles. Those miracles recognized as such, in the case of Moses and his superior magic (sticks and snakes, water from rocks, dividing waters), Jesus and his superior medicine (curing the sick, reviving the dead) or Muḥammad with his more intellectual miracle (the reception of the Qur'an), may strike us as perhaps somewhat less compelling than the cosmic and cataclysmic miracles evoked by al-Marwarrūdhī. For 'miracle' he uses the Qur'anic terms *āya* (literally, 'sign') and *burhān* ('demonstration, proof', also used in logic), rather than the technical term for a true prophet's miracle, *muʿjiza*, literally, 'what is inimitable', even though the miracles he enumerates are surely as inimitable as any. If such shocking events could not have convinced the Arabs, it means that the cadi considered the abhorrence of close-kin marriage as incontrovertible as any *a priori* knowledge, such as the belief that two and two equal four.

A priori knowledge cannot properly be proved logically. It is no different in the case of close-kin marriage. All that the two speakers, al-Marwarrūdhī and Abū l-Ḥasan al-Anṣārī can do is to give some corroborating evidence, apart from using strong language and a lot of rhetoric. The evidence is derived from nature, both animate and inanimate.

First, Abū Ḥāmid argues that animals, or more specifically large domestic animals (*bahāʾim*), naturally avoid it. When he says, 'we have found', it is left to the reader to guess whether Abū Ḥāmid knows it from personal observation of animal behaviour, or has found it in books. The latter is more likely. Contrary to what might be expected, some writers find relevant information on camels, not in Arabic but Greek works. Ibn ʿAbd Rabbih (d. 328/940) says in his great anthology *al-ʿIqd al-farīd* ('The Unique Necklace'): 'I have read in some book by the Greeks (or Byzantines, *al-Rūm*) that camels avoid their mothers and do not mount them'.[74] Al-Damīrī (d. 808/1405), author of a large encyclopedia on animals entitled *Ḥayāt al-ḥayawān al-kubrā* ('The Great Life of Living Beings'), ascribes this opinion to 'the author of the *Logic*', meaning Aristotle:

> The author of the *Logic* says that he (viz. the camel) will not mount his mother. He says that, long ago, a man covered a she-camel with a cloth and then let her son loose upon her. When the son became aware of what had happened, he bit off his yard. Subsequently he became so malicious towards that man that eventually he killed him. Another man did the same thing; when (the stallion) realized that it was his mother he killed himself.[75]

The story is indeed found in Aristotle's *History of Animals*, and followed by a similar passage about horses belonging to the king of Scythia, in which the fooled foal subsequently hurls itself down a precipice;[76] it is quoted by al-Tawḥīdī in his *al-Imtāʿ wa-l-muʾānasa* and attributed to Aristotle:

> A king had a mare which had foals. He wanted to make her pregnant by the most noble of them, but the foal declined and was unwilling. When the mother's head was covered, he mounted her. Once the piece of cloth was removed and he saw her, he galloped away and hurled himself into a wadi, killing himself.[77]

One may well wonder if there is any report of such a thing as observed by Arabs, Bedouin or otherwise. In fact, I have found only a single such report, on horses rather than camels, but its similarity to the previous story makes it rather suspect:

> Abū Yūsuf told: We were told by al-Awzāʿī, who said:
>
> We were near the coast[78] when a stallion was brought, that was made to mount his mother. He refused; so they put her into a room, hung a curtain in the door opening, and covered her entirely with a cloth. When

> the stallion had mounted her and had finished, he smelled that it was his mother. Then he set his teeth to the base of his yard, bit it off, and died.[79]

Interestingly, the informants, Abū Yūsuf and al-Awzāʿī, are neither Bedouins nor lexicographers, but two famous specialists in Islamic law, although it is not clear whether this is relevant here, since any explicit extrapolations of the principle into the realms of human custom or divine law are absent. The story is given merely as a curious bit of information. A laconic summary is found in a twelfth-century popular encyclopedia, *Mufīd al-ʿulūm wa-mubīd al-humūm* ('The Provider of Useful Knowledge and Remover of Sorrows'): 'A noble horse will not mount his mother or his sister'.[80] Although this work is full of pious and moralistic matter, this titbit of useful knowledge is given in a chapter on properties and characteristics of the natural world, without any lesson being drawn explicitly. The only one to do so is Abū Ḥāmid al-Marwarrūdhī. His source is unclear and the evidence somewhat shaky, but apparently he takes it for granted that it is a fact universally acknowledged. In fact, it has been shown that the animal world provides evidence for the existence of mechanisms that help to avoid close-kin matings, particularly in animals living in small, relatively closed groups, such as lions, monkeys, and apes. For instance, young males may regularly leave the group, or, if remaining in the group, may have a lower rank which makes mating with relatives more difficult.[81]

However, even if it turns out to be true that animals, particularly those considered noble by the Arabs such as horses and camels, avoid next-of-kin matings, this does not logically prove that humans should follow them. There are quite a number of habits displayed by these noble beasts that any decent Muslim would be eager to avoid. Abū Ḥāmid the lawyer's argument would only work if one was already convinced of the abhorrent nature of such matings. His colleague Abū l-Ḥasan al-Anṣārī, the Muʿtazilite theologian, may not be as eloquent and rhetorical as Abū Ḥāmid, but his arguments are stronger from a scientific point of view. Perhaps because he is also called an *adīb*, man of letters, he knows the verb *ḍawiya* and its meaning, and introduces the argument of stuntedness, quoting some of the sayings and verses that have been discussed in Chapter One. I do not quite understand why he thinks that the Bedouins only refer to mental debility rather than physical; the passage in question is not wholly coherent, and may be corrupt, the original drift being that the Bedouins, when they use the root *ḌWY*, refer *both* to bodily and mental or intellectual deficiencies. The lexicographers confirm this.

Abū l-Ḥasan al-Anṣārī finds proof also in the inanimate world, when he uses the analogy of the soil made fertile by the 'ploughing' of the winds that mix soil from distant places. The metaphor works all the better because in Arabic, as in English, man is made of the dust or clay to which he shall return. It is hardly incontrovertible proof, but one could argue that the argument contains a grain, or speck, of truth. After Abū l-Ḥasan's relatively short intervention, Abū Ḥāmid sums up by referring to Nature and Divine Law, both ignored by the pre-Islamic Magian marriage matchmakers.

That the Arabs are credited by Abū Ḥāmid with an above-average sexual libido (but appropriately restrained) is obviously meant to add to their glory. Bravely he also raises, unprompted, the awkward matter of infanticide practised by some Arab tribes in the pre-Islamic period. He links it with the Persian close-kin marriage. Rather than explaining both, like some modern sociologists, as resulting from economic constraints, Abū Ḥāmid suggests that both are practised with the misguided intention of avoiding shame. A Qur'anic verse that condemns the burying of infant girls (Q 16:59) also suggests that it was done to escape *hūn*, humiliation or shame. Shame is associated with women, especially unmarried virgins. To kill infant daughters, although wrong, is a better way of avoiding shame than marrying them off incestuously, in Abū Ḥāmid's view. It is a debatable point, and a convinced Zoroastrian might have argued the opposite. The comparison of the two different customs regarding daughters is the subject of an anecdote involving the Medinan poet Ismāᶜīl ibn Yasār, who died at an advanced age some years before 132/750. Of Azerbaijani descent, he made some anti-Arab poems, one of them including the following lines, the last words of which (*tadussūna safāhan banātikum fī l-turābi*) echo the Qur'anic verse on girl burial (Q 16:59: *am yadussuhū fī l-turāb*):

If you don't know about us and yourself, ask
  how we were in past times:
When we raised our daughters and you, stupidly,
  buried your daughters in the earth.

On hearing this, an Arab replies, 'What we intended for our daughters was not what you had in mind for them', silencing the poet. In a more explicit version of this anecdote, the reply is by Ashᶜab, who figures in numerous jokes:

—You are right, by God! The Arabs intended for their daughters something different from what you intended!

—What do you mean?

—The Arabs buried their daughters fearing disgrace, and you raised them in order to marry them.

The people laughed loudly, and Ismāᶜīl was so ashamed that if he could have sunk into the earth he would have done so.[82]

Like all the reports we possess on the Shuʿūbiyya polemics, the anecdote is told in a pro-Arab context, hostile to the anti-Arab faction. To the Muslim Arabs it goes without saying that burying daughters is less heinous than mating them; but it is not impossible that Ismāʿīl ibn Yasār was already hinting at the opposite view with his line.

There is one other case where daughter burial and sexual relations with a daughter come together. Qays ibn ʿĀṣim was a tribal leader of Tamīm and a contemporary of the Prophet. He is renowned not only as hero but as a paragon of generosity and *ḥilm* (wisdom, leniency and self-restraint), thus embodying all the traditional main virtues in Arab eyes.[83] Yet this celebrated figure was not only the most notorious of infant-buriers (the Qur'anic verses denouncing the custom, Q 81:8-9, are said to have been revealed especially about him),[84] but was guilty of sexually approaching one of his surviving daughters under the influence of alcohol.[85] Apparently it was not a very serious matter; details are lacking, it may actually have been a sister instead of a daughter, and it seems to have amounted to no more than some petting. Next morning, sober, he became the first Arab in pre-Islamic times to renounce alcohol. No explicit reference is made to Magian practices here, but the story serves to show that drunkenness and incestuous acts are naturally abhorred, even by pre-Islamic Arabs, whereas infant burial was not quite such a bad thing until Islam forbade it.

Even more frequently found than the topos of child burial in anti-Arab polemics is the fact that the diet of the Bedouin Arabs contains certain items that city-dwellers usually find repulsive, such as lizards and snakes. This theme is also part of al-Jayhānī's invective, as quoted by al-Tawḥīdī. The latter's superior, the famous vizier al-Ṣāḥib ibn ʿAbbād (d. 385/995), though himself probably of Iranian origin,[86] made an invective poem in reply to a Persian who had called the Arabs snake-eaters. The poem counters with the incest theme:

You who ignorantly blames the Bedouins
  because they eat snakes as their food:
As for the Persians, all night their 'snakes'
  slither into sister and mother.[87]

In al-Tawḥīdī's text, Abū l-Ḥasan al-Anṣārī compares the Persians unfavourably with the Indians, who are said to commit the same acts as they but without pretending to have received divine sanction. He refers to the so-called temple prostitution found in India, which is not exactly the same thing, although in some cases it may result in what normally would be considered incest. In medieval India Magian practices are absent, it seems. It is hard to generalize about such a vast subcontinent and its diverse civilizations. Roughly, the North contrasts with the South in that out-marrying characterizes the former, and in-marrying is dominant in the latter.[88] The great scholar al-Bīrūnī (d. after 442/1050), in his pioneering study of India, did his research in the North. His findings are that 'according to their marriage law, it is better to marry a stranger than a relative. The more distant the relationship of a woman with regard to her husband the better'. Collateral relations are forbidden unless the partners 'be removed from each other by five consecutive generations', in which case the prohibition is waived, though reluctantly.[89]

The Arabs' knowledge of the ancient Magian custom of *khwētōdas* was not directly derived from the *Avesta* or the various Pahlavi texts in which the practice is mentioned and recommended: no Arabic translations were made. It ought to be said that not all of the ancient texts are equally outspoken in their praise of the custom, and that the term *khwētōdas* is sometimes, in later texts, interpreted in the far more moderate sense of marriage between first cousins.[90] In one text, Zoroaster himself is said to have had doubts about the father—daughter relationship, this 'perplexing thing' which in his eyes is 'an evil'.[91] This, together with the absence of any clear evidence of the practice in Islamic times, seems to indicate that the more extreme form of close-kin marriage was to be upheld as a kind of religious ideal rather than to be put into practice. Bih-Āfrīd (or Wēhāfrīt) ibn Farwardīn, who led an uprising near Nishapur around 129/747 (soon crushed by Abū Muslim, the organizer of the Abbasid revolution), and who acted as a kind of Neo-Zoroastrian prophet, in fact spoke out against the practice.[92] In one of the older Arabic sources, *Mafātīḥ al-ᶜulūm* ('The Keys to the Sciences') by Abū ᶜAbd Allāh al-Khwārazmī (4rd/10th century) it is merely said that he 'opposed the Magians in many of their religious institutions';[93] later writers, al-Bīrūnī (d. *c.* 442/1050) and al-Shahrastānī (d. 548/1153), state that Bih-Āfrīd preached that certain old practices were henceforward prohibited, including fire worship, drinking wine, and consanguineous marriages with mothers, daughters, sisters, and nieces.[94] It is possible that al-Shahrastānī is merely interpreting the vague statements of earlier sources; even if correct, it does not prove that the practice was still common in the time of Bih-Āfrīd, but merely that he wished to reform Zoroastrian teachings on lines more compatible with Islam.

Al-Bīrūnī was informed by a Persian prince, Marzubān ibn Rustam ibn Sharwīn of Pirīm (second half of 4th/10th century), that it had all been a misunderstanding. Zoroaster had not commanded his followers to copulate with mothers. He had been asked by the leading scholars of his time what someone should do who, isolated from others, was left with his own mother: should he (by analogy with Lot and his daughters) ensure the survival of his line by bedding the only woman available? Zoroaster had ruled that it was allowed, and his fatwa was misinterpreted.[95]

Pre-Islamic Arabs with Magian Leanings

Arabic references that mention close-kin marriage amongst the Persians are usually set in the pre-Islamic past. The speakers in the text given by al-Tawḥīdī seem firmly convinced that the abomination of incest is an utterly un-Arab thing. Nevertheless, instances of intercourse between close kin and even institutionalized close-kin marriage are reported. The Greek geographer Strabo (d. AD 19) writes about the inhabitants of Arabia Felix (i.e. Yemen) that they hold all property in common. He continues:

> One woman is also wife for all; and he who first enters the house before any other has intercourse with her, having first placed his staff before the door, for by custom each man must carry a staff; but she spends the night with the eldest. And therefore all children are brothers. They also have intercourse with their mothers.[96]

Strabo adds a story of a princess whose fifteen brothers were in love with her and visited her in turn. The girl, exhausted, places a fake staff at the door, which makes them think she has a lover, but in the end her innocence is established.[97] It is impossible to say how accurate these reports are, but strong doubts would seem justified. Holding property and wives in common is a common motif in descriptions of barbarous peoples or heretical sects. Al-Tawḥīdī's speakers would doubtlessly add that, if the report contains a grain of truth, it does not concern the true Bedouin Arabs. Among the latter, however, there are a few cases which, unlike Strabo's story, are part of the Arabs' own tradition.

Ibn Qutayba tells the story of the pre-Islamic hero Ḥājib ibn Zurāra, like Qays ibn ᶜĀṣim a celebrated *sayyid* of Tamīm, like him famous for his mildness and self-restraint, and again like him guilty of behaviour abhorred in Islam, but eventually repentant:[98]

> Ḥājib ibn Zurāra visited the court of Kisrā (Chosroes, traditional name of the Sasanid emperor). He saw that they married their sisters and daughters, and he let himself be seduced into following their example. He embraced their religion and married his daughter. Later, he repented and said (in verse),
>
> God curse your religion, you uncircumcised one,
>   which allows us to marry sisters and daughters.
> I have ensnared my family in an evil deed[99]
>   and I have collared my neck with infamy.
> I have left on my shoulder a disgrace,
>   ugly things that will live on after death.

A girl covered by (*tajallalahā*) her old man:
A bad old man, a good girl![100]

The story looks like an embroidery, based on the reports of the visit of Ḥājib and some other Arab leaders to Kisrā as deputies of al-Nuᶜmān, king of Ḥīra.[101] The poetry does not sound authentic either. In his historical handbook *al-Maᶜārif* Ibn Qutayba merely remarks that Ḥājib 'married his daughter but then repented'.[102] Of interest is that Ḥājib is mentioned there as one of several of his tribe Tamīm who were Zoroastrians. Apart from him, three names are given: his father Zurāra ibn ᶜUdus, al-Aqraᶜ ibn Ḥābis, and Abū Sūd, grandfather of Wakīᶜ ibn Ḥassān.[103] Nothing about their marriage customs is known. It is striking that Ḥājib's incest has, apparently, not damaged his great reputation, persisting in Islamic times. In connection with Ḥājib it must be mentioned that his equally famous brother Laqīṭ, poet and *sayyid* (tribal leader),[104] is said by Abū l-ᶜAlāᵓ al-Maᶜarrī (d. 449/1058) to have married his own daughter Dukhtanūs (or Dakhtanūs) 'because he was a Zoroastrian, who at the court of Kisrā had embraced the latter's religion'.[105] Since no older sources confirm this, it seems obvious, however, that Laqīṭ has been confused with his brother.

Ḥājib ibn Zurāra's story is of a pattern with that of Qays ibn ᶜĀṣim, demonstrating that pre-Islamic Arabs, although ignorant of the true religion and going seriously astray in some cases, may in the end find the right course through their innate noble qualities. There is yet another pre-Islamic Arab who should be mentioned in this respect, even though his incestuous act was apparently neither inspired by nor subsequently linked with Zoroastrian practice or belief. Here is a translation of the story of al-Burj ibn Mus'hir ibn al-Julās, of the tribe of Ṭayyiᵓ, who was known as a poet;[106] Abū l-Faraj al-Iṣfahānī reports it in the words of Abū ᶜUbayda:

> Al-Burj had a sister called al-ᶜUfāṭa.[107] One day he was drinking with [his friend] al-Ḥuṣayn [ibn al-Ḥumām, also a poet, of the tribe Dhubyān]. He got drunk, turned to his own sister and deflowered her. He repented when he was sober again. Then he addressed his kinsmen (*qawm*) [who apparently were aware of what happened] and said,
>
> —What am I to you?
>
> —Our knight, our best man and leader!
>
> —If any of the Arabs learns what I have done, or if you tell anyone, I shall leave immediately and you will never see me again.
>
> And nobody came to know of it. But then a slave girl of some of the Ṭayyiᵓ came into the possession of al-Ḥuṣayn ibn al-Ḥumām. One day she saw al-Burj with him, while they were both drinking. When al-Burj had left, she said to al-Ḥuṣayn,

—That drinking companion of yours was drunk in your presence and then he did such-and-such with his sister! He was about to do the same to you whenever he came to you and got drunk ...

Al-Ḥuṣayn rebuked her and called her names, so she stopped talking.[108]

Subsequently, al-Burj carries out a raid on some protégés of al-Ḥuṣayn ibn al-Ḥumām, which causes a rift between the two. Some verses are exchanged, and al-Ḥuṣayn concludes his poem with a reference to al-Burj's infamous act:

... You mustn't think, al-ᶜUfāṭa's brother, that I
am ignorant of that matter concerning you.
They called you down, after you had made her shift wet,
from your mother's daughter, her skirt bloody.

In the ensuing conflict between the two and their clans, al-Burj and his men are defeated; some are killed and he himself is taken captive. Al-Ḥuṣayn forgives him for the sake of old times and frees him. When al-Burj returns to his people, he blames them:

—You have spread the news about what I did to my sister and you have shamed me!

Then he departed on the spot, leaving them and entering the land of the Byzantines. And until now nothing has ever been heard about him.[109]

Al-Iṣfahānī adds that according to another authority on pre-Islamic matters, Ibn al-Kalbī, al-Burj 'drank unmixed wine until it killed him'. A shorter and somewhat different version of this story is found in a work by Ibn Ḥabīb (d. 245/860), in a short chapter on 'Those Who Drank Unmixed Wine Until Death, out of Anger or Spite':

Al-Burj ibn Mus'hir al-Ṭāʾī woke up one night, having drunk. He heard his sister al-F.qāṭa urinate. He said [in rhymed prose],

—I can hear someone piss: a good lay for me that I can't give a miss.[110]

Then he jumped on her. She said,

—Damn you, I am your sister!

But he went on and deflowered her. The following morning he fled to Syria and stayed there, becoming a Christian. Subsequently al-Ḥuṣayn ibn al-Ḥumām made invective poetry on him, mentioning what he had done to his sister. Then al-Burj drank unmixed wine until he died.[111]

There is no happy ending to this story. Whereas the repentance of Qays ibn ᶜĀṣim and Ḥājib ibn Zurāra leads them to abandon sin and, eventually, to become good Muslims, al-Burj's repentance leads him first into exile,

Christianity, and finally death by means of what caused his sin in the first place.[112]

The motifs of wine and sister-rape recur in a story about the origin of the Magian close-kin-marriage.[113] ᶜAlī ibn Abī Ṭālib, explaining that the Zoroastrians are in fact to be considered 'People of Scripture' (*ahl kitāb*) together with Jews and Christians, tells the story of one of their kings (identified by ᶜAlī as Bukhtnaṣṣar or Nebuchadnezzar), who had intercourse with his sister when drunk. Like Qays and Ḥājib, he repents as soon as he is sober. 'Woe to you! what have I done and what is the way out?', he says to her. The sister, rather than trying to cover up the event, tells him to proclaim to the people that God has permitted marrying their sisters, hoping that they would accept this new rule. However, they were not easily persuaded, and after whip and sword had failed to impress them, the sister suggested digging a trench and burning the recalcitrant people. Even then, many preferred to be burned. The story is told to explain the rather cryptic reference in the Qur'an to 'the People of the Trench' (Q 85:4), who are more often identified with the Christian martyrs of Najrān in the Arabian Peninsula who suffered under the wicked king Dhū Nuwās around AD 520.[114] Wine as the cause of major sins is a recurrent motif in Muslim stories; one may compare, for instance, the story of the fallen angels Hārūt and Mārūt, where drinking, as a lesser sin, leads to greater ones.[115] As was mentioned in the introduction, some lexicographers defined the word *rahaq* as 'copulation with non-marriageable relations, as a result of drinking wine or something like it', as if such a heinous act as incest could only be committed while one's mind was clouded.

Arabic Historiography on the Majūs

When Arabic historical and literary sources mention close-kin marriage as a characteristic of Zoroastrianism, they do not bother to distinguish between theoretical belief or doctrine and religion as a practice in everyday life. They, too, often refer to the past, as does al-Yaᶜqūbī (d. 284/897) in his *History*:

> The Persians ... used to marry mothers, sisters and daughters, maintaining that this is a boon to them (*ṣila lahunna*) and a charitable act (*birr*) to them, as well as a pious deed to God concerning them.[116]

The words *ṣila lahunna* could also be interpreted as 'a bond with them'. *Birr* is the exact equivalent of Latin *pietas*, the kindness, piety, reverence and sense of duty that ought to exist, bi-directionally, between parents and children or between God and man. Al-Yaᶜqūbī uses positive terms to describe the custom and refrains from adding condemning comments.

In general, it is remarkable that most historians are reticent about the custom, either omitting polemical comments like al-Yaᶜqūbī, or not mentioning the custom at all. Al-Yaᶜqūbī was the first to write a universal history combined with chapters on various civilizations before Islam in an encyclopaedic manner. Speaking of the ancient, pre-Sasanian Persians, he mentions that 'there are verified reports concerning them that most people, as we see, reject and find repugnant. Therefore, we have omitted them, since it is our method to delete all repugnant things.'[117] One wonders what he refers to here. In any case, when he touches upon the incestuous custom, which must have been repugnant to him, he does not adopt a polemic stance.

Roughly the same structure as that of al-Yaᶜqūbī's *History* was adopted by Muḥammad ibn Jarīr al-Ṭabarī (d. 311/923) and al-Masᶜūdī (d. 345/956), both of whom wrote on a much grander scale. Yet in their lengthy sections on pre-Islamic Persia marriage customs are not discussed. When speaking of barbarians, unbelievers or heretics (on which see the next chapter), charging them with deviant and shocking sexual behaviour has always been popular, in any culture; but the Muslim Persians were generally not barbarians, unbelievers or heretics. Their Zoroastrian past tainted them to some extent, and could be used against them whenever it was opportune to do so, in anti-*shuᶜūbī* polemics, or generally in invective and jokes. It is striking, however, that many Arabic descriptions of the Persians and their Magian past dwell at length on their greatness, their wisdom and good manners, and are wholly silent on the embarrassing theme of incest. It could be that the historiographers were themselves Persians and therefore reluctant to dwell on such disreputable facts. The ethnic affiliations of both al-Yaᶜqūbī and al-Ṭabarī are uncertain;[118] but al-Masᶜūdī, who was an Arab, also deals with the pre-Islamic Persians at length without once referring to the practice.[119] It is true that he keeps referring to his *Akhbār al-zamān* ('Reports of Past Time', perhaps the most regrettable loss of Arabic letters) for more details, but if he had attached much importance to the incestuous practices, he would surely have mentioned them in his extant works. On a smaller scale, the Andalusian Arab Ṣāᶜid ibn Aḥmad (d. 462/1070) extols the Persian contribution to science and civilization in no uncertain terms in his survey *Ṭabaqāt al-umam* ('The Categories of Nations').[120] Although he mentions Zoroaster and Zoroastrianism (including Zurāra and his son Ḥājib's embracing of Magian practices),[121] there is not one word of condemnation. Abū Ḥanīfa al-Dīnawarī (d. 282/895), in his *al-Akhbār al-ṭiwāl* ('Long Reports'), gives relatively much attention to pre-Islamic Persia, but again he does not dwell on the topic of close-kin marriage, except when he discusses one celebrated case, without explaining that this was part of a widespread custom.

This case concerns the birth of Dārā (Darius), son of Bahman, in a story (also found in al-Ṭabarī) that aims at linking the origin of the Sasanid dynasty with its predecessor. Al-Dīnawarī tells the story as follows:

> They say that Bahman [ibn Isfandiyādh] had embraced the religion of the Israelites, but eventually he reverted to Zoroastrianism and married his daughter Khumānā (or Khumānī).[122] She was the most beautiful woman of her time. Bahman was on his death-bed when she was pregnant by him. He ordered that the crown be put on her belly, and told the leading men of the realm to obey her orders until she gave birth. If the child were a boy, they should confirm her rule until he had grown up and reached the age of thirty, and then the rule should be handed over to him.
>
> They say that Bahman's son Sāsān was at that time a handsome, intelligent, well-bred and virtuous man. He became the ancestor of the Persian kings called Akāsira [pl. of Kisrā/Chosroes], and therefore they are called Sasanids. People did not doubt but that he would rule as king after his father. When his father made Khumānā to rule, he disapproved strongly and left ...[123]

A somewhat later history of the Persian kings written in Arabic also tells the story in plain language, easily jumping from fatherly love to something more:

> ... She was the most beautiful woman of her time, in face and figure, and the most perfect in intelligence and virtue. So (*sic*) he loved her and married her, and thought the world of her (*lam yara l-dunyā illā bihā*) ...[124]

as if it were the most natural thing to do. The story is not found in every Arabic source where it might be expected. Al-Masᶜūdī[125] mentions Ḥumāya/Khumānā/Khumānī, daughter of Bahman, as well as Dārā, son of Bahman, and he tells that Khumānā/Khumānī, 'known as Shihrāzād, after her mother',[126] as a queen fought wars with the Byzantines and other kings, and was a good ruler to her subjects for thirty or more years before her brother Dārā took over. He fails, however, to explain that Dārā was more than her brother. When al-Ṭabarī tells the story he mentions the incest so casually that it escaped the attention of the recent translator:

> One authority said that Khumānī reigned after her father Bahman. When she was pregnant [by him] with Darius the Elder, she asked Bahman to crown the yet unborn child.[127]

The crucial words 'by him' (*minhu*), have been added by me. It is possible that al-Ṭabarī was reluctant to dwell on the incest element, to the point of not even providing a justification, because he did not wish to add more fuel to the debate on Arab or Persian superiority, or in order not to embarrass Persian readers; his own ethnic origins are unknown. A Persian version of the story, found in Ibn al-Balkhī's *Fārs-nāma* which was completed early in the 6th/12th century, also mentions the incest casually.[128]

In the universal encyclopedic history by al-Muṭahhar al-Maqdisī (*fl.* 355/966) it is told drily that 'Humāy became pregnant by her father Bahman shortly before he died'.[129] Both al-Ṭabarī and al-Maqdisī offer a sequel with motifs that are common in folklore: the newborn son is smuggled out of the palace and he is put afloat on the river in a cradle (al-Maqdisī) or a casket (al-Ṭabarī). After a shipwreck on the Tigris (al-Maqdisī) or the River al-Kurr, near Iṣṭakhr (al-Ṭabarī), the cradle is safely cast ashore and fostered by a fuller (in al-Maqdisī), or a miller (in al-Ṭabarī), and his wife, who know by the jewels on the boy that he is of noble birth. Eventually, as a comely lad he is recognized by his sister-mother 'whose milk began to flow and whose soul was stirred'. Her feelings, apparently, are motherly and there is no hint of further incestuous intrigues such as are known from Greek mythology, where Auge and her son Telephos, about to marry, are warned in the nick of time. Humāy tells her son-brother the truth and crowns him as king.[130]

This is the stuff of legend. It ended up in Arabic folk epic, in the Story of Fīrūz Shāh, son of King Ḍārāb, where, according to the summary by Malcolm Lyons, King Bahman rapes his daughter, called Ward Shāh (here it is apparently taken for granted that incest is wrong and there is no reference to Magian customs).[131] In Persian, it became part of high-status literature since the great 'national Persian epic', the *Shāhnāma* by Firdawsī (d. 411/1020) offers an elaboration of this story.[132] No rape there: his explanation of the father—daughter marriage is composed of two elements: it is on account of the girl's beauty and because it is 'in accordance with the custom which you call Pahlavi'.

The point of the story of the baby that is abandoned to the river could be to give an explanation of the long interval before the son succeeded his father. In Firdawsī's epic it is suggested that the mother wants the existence of her son to be kept secret not because it is a shameful affair, but because she wants to reign herself. However, one might think that in the eyes of al-Ṭabarī and al-Maqdisī, who do not justify the marriage as a Zoroastrian custom, the purpose of exposing the baby is simply what to a Muslim would be evident: the shameful incestuous birth must be hidden. Elsewhere in his work al-Maqdisī shows that he is aware of Zoroastrian marriage customs. In a section devoted to the doctrines and religious customs of the Majūs[133] he, for once, seems to speak of the present or at least the relatively recent rather than the remote past when he condemns the various kinds of Majūs, including the Bih-Āfrīdites (the followers of Bih-Āfrīd, mentioned above), the Khurramites ('there are no people as ravingly wrong and confused as these'),[134] the Manichaeans (al-Manāniyya), the Marcionites (al-Marqūniyya), and the Zoroastrians (al-Zaradūshtiyya). 'They allow the marriage of men with sisters and daughters, justifying this to those who oppose them on the basis of what

Adam, peace be upon him, did'.[135] Rather oddly, in a separate section on the Khurramites, having reviled them shortly before, he speaks of more positive personal acquaintance with them:

> As for those of them we have met in their territory, in Māsabadhān and Mihrajān Qadhaq, we found them to be extremely scrupulous about cleanliness and ritual purity, behaving very friendly towards other people, and doing them favours. We found that some of them allow marriage with any woman as long as it is with their consent, and who allow anything in which the soul finds pleasure and to which one is attracted by nature, as long as it does not result in harm to anybody.[136]

It is tempting, but obviously wrong, to imagine that the absence of commentary or condemnation on al-Maqdisī's part hides a secret approval of these modern-sounding ideas of consensus and mutual tolerance and respect. To a pious Muslim these matters are of secondary importance compared with God's commands.

*

The speech by Abū Ḥāmid al-Marwarrūdhī given by al-Tawḥīdī is perhaps the longest but not the only or the earliest reference to close-kin marriage in the debate on the superiority of Arabs and Persians. Al-Tawḥīdī quotes in another of his works a well-known early genealogist, Daghfal ibn Ḥanẓala (d. 65/685) as having said that

> the Arabs are superior to the Persians (*al-ᶜAjam*) in three things: because we preserve our genealogies and they let them get lost; we are chaste regarding our female relations, while they marry their mothers and sisters; and we possess a natural disposition for eloquence and clear speech.[137]

One suspects that the three things are in fact only two, or at least that the first two are firmly connected in Daghfal's mind. 'Preserving' or 'losing' is not merely a matter of recording and memorizing, for the words used (*ḥifẓ* and *ḍayāᶜ*) also imply 'keeping in good condition' and 'ruining', respectively. Using the word *ᶜiffa*, chastity, he expresses a moral judgment, but the genealogist in him speaks when he points out that close-kin marriage results in ruin (*ḍayāᶜ*) of lineages. Clarity is all, and perhaps it is no coincidence that the two terms Daghfal uses for the third characteristic, eloquent language, are also associated with the concepts of purity (*faṣāḥa*) and clarity (*bayān*).

Muḥammad ibn al-Kalbī (d. 146/763) praised the pre-Islamic Arabs because they anticipated Qur'anic prohibitions by not marrying mothers, daughters, or aunts maternal or paternal. The worst thing they did was to marry two sisters at the same time, or to marry their deceased fathers' wives.[138] In his *Kitāb al-ᶜArab* ('Book of the Arabs'), devoted to the virtues of the Arabs, Ibn Qutayba praises especially Quraysh, the Prophet's tribe, for preserving something of the old Abrahamic religion, inherited through Abraham/Ibrāhīm's son Ismael/Ismāᶜīl; these remnants included 'circumcision, ritual ablution, repudiation of women, manumission of slaves, and the prohibition of marriage with forbidden family members, through kinship, milk relationship, or affinity by marriage'.[139] Yāqūt (d. 626/1229) rephrases the same idea: the pre-Islamic Meccans

> were not like the uncouth[140] Bedouins. They used to circumcise their sons, to perform the Hajj at the Kaaba; ... they shunned marriages with a daughter, a daughter's daughter, a sister, and a sister's daughter, because of their sense of jealous honour and in order to keep aloof from the Magians.[141]

Zoroastrian Marriage as an Arabic Invective Motif

Most of the invective forms in which the topic of close-kin marriage appears are part of the general polemic of Shuᶜūbites and anti-Shuᶜūbites, the latter always dominant because they controlled and produced the sources that are at our disposal. The bulk of the material is not found in long discursive texts such as al-Tawḥīdī's session with the vizier, but in jokes and anecdotes. A joke may present incest as something pleasant:

> Someone said to a licentious fellow (*baᶜḍ al-mujjān*):
> —The good life is only had by the Zoroastrians! Father comes in and fucks, son comes in and fucks! [incest being implied in both cases, of course]
> —Shut up, don't let your womenfolk hear it, or they will renounce Islam![142]

But a joke cannot, of course, be taken seriously. It is in anecdotes, above all, that the Majūs are condemned or mocked for their allegedly incestuous practices. They are never, to my knowledge, directly addressed, but only figure *in absentia*. A typical anecdote, found in several versions, usually in sections about stupid people, is the following, here taken from al-Jāḥiẓ's work on the eloquence of the Arabs:

ᶜAwāna [d. *c.* 150/767] said: Muᶜāwiya [*reg.* 41-60/661-80] once appointed a man from the tribe of Kalb as governor. One day, the Majūs were mentioned when people were gathered with this person. He said,

—God curse the Majūs! They marry their mothers. By God, even if they gave me one hundred thousand dirhams I would not marry my mother!

This was reported to Muᶜāwiya, who said,

—God damn him! Suppose they gave him more than one hundred thousand, would he do it then?!

And he dismissed him from his post.[143]

The dismissal of this well-meaning governor seems rather harsh, which is perhaps why in some versions of this story it is omitted. Hardly historical, the point of the story is to show how unthinkable the matter should be to good Muslims. Another caliph, al-Maʾmūn (*reg.* 198-218/813-833) is involved in a rather bluntly-phrased story about a Christian dignitary and a Zoroastrian one:

Al-Maʾmūn was sitting with some theologians in his presence, as well as the Catholicus (*al-Jāthalīq*). The Mūbadh [or Mōbedh, Magian priest][144] arrived, and the Catholicus said,

—Commander of the Believers, would you like me to make you laugh at the Mūbadh?

He turned to the Mūbadh and said,

—This man claims that Paradise is in his mother's cunt, and that the more he copulates with her, the closer he gets to the Gate of Paradise!

Then the Mūbadh said,

—We used to do that, until we were told that your god came out of such a place.

Thus he silenced him, and al-Maʾmūn laughed, to the extent that his foot scraped the floor.[145]

Judging by the caliph's mirth the joke was successful, although it is not exactly obvious why the Magians, hearing about the birth of Christ, should therefore have discontinued their custom: one might think it would only confirm them in their belief. In a version given by al-Tawḥīdī the Mūbadh's reply is different and more logical: 'We used to suspect that this was true. But when we learned that your god came from that place, our doubts ceased.'[146] The story uses the well-known format of the debate between contestants before some kind of arbiter or authority. Although in this story the Magian defeats the Christian, it would be wrong to conclude that the point of the anecdote is to show that Zoroastrianism is superior to Christianity. To Muslim readers, it only serves to underline the superiority of Islam, whose supreme ruler is able to use the primates of other religions and make them act in his presence and on his behalf as foul-mouthed buffoons and jesters. Obscenity is cleverly exploited to ridicule points deemed offensive in each of the two rival religions: the absurdity, in Muslim eyes, of Christ's divine nature,[147] and the next-of-kin marriage of the Magians. To a Muslim, conscious incest can only be committed out of utter depravity or utter stupidity. 'He (Zoroaster) prescribed to them the fucking[148] of mothers and the ritual ablution with cows' piss when he saw how utterly stupid they were'.[149]

A Digression: Muslim Anti-Jewish Polemics

It is remarkable that when the Persians are derided for the incestuous practices of their ancestors, they are almost never described as suffering from the physical and intellectual degeneration that may result, even though the Arabs were well aware of the connection, as we have seen. For possible and somewhat doubtful exceptions, see the few invective lines by al-Farazdaq quoted below.[150] This state of affairs may be contrasted, for instance, with what al-Jāḥiẓ, in his *al-Radd ʿalā l-Naṣārā* ('Refutation of the Christians'), says about the Jews, calling them uglier, weaker and more stupid than Christians as a result of their inbreeding:

> The Christians, with all their misshapenness (*masākha*), are nevertheless not as misshapen as the Jews, and the only reason is that an Israelite will not marry except with another Israelite. All their marriages are between themselves and restricted to themselves, without any admixture of strange women, nor have males of foreign races had intercourse with them. They have not produced noble offspring in terms of intellectual ability, physical strength, or charm. As you know, these same things may be observed in horses, camels, donkeys and pigeons.[151]

The choice of the word *masākha*, rather than *ḍawā*, for instance, seems prompted by the context, for its exact meaning is 'transformation into an ugly shape', and it is precisely the Christians and the Jews who have been punished with *maskh*, being changed into monkeys and pigs, according to Muslim tradition.[152] Although *masākha* could refer to physical change only, al-Jāḥiẓ makes it clear that in this case the degeneration as a result of inbreeding affects the intellect (*ʿaql*) as well as bodily strength (*asr*). The third term that he uses, *milḥ*, has been variously and mostly wrongly interpreted. It has several meanings in addition to 'salt'. The editor, ʿAbd al-Salām Muḥammad Hārūn, explains it as 'suckling and milk (*al-raḍāʿ wa-l-laban*)' and Finkel translates it as 'superior lactation'; but this oddly specific fact sits uneasily with the two more general preceding concepts. Hawke has 'shrewdness',

Müller has 'Geist' and Allouche, on unexplained grounds, 'science'. The dictionaries also offer 'fat' or 'plumpness'. There can be little doubt that one has to connect it with the word *malāḥa*, implying a combination of pleasant outward appearance and pleasing behaviour ('attractiveness, charm, elegance, or grace'), seeing that al-Jāḥiẓ uses the word *milḥ* in this sense many times, speaking of people or animals.[153] Since al-Jāḥiẓ explicitly mentions the absence of outbreeding on the male as well as the female side, and stresses the physical, intellectual and behavioural consequences, his statement is altogether the most comprehensive condemnation of persistent inbreeding. Why are the Jews singled out for this treatment, and not the Persians, whose close-kin marriages could have had far more disastrous results? No doubt because, firstly, in al-Jāḥiẓ's time the Zoroastrian *khwētōdah* was largely a thing of the pre-Islamic past and endogamy was not practised by the Persians in general; and secondly because the Jews, unlike the mostly Muslim Persians, qualified as Most Despised Nation among the Muslim Arabs. Whereas the canon law of the Christians was much more restrictive concerning marrying kin than the Muslim regulations, the Jews allowed unions considered incestuous by the Muslims. Al-Masᶜūdī relates that in the course of a discussion on religious matters, held in the presence of the Egyptian ruler Ibn Ṭūlūn (*reg.* 254-270/868-884), a Copt accosted a Jewish doctor:

> —Who are you, and what is your religion?
> —I am Jewish.
> —A Zoroastrian, then!
> People protested,
> —How could that be, since he is a Jew?
> —Because they allow marrying their daughters in some situations. For their religion teaches that a man may marry the daughter of his brother, and it prescribes that they should marry the wives of their brothers when the latter die. Thus, if the wife of his brother happens to be his daughter, he is forced to marry her. This is one of their secrets that they keep hidden and do not make public. Is there anything in Zoroastrianism that is more abominable than that?
> The Jew disavowed this and denied that this was part of his religion, or that anyone of the Jews knew about this. However, when Ibn Ṭūlūn investigated the truth of the matter, he found that the same Jewish doctor had in fact married his brother's daughter, who was his own daughter.[154]

The unlikely conclusion of this report is obviously a piece of anti-Jewish polemic, but the point raised by the Coptic speaker is interesting. He points to a possible result of the levirate, the Jewish custom of marrying a childless brother's widow, and the fact that a man may marry his niece.[155] Knowing the Rabbis' thoroughness and fondness for such hypothetical cases, it is very unlikely that they had not already foreseen the possibility and dealt with it accordingly. Al-Masᶜūdī himself remarks that the Jews deny the allegation that it would be possible to marry one's own daughter, even though the majority of them allow marrying one's niece.[156] The Copt continues his attack on the Jews, mentioning in passing the story of Lot who, intoxicated by wine, unwittingly impregnated his own two daughters on two consecutive nights.[157] This well-known story (see Gen. 19:30-38) is used against the Jews, not in order to show that incest was known even among their patriarchs, but to show that their version of the revealed text is dreadfully corrupt and distorted. After all, the story of Abraham, Lot and the other patriarchs is also part of traditional Muslim Arab history; and Muslims are, on the whole, much less inclined to accept that Rightly Guided prophets and apostles could have had failings than the rather more humane authors of the Hebrew Bible.

The most outspoken critic of the alleged distortions of the Jews in their biblical text is the fiercely polemical Ibn Ḥazm, whose literalist rationalism makes him blind to the narrative merits that human failings may have, and who zealously guards the reputation and impeccable genealogy of patriarchs and prophets. He introduces his comments on the passage on Lot and his daughters by saying that 'it contains shameful and wicked things which will make the skins shiver', when heard by true believers who are aware of the respect that is due to the prophets.[158] The first absurdity is the false justification used by the two daughters: 'Our father is old, and there is not a man in the earth to come in unto us after the manner of all earth.' This, says Ibn Ḥazm not without ground, is blatant nonsense. More importantly, the story cannot be true, for God would not have allowed one of His prophets to commit, even unwittingly, such a heinous act.

> And if they say that he is not to be blamed for this because he did it while he was drunk and he did not know who they were, then we reply: What did he do then when he saw that they were pregnant; when he saw that they had given birth to two sons as a result of improper conduct; when he saw how they raised these bastard boys? These are perpetually shameful things, the procreation of Manichaeans, that are extreme in their contempt of God Almighty and His Apostles, may God preserve them.[159]

Finally, he argues, it is unthinkable that these two sons (eponymous ancestors of the Moabites and the Ammonites), 'these bastards, hatchlings of fornication)' could ever have been recognized as Lot's sons, inheriting land just like the sons of the other patriarchs.

Ibn Ḥazm did not have to wait long before he found more grist to his mill. Immediately following the story of Lot and his daughters, Genesis 20 relates that Abraham called his wife Sarah his sister, explaining subsequently that she is his father's daughter, though not his mother's. While the father—daughter incest of Lot is obviously deemed shameful to some extent even in the Hebrew text, since Lot has to be tricked into it, nobody in the Genesis story seems to take offence to Abraham's sibling marriage. Abraham has the obvious excuse that he could not have been aware of Moses' laws and Leviticus 18:9: 'The nakedness of thy sister, the daughter of thy father, or daughter of thy mother, whether she be born at home, or born abroad, even their nakedness thou shalt not uncover.' Ibn Ḥazm, however, to whom Abraham/Ibrāhīm was in a sense the first true Muslim, will have none of this. He tells that he discussed the passage with 'Ismāᶜīl ibn Yūsuf al-kātib, known as Ibn al-Naghrālī', otherwise known as Samuel the Nagid or Ibn Nagrila (d. 1056). It is interesting to see that this famous Jewish poet and prince, apparently embarrassed by this story, tried to eliminate the sibling relationship by suggesting that the word 'sister' in Hebrew may be applied to more distant female relations. Ibn Ḥazm was quick to demolish this feeble attempt, pointing out that Abraham's own words leave no doubt that 'sister' meant 'father's daughter' in his case. It is clear to Ibn Ḥazm that one must conclude that the text is falsified.[160] To Ibn Qayyim al-Jawziyya, who like Ibn Ḥazm denounces the story of Lot and his daughters as gross slander, the fact that Abraham tells King Abimelech that Sarah is his sister, thus hiding his marriage to her, proves that marrying one's sister was already prohibited in those days.[161]

Another kind of Muslim sensitivity is hurt when, soon after this, Ibn Ḥazm comes across Reuben who marries Bilha, his father's concubine (Gen. 35:22),[162] or various instances of the levirate.[163] 'God forbid', he comments, that God should forsake His prophet and not protect him against these disgraces that affect the inviolability (*ḥurma*) of his wife and daughter'. The harm lies not so much in the genealogical confusion that result from such unions, as in the disrespect to the *pater familias*. Summarizing, Ibn Ḥazm exclaims:[164]

> By God, I have never seen a nation that affirms belief in prophethood yet attributes to the prophets all these things that these unbelievers attribute to them. First they impute to Ibrāhīm/Abraham that he married his sister, who gave birth to his son Isḥāq/Isaac. Then they charge Yaᶜqūb/Jacob with marrying one wife who then provided him with another woman who was not his wife, and who bore him children ... Then they charge Rūbān/Reuben, the son of Yaᶜqūb/Jacob, with fornication with his stepmother, wife of his father, the prophet, and the mother of his brothers. Then they impute to Yahūdhā/Judah that he fornicated with the wife of his two sons, who became pregnant and gave birth to a bastard child,[165] from whom Dāwūd/David and Sulaymān/Solomon are descended. Then they impute to Yūshaᶜ/Joshua, son of Nūn that he

married Raḥab, the notorious harlot who devoted herself to whoredom with every male on two legs in the town of Jericho.[166] Then they charge ᶜImrān/Amram, son of Quhath/Kohath, son of Lāwī/Levi, with marrying his aunt, the sister of his father, who was called Yūḥābadh/Jochebed, who was born to his grandfather [Lāwī/Levi] in Egypt and who gave birth to Hārūn/Aaron and Moses.[167]

Magian Marriage in Lampoons, Love Poetry, and Literary Riddles

In the passage quoted above Ibn Ḥazm does not refer to the Zoroastrian customs. In popular stories, anecdotes, jokes, and poems, however, the association between the Majūs and incestuous unions is relatively frequent. It is related that the profligate Umayyad caliph al-Walīd ibn Yazīd (*reg.* 125-126/743-44), bad ruler but gifted poet, deflowered one of his daughters in the presence of one of her maids; the word used, *ḥāḍina* 'nurse', seems to indicate that the girl was still very young. The woman cries out: 'This is Zoroastrianism!', but al-Walīd tells her to shut up and recites a famous verse: 'He who regards people's opinions will die of grief / but a daring man will attain pleasure'. Although the story has a chain of authorities going back to the famous scholar Hishām ibn al-Kalbī, Abū l-Faraj al-Iṣfahānī, who quotes it, doubts its truth. As the reason for his scepticism he does not mention that many flagrant and dubious stories were attributed to the Umayyad caliphs and to al-Walīd ibn Yazīd in particular during the reign of their successors, the Abbasids, but merely the fact that the line he is said to have quoted is in fact by a later poet, Salm al-Khāsir (d. 186/802), who could not have been known to al-Walīd.[168] The incident is not mentioned by other sources, although some late ones speak in vague terms about al-Walīd's 'ravishing those made inviolable by God',[169] and others specify that he married his father's wives.[170]

Apart from the lines by the repentant Ḥājib ibn Zurāra quoted above, I have found only one pre-Islamic instance of the invective motif with an allusion to Magian marriages. The early poet Aws ibn Ḥajar (6th century) lampooned some tribesmen of Qays ibn Thaᶜlaba (who lived in Eastern Arabia) for marrying their stepmother Fukayha, saying that 'the Persian custom (*al-fārisiyya*) is not rejected among you'.[171] The employ of *al-fārisiyya*, implying Zoroastrianism, is unusual. The poet clearly insinuates, probably without foundation, that Fukayha was their biological mother.[172]

After the Islamic conquest the references to the Zoroastrians increase in number. Comparisons to the Majūs in lampoons do not always hint at sexual matters; al-Jarīr (d. *c.* 111/729), whose invective abounds in obscene abuse, concludes a poem against a clan in a subdued mood with 'Do not boast, for the religion of Mujāshiʿ is that of the Zoroastrians, who circumambulate an idol'.[173] Rather different are verses by his great rival al-Farazdaq (d. *c.* 110/728) on the clan of Jaʿfar ibn Rabīʿa:

No husband of a Jaʿfarī woman dies but
her son, on reaching puberty, will visit her ...

The commentator clarifies: 'meaning that the son takes the place of the father';[174]

... Their bodies know that Jaʿfar are
Zoroastrians, their cunts and pricks.[175]

It is likely that the poet blows up the matter, from incest by affinity (marrying stepmothers) to consanguineous incest. It is tempting to think that the reference to 'bodies' hints at stuntedness, but in this kind of invective one would have expected a more explicit wording. Another possible but vague hint at stuntedness is offered by lines in another poem by al-Farazdaq:

He has donned the cloak of baseness when (still) in his mother's belly;
his arms and fingers testify to that,
Just as the hands of the Zoroastrians testify against them ...[176]

The commentary on the first line explains: 'He means that he has short and base arms and fingers' (whatever 'base', *laʾīm*, implies here). Unfortunately the second line is not elucidated.

A contemporary of Jarīr and al-Farazdaq, Ziyād al-Aʿjam (d. *c.* 100/718), either a Persian or a Persianized Arab,[177] was derided by Kaʿb al-Ashqarī (d. *c.* 95/714), an Arab, as

An uncircumcised one, who prays after having fucked his mother,
thinking that's permitted in the religion of the Zoroastrians.

Ziyād ably avenged himself by replying, 'So she informed you that I am uncircumcised?'.[178]

When the blind poet Bashshār ibn Burd (d. *c.* 167/784) is allowed to converse with the slave-girls of the caliph al-Mahdī, they say, 'If only you were our father, then we would never be separated from you!'. The poet replies, 'Yes, and if only Kisrā's religion were mine, then'. The caliph is amused.[179] A certain man from Homs in Syria, according to an anecdote told by al-Tawḥīdī, 'once looked at his daughter and was pleased with her buttocks. "My dear child", he exclaimed, "How blessed we would be if we were Magians!"'[180] Al-Tawḥīdī explains that to correct the solecism *ṭūbatanā*, instead of *ṭūbā lanā*, would spoil the telling of this joke about this 'ignoramus' (*jāhil*).

The following lampoon on an unknown person by Abū ᶜAlī al-Muḥassin ibn Ibrāhīm ibn Hilāl al-Ṣābiᵓ (d. 401/1010), quoted by Yāqūt, is perhaps the richest and most explicit of its kind:[181]

Shall I lampoon a Zoroastrian who, if I told him
 to fuck his mother openly, would not eschew it as a sin?
When she is mentioned to him his heart is thrilled
 and he has an erection, yearning for her, infatuated.
He longs for her with two longings, for he
 would be husband to her, and is already her son.
He paid her for the debt for sucking her breast with his prick:
 he displays (?) his genitals to her, and she her mouth to him.[182]
Now if she were knocked up, made pregnant one day,[183]
 the baby would be a brother and a son to him if he traced his pedigree.
He fucks distant and near relations, thus deeming permissible
 what God has made forbidden.
When people of various religions pray to their Lord,
 he is the first to jabber in his prayer, muttering.[184]
He backs out of the hardships that have been imposed on others,
 and considers pleasures his just reward and gain.

It should be noted that the poet, although a member of a distinguished family of scholars and literati, was a pagan, of the planet-worshipping religion of the Ṣābiᵓa that survived in Ḥarrān/Carrhae for several centuries in the Islamic period; it is said that they did not marry near kin.[185] Yāqūt tells that he has read the poem in al-Muḥassin's handwriting, in an anthology compiled by the latter for his son Hilāl, the famous historian (who converted to Islam), and attributed to 'a modern poet of our time'. After the father's death the son had added in the margin: 'These lines are by Abū ᶜAlī al-Muḥassin ibn Ibrāhīm ibn Hilāl, God rest his soul.' It is a pity that we do not know the victim of this lampoon, or whether he was a genuine Zoroastrian or perhaps someone suspected or merely accused of having more than filial feelings towards his mother. It is, of course, a golden rule in studying Arabic lampoons never to take the accusations at face value, but when a poem, like the present one, dwells on a theme at some length, there must be a reason for it, however slight or innocent.

The verses quoted here do by no means exhaust the invective use of the incest motif; here I have only given those that connect it overtly with Zoroastrianism. As for those that do not, they will be discussed in Chapter

Four. The few references to the incest motif that preceded in this section are either invective and satirical or jocular. The motif is also found in contexts that are, if not entirely serious, at least semi-serious. A borderline case is a line in a short love poem by Abū Tammām (d.231/846), admiring his beloved:

... if her father saw her, he would say,
smitten with love, Would that I were a Zoroastrian![186]

At first glance the poet seems to use the motif without apparent irony. Yet it may be that the poet is not wholly serious, for there is a play on words: the line is introduced by the common formula of admiration *bi-abī* '[I would ransom her] with my father['s life]', as if the poet would sacrifice his own father while in a sense identifying himself with the girl's father. When the famous singing-girl Faḍl sees the caliph al-Mutawakkil (*reg.* 232-247/847-861) playing with his daughter, the caliph quotes this line and asks her who made it. She tells him, wrongly, that it was Abū l-ᶜAtāhiya (d. *c.* 211/826); the caliph gives orders to send ten thousand dirhams to him, and when he is told that the poet has died, he gives orders to spend it on his tomb and on a surviving son.[187] Al-Mutawakkil's contemporary, ᶜAbd al-Ṣamad ibn al-Muᶜadhdhal (d. *c.* 240/854), elaborates the motif in a poem on a slave-girl that he used to call his 'daughter':

I love my little daughter with a love that, I think,
is greater than (ordinary) love for daughters.
I find myself being fond of pinching your cheek,
to suck your lips and gums,
To press your belly against mine,
to pull your loose-hanging locks, embracing you,
And something nice that I will not mention,
which a lucky man gets from a girl.
When we meet, I find the rule of Zoroastrians
as lawful as drinking the water of the Euphrates.[188]

Al-Mutanabbī (d. 354/965) uses the motif in the following verses:

O sister of him who 'embraces' knights in battle:
your brother is truly gentler and more compassionate than you:
He stares at you, but chastely, while thinking
that the Zoroastrians are right in their rulings.[189]

He uses the common metaphor 'embracing' for attacking with the sword; the brother is thus described as kinder than the cruel but beautiful beloved sister. Naturally, there is an implied paradox in that a stare that is accompanied by thoughts of incest can hardly be called 'chaste', except in the very literal sense of not referring to actual carnal intercourse.

Taking the metaphor a step further, from the world of human beings to the realm of things, the poet Muslim ibn al-Walīd (d. 208/823) calls wine

a Zoroastrian's daughter, whose father is her spouse:
her genealogy does not go beyond the river.[190]

He refers to the customary mixing of wine (feminine in Arabic) with water (masculine); the grape juice is ultimately derived from the water with which the vine has been irrigated, so that wine is the daughter and the water is the father/spouse. This plausible interpretation is given by a later anthologist.[191] The 4th/10th-century commentator of the *Dīwān*, on the other hand, explains, mistakenly I believe, that the wine merchant is the wine's spouse by virtue of having bought it, and its father since he has 'raised' it (*rabbāhā*); he interprets *al-nahr* as a place name. A similar metaphor by Muslim speaks of

A fine ruddy wine, daughter of a fine yellow
wine, not having been pressed:
Two sisters, one being the daughter of her sister,
both of them leaving a healthy man sick (i.e. drunk).[192]

The point seems to be that one of the two wines is made from juice that trickles from the grapes without pressing, and thus is the 'daughter' of the juice that remains in the grapes that was once its 'sister'. There is no mention of Zoroastrians here, or in the line by the Andalusian poet Muḥammad ibn Safar, who may have been inspired by Muslim ibn al-Walid in the following line, in which he describes the bubbles resulting from the mixing of wine with water:

Do not find its fury odd: it resents that her father has become her husband.[193]

The incest motif applied to things is already found in the poetry of the last great Bedouin poet, Dhū l-Rumma (d. 117/735), who, as a true Bedouin, connects it with the idea of stuntedness rather than Zoroastrianism, and may have been thinking of camels instead of people. In a striking poem full of riddles he offers the following enigmatic description:

Her brother is her father, though stuntedness (*ḍawā*) does not harm her;
and the leg of its father is its mother, having been cut off.[194]

It is not a true riddle, for the solution is already suggested in lines that precede, which compare a 'spark' to a little child engendered by two parents.[195] The poet speaks of the fire that is engendered by rubbing two pieces of wood cut from the same tree: the one on top, the fire-stick (*zand*), is the 'father', to be rubbed in a notch made in the lower piece (*zanda*). This piece, here called 'leg', is the trunk from which it has been cut and thus called the 'mother'. The sexual metaphor readily offers itself in view of the technique as well as the vocabulary. The poet and lexicographer Ibn Durayd (d. 321/933) took up the same motif in order to accommodate the word *ḍawā* in his long poem *al-Maqṣūra*, so called because all its *rajaz* couplets rhyme in -*ā* (*alif maqṣūra*):[196]

> One that has been brought forth—the mother of his father being his mother,
> His body not impaired by stuntedness—
> I made to lie upon his brother's daughter, who revealed
> A child with whom one can make a fire or roast.[197]

The commentator, al-Tibrīzī, explains that 'one that has been brought forth' is a branch; that 'the mother of his father' is either the earth that produced both trunk and branch, or the trunk itself, from which the fire-stick is cut. When the poet and critic Ḥāzim al-Qarṭājannī (d. 684/1285) surpasses Ibn Durayd with a *maqṣūra* poem of more than one thousand couplets, he mentions *ḍawā* explicitly in connection with camels. He connects two familiar motifs, the emaciation of camels through travel, and the wasting of lovers' bodies:

> The bodies of ruddy camels are infected by [the lovers'] bodies
> that can hardly be seen because of their extreme *ḍawā*.[198]

Making stuntedness a kind of contagious disease, metaphorically, is obviously a poetic licence. In any case, connotations of inbreeding or incest are absent here, or at best remote.

*

Notwithstanding the possible physical disadvantages of next-of-kin marriage, there is one bizarre fact that would seem to indicate a medically positive effect, at least according to the Zoroastrians themselves. In connection with a disease called *namla* 'ant', a kind of skin ulcer or pustules said to occur variously in the side (*al-janb*)—perhaps shingles—, on the back of the hand, or the legs, it is said the Majūs believe that it can be cured if a man born from a union between father and sister traces lines over the pustules (*khaṭṭa ʿalā l-*

namla). Hence, we are told, there is an Arabic saying 'someone traces lines over the ants', used to insinuate that he is a Zoroastrian. In support an anonymous line of verse is quoted in which the poet says proudly of his clan, 'We do not trace lines over ants', as if to say, we are no Zoroastrians who mate with their sisters.[199] Needless to say, the physicians ignore this 'cure'.[200]

Muslim Heresiography on the Zoroastrians

In the text by al-Tawḥīdī the theme of Zoroastrian incest is employed above all in the debate on Arab *v.* Persian superiority. It is abundantly clear from this and many other passages quoted above that this debate cannot be separated from the religious debate on the superiority of Islam *v.* Zoroastrianism, but here the matter of incestuous marriage is, at best, a side issue. Although both Islam and Zoroastrianism are perhaps best considered as religions of orthopractice rather than orthodoxy, being more concerned with rituals and matters of purity than with doctrinal systems, it is precisely doctrine that is foremost in religious polemics. Muslim scholars often show a certain uneasiness about the fact that Zoroastrians are awarded the same status of 'protected religious minority' (*dhimma*) as those who profess one of the monotheistic religions, the 'People of the Book' (*ahl al-kitāb*), viz. Jews and Christians, even though Zoroastrian belief cannot be described as truly monotheistic, nor are its scriptures recognized by Muslims as standing in the same tradition as their own or those of Jews and Christians. Fakhr al-Dīn al-Rāzī, in connection with the Qur'anic rules on incest, calls Zoroaster 'the apostle of the Majūs' but adds that most Muslims agree that he was a liar.[201] In this respect the Zoroastrians are like the pagan, planet-worshipping Sabians of Ḥarrān, whose privileged status in Islam is due to a felicitous confusion with a rather obscure sect also called *Ṣābiʾa*, 'Baptists'.[202] There was no confusion in the case of the Zoroastrians; their status was the result of practical considerations. The Qur'an mentions them only once (Q 22:17), without condemning them for any specific beliefs or customs. It lumps them together with almost anyone else on earth: «they that believe, and those of Jewry, the Sabaeans, the Christians, the Magians and the idolators»,[203] adding that God will separate them on the Day of Judgement. The only 'canonical' statement attributed to the Prophet Muḥammad involving Zoroastrianism, his famous saying about parents being the ones who 'Judaicize, Christianize, or Zoroastrianize' their child, is equally neutral in tone.[204]

When Muslim religious scholars attack Zoroastrianism, it is above all because of its fire-worship and its recognition of two primeval principles, Good and Evil, instead of one God who is responsible for both good and evil.

Nevertheless, when attacking and vilifying opponents, arguments and insinuations that involve deviant sexual matters are eagerly deployed. Thus in the work *Akhbār al-zamān*, wrongly ascribed to al-Masᶜūdī, we read that the custom had a devilish and Faustian origin:

> It is said that Ardashīr (Artaxerxes) saw his Satan in a dream. He said to him, 'Teach me knowledge that will be useful for me'. Satan answered, 'On condition that you marry your mother, for she is your closest relative'. This he did, and it became the religion (or custom, *dīn*) of the Zoroastrians. The Persians allege that marrying one's sister dates from the time of Adam; subsequently their heretics (*zanādiqatuhum*) gave them free rein to marry their mother. 'She is more entitled to it than a sister,' they told them. So they did.[205]

Ibn al-Jawzī, in his polemical work *Talbīs Iblīs* ('The Deception of the Devil'), says,

> Al-Jāḥiẓ says: Then came Zoroaster, from Balkh. He is the leader [or rather 'founder of the religion', *ṣāḥib*] of the Zoroastrians. He maintained that revelation had come over him on Mount Sīlān,[206] and he preached to the inhabitants of those cold regions, who only knew cold, threatening them with a great increase in coldness (as divine punishment). He affirmed that he had been sent only to the mountains. He prescribed for his followers ritual ablution with urine, copulation with mothers, worshipping fires, and other disgusting things.[207]

The passage is a rewriting of a section on coldness in *al-Ḥayawān* ('Living Beings') by Jāḥiẓ;[208] but there al-Jāḥiẓ is not primarily bent on attacking the Zoroastrians, and the sentence on urine and mother—son incest is an addition by Ibn al-Jawzī. Elsewhere in the same work Ibn al-Jawzī expands his polemic against the Magians, repeating that

> they wash their faces with cows' urine by way of blessing (the older it is, the more blessing), and they consider it permissible to marry mothers. They say: a son is the one most fit to allay his mother's lust; and when the husband dies, then his son is the one most entitled (*awlā*) to the wife.[209]

He goes on to describe how Mazdak, the revolutionary leader during the reign of the Sasanid ruler Qubādh (488-531), abolished marriage impediments altogether, allowing men to have intercourse with any woman and putting this sexual communism into practice with the wives of King Qubādh, hoping to make people follow his example. Qubādh's son Anūsharwān, crying before

Mazdak and his father, then implores them to give his mother to him instead. When Mazdak refuses, Qubādh asks him, 'But don't you maintain that a believer should not be denied the gratification of his sexual lust? So why do you deny this to Anūsharwān?' Then he gave her to Anūsharwān, who, once he reigned as king, put an end to Mazdak and his sect.[210] This lurid story, which has ancient roots in anti-Mazdaean polemics, is used to show that while Zoroastrianism is bad, there are even worse religions.

Certainly worse, in Muslim eyes, than being a Zoroastrian was to be a Manichaean or an adherent of Mazdakism.[211] Persecution of Manichaeans, called *zanādiqa* (sing. *zindīq*), which is often loosely applied to anyone considered a heretic, took place during the reigns of al-Mahdī (158-169/775-785) and his son al-Hādī (169-170/785-786). It is during this period that one comes across a case of alleged incest. Al-Ṭabarī tells in his *History* that in the year 169/785-86 Fāṭima, daughter of Yaᶜqūb b. al-Faḍl b. ᶜAbd al-Raḥmān b. ᶜAbbās b. Rabīᶜa b. al-Ḥārith b. ᶜAbd al-Muṭṭalib (a distinguished lineage, being of the Prophet's clan, Hāshim), confessed to being pregnant by her father.[212] She, her father and her mother had been accused of being *zanādiqa*. Her father had been personally interrogated by al-Mahdī, had duly confessed, and had been discretely killed by being smothered under a carpet. His daughter Fāṭima was found to be pregnant. A contemporary witness relates:

> Fāṭima was taken to al-Hādī—or, before, to al-Mahdī—together with Yaᶜqūb ibn al-Faḍl's wife, who was not a Hāshimite; her name was Khadīja. Both confessed to being heretics; and Fāṭima confessed that she was pregnant by her father. The caliph sent both women to Rayṭa bint Abī l-ᶜAbbās [al-Mahdī's senior wife]. She looked at them, both with their eyes made up with kohl and [their fingers or faces] dyed with henna, and rebuked them, the girl in particular. 'He forced me,' said she; but Rayṭa replied, 'Then why the henna, the kohl, and this cheerful apparel, if you were forced?', and she cursed them. I was informed that they were so frightened that they died: they were beaten on the head with a thing called *ruᶜbūb*,[213] and were so frightened that they died.

Whether or not father and daughter were in fact Manichaean *zanādiqa*, their confessions of heresy and incest do not sound very convincing and it is possible that the pregnant girl, apparently unmarried and therefore in serious trouble in any case, accused her father in order to please her interrogators, who would gladly impute irregular sexual customs to heretical opponents.

Incest in Sects

Muslim heresiographers have also accused certain Islamic sects of practising incest. The word 'Islamic' means here that the adherents consider themselves as belonging to Islam. The heresiographers whose writings have become standard works, naturally representing the majority view, agree that the alleged incestuous practices put them outside the pale of Islam. In his work on the doctrines of Islamic sects and movements the great theologian al-Ashᶜarī (d. 324/935) quotes a certain al-Karābīsī[214], according to whom the ᶜAjārida (followers of Ibn ᶜAjarrad) and the Maymūniyya (followers of a certain Maymūn) allow marrying granddaughters and great-nieces, 'saying that God has (only) forbidden daughters and nieces'.[215] These two groups are classified among the politico-religious movement of the Khārijites, and were active in 2nd/8th-century Khurāsān, in the East. According to a later heresiographer, ᶜAbd al-Qāhir al-Baghdādī (d. 429/1037), this Maymūn had adopted some doctrinal views of the Muᶜtazilite movement and those called Qadarites, believers in free-will, views that by al-Baghdādī's time had fallen from grace. However, he adds, in a passage that with its reference to Qur'anic regulations anticipates our Chapter Three:

> He exceeded the Qadarites and the Khārijites, by a straying from the truth which he derived from the religion of the Zoroastrians: he allowed the marriage of granddaughters and the daughters of children of brothers and sisters. He argued that when God mentions the prohibition of marrying women on the basis of consanguinity, He only mentions mothers, daughters, sisters, aunts maternal and paternal, daughters of a brother and daughters of sisters; but He does not mention daughters of daughters, nor daughters of sons, nor daughters of brothers' sons, nor daughters of sisters' sons. If he were to pursue this analogy to include mothers of mothers and mothers of fathers and grandfathers, he would be a wholehearted[216] Zoroastrian. If, however, he does not allow the marrying of grandmothers and thus extends the sense of 'mothers' to include grandmothers, then he must extend the sense of daughters of one's own loins to include daughters of children: if he does not pursue his analogy in this matter, his reasoning becomes defective ... He who holds marriage with unmarriageable kin to be lawful thereby becomes a Zoroastrian; and a Zoroastrian cannot be reckoned among the sects of Islam.[217]

Maymūn's views may have been adopted from the Zoroastrians, as W. M. Watt has proposed[218] and as Abū l-Muẓaffar al-Isfarāyīnī (d. 471/1078) said before him.[219] It is true that these Khārijites were active in Iran and Khurāsān (the meaningless reading *Sh.khriyya* in ᶜAbd al-Qāhir's text is probably a corruption of *Sijziyya*, referring to Sijistān or Sīstān, south of Khurāsān). It is not at all certain that these sectarians were Persians. If they were mainly Arabs, it is not so very likely, in view of the proud intolerance and bigotry of the early Khārijites, that they would have adopted practices of second-rate citizens who were neither Muslims nor Arabs. However, whether they were Arabs or Persians, it is also possible that Maymūn's views are simply the result of a very literalist reading of the Qur'anic text, as al-Baghdādī's passage suggests, rather than vestiges of Zoroastrianism.

Doctrinally the opposite of the Khārijites, some extreme Shīᶜites (the various Ismāᶜīlī sects and movements) have also been accused of adopting Zoroastrian marriage customs. Politically and religiously far more dangerous and influential by the 4th/10th century than the Khārijites, the extreme Shīᶜites were the butt of very hostile attacks from the Sunnites, and it is not surprising that the accusations are proportionally more serious. ᶜAbd al-Qāhir al-Baghdādī says of the so-called Bāṭiniyya, the Ismāᶜīlī branch of the Shīᶜa:

> Having interpreted the foundations of religion on the basis of polytheism, they also have deceitfully interpreted the rulings of revealed Law (*al-Sharīᶜa*) in manners that lead to the cancellation of this Law, or to something resembling the rulings of the Zoroastrians. That this is in fact their intention is proved by their interpretation of the Law when they allow their followers to marry daughters and sisters, and allow drinking wine, and all sorts of sensual pleasures.[220]

In a subsequent passage he quotes from a letter allegedly by ᶜUbayd Allāh ibn al-Ḥasan al-Qayrawānī (the founder of the Fāṭimid dynasty, who called himself al-Mahdī) to a follower:

> Nothing is as astonishing as a man pretending to be intelligent, who has a pretty sister or daughter, who has no wife as pretty as she, and who then declares her forbidden to himself and marries her to an unrelated man! If this ignorant man were intelligent he would know that he himself has more right to his sister or daughter than this stranger. And that is only because their leader (*ṣāḥibahum*, apparently Muḥammad) has forbidden nice things to them and has scared them with the Unseen who cannot be imagined, that is, the God they claim exists ...[221]

The same argument in favour of incest is found elsewhere. In an anonymous anti-Islamic poem quoted by Abū l-ᶜAlāᵓ al-Maᶜarrī as being sung by singing-girls for Manṣūr al-Ṣanādīqī, also known as Manṣūr al-Yaman or Ibn Ḥawshab, 'prophet' of the 'Manichaeans' (*zanādiqa*)—in fact the Ismāᶜīlī or Carmathian movement—active in Yemen around 270/883-884:

Hey girl, pick up your tambourine and play,
 spread the praises of this prophet.
The prophet of the clan of Hāshim (Muḥammad) has gone,
 and the prophet of Yaᶜrub[222] has come.
We do not want to run at al-Ṣafā [during the Muslim pilgrimage]
 or to visit the tomb [of Muḥammad] in Yathrib (Medina).
If people perform the ritual prayer, do not stand up;
 and if they fast, then eat and drink.
Do not deny yourself those believers
 who are related or unrelated.
For why should you be allowed to marry a stranger
 but be forbidden to your own father?
Doesn't a plant belong to him who reared it
 and who watered it in a year of drought?
And wine is only like the water falling from clouds,
 permissible! Hallowed be this faith![223]

This poem (also quoted in a fiercely polemic work by the 5th/11th-century Yemeni heresiographer Muḥammad ibn Mālik[224]) could have been made in jest, just as Abū Nuwās probably made his antinomian poems at least partly in jest; it does not present incest as something horrible. The same imagery of the plant, which to the gullible might sound persuasive, is found embedded in a cautionary tale that is intended to show the depraved nature of him who used it. According to this tale, the last ruler of the harbour town Qalhat in Oman had an affair with his daughter and defended himself against his critics, saying, 'Why should I give to others the ripest fruit of my own garden?'. So his city was destroyed, the instrument of God's vengeance having been either 'an earthquake, a tidal wave, or the Portuguese'.[225] A modern version is found in an Arab folk tale in which the father argues to the judge that he is entitled to marry his daughter because she is 'a tree that I've cared for, feeding and watering it'.[226] And the plant metaphor still lives on, applied to first-cousin marriage rather than incest: Abdelwahab Bouhdiba relates that in Qairawan such unions are invariably justified with 'It is pure madness to give one's wealth to others', or 'Why irrigate the jujube tree? Priority for water belongs to the olive tree'.[227] The botanical metaphor, however, has also been used to recommend out-marrying, as when an unknown poet says,

If you want good children, then marry a stranger
 and do not seek a union with close relatives.
For one picks tasty and good fruit
 from an alien branch that is grafted.[228]

Chapter Three: Islamic Incest Regulations

Pre-Islamic Ignorance

In spite of a few notable and relatively short-lived exceptions, virtually every culture has incest taboos. They have been listed among 67 'universals of culture' by an American anthropologist, among such diverse things as calendars, dancing, food taboos, games, joking, kinship nomenclature, language, law, marriage, trade, and weaving.[1] Many cultures and religions, among them Islam, incorporate important taboos in their written laws.

In a work on sexuality in Islam, Abdelwahab Bouhdiba says that 'Islam offers the widest possible view of incest'.[2] This is obviously incorrect, for some societies or religions have or had a much wider interpretation of the idea of incest. Christian canon law, for instance, is much more restrictive and at one stage, in the eleventh century, forbade not only marrying one's blood relations to the seventh[3] degree, but also one's in-laws, the in-laws of one's in-laws, and the in-laws of the in-laws of one's in-laws;[4] in addition to consanguinity and affinity, spiritual kinship (godparents, godchildren) formed a barrier to marriage. Bouhdiba's statement is probably inspired by the unique Muslim rule concerning milk-relationship. The Arab Muslims themselves were aware of the existence of systems that were much stricter than their own, such as those of the Chinese and the Indians.[5] The Ṣābiʾans, too, that syncretistic sect that survived in Ḥarrān in Northern Mesopotamia, seem to have been more strict than the Muslims; at least that is suggested when Ibn al-Nadīm, writing towards the end of the 4th/10th century, says that 'they do not marry close kin'.[6] The relevant Islamic regulations go back to the very beginning of Islam, since the Qur'an itself provides the basic rules, which are relatively unambiguous and needed little further exegesis. Much has been written on the extent to which Islam changed or confirmed the existing customs in pre-Islamic Arabia. Data on these customs are scanty and have been exploited by writers who had certain axes to grind, such as those who wished to demonstrate that Islam brought great improvements in the position or women or of people in general, or those, like G. A. Wilken and W. Robertson Smith, who intended to prove that a matriarchal society had changed into a patriarchal one. As for the forbidden degrees of marriage, early Muslim authorities explain that the main differences between pre-Islamic and Islamic customs concerned the marriage of stepmothers and sons, and being married to two sisters simultaneously. Muḥammad ibn al-Sāʾib al-Kalbī (d. 146/763) praises the Arabs in the Jāhiliyya, the period of the 'ignorance', for anticipating Qur'anic prohibitions:

The Arabs, in the time of their Ignorance, held things for forbidden that the Qur'an was to declare forbidden. They did not marry daughters or mothers, nor sisters or aunts from the mother's side or the father's side. The worst thing they used to do was to be married to two sisters at the same time, or to succeed one's deceased father as husband to his wife. They used to call someone who did this *ḍayzan*. Aws ibn Ḥajar al-Tamīmī [the pre-Islamic poet] said, deriding some people of the tribe of Qays ibn Thaᶜlaba, who married their father's wife in turn, three of them, one after the other:

The Persian custom is not rejected among you:
each one of you is a *ḍayzan* to his father.
Fuck Fukayha, walk round her bower
like a giraffe, strutting arrogantly.[7]

(...) If a man died, leaving a wife, or divorced his wife, his eldest son would stand up and throw his cloak over her if he wanted her. If he did not want her, one of his brothers would marry her, with a new bride-price.[8]

Ibn Ḥabīb (d. 245/860), who has a nearly identical passage,[9] adds that 'Islam has separated men from the wives of their fathers; they are numerous'. He mentions names of some who married their fathers' wives and were separated as a result of the new Islamic rule:[10] Manẓūr ibn Zabbān, who married Mulayka bint Khārija;[11] Tamīm ibn Ubayy ibn Muqbil, who married Dahmāᵓ; or Muḥṣin ibn Abī Qays ibn al-Aslat, who 'inherited' his father's wife Kubaysha bint Maᶜn. Ibn Qutayba also mentions a few cases that happened before Islam could interfere,[12] such as Āmina bint Abān ibn Kulayb. She was married to Umayya ibn ᶜAbd Shams, the eponymous ancestor of the Umayyads, and upon his death she married Abū ᶜAmr, his son by a different wife. She had children by both father and son.[13] Jaydāᵓ bint Khālid was first married to Nufayl ibn ᶜAbd al-ᶜUzzā (their son was al-Khaṭṭāb, father of the future caliph ᶜUmar); after Nufayl's death she married his son ᶜAmr and had a son by him, called Zayd, 'a seeker after the true religion'.[14]

Ibn Ḥabīb also states that the Arabs used to marry two sisters: such as Abū Uḥayḥa Saᶜīd ibn al-ᶜĀṣ, who married Ṣafiyya and Hind, daughters of al-Mughīra ibn ᶜAbd Allāh; Qusayy (Thaqīf ibn Munabbih), who married Āmina and Zaynab, daughters of ᶜĀmir ibn al-Ẓarib; and Hinnām ibn Salama, whose wives are not named.[15]

As Robertson Smith has observed, in a version by Abū l-Fidāᵓ (d. 732/1331) the text by Ibn al-Kalbī quoted above is twisted in order to make the pre-Islamic customs even more like the Islamic ones: 'It was a most disgraceful thing in their eyes to marry two sisters at once, and they fixed ignominy on him who married his father's wife, calling him *ḍaizan*.'[16] Robertson Smith denies that *ḍayzan* was a name of contempt, mentioning that it was used as a personal name and that the native lexicons give various explanations. It seems likely, however, that it was an opprobrious word. The dictionaries explain it, among other things, as 'partner', or, less neutrally, 'someone who pushes away (*yuzāḥim*) his father concerning his wife', or 'someone who pushes others at the water basin'. In pre-Islamic legend, al-Ḍayzan is the name, or nickname, of a ruler of Hatra (al-Ḥaḍr), who was also called Sāṭirūn or Sanatruk.[17] Interestingly, one source tells us that although he was a good ruler, 'he deemed it permissible to marry daughters and sisters'.[18] His beautiful but treacherous daughter al-Naḍīra—we know that she was spoilt by her father, but there is no explicit mention of an incestuous relationship here—became the prototype of the Princess on the Pea (a myrtle leaf in her case), in a sad story found in several sources.[19]

Against the tendency of presenting the pre-Islamic Arabs as being very close to Islam already, others restrict this virtuous behaviour to the inhabitants of Mecca, contrasting them with the Bedouins, as did Yāqūt in the passage quoted above.[20] A book or treatise by the prolific al-Madāʾinī (d. *c.* 228/843) has the lengthy title *Those who married two sisters, those who married a stepdaughter, those who married more than four women and those who married a Zoroastrian woman*;[21] it is lost, so it is unknown if the compiler had a particular axe to grind. In view of al-Madāʾinī's preoccupations it is likely to have dealt with the Arabs, in pre-Islamic times and probably the early Islamic period. It is perhaps significant that the categories listed in this title, all relating to forms of marriage forbidden in Islam, do not include the more serious forms of incest. Robertson Smith, keen to prove the survival of matrilineal kinship among the Arabs which does not recognize kinship through fathers, summons evidence from other cultures of marriage with a non-uterine half-sister: the ancient Greeks in Athens, the Israelites (Abraham and his wife Sarah, Amnon who could have married Tamar), the Phoenicians; he adds that 'the same thing appears at Mecca'.[22] Only one example is given, however: ʿAwf b. ʿAbd ʿAwf (the father of the famous companion of the Prophet, ʿAbd al-Raḥmān b. ʿAwf) is said to have married his paternal sister al-Shifāʾ.[23] The sources are not very explicit and there may be some confusion here.[24] If the case is genuine, it seems to be exceptional, and one should not, as Robertson Smith did, state categorically that 'marriage with a sister not uterine was allowed',[25] or, even more generally, that 'It is safe therefore to say that there was no bar to marriage in the male line'.[26] Perhaps in order not to sound too crass, he allows one possible exception ('unless probably that a man cannot marry his own daughter'), but if his theory is accepted it is not at all clear why this exception should apply.

Marrying one's stepmother or two sisters simultaneously, though un-Islamic, does not amount to incest in the strict sense of consanguineous union. The main objection to such unions is social rather than biological: the former could easily be seen as disrespectful towards the father, the second is supposed to lead to rivalry between siblings, and both forms, if productive, will result in odd degrees of kinship, but not necessarily in inbreeding and its concomitant dangers. In an interesting attempt to combine the social and the biological, Françoise Héritier sees the fear of mixing 'identical' bodily fluids (for two sisters are identical in this sense, as are a woman and her mother or a father and his son) as lying at the basis of all incest taboos. Thus what is normally considered the primary form of incest is, according to her, possibly an offshoot of the secondary form, as she makes clear in the title of her monograph *Two Sisters and Their Mother* .

In general, as far as may be ascertained, inbreeding was not very common in pre-Islamic times. It is difficult to obtain precise information. The genealogies of tribes and clans in the pre-Islamic and early Islamic periods, though very detailed, are notoriously unreliable, loaded as they are with politics and sentiments; an alliance between tribes was often cemented by fabricating a common ancestor. Moreover, the genealogies normally present the male lines only and give very little information on females. Among the exceptions are the lineages of the Prophet Muḥammad and other prominent early Muslims. Thus Ibn Ḥabīb gives Muḥammad's ancestors in the all-female line, going back seven generations.[27] Similar but shorter matrilinear lines are given for Abū Bakr, ᶜUmar, ᶜUthmān, ᶜAlī, and al-Ḥasan.[28] Only two lines are given in full in these lineages: the all-male and the all-female, out of the theoretical maximum of 128 (2^7) lines of ascendants that go with a full picture of seven generations in Muḥammad's case. Therefore it is hazardous to draw any firm conclusions. Yet the general picture that emerges from this admittedly limited sample is clear: there may have been 'irregularities' by Islamic standards, such as the above-mentioned stepmother-marriages, but the spouses are not closely related and even first-cousin unions, often assumed to be dominant in Arab society, are almost absent as far as can be observed. In the Prophet's lineage, one finds that his great-grandmother Umm Ḥabīb and her husband ᶜAbd al-ᶜUzzā had a great-grandfather (Quṣayy) in common; ᶜUthmān's maternal great-great-grandmother Ṣakhra bint ᶜAbd ibn ᶜImrān married her first cousin ᶜAmr ibn ᶜĀʾidh ibn ᶜImrān.

Forbidden Degrees in the Qur'an

The main text containing the Qur'anic regulations on marriage impediments is found, appropriately, in the sura called 'Women'. Appropriately, at least, in pre-modern male discourse, where everything is usually discussed from the point of view of the man. In the present study I cannot but adopt this asymmetry. The forbidden degrees are usually expressed in the feminine: one finds the term *muḥarramāt*, women that are forbidden (to a man), but not normally *muḥarramūn*, men forbidden to a woman. The inequality is not only a matter of viewpoint or terminology, for Islamic marriage laws are themselves essentially asymmetrical, most obviously in allowing polygyny but not polyandry.

Here follows Arberry's translation of the relevant *āyāt* ('verses') from the fourth sura of the Qur'an:[29]

> (4:19) O believers, it is not lawful for you to inherit women against their will; neither debar them, that you may go off with part of what you have given them, except when they commit a flagrant indecency. Consort with them honourably; or if you are averse to them, it is possible you may be averse to a thing, and God set in it much good. (...)
> (4:22) And do not marry women that your fathers married, unless it be a thing of the past; surely that is indecent and hateful, an evil way.[30]
> (4:23) Forbidden to you are your mothers and daughters, your sisters, your aunts paternal and maternal, your brother's daughters, your sister's daughters, your mothers who have given suck to you, your suckling sisters, your wives' mothers, your stepdaughters who are in your care being born of your wives you have been in to—but if you have not been in to them it is no fault in you—and the spouses of your sons who are of your loins, and that you should take to you two sisters together, unless it be a thing of the past; God is All-forgiving, All-compassionate.

As with any Qur'anic passage, it is obviously impossible to discuss, or even to read, all that has been written by exegetes, jurists, lawyers, mystics, ethicists and rhetoricians, to mention only the more relevant categories. I have tried to look at what are generally recognized as the more important or authoritative sources. As for Qur'anic exegesis I have relied in particular on one very informative source, the great Qur'an commentary by Fakhr al-Dīn al-Rāzī (d. 606/1209), a Sunnite polymath, theologian and exegete, and very much at home in philosophy as practised by al-Fārābī and Ibn Sīnā.[31]

The corpus of legal treatises, handbooks and compendia is stupendously large. In consulting particular works I have been led by relevant and less relevant factors, such as importance, influence, and availability. Although Islam has never had a unified and uniformly acknowledged code of law, and there are several legal schools that are roughly geographically distributed over the Islamic world, each with its own set of authoritative legal textbooks, there is nevertheless unanimity on most essentials. The organization of the material is also mostly identical, and the wording and formulations are very similar or identical not only within each of the major schools but in general. Moreover, these major schools (in Sunnite Islam being the Mālikī, Ḥanafī, Shāfiᶜī and Ḥanbalī schools, each called after a prominent early authority) are aware of each other and show a fair measure of mutual respect. Except in the shortest manuals the authors regularly refer to the points of difference and dispute. All expositions of Islamic law have a chapter on marriage that contains a section on the forbidden degrees;[32] they all have a chapter on 'prescribed punishments' (*ḥudūd*, sg. *ḥadd*) for certain crimes, of which *zinā* ('fornication') is one. It is in these sections that one finds much on what could be termed incest. The jurists are generally far more interested in dealing with possible cases, hypothetical or with practical import, than in providing thoughts on the underlying justifications and the ethical implications of the legal rules. In this study I am concerned only with the latter; consequently my harvest is relatively meagre. There is another source of information on Islamic law, the collected fatwas or legal opinions of scholars acting as *muftī*. Often they reflect everyday practice rather better than the legal handbooks, even though some of the questions put to the *muftī* could have been invented just as letters to agony aunts are sometimes made up. In any case, the collections consulted did not yield any information on the occurrence of incest in the normal English sense, whereas the 'milk-incest' peculiar to Islam is a recurrent preoccupation. This is understandable; true incest is not often made public as it is deemed far more shameful than mistakenly marrying, or intending to marry, someone with whom a milk-relationship is suspected. It is in the nature of a taboo that it affects not only the perpetration of certain acts but also speaking about them.

When dealing with Islamic law, and penal law in particular, one should be aware that the texts deal with an ideal. At any time in the history of Islam there has been a gap between this ideal and practice, since it was easy for rulers to impose penalties of their own devising, which were sometimes more lenient but often harsher than those prescribed by Islamic law. Since juridical archives are lacking in medieval times, there is virtually no information about legal practice regarding incest as a crime. The Islamic principle of 'commanding right and forbidding wrong'[33] is, naturally, a task of the just ruler, but ordinary people could also use the principle to voice their opinion or even to take action if they noticed anything untoward, to the extent of interfering with people's privacy. Michael Cook, in his comprehensive monograph of this principle and its practice, mentions many cases of people feeling morally outraged by perceived sexual irregularities such as 'ordinary' fornication, adultery, prostitution, rape or sodomy; yet incest is not mentioned once.[34] If it occurred at all, it was well-hidden.

The following takes up the several constituent parts of the two Qur'anic verses translated above, in order of appearance.

Stepmothers

By common consent among Muslim and non-Muslim scholars the Qur'anic passages on the forbidden degrees are said to date from the Medinan period, when Muḥammad had to combine the functions of Prophet and Lawgiver. The precise occasion for their revelation[35] cannot be determined. In the sub-discipline of Qur'anic studies called *asbāb al-nuzūl*, 'occasions of revelation', Muslim scholarship has connected the first passage, which seems to concern a kind of levirate system, with a specific event, although early traditions do not refer to a particular occasion. In al-Bukhārī's *al-Ṣaḥīḥ*, Ibn ᶜAbbās (the Prophet's cousin, considered the foremost early authority on Qur'anic exegesis) explains the verse in general terms:

> When someone died his nearest relatives (*awliyāʾuhu*) were entitled to his wife: if one of them wished, he married her, or if they wished, they made her marry (someone else). And if they wished, they did not make her marry; for they were more entitled to her than her own people. Then this verse was revealed about this.[36]

The 'nearest relatives' are primarily the deceased's brothers, who could 'inherit' the marriage. It should be mentioned that not everyone has seen in the Qur'anic text a reference to the levirate marriage. Richard Bell, who translates «it is not permissible for you to heir women against their will», attaches a note: 'Ambiguous; usually taken as referring to an old Arab custom of inheriting wives; but more probably refers to putting pressure on a wife to compel her to bequeath her property to her husband',[37] and he has some Muslim precursors in this opinion.[38]

If brothers could be said to 'inherit' a marriage in pre-Islamic times, so could a son, and Q 4:19 has also been interpreted in this manner,[39] although in that case the more explicit Q 4:22 would not have been necessary. As we have seen, this issue was altogether more sensitive, and it is here that specific cases are mentioned that occasioned the revelation. Al-Ṭabarī, author not only of the great *History* but also of the greatest early Qur'anic commentary, reports that Q 4:22 was revealed in connection with the case of several individuals: of Abū Qays ibn al-Aslat,[40] who succeeded his father as spouse of Umm ᶜUbayd bint Ḍamra; al-Aswad ibn Khalaf, who married his father's wife Bint Abī Ṭalḥa; Ṣafwān ibn Umayya, who married his father's wife Nāḥiya bint al-Aswad; and Manṣūr ibn Zayyān [*recte* Zabbān] ibn Sayyār, who married Mulayka bint Khārija.[41] Some of these names we have come across in Ibn Ḥabīb's discussion of the custom. Instead of Abū Qays ibn al-Aslat and his father, Ibn Ḥabīb mentions the next generation, Muḥṣin ibn Abī Qays, as having 'inherited' his father's wife (it is uncertain whether there is some confusion or whether the habit ran in the family). According to Ibn Ḥabīb, it was after Muḥsin had first claimed his right by throwing his cloak over Kubaysha bint Maᶜn and then, changing his mind, neither consummated the marriage nor provided for her maintenance, that the Prophet intervened, telling her to return to her own people. 'If God makes something happen concerning you, I shall let you know', he told her. Promptly, Q 4:22 was revealed, as well as 4:19.[42]

The Qur'anic text is particularly emphatic in its condemnation of marrying stepmothers, not only by keeping it apart from what follows by verse-separators, the tags 'rhyming' by assonance (22: *sāʾa sabīlā*, 23: *inna llāha kāna ghafūran raḥīmā*), but also by calling it indecent, hateful, and evil, whereas the far more extreme cases enumerated in what follows, and which concern consanguinity instead of affinity, are not accompanied by any strongly negative divine comments. The reason is obvious: only a controversial matter would need special rhetoric. The exegetical and legal literature mirrors this emphasis by generally giving more space to this forbidden marriage than to any other. The marriage with one's father's wife has acquired the nickname *nikāḥ al-maqt*, 'hateful marriage'. It sounds as if this idiom is derived from the Qur'anic verse, although Muslim authorities suggest that it precedes it; al-Zamakhsharī explains:

> They [viz. the pre-Islamic Arabs] used to marry their stepmothers. Some decent and virtuous people among them hated this and called it 'hateful marriage; someone born from such a union would be called *maqtī*. That is why the Qur'an has «hateful», as if to say that it is an indecent thing in God's religion, an exceedingly ugly practice, hateful to (people with) decency. Two kinds of ugliness: it could not be exceeded.[43]

With the last sentence al-Zamakhsharī refers to the domains of religious prescriptions (*dīn*) and common virtue or decency (*murūʾa*), the latter of which could also be found among the pre-Islamic Arabs. The existence of the word *maqtī* is confirmed by the lexicographers (some of whom say that it is not only applied to the offspring but also to the one who marries his stepmother); I have never seen it in any pre-Islamic text, however.[44] Abū ᶜUbayda, commenting on Q 4:22, gives not only *maqtī* but also the variant *maqtawī*, a form irregularly formed from the root QTW.[45] The lexicographers explain it as 'servant', but they do not connect it with the term *maqtī* or with stepmother-marriage.[46] Al-Zamakhsharī's words suggest that he believes that the practice was 'hated' by the Arabs already before the prohibition was revealed, and that thereafter a religious sanction was given to this aversion.

Fakhr al-Dīn al-Rāzī (d. 606/1209), even more precise than al-Zamakhsharī, justifies the Qur'anic use of three negative terms by distinguishing between three domains: the marriage in question is «indecent» according to reason, «hateful» according to revealed law, and an «evil way» according to custom;

the allocation of the three qualifications looks somewhat arbitrary.[47] Many authorities go as far as to state that completed sexual congress is not even a necessary condition, a mere caress or lustful look being enough. The argument is that *nikāḥ*, according to one explanation, means 'being joined together with pleasure', and a lover's meeting is a form of such being together. Therefore, as Abū Bakr ibn al-ᶜArabī says, 'When (a son) and his father look at (a woman) lustfully, she is forbidden to both of them.'[48] The Ḥanafites rule that if a man touches a woman lustfully, her mother and her daughter are forbidden to him;[49] Ibn Ḥanbal (d. 241/855) ruled that if a man touches, kisses or undresses a female slave lustfully, she is forbidden to his son.[50] The Shāfiᶜites seem to be more lenient in this matter, which offers a good opportunity to the jurists to indulge in detailed discussions, including the definition of those categories that count as objects of lust (a girl of nine or older always, a girl of five or younger never, and between five and nine if she is plump, according to an authority).[51]

The custom of marrying a stepmother may be condemned in strong terms in both Qur'an and exegetical literature, but one finds very little in the way of explicit justification of the prohibition. Obviously, this was not deemed necessary. Usurping a father's harem, mating with his spouses or concubines during his lifetime is an obvious act of rebellion, perpetrated by many sons in lore and history, and made all the more attractive as a result of the common habit of marrying wives much younger than oneself, which would regularly make stepmothers of an age with their stepsons. Absalom, who followed Ahithophel's advice and 'went in unto his father's concubines in the sight of all Israel', provides one of the better-known examples.[52] According to a somewhat strange report the Umayyad caliph Muᶜāwiya (*reg.* 41-60/661-680) made use of the taboo when he, symbolically and publicly, 'placed his rod' on the vulva of a naked slave-girl, in order to make it impossible for his son to have her, and saying to a courtier, 'Take her for one of your of your sons, since she is not permissible for Yazīd after what I have done to her'.[53] A certain Ṣāliḥ ibn Maḥmūd, not otherwise known, is said to have asked his father to marry him to one of the latter's wives, or ex-wives:

—Marry me to one of the mothers of your children!
The father said,
—Damn you, they are like your mother!
—But a man has only one mother, and mine has died.[54]

Obviously meant as a joke, quoted amidst other jokes on stupid people, this anecdote seems to reinforce the preposterousness of marrying a stepmother. At the same it is tempting to interpret it as mildly subversive: after all, many fools are wise fools who expose follies and inconsistencies in normal, accepted ideas. A man has only one true mother: why impose unreasonable restrictions? It is unlikely, however, that such a reading would have occurred to medieval readers.

To marry a father's wife after his death is of course a somewhat different matter, but it could still be considered, if not rebellious, then at least disrespectful. Especially, one might say, if one has first killed one's father, as in the story of the Persian king Shīrawayh (or Shīrōye), found in an Arabic source. Having killed his father, he wished to marry the latter's wife Shīrīn. She pretended to consent but killed herself by sucking a poisoned ring herself, leaving her would-be husband another poisoned ring with a note promising great aphrodisiacal powers; the intended result followed soon afterwards.[55]

The oblique tie established between son and stepmother if they marry could lead to unusual degrees of kinship if offspring ensues; an aversion to such oddities and complexities might have formed another reason for disliking the custom. One might almost consider it an aesthetic uneasiness about deviance and asymmetry, a preference for horizontal ties (as between cousins) rather than 'oblique' ties, across generations. The obliqueness is a genealogical concept, which in reality will often be 'straightened' or made more 'horizontal' because the age of the stepmother will very often be on a par with the stepson, as said above. In any case, if such an intellectual aversion to oblique unions existed, it would have been a far less important factor than practical, economic and social considerations, such as those relating to inheritance, not only of property but of duties and obligations too. The customs and laws of inheritance, already intricate enough, could do without further complexity such as conflating into one person the genealogical functions of stepmother and wife. I am therefore not as dismissive of this argument as an explanation of incest taboos in general as some are. Robin Fox has called it 'too silly to dwell on', arguing that one can be only one person at a time.[56] But even if that is true, one may have to be two different persons at different times, and that could lead to conflicting interests, imagined or real. Another, rather ingenious explanation favoured by a number of French anthropologists is based on the assumed aversion to mixing fluids: the *maniyy* of the woman (the same word that is used for the man's sperm) is mingled first with that of the father and then with the son; it will then also be part of the woman's milk (on which see also below). As Édouard Conte explains,

> If the widow, together with having a sexual relationship in this new union, continues to suckle a child engendered by the ex-husband, the substance of the deceased could be found in the milk of his own son. According to this hypothesis, which has connotations that are incestuous and homosexual at the same time, the inheritor-husband, half-brother, becomes adoptive father of the suckled child, by equally becoming the nursing father. This seemed 'an evil way' in the perspective of Islam.[57]

This may sound convincing if one believes in the overriding importance of the idea of bodily fluids in the minds of the early Arabs, or indeed if one thinks, as does Françoise Héritier, that all incest taboos are based on an aversion to identical bodily fluids being mixed.[58] The analysis seems somewhat contrived, but it must be admitted that it offers an explanation of a few oddities in the Islamic rules. The sperm of a father is thought to be 'identical' to that of his son and may therefore not be mixed in one womb. By this reasoning, the worst part of Oedipus' 'crime' is not that he slept with his mother, but that he mixed his seed with his father's.[59]

If such principles involving bodily fluids were held unconsciously, they were never expressed overtly by the medieval Arabs. Perhaps the nearest to an explanation of the 'hatefulness' of marrying one's stepmother is a psychological justification given by Fakhr al-Dīn al-Rāzī: such a marriage is called hateful (*mamqūt*) and its offspring *maqtī* 'because the wife of the father is like one's mother, and marrying mothers is one of the most horrible things according to the Arabs. Therefore, since this type of marriage resembles that, it was necessarily loathsome to them.'[60] By the same token, the Prophet's wives, called metaphorically the Mothers of the Believers in the Qur'an (Q 33:6), were barred, unmetaphorically, from remarrying after his death (Q 33:53).

Just as for the prohibition of the custom, there must have been a justification for its existence in pre-Islamic times. Again one seeks in vain for explicit statements. No doubt social and economic considerations would make it desirable in some cases to provide for widowed women, but our limited data do not allow us to draw any conclusions about the reasons for its occurrence in general or in the few individual cases of which we know.

In connection with the prohibition there are a number of questions that had to be resolved. Does «(women) that your fathers married» refer only to a man's legal spouses and concubines, or does it include any other women with whom he has had illegal intercourse? The authorities of the various legal schools give different answers.[61] Abū Ḥanīfa, arguing that the original meaning of the verb *nakaḥa* is 'to copulate' rather than 'to conclude a contract of marriage', includes adulterous partners. However, it is not difficult to find instances, in the Qur'an or elsewhere, where *nikāḥ* must refer to legal marriage (Q 33:49 is a good example); and al-Shāfiʿī answers the question with a negative.

The precise implications of the exception, «unless it be a thing of the past», were also the subject of some debate. Mostly it is taken to mean that such unions, if concluded before the Qur'anic injunction appeared, would be forgiven by God and would not be considered a sin, although the partners should be separated. As Ibn Ḥabīb and others tell us, this did in fact happen.

In the case of a mistress or a concubine, rules were apparently not too rigid in practice. An example is the famous singer ʿArīb, also an accomplished poet, sometimes said to be a daughter of the Barmakid vizier Jaʿfar ibn Yaḥyā. She died at an advanced age in 277/890 and boasted of having had sexual relationships with seven or eight Abbasid caliphs.[62] If that is true, comments Ibn Ḥazm, they include father and son.

Mothers, Daughters, Sisters, Aunts, Nieces, et aliae

The following, long *āya* (one is reluctant to call such a prosaic enumeration a 'verse') is the central text in the matter of Muslim rules concerning incest. Besides affinity (*ṣihr*) and consanguinity (*nasab*) a wholly new category is introduced, that of milk-relationship (*raḍāʿ*). Like any part of the Qur'anic text, the passage has had its share of exegesis. Much of it is straightforward and not particularly controversial. Thus it is regularly pointed out that what is forbidden, *ḥarām*, is not 'your mothers and daughters' etc., but, strictly speaking, 'marrying, or mating with (*nikāḥ*), your mothers and daughters', etc.

Strangely, at least one exegete did not accept this obvious interpretation, and considered this verse *mujmal*, 'generalized', a technical term in Qur'anic scholarship implying some kind of ambiguity and unresolved interpretative uncertainty. Being forbidden cannot, in Arabic legal thought, be predicated of a thing but only of an act. Since such an act is not explicitly mentioned in the Qur'anic text, it must be understood and supplied. As Fakhr al-Dīn al-Rāzī states, a certain al-Karkhī, whom I have not been able to identify, apparently thinks there is a choice between various matters, and no obvious choice; one wonders what kind of acts he had in mind. It is not clear whether it was his intention to ignore related females altogether, or to ignore the prohibition itself. Al-Rāzī, understandably, rejects this reasoning as a feeble kind of sophistry (*sūfisṭāʾiyya*). The general consensus is, of course, that the relevant act is easily supplied from the words *lā tankiḥū*, 'do not marry', in the preceding verse, and that even if the context were ignored, common usage (*ʿurf*) would be sufficient here.[63] Al-Rāzī, thorough as ever, raises other points concerning the syntax. The verbal form *ḥurrimat* ('forbidden ... are') is a passive and the agens (by whom it was forbidden) is not mentioned; theoretically, it could have been anyone who uttered the interdiction. That God is in fact the one who establishes the prohibition can only be a matter or consensus; it cannot be proved. Fortunately, consensus (*ijmāʿ*) is a recognized and essential source of Islamic law. Similarly, it has to be agreed by consensus that the prohibition concerns everyone, not merely those who were present during its revelation, and that it is valid forever and not for a limited period, or only for the past, as the perfect or past tense *ḥurrimat* might suggest: it could also be translated as 'forbidden .. have been'. The use of a finite verb in the past tense could also suggest that an innovation is intended, and that before the revelation of the verse incest was permitted. Al-

Rāzī also points out that 'forbidden to you are your mothers', which employs plural second person pronouns, could theoretically mean that *all* mothers are forbidden to *all* people addressed, but that it should be understood in a personal sense, each and his own mother, and similarly for the other categories. All this goes to prove, he concludes, that the external or literal meaning of the wording taken by itself is not sufficient to establish the prohibition. This exercise in close reading, condemned by Abū Ḥayyān al-Gharnāṭī (d. 745/1344) as unnecessary and irrelevant,[64] is perhaps meant as a critique of Dāwūd al-Iṣfahānī and his literalist or 'Externalist' (Ẓāhirī) school of thought, which did not recognize the existence of the *mujmal* (general, ambiguous) category in the Qur'anic text and believed that the text is always self-sufficient.[65]

The categories that are enumerated in the verse, though generally clear enough, call for some comments. As the exegetes and jurists point out, 'mothers' should be interpreted as any female forebear, whether from the father's side or the mother's, so as to include grandmothers (*jaddāt* sg. *jadda*) and even earlier generations, if this can be imagined.[66] Such an interpretation is not difficult, for in Arabic 'mothers' and 'fathers' are regularly used in such a sense. Even here, some literalists have claimed, as al-Rāzī says, that *ummahāt* (plural of *umm*) should only be taken in its original and literal sense as 'mothers', excluding grandmothers, in which case the prohibition to marry the latter rests on consensus rather than on the Qur'anic text. The great jurist Ibn Ḥazm, though a 'literalist', has no difficulty in interpreting *umm* as any female ancestor, finding evidence in the words of God and the Prophet: in the Qur'an mankind is often addressed as «children of Adam» and Muḥammad refers to all women as 'Adam's daughters'.[67] The same applies to *banāt*, 'daughters', which is normally taken to include granddaughters, great-granddaughters, and so forth. What to us, and to most early Muslims, seems a logical step may not have been so originally. Édouard Conte argues that the Prophet Muḥammad's Arab contemporaries who first heard the Qur'anic text may not have taken it for granted; he believes that extending the sense of the words 'mother' and 'daughter' (and, as we shall see, 'sister') was the work of the Qur'anic exegetes and Islamic jurists who were keen to replace the 'Arab' marriage system with the Islamic one, in which consanguineous marriage was restricted.[68]

The jurists disagree about daughters born out of wedlock, from adultery or fornication. In Christian canon law there could be no doubt: sex makes partners 'one flesh', as the Bible (Gen. 2.24, Eph. 5:31) puts it, and thus creates prohibited degrees just as does marriage.[69] Most Muslim scholars are of the same opinion. According to Abū Ḥanīfa (d. 150/767) and his school such an incestuous union is forbidden. Thus al-Kāsānī (d. 587/1189), an authoritative Ḥanafite scholar: '«and your daughters»: regardless whether it is a daughter born in wedlock (*nikāḥ*) or from fornication (*sifāḥ*),[70] because the

Qur'anic text should be taken in a general sense'.[71] Ibn Ḥanbal, asked by his son ᶜAbd Allāh about marriage with a daughter born out of wedlock, is explicit: 'God forbid that a man marry his own daughter! This is an evil doctrine.'[72] However, al-Shāfiᶜī (d. 204/820) holds that marrying such a daughter is not forbidden to her natural father. This rather startling judgement of a man who was perhaps the greatest legal scholar of Islam of all times is the logical conclusion of the well-known rule that 'the child belongs to the marriage bed', irrespective of biological paternity. Thus, for the law she is not his daughter. We shall come across similar cases where Islamic law is at variance with what would seem to be accepted ethical rules,[73] for one must assume that al-Shāfiᶜī would have condemned a wittingly concluded marriage between natural father and daughter. Al-Rāzī, himself a Shāfiᶜite, sets out the argumentation in some detail:

> We say: she is not a 'daughter' for several reasons. Firstly, Abū Ḥanīfa must hold it she is his daughter basing himself *either* on the true state of things, which is that she is created from his semen [lit., 'water'], *or* on the fact that the law judges the parentage to be established. The former is invalid according to his school, in accordance with the reasoning by means of opposite extremes.[74] If one were to buy a virgin slave-girl, to deflower her and to keep her in one's house, upon which she would give birth to a child, then this child is known to be created of his semen, yet Abū Ḥanīfa will not confirm the relationship except after the avowal of paternity (*istilḥāq*). If the reason [for this opinion] were the fact that the child is created from the father's semen, Abū Ḥanīfa would not have hesitated to confirm the relationship without avowal of paternity. Alternatively, if a man in the East marries a woman in the West and a child is produced [even though they have never been together], then Abū Ḥanīfa would confirm the relationship here, even though the child is indubitably not created from his semen. Thus it is proved, by means of reasoning by opposite extremes applied to Abū Ḥanīfa's view, that it is invalid to make the fact that a child is created from someone's semen a reason for parenthood. If we hold that paternity is confirmed on the basis of the law [rather than 'reality'], then, according to the consensus of the Muslims there is no paternity of the adulterer *vis-à-vis* his child, and if the child claims to be his child, the judge must forbid this claim. Therefore, such a claim of paternity is not possible, neither on the grounds of reality nor of the law.
>
> Secondly, one must hold fast to the words of the Prophet: 'The child belongs to the marriage bed; stoning to the fornicator.'[75]

Al-Rāzī argues further that if such a daughter were to be recognized legally, there would be other complicating consequences, such as her right to inherit, the father's right to act as her guardian and provide for her, his right to be alone with her, normally allowed only with one's *maḥārim* or non-marriageable relations. His conclusion is therefore that a father may marry a child engendered by him out of wedlock. It is easy to see that this rule may be the most practical one in a society in which fatherhood cannot be proved as easily and indisputably as in the modern world since only very recent times. Whatever his personal feelings may have been about such a union, al-Rāzī does not offer them.

The opinion of the Shāfiᶜites was also held by some Mālikites, who do not agree among themselves in this matter,[76] whereas the other legal schools declared it forbidden in spite of the possible complications. The Ḥanbalite jurist Ibn Qudāma (d. 620/1223) discusses the matter in more detail, for there are other categories of relatives from adulterous affairs and fornication (*zinā*) than merely one's daughter:[77]

> It is forbidden for a man to marry his daughter from fornication, or his sister [born from his father's fornication],[78] or the daughter of his son, the daughter of his daughter, or the daughter of his brother or of his sister (born) from fornication. This is held generally by jurists. Mālik [ibn Anas, d. 179/796, founder of the Mālikite legal school] and al-Shāfiᶜī, according to the reigning opinion in the latter's school, allow all these unions, because the woman (in every case) is legally a 'stranger' (*ajnabiyya*) to the man, and not related to him by law; there is no inheritance between them, she is not (automatically) freed when he becomes her owner,[79] he is not bound to provide for her maintenance, and she is not forbidden to him, like all other 'strangers'. We, however, hold on to God's words, «Forbidden to you are your mothers and daughters», and this woman (as described above) is his daughter, for she is a female created from his semen: this is the sense in reality, which does not vary with legitimacy or illegitimacy. Evidence for this opinion are the Prophet's words regarding the wife of Hilāl ibn Umayya: 'Look at him!'—meaning her child—'If she gives birth to him and he looks thus, then he is the son of Sharīk ibn Saḥmāᵓ'—meaning the fornicator.[80] Furthermore, because she is created from his semen, and thus resembles a daughter created from (illegal) intercourse committed *bona fide* (*waṭᵓ al-shubha*); and because she is 'flesh of his flesh' (*biḍᶜa minhu*). Therefore she is forbidden to him, like a daughter born in wedlock.[81]

The next category in the Qur'anic passage, 'sisters', needs only little clarification. The term includes sister german (full sister) as well as half-sister (either uterine sister or sister from the father's side only). As for 'aunts', the Qur'anic text has the two Arabic words: *ᶜammāt* (sg. *ᶜamma*) for paternal aunts and *khālāt* (sg. *khāla*) for maternal ones. Al-Wāḥidī points out that, since the sister of any male ancestor, from father's or mother's side, is called *ᶜamma*, and the sister of any female ancestor is called *khāla*, the categories are to be extended through the ascendants, including great-aunts, just as 'mother' is taken to include any female ascendants.

Nieces complete the forbidden degrees by consanguinity. Here, too, the jurists and exegetes extend the concept, this time in descending line just as in the cause of daughters. It is here that Islam is stricter than Judaism, which allows marrying nieces, whereas Christianity is stricter than Islam in generally not favouring marrying first cousins. The prolific theologian, preacher, and Ḥanbalite jurisconsult Ibn Qayyim al-Jawziyya (d. 751/1350), in a long series of objections to opinions that point out perceived illogicalities in Islamic law, argues that the Qur'anic rules provide the happy medium between the Zoroastrians who respect no restrictions, and those who would equate close-kin and remote kin by banning marriage with either, and who would thus impose great 'difficulty and distress' on a society in which relation with paternal cousins is so important as it is to the Arabs. Islamic law, in contrast, has 'the closest connection to sound reason and correct natural disposition'.[82]

Milk-Relationship

Something of a novelty is introduced with the words «your mothers who have given suck to you and your suckling sisters». There are several references in the Qur'an to breast-feeding, and it is abundantly clear that milk from mothers or wet-nurses was at least as important in pre-Islamic society as it is elsewhere, but there is nothing to prepare us for the introduction of a whole new category among the forbidden degrees, that of milk-relationship or fosterage (*raḍāᶜ*, *riḍāᶜ*, or *raḍāᶜa*).[83]

Being suckled together 'creates fraternal bonds which have a widespread social and moral effect', as J. Chelhod writes,[84] and it is considered a 'vital element' on a par with blood. Indeed, the Qur'anic rule is obviously based on the idea that the milk is somehow formed from the blood of the womb,[85] while there are also statements in Hadith reports that make a connection between the wet-nurse's milk and her husband's semen.[86] Bouhdiba even speaks of the 'mystical, affective quality' of the Islamic regulations of the forbidden degrees and the 'magical view of incest', in connection with the role of milk.[87] Genealogy, in medieval science and law, is a confusing mix of liquids: the man's semen (*maniyy*, often called 'drop', *nuṭfa*, the word used twelve times in the Qur'an), the woman's contribution (by many authorities also called *maniyy*), milk, and blood.

According to Chelhod the Qur'anic prohibition is rooted in pre-Islamic Arabia; as evidence he points to the story of the poet-hero ᶜAntar, whose rival insinuated that ᶜAntar's sweetheart ᶜAbla was suckled by his mother, thus attempting to prevent their marrying.[88] This is far from convincing, because Chelhod has based himself on the popular epic-romance on the hero, which, although incorporating much ancient lore, is obviously shaped in Islamic times, much later than the stories on the pre-Islamic poet called ᶜAntara rather than ᶜAntar. There is no ancient source for the episode of the thwarting of the hero's marriage plans. On the other hand, it has been observed that the rather casual manner in which the milk-relations are listed together with the other forbidden degrees seems to suggest that the matter was not unfamiliar to those addressed.[89] But the casual mention may also be a rhetorical trick of the lawgiver to pass off a novelty as something normal. The Muslim jurists tried to present the new ruling as something that the pre-Islamic Arabs had in fact anticipated: 'They used to make much of the matter of *raḍāᶜ*, just as they did with consanguinity (*nasab*)', as al-Sarakhsī maintains.[90] Giladi thinks that the Prophet may have wanted to encourage out-marrying; he also demonstrates that there was some early opposition to the strict adherence to the equation of milk with blood.[91] Montgomery Watt has speculated that the Qur'anic rule reflects a concession to matrilineal groups: 'Possibly some of those which practised forms of polyandry avoided undue endogamy by making certain degrees of milk-relationship a barrier to marriage'.[92] Hard evidence for this is absent, however. As I see it, there may be a connection with the Westermarck thesis. Being suckled together will normally imply growing up closely together in the crucial first years, and therefore greatly increase the likelihood of mutual sexual aversion at a later age. Emotionally, milk-siblings are like genetic ones. Islamic law merely stated explicitly what is engrained already in human nature. In terms of genetic evolution the prohibition of marriage between milk-relations is pointless; in terms of psychology it is not. As Françoise Héritier-Augé has demonstrated, the Islamic rules of milk-relationship do not amount to giving female milk the same status as male semen: even in the rules of *raḍāᶜ* it is the latter that is ultimately decisive; 'milk comes from the man'.[93]

There is no need to dwell at much length on the origin and implications of the prohibition, since a number of recent studies deal with milk-relationship in Islam. The recent monograph on breast-feeding in Islam by Avner Giladi discusses the matter in detail; it includes a separate chapter on the legal implications.[94] He notes that with the rule against marriage of milk-relations the Qur'an brings something unique, but cannot offer more in explanation of the origins of, and the motivation for, the novelty.[95] Héritier-Augé discusses the strange ways in which milk-relationship and blood-relationship are different according to Muslim law, even though it is often professed that milk and blood are alike.[96] In a richly documented article, Mohammed Hocine Benkheira argues that among early jurists a struggle took place which, at least among the Sunnites, resulted in the triumph of the concept of 'bilinearity'.[97] The Qur'anic prohibition simply identifies a nurse of a child as its mother, in terms of marriage impediments. According to Benkheira, the jurists saw a lack of symmetry: biological motherhood is established incontrovertibly, and biological fatherhood is established by reasoning. So far, so good; but a woman can breast-feed a child not biologically hers and thus become its 'mother', so why cannot a man do the same? 'It is this question which the doctrine of *laban al-faḥl* ["the stallion's milk", or the milk of the male] has attempted to solve: there are also milk-fathers'.[98]

Al-Rāzī's exegesis of the relevant Qur'anic words begins with an explanation of the metaphorical use of 'mother' meaning wet-nurse or foster-mother; then, in a passage translated by Giladi,[99] he extends the principle so as to make milk and blood relationship equally strong in effecting an impediment to marriage. This is in accordance with the general opinion of Muslim commentators and jurists, who have inferred from these few Qur'anic words that blood and milk are wholly equal in this respect, even though the Qur'anic formulation for the former is more detailed than for the latter. In this they found or fabricated support in a *ḥadīth* attributed to the Prophet: 'What is forbidden on the basis of milk-relationship is the same as what is forbidden on the basis of blood-relationship.[100] Others point out, however, that in some cases there is a difference between blood and milk: a man may marry the milk-sister of his own son, but not his half-sister; and one cannot marry the mother of one's half-brother, but it is possible to marry the mother of one's milk-brother.[101] As said above, Héritier-Augé and Benkheira discuss this in detail and offer explanations of the discrepancy between the matters of blood and milk.

Much medieval ink has been spilt on establishing the minimum amount of milk, expressed in numbers of sucks or sucking sessions. Opinions vary from the ultra-strict (one sucking is enough to establish milk-relationship) to more lenient views which see no harm in one, two, or less than five suckings. It was not merely a matter of ink and theory, however, but one of great practical importance: Giladi relates numerous cases culled from fatwa collections, which reflect real life better than the sophistry and the imaginary casuistry of the legal theorists. Some of these cases make amusing reading but could have had serious consequences, such as the case of the baby briefly held by the mother's female friend in the public bath, and who was discovered with her nipple in its mouth: was any milk consumed, or not?[102] Another matter that needed sorting out was the way the milk is ingested: suppose it were not sucked in the usual way but administered as an enema, which, after all, would break one's fast? Here, too, the authorities are of different views.[103]

Then there is the question of non-human milk. Animal milk, although considered second-best only for infants, was used and was of course, in its different forms, part of the staple diet of the Bedouins. Most jurists held milk-relationship cannot be brought about by animal milk. After all, one could argue that since blood-relationship cannot occur between two different species, a milk-relationship cannot be established through the milk of an alien species. One may compare the opinion, quoted by al-Jāḥiẓ,[104] that a kid suckled by a pig may be eaten by Muslims, in spite of the Islamic prohibition of eating pork. Nevertheless, here too some held deviant opinions. The famous Hadith compiler al-Bukhārī (d. 256/870) had to give up his post as *muftī* and had to leave Bukhara because he judged that children who had received milk from the same animal were barred from marrying each other.[105]

Mothers-in-Law

Mother-in-law avoidance is not only the stuff of mostly bad jokes but a widespread practice in kinship.[106] Various explanations, psychological and social, may be invented for the aversion to marrying one's mother-in-law. Moreover, in a society where in-marrying is common and marrying one's father's brother's daughter is considered the recommended option, it is easy to imagine that one's mother-in-law is a rather close blood-relative; she could in fact be, at the same time, one's father's sister, for instance (in which case she would be forbidden in any case). The Qur'anic rule makes a mother-in-law forbidden even if she is not perceived as consanguineous; as suggested above, part of the explanation may lie in the aversion against oblique ties in general. The body-fluids theory of incest has a ready explanation: mother and daughter share the same substance, which must not be mixed by intercourse with the same man. The commentators and jurists duly extend the category of mother-in-law to include all her female ascendants. A difference of opinion is found concerning the consummation of the first marriage. To a minority, this is a necessary condition of the impediment, since they take the words «(those) you have been in to» to refer not only to the stepdaughters but to the mothers-in-law too, which is syntactically possible but which is refuted by al-Rāzī at length, on syntactic rather than sexual or social grounds.

Stepdaughters and Daughters-in-Law

What Arberry translated as «your stepdaughters who are in your care» could also be rendered as 'your foster-daughters who are in your laps'. The word *rabāʾib* (sg. *rabība*) is derived from the verb *rabba*, which means both 'to be master of' and 'to raise, bring up', and the word *ḥijr* 'lap' is often used metaphorically for 'care'. Naturally, the commentators have tried to explain why the word «your stepdaughters» is qualified by two different things here, the phrase «in your care» and the clause «being born of your wives you have been in to». 'Now if you asked, "What is the point of «in your care»?"', says al-Zamakhsharī in his characteristic Q&A manner, 'Then I would say that it serves to explain the prohibition'. He goes on to speak of the mixing, the intimacy, the love and compassion (*khulṭa, ulfa, mawadda, raḥma*) that arise and which put foster-children on a par with biological children. He does not make being in one's care a condition of the prohibition, although others do.

The clause «being born of your wives you have been in to» is obviously a necessary condition, as the sequel makes clear. The commentators are generally agreed that «been in to» means sexual intercourse, although some consider mere petting, or seeing the woman naked, a sufficient cause. Al-Rāzī, as a Shāfiʿite, again argues that the sexual contact refers to wedlock, and that the verse does not include women with whom one has illicit sex.

He could have found some support for this distinction in the following category, the last oblique tie that is prohibited, for the expression used for «spouses of your sons», *ḥalāʾilu abnāʾikum*, could also be translated (as Bell did) as 'lawful (wives) of your sons'. The word *ḥalāʾil*, sg. *ḥalīla*, is cognate with *ḥalāl* 'lawful', and it is generally taken to refer to official wives as well as to legal concubines, although the Ḥanafites are an exception. The qualification «of your loins» excludes adopted sons. This is of some relevance to Muḥammad's own life, since he married Zaynab bint Jaḥsh, the daughter of his paternal aunt, after his adopted son Zayd ibn Ḥāritha had divorced her; for this he was criticized by some 'Hypocrites', the term for those early Muslims who followed the Prophet only half-heartedly or outwardly, and Zayd himself had some scruples about divorcing his wife under pressure after the Prophet had become enamoured of her. Fortunately and conveniently, a few Qur'anic verses were revealed in connection with the affair (Q 33:5, 33:37-40). These verses mention Zayd and Muḥammad by name and explicitly say that Muḥammad «is not the father of any one of your men». As a result, on the basis of this Qur'anic text, adoption was rejected by Islamic law.[107] The affair was to become a standard topic in Christian anti-Muslim polemics and Muslim apologetics.

It is to be noted that in the case of stepdaughters consummation of the marriage with their mother is explicitly mentioned in the Qur'anic verse, whereas it is not in the case of the spouses of sons. The latter case could be said to have been left vague, a situation undesirable in legislation. In this connection an oddity of Arabic lexicography should be mentioned. In legal texts dealing with the various categories of forbidden degrees a distinction is often made between women that are intrinsically forbidden, such as mother, sister, daughter, and those that are only accidentally so, including stepmother, mother-in-law, daughter-in-law. For the first category one sometimes find a special term: *mubham*, the 'normal' meaning of which is in fact 'obscure', 'vague' or 'ambiguous'. It is strange that precisely this term should have been applied to a category that is supposedly *not* obscure or ambiguous. Although the term is rarely found in legal texts or Hadith, it was used by al-Shāfiʿī.[108] Ibn Manẓūr's great dictionary has a lengthy passage on it, in which he explains that *mubham* does not mean 'obscure' or 'difficult' here, but 'unqualified, to be taken in a general sense';[109] it is in fact a technical term in Qur'anic exegesis[110] and does not specifically refer to a category of the forbidden degrees, as some dictionaries would make us believe.

Two Sisters

As said above, being married to two sisters at the same time was one of the main differences between pre-Islamic customs and Islamic marriage law. One sometimes finds the opinion that before the coming of Islam the rules were simply different. Thus, after telling that Jacob/Yaʿqūb was married to two sisters, Rachel/Rāḥīl and Leah/Liyā, al-Maqdisī comments, 'At that time one could be married to two sisters'.[111] This is clearly a neutral statement, not meant to expose the patriarch as a sinner. Similarly, al-Thaʿlabī explains that this was the normal custom until Moses came to reveal the sacred law.[112] More often, especially when speaking of the pre-Islamic Arabs, the old custom is condemned. Together with marrying one's father's wife it has been called the 'worst' (*aqbaḥ* or *ashnaʿ*) thing that the pre-Islamic Arabs did, although in context this is often said not in order to blacken them, but rather to stress that unlike other nations they never allowed next-of-kin marriage. Nevertheless, it is condemned in Islam and it is not immediately obvious why. It does not in itself involve any inbreeding, it lacks the shamefulness-by-association of marrying a stepmother, and it does not result in serious role conflicts, it seems. The children from such a dual union would have a stepmother who is also a maternal aunt: it is not easy to see how this could be upsetting to anyone. In popular stories, the prohibition is blithely ignored.[113] The commentators and jurists, as usual, give much attention to a host of formal problems, but most are silent on why the practice was bad. There are some exceptions, however, among them al-Sarakhsī (d. 483/1090), author of the large Ḥanafite work *al-Mabsūṭ*. He explains that the natural bond (he uses the word *raḥim*, 'uterus, kinship') between sisters is likely to be severed if they become rival wives,[114] thus echoing Lev. 18:18 ('Neither shalt thou take a wife to her sister, to vex her'). Such rivalry is implied in the Arabic word for 'second (or third, or fourth) wife' or simply 'rival wife', *ḍarra*, which is regularly connected with *ḍarr* 'damage, hurt, injury'.[115] The concept of cutting the bonds of kinship will recur in some of the following discussions on marriage impediments. A modern reader is tempted to read al-Sarakhsī's remark as an implicit condemnation of polygyny in general. It should be added that the Qur'anic rule was extended by all legal schools, by also forbidding the combination of a wife with her aunt paternal or maternal. An elegant, though rather oddly sounding formulation of the prohibition makes it forbidden to be married simultaneously to two women who, *if one of them were male*, could not marry each other.[116]

To the French anthropologists mentioned before the two-sisters prohibition, far from being a minor difference between the pre-Islamic and the Islamic marriage customs, is a corner-stone of the Islamic system. Édouard Conte argues that this system sought to reduce the tendency of the 'Arab' system to transform maternal relationships into paternal ones, and thus to cement alliances between clans: 'a sole union of this type could be an occasion for the members of a group dwelling together, or for political allies that are recently associated, to multiply rapidly the consanguineous marriage options of all kinds'.[117] For different reasons that have been outlined before, Françoise Héritier also considers the prohibition a central one in the complex system of incest taboos.

The two-sisters rule is another instance of the gender asymmetry in Islamic law: there is no male equivalent, no 'two-brothers rule', since any polyandrous marriage or concubinage is ruled out anyhow. The asymmetry is exploited in a joke:

> Al-Faḍl b. ʿAbd al-Raḥmān[118] was asked,
> —Why don't you get married?
> —My father has given a slave-girl to me and my brother.
> —No, really! Has he given one girl to you and your brother?!
> —What do you find so odd in that? Our neighbour Abū Ruzayq, the judge, has two slave-girls.[119]

It would be tempting but wrong to read this as a subversive comment on Islamic laws of marriage and concubinage. It is an example of jokes on stupid people, and therefore included in Ibn al-Jawzī's book *Akhbār al-ḥamqā wa-l-mughaffalīn* ('Stories of Stupid People and Simpletons').[120] Only an utter fool or a depraved man would stoop to sharing a woman; it is taken for granted that women would be content to share a man.

*

With the two sisters, the Qur'anic verse ends, even though the syntax and the sense are continued in the following verse, which opens with yet another category of forbidden women, the one that in ordinary daily life is by far the most important: «And wedded women (*wa-l-muḥṣanātu*)». The passage on the forbidden women from sura 4 is the only one in the Qur'an that deals explicitly with the incest taboo. Some commentators have seen an allusion to it in Q 25:54, in which God is said to have created mankind 'as *nasab* and *ṣihr*', or related by descent and by marriage. Al-Farrāʾ (d. 207/822) explained *nasab* and *ṣihr* as those persons one is not allowed to marry and those one may marry, respectively, the latter category including 'paternal and maternal cousins and similar relatives whom one may marry',[121] but he is attacked by others, to whom the term *ṣihr* encompasses both forbidden and allowed degrees,[122] and whose interpretation prevailed.

Exegetes and jurists have classified and counted the various kinds of marriage impediments. 'There are fourteen: seven through consanguinity, two through milk-relationship, four by affinity, and one by combination'.[123] Or, 'There are seventeen (forbidden) women: mother, daughter, sister, paternal aunt, maternal aunt, brother's daughter, sister's daughter, milk-sister, father's mother, wife's daughter, i.e. foster-daughter, son's wife, father's wife, two sisters combined, wedded women who have husbands, Zoroastrian women, slave-girls of the People of the Book (i.e. Jews and Christians); (altogether) seven by consanguinity, two by milk-relationship, six by affinity, and two by religion.'[124] Many authorities remark that these categories still do not exhaust the forbidden women: to a man who is married to the maximum of four women, any other free woman is forbidden. Moreover, a marriage between a Muslim and an unbeliever is often deemed forbidden, on the basis of Q 2:221 (Arberry's translation): «Do not marry idolatresses, until they believe». Finally, the Qur'an stipulates that one should not marry a fornicator unless one is one oneself: «The fornicator shall marry none but a fornicatress or an idolatress, and the fornicatress—none shall marry her but a fornicator or an idolator; that is forbidden to the believers» (Q 24:3). The legal scholars had some difficulty with this rule, understandably, and it was generally deemed to have been abrogated by later passages.[125]

Islamic law has no definitive codex in which the regulations are formulated authoritatively and as unambiguously as possible, and which is accepted by all Muslims. Instead, there are numerous compendia recognized by the main legal schools. The relevant Qur'anic text, although relatively clear on the forbidden degrees, cannot be adopted wholesale; its purport, extended or modified in accordance with accepted Hadith and other consensually accepted rulings, is couched in the jargon and format employed by the jurists. This is, by way of example, how the forbidden degrees are enumerated in a very concise and popular compendium of Ḥanafī law, *Multaqā l-abḥur* by Ibrāhīm al-Ḥalabī (d. 956/1549):[126]

> Chapter on the forbidden women. Forbidden to a man are his mother and his grandmother and her ascendants, and his daughter and the daughter of his child and her descendants, and his sister and her daughter, and the daughter of his brother, and (these daughters') descendants, and his paternal aunt, and his maternal aunt, and the mother of his wife unconditionally, and the daughter of a wife with whom he has had intercourse, and the wife of his father and of his ascendants, and of his son and of his

> descendants; and all (these categories are also forbidden) on the basis of milk-relationship; and (it is forbidden) to combine two sisters in marriage ... or concubinage. If he marries the sister of his concubine with whom he has already had intercourse, he must not have intercourse with either of them until he declares the other one of them forbidden. If he marries two sisters in two different marriage contracts without knowledge of the first woman, he must make a separation between himself and the two women ... And (it is forbidden) to combine (in marriage) two women who, supposing one of them to be male, would be forbidden to each other, in contrast to combining a woman and the daughter of her husband who is not her own daughter. Fornication causes an impediment by affinity, as does lustful touching by one of the two parties, or the man's looking at the woman's private parts, or the woman's lustful looking at the man's penis. A female younger than nine years old is not considered the object of lust ... [127]

Legal impediments are more easily created than one might think. Naturally, marriage or sexual congress with a woman turns her female close kin (mother, daughter, sister) into forbidden partners to the spouse. Many jurisprudents, however, agree that sexual petting short of full intercourse, even a mere lustful gaze at a naked or partially naked female, has the same effect. This was pointed out above in the section on stepmothers, but the application of this principle extends further, as is implied in the passage just quoted from *Multaqā l-abḥur*. The various schools differ as to the details. In some cases the consequences look grotesque, as in the following fatwa of a Mālikite jurisconsult:

> Abū Muḥammad was asked about someone who extended his hand towards his wife, intending (sexual) pleasure (*ladhdha*), but touching his daughter instead. He answered: If he did not let his hand rest on her but removed it instantly, then it has no consequence for him. But if his hand stayed where it was and he felt pleasure, not knowing who she was, then her mother is forbidden to him. And if he was aware that she was his daughter and he laid his hand on her for the sake of pleasure, then he has committed a heinous thing.[128]

This resembles what Sufyān b. ᶜUyayna (d. 198/813) allegedly said: if a man kisses his daughter lustfully, thinking she is his wife, then his wife is forbidden to him (Ibn Ḥanbal comments that he personally would not forbid it unless intercourse with the daughter had taken place).[129] Ibn Ḥanbal, asked about a man who lustfully touches an immature girl, ruled that as a consequence the man's son could not lawfully have intercourse with the girl.[130] Another ruling, transmitted by the Shīᶜite scholar Ibn Bābawayh (d.

381/991), says that a man may not marry the midwife who has delivered him as a baby, nor her daughter, 'for she is as one of his mothers'.[131] Quite extreme sounds an opinion ascribed to ᶜAlī b. Abī Ṭālib: 'If a woman touches the body of her daughter [one would rather have expected: her son] who has reached the age of six years, it is a form of fornication'.[132]

Foundlings

In pre-modern Western Europe there was some concern about the danger of incest committed unknowingly with children who had been abandoned as infants and could have ended up in brothels. It was this topic that inspired John Boswell to write his monograph on the foundling in European history.[133] In several influential stories an abandoned male child later becomes involved with incest, Oedipus being the best known example. Incest might not only be the result but also the cause of abandoning infants, if these were the offspring of conscious incest. The stories of Albanus (or St Alban) and Gregorius illustrate both sides, for they are born of incest and later unwittingly become involved in incest again.[134] The scholastic specialists might say, as they do in Islam, that incest committed without knowing is no sin, but in the popular mind no such distinction is made between conscious and 'tragic' or unwitting sinning.[135] In Jewish law the risk of unwitting incest thus committed was apparently considered too slight to bother about much, yet there were some marriage restrictions, since those groups whose purity was essential, such as priests and Levites, were not allowed to marry foundlings.[136]

Since genealogy is such an important issue both in Arab society and in Muslim law, it could be expected that the status of a foundling, whose genealogy is in principle unknown, gave rise to problems. A separate chapter on the foundling (*laqīṭ*) is found in every manual of Islamic law. Among the points that are regularly discussed are the social status of the child (is he or she free or a slave?), the property of any possessions that may have been left with the child, the religion of the child, and what happens if someone claims paternity or maternity. To my knowledge, however, nobody raises the possibility that marrying a foundling could well be incestuous, especially if one assumes that a child is often abandoned within the community in which it is born rather than in a remote region. Apparently, it is taken for granted that there is no consanguineous relationship unless it is proved to be otherwise. It was obviously undesirable to prohibit any marriage of someone with uncertain genealogy on the small chance of an incestuous bond, for in that case no foundling could ever marry—celibacy being frowned upon in Islam instead of deemed a virtuous option, as in Christianity. In addition, it could be argued that no paternity is ever wholly reliably established, before the advances of modern science, so the case of the foundling does not differ in principle from anyone else.[137] That medieval Christianity was more concerned with the dangers of incest with foundlings than Islam may be explained in part by the rather wider interpretation of incest in the former, extending to the seventh degree of kinship, whereas in Islam the danger was less acute. It could, of course, be argued that it is perhaps the other way round: a greater fear of incest gave rise to more restrictive marriage laws. Why medieval Islam, on the whole, seems less obsessed with incest than contemporary Christianity is a difficult question that will be raised again and tentatively answered towards the end of this study.

Punishments

Incest is not a concept that has a clearly separate status in Islamic law and there is no single Arabic term that covers it. In principle, all illicit sexual relationships fall under the term *zinā*, usually translated as fornication or adultery, but more strictly to be understood as unlawful sexual intercourse.[138] The penalties for *zinā* do not make any clear distinction between incestuous and non-incestuous fornication, although we shall see that incest is sometimes treated as a special case. Generally, fornication is considered worse if it is incestuous; Ibn al-Jawzī calls it 'among the most monstrous (*min afḥash*)' kinds of fornication.[139] Nevertheless, on the basis of legal technicalities the punishments for incest may be less severe than for ordinary fornication, as will be explained below. The penalties for *zinā* may take two forms, one as punishment in the Hereafter and the other in this world. The former category is not clearly formulated in the Qur'an or in Prophetic Tradition (Hadith); the law is concerned only with the latter. Hadith literature contains some lurid depictions of what awaits fornicators in Hell. Some of those have been collected by al-Dhahabī (d. 748/1348) in his book on 'grave sins' (*al-Kabāʾir*), which is not a legal text. He remarks that 'fornication with one's mother, sister, stepmother, or with (other) unmarriageable women is the worst form of *zinā*',[140] without quoting Prophetic traditions with punishments specially reserved for the incestuous deceased: one can only imagine that their torments will be even more horrid than those of ordinary fornicators. A tradition put into the mouth of the Prophet, quoted by several authors, categorically states that those who commit incest will not enter Paradise.[141] Al-Dhahabī, however, adds an often-quoted tradition on the worldly punishment of culprits, about a man who claims that the Prophet ordered him to kill a man who had wedded his stepmother, a case to which we shall come back.

In Judaism, at least according to the Old Testament and Talmudic prescriptions, the punishments for incestuous sexual intercourse are harsh. Al-

Maqdisī, summarizing Jewish law, speaks of burning for incest with a mother-in-law, a stepchild, or a daughter-in-law,[142] which seems incomplete and inaccurate, since the Talmud mentions stoning for incest with mother, stepmother, and daughter-in-law (Sanhedrin 7:4), burning in the case of stepdaughter, step-granddaughter, mother-in-law, daughter, granddaughter (Sanhedrin 9:1), and flogging in other cases; incest, with murder and idolatry, is not even allowed in order to save one's life.[143] The Islamic penalties for *zinā* in general are potentially very severe too, consisting of lashing or stoning for various kinds of *zinā*, depending on the culprit's marital status. The burden of proof, however, is almost impossibly heavy (four witnesses must have observed sexual penetration) and there are harsh punishments for false or unproved accusation of unlawful intercourse (*qadhf*). Since incest would normally take place in private domestic circumstances, kept hidden either by mutual consent or by familial pressure and, even if witnessed, often kept in the nuclear family, it is unlikely that many cases would be brought to court. Similarly, in the medieval West, where archives are more abundant than in Islam, very few cases are found in ecclesiastical court records of incest in the nuclear family.[144] If ordinary fornication is very difficult to prove according to the strict demands of Islamic legal proof, proving incest will, if anything, be yet more difficult. As with ordinary *zinā*, confession is the surest proof, but this is a rare event. The 'confession' of Fāṭima bint Yaᶜqūb, mentioned above,[145] should not be taken seriously and the alleged perpetrators were executed not on the basis of the Islamic penalty for incest but as heretic rebels.

The legal handbooks, while demonstrating a great eagerness to deal with punishments for fornication in general, do not give much special attention to incest when they discuss penal law. Shīᶜite law differs from Sunnite law in that a death penalty can be imposed where the latter would not do so (e.g. in the case of someone who is not and has never been married) if there are aggravating circumstances, including incest.[146]

The Sunnites, too, can be severe. 'He who fornicates with his sister, while knowing it to be forbidden, must be killed', as Ibn Taymiyya (d. 728/1328) said in a fatwa, without any qualification as to the marital state of the perpetrator.[147] His proof consists of the same *ḥadīth* that al-Dhahabī had mentioned, about the Prophet's ordering someone to behead a man who had married his father's wife. This story is often quoted.[148] Apparently Ibn Taymiyya reasons that incest, knowingly committed, between brother and sister, being more closely related, deserves at least as severe a punishment as marrying a non-consanguineous but forbidden woman. If it was done unwittingly and subsequently discovered to be illicit, the marriage is to be annulled. In the story in question, told by al-Barāᵓ (a contemporary of the Prophet), however, a man actually arranges a wedding feast for his marriage to his father's wife. Since he can only have done this knowingly, he was to be beheaded and his property confiscated.[149] Not everyone was equally severe. One authority said, 'I do not think such a man [who knowingly marries a woman within the forbidden degrees] receives a *ḥadd* punishment; rather a *taʿzīr* punishment'; the former is the harsh mandatory penalty prescribed in clear-cut cases, the latter a discretionary and usually less severe punishment. Aḥmad ibn Ḥanbal was a hard-liner in this matter: upon hearing this opinion, he comments: 'How repulsive this doctrine must be to God!', and adds that the man must be killed if he acted intentionally.[150] The Ḥanbalite Ibn Qudāma also favours the death penalty, while mentioning the opinion of others who demand *ḥadd* (which is not necessarily a death penalty) or merely discretionary punishment.[151] The Shāfiʿites agree that the mandatory *ḥadd* punishment is appropriate in this case, as is argued for instance by Bahāʾ al-Dīn ibn Shaddād (d. 632/1235), better known as Saladin's biographer. Quoting two versions of the anecdote told by al-Barāʾ, he concludes that 'copulation with non-marriageable persons is not permitted in any situation or manner and is plain *zinā*.'[152] It does not make any difference, as the Shāfiʿite al-Māwardi (d. 450/1058) says in his massive *al-Ḥāwī*, whether or not a semblance of legality was created by means of a wedding contract.[153]

The Ḥanafites, however, do not agree. The Ḥanafite jurist al-Manbijī (d. 686/1287) gives compelling reasons why the story told by al-Barāʾ cannot be used to demand capital punishment for merely marrying one's stepmother: killing with the sword and confiscation of property are appropriate for fighting apostates, not for punishing adulterers. The man in question was openly challenging the Prophet's authority and the crime for which he was killed was apostasy, not *zinā*;[154] this was in fact already suggested by Ibn Ḥanbal, who said that the Prophet had rightfully ordered the man to be killed, '*like the apostate*';[155] similarly, the Ḥanbalite Ibn Taymiyya says in a fatwa that a man who marries his biological daughter born out of wedlock should be killed, 'qualifying as an apostate'.[156] The Ḥanafite jurist al-Kāsānī summarizes the view of his school. He argues that the term *zinā* cannot be used in many cases, such as intercourse with a Zoroastrian woman, an apostate woman, a manumitted slave, a woman with whom one has a relationship of a forbidden degree through affinity or milk-relationship, even if all these are forbidden. He continues:

> Similarly, when one marries a woman of the forbidden degrees or a fifth wife, or one's wife's sister, and then has sexual intercourse with her, the *ḥadd* punishment is not applied according to Abū Ḥanīfa, even though the man knows it to be forbidden; he is to receive discretionary punishment (*taʿzīr*). But according to the two [other Ḥanafī authorities, al-Shaybānī and Abū Yūsuf] and al-Shāfiʿī, *ḥadd* does apply to him.[157]

The ensuing explanation of Abū Ḥanīfa's view is that precisely because a marriage was concluded, even though it is a forbidden one, the sexual act is no longer a straightforward case of *zinā*,[158] and the *ḥadd* punishment cannot be applied, regardless of whether the man mistakenly thinks the marriage is permissible and thus claims *bona fides*,[159] or knows that it is forbidden. According to Abū Ḥanīfa, the term fornication (*zinā*) cannot be applied here, and the case may be compared to that of the Zoroastrians, who marry their mothers and sisters, which is not called *zinā* in Islamic law and is not punished with *ḥadd*.[160] In this view, an incestuous marriage constitutes a *shubha*, a 'semblance' or 'ambiguity', the technical term for a forbidden act that resembles a lawful one. No matter whether the marriage was in fact invalid (*bāṭil*), which is the majority view, or perhaps 'merely' defective (*fāsid*)—al-Kāsānī gives arguments for both views—, the perpetrator should be given the benefit of the doubt, assuming that he may have acted in good faith. If he was aware of the prohibition of marrying within the forbidden degrees, he should be punished with *taʿzīr*, discretionary punishment, but not with *ḥadd*, for as long as the incest was committed in a marriage he has not committed straightforward adultery. It is obvious that if and when incest occurs in society, it is extremely unlikely to be thus 'sanctioned' by a formal marriage, and that in the great majority of cases it occurs out of wedlock. These cases do not particularly interest the jurists, for they are clearly cases of *zinā*, straightforward fornication unproblematical from a legal point of view, and the fact that they may be morally more objectionable than ordinary illicit intercourse does not concern them as jurists. Neither does it matter much to them whether the sexual deed was performed with mutual consent or as rape, forced upon an unwilling partner. An example of the latter is found in a story adduced by Ibn Qudāma[161] and also given by Ibn Qayyim al-Jawziyya.[162] The Umayyad governor al-Ḥajjāj (d. 95/714), confronted with a case of rape of a woman by her brother, is uncertain about what to decide. When some surviving Companions of the Prophet are asked, one of them claims to have heard the Prophet say, 'Whoever transgresses against the believers, smite his middle with the sword! (*ḥuṭṭū wasaṭahu bi-l-sayf*)'. This manner of execution, evoking the gruesome *tawsīṭ* practised in Ayyubid and Mamluk times, sounds anachronistic and out of character in a story about the Prophet; another source, more plausibly, reads 'head' instead of 'middle'.[163] Ibn Qudāma, who is not worried by the version he quotes, adds another saying attributed to the Prophet: 'Whoever copulates with an unmarriageable kinswoman, kill him!', and has therefore no difficulty in recommending the death penalty.

It has already been remarked that the formal nature of Islamic law has consequences that may seem odd from the viewpoint of Western or modern morality. Those forms of incest that have in recent decades been exposed in Western countries as being more frequent than was hitherto suspected or admitted, namely of parents with their children, forms that are generally considered as being particularly depraved, are not very conspicuous in traditional Muslim society or jurisprudence. Bousquet observed that in Islamic law it is a less grave crime to sodomize one's own prepubescent son than it is for a widower to have sexual intercourse with a betrothed widow before marriage.[164] In this connection it should be added that for Islamic law anal intercourse, though forbidden even in marriage by most schools, nevertheless counts as sexual intercourse; in support of this it is regularly remarked that the word *farj*, 'pudendum', could refer to the anus as well as to the genitals, male or female. This has some interesting consequences for the rules on marriage impediments. If a man has intercourse with a young man,[165] Ibn Qudāma states, he is not allowed to marry the latter's mother and daughter, according to some Ḥanbalite authorities; likewise, the perpetrator's mother and daughter are forbidden to the passive partner.[166]

Some Muslim scholars, too, were aware of the apparent lack of proportion in the prescribed punishments. Al-Manbijī points out that an ordinary case of adultery is to be punished with the proper *ḥadd*, i.e. stoning or flogging depending on the status of the culprits, whereas marrying one's stepmother is not punishable with *ḥadd*. He continues, imagining that someone might object: 'But if this is not adultery, it is surely worse (*aghlaẓ*), and all the more calling for the *ḥadd* to be imposed!"' Then one should answer that punishments are applied on the basis of *tawqīf*, meaning that they are given 'from above' rather than developed by human reasoning. After all, to accuse someone wrongly of being an unbeliever is surely worse than a false accusation of adultery; yet in Islamic law only the latter is punishable with *ḥadd*. Thus, al-Manbijī concludes, 'it is proved that analogous reasoning does not apply to legal punishments. God knows best'.[167] The last words hint at a doubt. In fact, the 'illogical' result of Bousquet's example and other cases is built on logical reasoning. Illicit intercourse (*zinā*) is defined as sexual intercourse with living humans normally considered sexually attractive. This means that necrophilia, bestiality and intercourse with very young children, although considered punishable as disgusting deviances, do not strictly count as *zinā* (note that homosexual intercourse with adolescent boys does not fall in the same category, since they are considered sexually attractive to normal men). Similarly, sexual cravings for one's close kin are not considered as natural; hence, incestuous relationships do not always and automatically count as ordinary *zinā*. Traditional Muslim society, which separates the sexes as much as possible, and which takes it for granted that, if a man is together in private with an unrelated woman, the worst is likely to follow, allows a man to be together with his *maḥārim*, unmarriageable relations. 'A man may not be alone with a woman except when he is unable to marry her (*dhū maḥram*)', as an authoritative saying of the Prophet puts it.[168] In a household with an extended family this would severely restrict the freedom of interaction between family members that could marry each other; interestingly, a solution has been found by women who would suckle, for instance, their husbands' younger brothers, thus creating milk-relationships that would enable more girls to move around unveiled in the house.[169]

Ibn Qayyim al-Jawziyya takes up the point of mankind's natural inclination in a discussion of homosexual intercourse. Some of those who argue that the *ḥadd* punishment is not applied to those who practise it, justify this by saying that a natural inhibition (*wāziʿ ṭabʿī*) found in ordinary people is enough and makes prescribed punishments unnecessary, just as there are no such sanctions on eating excrement or drinking urine and blood. Most scholars, however, says Ibn al-Qayyim, reply that 'wicked souls' do indeed show such perverse tendencies, so that *ḥadd* punishment is even more appropriate than in the case of adultery. Therefore, he concludes,

> it is necessary to apply *ḥadd* punishment to someone who copulates with his mother, his daughter, his maternal aunt or his grandmother,[170] even though souls possess a natural inhibition and restraint from this. Indeed, the *ḥadd* for all these cases is capital punishment, regardless of whether one is a virgin or a non-virgin, according to the most correct opinions, viz. those of Aḥmad (ibn Ḥanbal) and others. And this in spite of the fact that the aversion (*nafra*) of (normal) souls from this is much stronger than the aversion from (intercourse with) beardless boys.[171]

In his monograph on love, *Rawḍat al-muḥibbīn* ('The Garden of Lovers'), Ibn al-Qayyim quotes a story about a man who had married his maternal aunt. Brought before the caliph ʿAbd al-Malik (*reg.* 65-86/685-705) he defends himself in vain by saying that he thought she was permitted to him. The caliph does not allow such gross ignorance in a Muslim and Ibn al-Qayyim adds, 'I think that he ordered him to be killed'.[172] This harsh ruling is exceptional. Ibn al-Qayyim continues with quoting the opinion of Aḥmad ibn Ḥanbal, who prescribes a death sentence and confiscation of one's possessions only for incest committed intentionally and knowingly; if committed while not knowing about the prohibition, the partners must be separated.[173]

The Ḥanafites are generally more lenient and are inclined to limit the imposition of *ḥadd* punishment as much as possible. The other schools are generally more strict in classifying incest as ordinary *zinā*. The Mālikites prescribe the ordinary *ḥadd*, stoning or flogging and banishment, for incest with one's mother, aunt, sister, or one's son's slave-girl.[174] The Shāfiʿite al-Qaffāl al-Shāshī (d. 507/1114) states that 'when a man marries a relative with whom he may not marry and consummates the marriage, while being convinced that she is forbidden to him, the *ḥadd* punishment is obligatory; but in Abū Ḥanīfa's opinion the *ḥadd* is not applied to him.'[175] Ibn Ḥazm gives the various opinions in some more detail:

> People have different opinions on this matter. Some say: He who marries his mother or his daughter or his *ḥarīma*,[176] or fornicates with any of these: these cases are all alike and all are *zinā*. The marriage does not count as a marriage. If he knows it to be forbidden, the *ḥadd* for adultery applies to him in full. A child [born from such a union] is not reckoned to be his. This is the opinion of al-Ḥasan [al-Baṣrī], Mālik, al-Shāfiʿī, Abū Thawr, Abū Yūsuf and Muḥammad ibn al-Ḥasan [al-Shaybānī], the latter two being followers of Abū Ḥanīfa. Mālik, however, made a distinction between sexual intercourse with a marriage contract and that with slave-ownership[177] (...) Abū Ḥanīfa said that no *ḥadd* applies in all these cases, nor to him who marries the mother who bore him, or his daughter, his sister, his grandmother, his paternal aunt, his maternal aunt, his brother's daughter, his sister's daughter, if he knows their closeness of kin to him and knows that they are forbidden to him, and has intercourse with all these: then the child is recognized as his, the nuptial gift (*mahr*) is obligatory, and no *ḥadd* but only *taʿzīr* (discretionary punishment) with less than forty lashes is applied to him. This is also the opinion of Sufyān al-Thawrī. Both said that if he has intercourse without a marriage contract, it is *zinā*, and the *ḥadd* applies to him as it would to any fornicator.[178]

Ibn Ḥazm continues with a lengthy argumentation against the Ḥanafite view, and concludes that the *ḥadd* should be applied if fornication with close kin has taken place while knowing of its illicitness. Marrying one's stepmother should be punished with death, even if the culprit is not *muḥṣan* (someone who has been married before), and confiscation of property.[179] Equally harsh are the Shīʿites generally. Al-Qāḍī Nuʿmān (d. 363/974) says in his *Daʿāʾim al-Islām* ('Pillars of Islam'), the principal source for Fāṭimid law, that intercourse with an unmarriageable relation is punishable with death, quoting a tradition going back to ʿAlī ibn Abī Ṭālib, who ordered a man to be executed by stoning for having fornicated with his stepmother, even though he was not a *muḥṣan* (being which would have saved his life if it had concerned ordinary adultery).[180] An authority of the Twelver-Shīʿa (or Imāmī Shīʿa) confirms that 'there is no difference of opinion on capital punishment being compulsory for incest with consanguineous relatives', adding that other authorities include incest with stepmother and stepdaughter.[181]

Islamic Law and Zoroastrian Marriage

Zoroastrians are often mentioned in Islamic legal texts. As said earlier, in Chapter Two, they are granted protected status (*dhimma*), together with Jews, Christians and Ṣābiʾans, and are sometimes reckoned among the so-called People of the Book, or Scripture, even though many authorities deny them this status since the Zoroastrian scriptures, unlike those of the Jews and the Christians, are not recognized as being inspired by God. The protection was granted provided that a certain special tax, called *jizya*, was paid. The protected religious communities were allowed to carry on with their own customs and institutions as long as they did not go against the interest of the Islamic state or the Muslim community. Islamic law discusses those matters where Muslims are, or could be, directly involved with Zoroastrians. Mixed marriages of Muslim men with Christian or Jewish women are generally allowed, although disapproved by many. Marrying Zoroastrian women or taking them as concubines, however, is forbidden by virtually all authorities; only Abū Thawr and Ibn Ḥazm allowed it.[182] The prohibition is never justified, as far as I can see, by the incestuous marriage customs of the Zoroastrians, but inspired by doctrinal reasons: the Zoroastrians may have protected status but are generally denied to be People of Scripture and therefore on a par with other polytheists and idolators.

However, some scholars felt uneasy about tolerating what Muslims always considered an abomination. Ibn Qayyim al-Jawziyya discussed the question at some length in a monograph on the protected communities.[183] These communities are allowed to continue with their practices and to conclude their 'defective marriages' (he uses the technical term *fāsid*, not quite identical with *bāṭil* 'invalid') on two conditions. The first is that they do not appeal to Muslim authorities: tacit toleration is one thing, but explicitly condoning when asked to do so is impossible. Secondly, the minority community must believe that the marriage is valid according to their own religion. This opinion had already been voiced by many early jurists. Al-Shāfiʿī had allowed the protected communities to marry within their own group according to their own rules, 'as long as they do not appeal to us'; in case they convert to Islam afterwards, the marriage is not to be annulled if it would have been valid by Islamic rules from the start. Otherwise, it is to be annulled.[184]

Apparently, some Muslims baulked at the thought of allowing Magian close-kin unions to continue, even if it remained an internal matter among the Zoroastrians. Ibn al-Qayyim reports two conflicting opinions attributed to Aḥmad ibn Ḥanbal. One of these allows it, referring in support to rulings of the Prophet concerning the Zoroastrians in eastern Arabia. However, seeing that adultery, homosexual intercourse and usury are in fact forbidden even to the protected communities in all circumstances, one could argue that marrying one's mother or daughter should also be forbidden, since it is a worse crime. The reply would be that one should consider the impact on the Muslim community: adultery, usury and homosexuality are all found in the Muslim community, and these crimes should be fought at all costs because they are, as it were, infectious. Close-kin incest, on the other hand, is an evil that supposedly does not occur among normal Muslims, and there is therefore no danger that the Magians' bad example will be followed. It is also argued that the Zoroastrians, against paying their special tax, are allowed to persist in their unbelief, and unbelief is surely even worse than incest.[185] It is, in principle, not different from allowing the Jews to marry their nieces.

The second opinion is not to allow it, which is what the second caliph ᶜUmar ibn al-Khaṭṭāb had done when he decreed that Zoroastrian close-kin unions should be dissolved. Ibn al-Qayyim ventures that this apparent conflict between the Prophet himself and ᶜUmar, to Sunnites perhaps the second most important authority in Islam, is due to the latter's reasoning that the political situation had changed in the meantime. In the Prophet's time, the Zoroastrian Sasanian empire still existed, Islam had not yet become an empire, and Islamic rules could not be imposed and enforced rigorously. The great conquests under ᶜUmar's reign changed all that. Ibn al-Qayyim leaves no doubt that he approves of ᶜUmar's view, even though he is reluctant to oppose an opinion attributed to Aḥmad ibn Ḥanbal, the founder of his school:

> This is among his best and strongest independent judgements [i.e. not based on a Qur'anic or Prophetic ruling], one that is most beloved by God and His messenger, for it is one of the vilest acts, hated by God and His messenger, that a man should marry his mother, his daughter, or his aunt. There cannot be any doubt that to remove this practice from existence is dearer to God and His messenger than to confirm it ... [ᶜUmar's view] is dearer to us than what is reported on this matter on the authority of Aḥmad (ibn Ḥanbal), al-Shāfiᶜī, Mālik, and similar authorities.[186]

Nowhere does Ibn al-Qayyim refer to cases in his own time; it is likely that the matter had only theoretical relevance. Al-Sarakhsī is of the opinion that the story of ᶜUmar's decree, even though it is found in several Hadith collections,[187] is not well-known (*mashhūr*, a technical term of the Hadith scholars), unlike that of the Umayyad caliph ᶜUmar ibn ᶜAbd al-ᶜAzīz (reg. 99-101/717-720). This second ᶜUmar, noted for his uncompromizing attitude towards non-Muslims, had consulted the famous al-Ḥasan al-Baṣrī on the matter, writing to him: 'Why is it that the Rightly Guided Caliphs [the first four caliphs] left the people of the protected religions as they were, marrying women of forbidden degrees, buying alcoholic drinks and pigs?' Al-Ḥasan replied that by paying the *jizya* tax they acquired the right to be left in peace as to their belief; the Caliph should not change this: 'You are a follower, not an innovator'.[188] From that time onwards, al-Sarakhsī adds, rulers and judges did not interfere with the non-Muslims even if they were aware of their practices.

It would be foolhardy for any traditional jurist to omit part of the Sharīᶜa for the trivial reason that the condemned practice no longer occurs. Thus we still come across incestuous Zoroastrians in the compilation of Islamic law made in the 'twenties of the past century by ᶜAbd al-Raḥmān al-Jazīrī: '...

marrying someone within a forbidden degree, such as one's mother, sister, or daughter, like the Majūs do.'[189]

Justifications

This is not the place to discuss the details in which the law schools vary. For a survey in a Western language, one could consult the work of Linant de Bellefonds or the more recent compendium by Bakhtiar.[190] More relevant to the present study are the relatively rare occasions on which writers express an opinion on the reasons for the prohibition of incest. Some justifications have already been quoted and discussed above, in the sections on the several forbidden degrees. A pseudo-explanation that is not rarely given is that incest goes against a 'sound natural disposition' (*fiṭra salīma*) which rejects incest. We have already come across this opinion, which does not explain much, in the words of al-Marwarrūdhī quoted above, in Chapter Two, or of Ibn Qayyim al-Jawziyya who also appealed to man's *fiṭra*,[191] and his natural inhibition. Most exegetes and lawyers simply do not raise the question. The easiest way of dealing explicitly with this problem is to deny the existence of a rational explanation. Ibn Kammūna (d. 683/1284), a Jewish convert to Islam from Baghdad who wrote an interesting work on comparative religion, said of the Zoroastrians:

> Their permissiveness about marriage with sisters and daughters is not a rationally inadmissible practice; the prohibition of such marriages is one point of the revealed precepts, and this kind of marriage has been disreputable among us because most religions known to us forbid it.[192]

A similar view is held by al-Rāghib al-Iṣbahānī (5th/11th century):

> Know that reason by itself is of little avail and hardly able to arrive at the knowledge of general concepts, beyond particularities (...) Reason will not let us know, for instance, that pig's flesh, blood, and wine are forbidden (...) or that one should not marry women within the forbidden degrees, or that one should not have sexual intercourse with a woman during menstruation.[193]

Mystics are usually credited with an inclination towards reading deeper, spiritual meanings in the holy text. It is striking, therefore, that the important Sufi authority al-Qushayrī (d. 465/1072) declares it impossible to give a reason for the prohibition on incest. Although he has an explanation of the prohibition of marrying one's father's wife (see below), he says of Q 4:23:

> It is impossible to contrive to extract the motives that led to this prohibition, because the Revealed Law is not given any justification (*al-sharʿ ghayr muʿallal*). God, the Exalted, forbids what He wishes to whom He wishes. The same applies to allowing things. The divine precepts have no 'reason' (*ʿilla*) whatsoever. If these forbidden women had been made allowed, this would have been possible.[194]

Al-Jāḥiẓ, a rationalist normally eager to explain things or to discuss rival explanations, can only point at God's commands in this matter:

> Women are a 'tillage ground' for men (...) Were it not for the trial and tribulation involved in the fact that certain things are illicit and others licit, and in the keeping of offspring free from doubts of adulterous parentage, and [in the need to ensure] the falling of inheritances into the hands of the legal heirs, no man would be more entitled than any other to any one woman (...) In fact, the situation would have been as the Magians assert it to be, [when they say] 'To a man belongs the closest, and then the next-closest to him by blood or kinship among women.' But religious duty has occasioned the test [of distinguishing some women as illicit for men in general], and has made the general rule subject to particular limitations.[195]

In any revealed religion there will be doctrines and precepts that cannot fully be explained rationally. Notwithstanding this, many Muslim theologians have declared Islam to be extremely rational. God is wise, merciful, and «desires ease» for His servants (Q 2:185), therefore one may assume that precepts and restrictions that may seem pointless, even burdensome, are there with a reason other than merely being a test of obedience. Regarding the incest prohibitions, one finds at least some attempts. William H. Durham has summarized the various theories that have been advanced and are still being advanced in human culture in general as explanations of incest taboos and prohibitions. Firstly, the theory that incest disrupts family harmony; secondly, that the taboos stimulate group alliance and cooperation; thirdly, the psychoanalytic theory that natural incestuous impulses are to be repressed; fourthly, the Westermarckian aversion theory; and lastly, the inbreeding or 'bad stock' theory.[196] In previous chapters I have shown that four of these five theories, in some form or other, were present among Arabs and Muslims in the past—that the psychoanalytic theory is the only absent one should surprise nobody. Islamic jurists broadly reflect the same ideas.

Al-Sarakhsī appeals to reason (*ʿaql*) which concurs with divine precept and mentions a psychological justification:

> The most correct opinion is to say that these (categories of) forbidden women are established by a Qur'anic text, while (at the same time) approved by the reason of intelligent people, too, when they reject evil practices. An intelligent person is eager to protect his mother and his daughter and to defend them against shame and disgrace, just as one is eager to defend oneself against these. Marriage (*nikāḥ*) means exposing oneself to copulation (*waṭ*ʾ), and an intelligent person shuns this deed regarding his mother and daughter as much as he shuns it regarding himself (...) Likewise he will reject it concerning the wife of his father, who raised him, being like a mother in the sense of raising him; and concerning his daughter-in-law, who has the status of a daughter to him and whose child will be a (grand)child to him.[197]

The same argument in different wording is given by al-Rāzī, speaking of son—mother and father—daughter incest,

> Scholars have said that the reason for this prohibition is the fact that copulation is a form of humiliation and abasement. People are ashamed to speak of it and only refer to it in private. Most forms of insult make use of it exclusively. Since this is so, one must protect mothers against it, because the kindness bestowed by a mother on her child is the greatest kindness that exists; so she has to be protected from this humiliation. A daughter takes the place of a part of oneself. The Prophet—God bless and preserve him—said, 'Fāṭima is a bit of myself'. Thus one must protect her from this humiliation, since intercourse with her is a kind of humiliation. The same may be said of the remaining (categories). God knows best.[198]

The Ḥanafite al-Kāsānī argues that the inevitable 'roughness' (*khushūna*)[199] that happens from time to time between marital partners would, if close-kin partners were wedded, lead to the 'severing of kinship' between them, which is forbidden. He uses a common term, *qaṭ*ᶜ *al-raḥim*, literally 'cutting the womb', always considered to be among the worst things that one could commit. He, too, stresses the respect due to a mother, incompatible with using her as a sexual partner, in which case she would owe obedience to her own son where the reverse is proper: 'This would lead to a contradiction'.[200]

It seems that al-Shāfiᶜī refers to the same ideas when he calls the divinely laid down precepts against incest a 'blessing' (*ni*ᶜ*ma*) from God, while cleverly exploiting the several related meanings of the word *ḥurma*: the quality of being forbidden; inviolability; and deference or respect:

> God has affirmed the marriage impediment (*ḥurma*) through consanguinity and affinity and made this one of His blessings bestowed on His creation. Thus if certain women are forbidden to men, this is through the

> inviolability (*ḥurma*) that men owe to them ... The prohibition (*taḥrīm*) of marriage is as blessing, not a punishment (*niʿma lā niqma*).[201]

All this should not be taken to mean that the sexual act is as inherently shameful in Islam as it is, for instance, in traditional Christianity. It is understood, of course, that copulation humiliates and abases only the one who is penetrated, not the penetrator; the same is valid for homosexual intercourse as it appears in Abbasid invective poetry. There is one difficulty with al-Rāzī's explanation. If it is taken for granted that women should marry and thus be subjected to this 'abasement', one could say, for the sake of argument, that it would be kinder and more protective to the woman if the deed were done by someone familiar—a father, a brother—rather than by a stranger. Al-Rāzī's concluding formula may be an indication of his own doubts about this theory, whose proponents he does not mention. Al-Qushayrī, who could or would not think of a human reason to forbid incest, at least has one to explain why marrying one's father's wife is bad: it is in human nature to dislike the idea that one's bed is to be shared with another; thus sons, respecting the rights of their fathers, are forbidden to marry stepmothers.[202] The Shāfiʿite scholar al-Kiyā al-Harrāsī (d. 504/1010) explains that the prohibition, cast in strong Qur'anic terms, to marry one's stepmother is not intended to make life difficult for the son: it expresses the respect for the father and for the stepmother who is like a real mother, just as one's daughter-in-law is like a real daughter.[203]

That a marriage is not conceived as a union between equal partners is of course not a surprise. In medieval Arabic a wife is said to be 'under' (*taḥt*) her husband, evoking not so much a crude physical image as a notion of being inferior and under the husband's authority. 'Marriage is slavery (*riqq*), so everyone of you should look closely to whom he enslaves his daughter' is a saying sometimes attributed to, of all people, the Prophet's favourite wife ʿĀʾisha, and attributed by al-Ghazālī to the Prophet himself.[204] The assumed link between 'noble' (*najīb*) offspring and strange women, explained in Chapter One, could be read in conjunction with an unpleasant saying found in several anthologies: 'If you want to produce a noble son, make your wife angry, then mount her'.[205] The plight of a bride who is a 'stranger' is often described in stories and poems, and it is not surprising that one finds women preferring marriage with a close relative, even if sexual attraction is absent. In a telling anecdote, a young and beautiful woman married to an ugly old man explains the situation saying, in an epigram, 'I took to him because he was a relative (*dhū qarāba*)'; the rest of her poem makes it clear, however, that she regrets her choice.[206] In a story set in pre-Islamic times the daughter of Aws ibn Ḥāritha ibn Laʾm al-Ṭāʾī rejects a respectable suitor recommended by her father, saying 'I do not want him. I have a difficult character, which relatives (*qurabāʾ*) may be able to endure, but not strangers (*buʿadāʾ*)'.[207] In a variant of this story, the girl says:

> I am a woman with a face that is a bit ugly and my character is rather weak. I am not his father's brother's daughter, who would observe the bonds of kinship, and he is not your protected neighbour, who would be ashamed of you. I fear that he will find something to dislike in me and divorce me.[208]

The most extended discussion of the possible benefits of the prohibition known to me from before the twentieth century is found in an author who, rather than late medieval, should perhaps be considered an early modern one, for Shāh Walī Allāh al-Dihlawī (d. 1176/1762) has been called a revolutionary thinker and the founder of Islamic modernism.[209] In his *magnum opus* in Arabic, *Ḥujjat Allāh al-bāligha* ('God's Convincing Proof'), he points out that God confirmed the prohibitions that were already observed by the pre-Islamic Arabs, while tidying up the few irregularities practised by them. The prohibitions are said to have several beneficial aspects; the author lists them in a somewhat rambling passage which does not so much advance new arguments as bring together and elaborate points that had been made before.[210] He argues that sexual attraction between close relatives would make everyday life impossible: 'One may observe how a man, struck by the charms of a strange woman, falls hopelessly in love and plunges into dangerous situations because of her. Now what do you think of a man being together with that woman, seeing her charms night and day?'. He does not explain why, as a general rule, people are not sexually attracted to their close kin even though they are able to see their 'charms' daily. He argues that a married woman, in case of conflict, has the support of her male relatives; if her husband were such a relative, there would be a conflict of interests and she would suffer as a result. If animals shrink from mounting their mothers and foster-mothers, men should shrink from it all the more. Avoiding the cutting of ties of kinship is another reason for the prohibition; this applies, for instance, to the marriage with two sisters, who would naturally turn into rivals.

The same applies, Shāh Walī Allāh continues, to closeness through affinity. If a woman were to desire her daughter's husband, or a man his daughter-in-law or stepdaughter, this would lead to all kinds of intrigues, even murder. 'If you have heard the stories of the ancient Persians, or if you had investigated the cases of your contemporaries who do not hold fast to the right Path, you would find innumerable serious matters full of perdition and iniquity', he adds, with a rare acknowledgment of the fact that such things happen at the time of writing.[211]

It might seem from the above that the exegetes and jurists are completely oblivious of the view, held by the ancient Bedouin Arabs, that incestuous unions may produce physical degeneration, if not caused by one individual act then at least in the long run if practised over several generations. It is true that, to my knowledge, the jurists never mention this aspect when they discuss the forbidden degrees. Nevertheless there is one school, that of the Shāfiᶜites, that regularly shows awareness of the biological aspects of inbreeding; not in the section of the forbidden degrees, but in the introduction of the chapter on marriage. In Chapter One we saw that al-Ghazālī, a Shāfiᶜite, lists the desirable qualities of a bride, one of which was not being too closely related to the bridegroom. He does this in his most influential work, *Iḥyāʾ ᶜulūm al-dīn* ('The Revivification of the Religious Sciences'), not a legal handbook, but dealing with many legal matters; he does not fail to mention the forbidden degrees, in an elegantly concise formulation.[212] The Shāfiᶜite manuals, including those by al-Ghazālī,[213] regularly have a similar passage on the desirable qualities of the bride, recommending that she be not closely related (*laysat qarāba qarība*). They do not explicitly link it to the matter of the forbidden degrees. The familiar view is repeated: a child from a union between close relatives tends to be puny—most use the word *naḥīf*, occasionally one finds *ḍāwiyy*; this is caused by the weakness of sexual desire in such cases.[214] On rare occasions the same discussion is found in non-Shāfiᶜī works: after all, the several schools did not exist in isolation and they were aware of one another. Thus the Ḥanbalī Ibn Qudāma says that an unrelated woman may be chosen as bride in order to produce good stock and he quotes the usual sayings about stuntedness and weakness.[215]

They do not all of them, however, accept the recommendation without questioning it. Al-Shirbīnī mentions that the saying attributed to the Prophet in which he warns against producing stunted offspring is not a reliable *ḥadīth* and he quotes al-Subkī (d. 773/1372), who said that therefore the recommendation does not stand, for lack of proof, and in view of the fact that the Prophet married his own daughter Fāṭima to his paternal first cousin ᶜAlī. He also quotes a certain al-Zanjānī,[216] who justifies the recommendation, saying that 'among the purposes of marriage is to effect unions between tribes, for the sake of mutual support and assistance'. He concludes that it is best to interpret it as a recommendation to marry outside one's nearest kin or family. After all, he adds, Fāṭima's marriage to her father's father's brother's son was not the closest imaginable, and the Prophet's own marriage to Zaynab, daughter of his maternal aunt, could be interpreted as a demonstration of the licitness of such a union.[217] Al-Ibshīhī, compiler of a popular encyclopedic anthology and likewise a Shāfiᶜite, cites an anonymous four-line didactic epigram, meant as a mnemonic device that lists the recommended qualities of a bride. Among other things, she should be 'a stranger (*gharība*), not of the family of the suitor'; the poem asserts that 'there are well-established *ḥadīths* on this, known to those who have studied the (religious) sciences.'[218]

Mother's Back

Although Muslim penal law does not normally recognize gradations of incest, it is obvious that some forms are deemed worse than others in society. The Qur'an may not single out mother—son incest as particularly abhorrent, yet there are indications that it was considered thus. A form of repudiation, presumably old, which is rejected by Islam, is called *ẓihār*, a verbal noun derived from the word *ẓahr* 'back', and referring to the use of a formula whereby a man says to his wife, 'You are to me as the back of my mother (*anti ʿalayya ka-ẓahr ummī*)',[219] implying that she is as untouchable to him as his mother. It should be noted that using this formula is normally taken to be a form of repudiation or divorce, even though the wording allows it to be interpreted as a vow of continence, rather than divorce.[220] Using 'back' as a euphemism in this manner is unusual. The word is used, say some, so as not to mention the *pudendum*.[221] Some exegetes and lexicographers take it literally, as if the expression meant that if the mother's back is declared forbidden, all the more so are her other body parts; others believe the word 'back' refers to *coitus a tergo*, as if this were the normal position for intercourse in pre-Islamic Arabia. Among the attempts to translate the term *ẓihār* into English one finds 'incestuous comparison',[222] and, somewhat quaintly, 'injurious assimilation'.[223] The Qur'an refers to this practice in sura 58 vss. 2-3:

> «Those of you who say, regarding their wives, 'Be as my mother's back,' they are not truly their mothers; their mothers are only those who gave them birth, and they are surely saying a dishonourable saying, and a falsehood.
>
> (...) And those who say, regarding their wives, 'Be as my mother's back,' and then retract what they have said, they shall set free a slave, before the two touch one another (...)»[224]

Although the last verse seems to state that the repudiation takes effect, temporarily at least, yet according to Islamic law the *ẓihār* is not recognized as repudiation and does not dissolve the marriage, even if it makes intercourse illegal until some penitence has been done or a religious fine paid; it is considered a bad thing that deserves an especially heavy expiation.[225]

Lexicographers and jurists point out *ẓihār* does not necessarily refer to the mother. Ibn Manẓūr gives, in addition to the customary version, one that extends the expression to any forbidden degree: *'hiya ᶜalayya ka-ẓahr dhāt raḥim'*;[226] Ibrāhīm al-Ḥalabī defines *ẓihār* as

> the comparison of one's wife, or any limb or part of her standing for all of her, to a part that one is forbidden to view, belonging to women in a forbidden degree to him, even if only through milk-relationship. Thus if one says to her: 'You (or your head, or half of your body, etc.) are to me as the back (or belly, or thigh) of my mother (or as the back of my sister, or my paternal aunt, etc.)'.[227]

This legalese cannot hide the obvious fact that it is the 'greater incest' involving the mother which is at the bottom of the custom. It is difficult to say how often the formula was actually uttered in Islamic times, but it is striking how frequently *ẓihār* is discussed by the jurists.[228] The efforts of jurists are probably prompted above all by the mentioning of *ẓihār* in the Qur'an and less by its occurrence in actual cases, which, if found at all, must have been overwhelmingly outnumbered by the triple divorce formula, bane of many a marriage and the delight of specialists in legal casuistry.

Robertson Smith argued that pre-Islamic *ẓihār* 'was not meant to hurt but to benefit the wife' and that she was 'invested with all the legal attributes of motherhood': in fact, involving a kind of adoption as a son.[229] The motives for such a procedure are difficult to imagine, and corroborative evidence is absent. The Qur'anic verse that precedes the passage on *ẓihār* and apparently introduces it refers to a woman pleading with the Prophet and complaining to God about her husband, who had rashly uttered the formula, much as later Muslims would use the triple divorce formula (the commentators identify the couple as Khawla bt Thaᶜlaba and Aws b. al-Ṣāmit).[230]

Revealing One's Adornment

There is a Qur'anic passage that somewhat resembles the one in sura 4 in having a list involving kinship and family relationships, this time not of 'forbidden degrees' but specifically allowing something in connection with them which is forbidden to others. What is allowed or forbidden here is not marriage or incest, but 'revealing one's adornment'. Here are the relevant verses from sura 24 ('Light'), in Arberry's translation:

> (24:30) Say to the believers, that they cast down their eyes and guard their private parts *(furūj)*; that is purer for them. God is aware of the things they work.
> (24:31) And say to the believing women, that they cast down their eyes and guard their private parts *(furūj)*, and reveal not their adornment *(zīna)*

> save such as is outward; and let them cast their veils over their bosoms, and not reveal their adornments save to their husbands, or their fathers, or their husbands' fathers, or their sons, or their husbands' sons, or their brothers or their brothers' sons, or their sisters' sons, or their women, or what their right hands own,[231] or such men as attend them, not having sexual desire, or children who have not yet attained knowledge of women's private parts (*ʿawrāt*); nor let them stamp their feet, so that their hidden ornament may be known.

This is not about marriage or sexual intercourse, but a sexual element is of course involved. It seems rather confusing that three terms are used for things not to be shown: *furūj* (private parts), *ʿawrāt* (pudenda), and *zīna* (adornment). The first two may be used for men and women, although the *ʿawra* of a woman differs from than of a man.[232] The word *zīna* is always explained literally, as jewels, rings and clothes. Thus stamping the feet, it is said, might reveal the anklets which, according to one commentator, 'produces an inclination in men'.[233] The various categories of persons in the passage include most of the forbidden degrees, with some differences, since the husband is by definition not a *maḥram*, nor is there any mention of milk-relationship. Moreover, the list, although mostly mentioning men, includes women, which means that marriage is not the point here. The passage shows that it is taken for granted that the 'forbidden degrees' can be trusted not to get sexually excited if they see more of a woman's body than others. In fact, the Qur'an thus recognizes what is, apparently, a law of nature.

An Early Case of Necessary Incest

In the Qur'anic text the various categories of incest are listed without any distinctions. As indicated above, there are no degrees of forbiddenness and the order in the holy text is in fact somewhat arbitrary, apart from the fact, as Abū Ḥayyān observes, that in view of the preceding passage on stepmothers it is logical to begin 4:23 with mothers,[234] and that within vs. 23 there is some semblance of order (consanguinity, milk-relationship, affinity).[235] Neither in the Qur'an nor in the legal textbooks are the categories graded: the 'greater incest', of parent with child, is never, at least not explicitly, said to be intrinsically worse than the 'lesser incest' between siblings, or incest with more remote kin such as with aunt or niece. The only kind that is condemned in stronger words than other kinds is, as we have seen, marriage with one's father's wives. In principle, all kinds of incest are forbidden equally strictly, and have always been so according to God's law.

There is one exception to this last clause, however. Belief in the creation of a first human couple who between them produced children from whom all mankind is descended makes it necessary to assume that some form of sibling incest took place, and that, apparently, Divine Law had not yet declared this forbidden (so that, strictly speaking, it cannot be called incest, since this term implies a prohibition or condemnation). The Jews, who believe in the immutability of Gods laws, are castigated for this belief by Ibn al-Jawzī: 'They say that the Laws cannot be abrogated, whereas they know that it was part of Adam's religion to allow marrying one's sisters'.[236] Fakhr al-Dīn al-Rāzī summarizes the view of most Muslims and mentions an attempt to circumvent this rather awkward fact:

> The prohibition of marrying mothers and daughters was established from the time of Adam to our time. In no divinely inspired religion is it confirmed that it is permissible to marry them. It is true that Zoroaster, the apostle of the Majūs, declared it permissible, but most Muslims agree that he was a liar. As for marrying sisters, on the other hand, it is reported that this was allowed in the time of Adam; but God decreed that it was allowed only out of necessity. I have seen one authority who denied this, saying that God used to send houris from Paradise to be married to Adam's sons. But this is unlikely, for if the wives of his sons and the husbands of his daughters were inhabitants of Paradise, then their progeny would not be the children of Adam only, and by general consensus that is untrue.[237]

The attempt to eliminate the incest from the creation story is found, for instance, in the *History* by al-Yaʿqūbī (d. 284/897). After giving the more common account, he adds that some relate a variant, in which Abel (Hābīl) is married to a houri (*ḥawrāʾ*) from Paradise, and Cain (Qābīl) gets a female jinni (*jinniyya*).[238] This variant is also found in a work by a leading Shīʿite authority, Ibn Bābawayh (or Bābūya) al-Ṣadūq (d. 381/991).[239] His story is that Adam married his two sons Seth and Japheth to two houris from Paradise, sent down by God for that purpose. The son born to Seth and the daughter born to Japheth married in due course. 'It is from these two that the elect prophets and messengers (of God) are descended. God forbid that this should have happened as some say, between brothers and sisters!'. In fact, all mankind after the Flood are descended from Seth, since Abel died without offspring and Cain's descendants all perished in the Flood. Ibn Bābawayh also quotes a version according to which two unnamed sons of Adam were married, one to a houri and the other to a female demon (*ibnat al-jānn*); the former union is responsible for any beauty and moral excellence in mankind, the latter for all badness. Here too, although not explicitly as in the first version, the story is at least partly meant to deny incest. With the legal and moral implications of the story of the first humans we move on the borderlines of law, legend and literature.

Chapter Four: Incest in Legend and Literature

An Early Case of Necessary Incest (Continued)

The story of Adam and Eve's children, which ended the preceding chapter, is not found in the Qur'an—or, for that matter, in the Hebrew Bible in this form—but it is widely known in Arabic sources, having found its way there from rabbinical literature and Christian material, in particular the famous Syriac *Treasure Cave*, which dates from around the sixth century.[1] This and similar Arabic stories, meant to explain and complement the stories or histories of the Old and New Testament as well as the Qur'anic stories set in pre-Islamic times, are known collectively as the *Isrāʾīliyyāt* or 'the matter of Israel'. Several collections deal with the legends of the prophets before Muḥammad, from Adam to ʿĪsā/Jesus. Their status varies: often entertaining, the stories were sometimes denounced by scholars sceptical of their authenticity. Their popularity, which made them suspect to some, was not restricted to the populace: the best-known compilation was written by a serious scholar, al-Thaʿlabī (d. 427/1035), as a corollary to his commentary on the Qur'an.

In a sense, the very first human marriage could be called incestuous. Eve was created from Adam (the story of the rib is not found in the Qur'an but was known to the Muslim Arabs[2]). If, rather incongruously, myth and biology are combined, Eve could be said to have been Adam's clone, his daughter and his wife. Muslim exegetes, however, unwilling to engage in mythical or metaphorical interpretations and unaware of modern genetics, never considered this as a form of incest. It is different in the case of their offspring.

At the end of the previous chapter we saw Seth and Japheth being mentioned as luckily escaping the horror of incest, according to a religious scholar. This is entirely understandable in the particular context, for all humanity after the Flood traces back its ancestry to Adam's third son Seth/Shīth. Nevertheless, the more famous children of Adam and Eve were surely the ill-fated Cain and Abel (Qābīl and Hābīl in Arabic), a consequence of the dramatic account in Genesis and its subsequent narrative developments. This greater popularity is reflected in Arabic literature, where the two brothers are involved in the earliest case of sibling incest.[3] Qābīl has a twin sister called Qalīmā or Aqlīmā,[4] and Hābīl has a twin sister variously called Labūdhā, Labūdā, or Layūthā, among other forms.[5] Their father, obeying God's instructions, orders them to cross-marry, each child with a child from a different birth, obviously in an attempt to minimize the incest; an attempt that, if without biological grounds,[6] could be said to be psychologically justified. Al-Masʿūdī explicitly comments that Adam acted in order to prevent close-kin marriage as scrupulously as possible, forced by the circumstances and unable to observe the desired 'disparity and mutual strangeness (of the partners)'.[7]

Hābīl is happy with this arrangement (al-Thaʿlabī adds that this was because Aqlīmā was 'the prettiest and best of women', which in these primeval circumstances does not necessarily mean much), but Qābīl is angry and claims to have more right to his own twin sister, arguing in addition that they belong together since they were conceived and born on earth while the earlier twins were born in Paradise. He also denies that his father is following God's command and claims that it is merely his own view. It cannot be denied that he has a point there: the argument of being more entitled, closeness in birth leading to closeness in marriage, has a certain logic. Adam is angry with Qābīl,[8] but his paternal authority is apparently less than absolute and he tells his sons to make a sacrifice to God, and see which offering is accepted, thus deciding who shall have the wife-sister of his choice. As one knows from Genesis 4 or sura 5:27-32, this leads to the first murder in human history. Qābīl, incensed because his offering has been rejected, says to his brother, 'By God I'll kill you, because God has accepted your offering and rejected mine, so that you will marry my pretty sister and I will marry your ugly sister, and people will say that you are better than I!'.[9] After the murder he leaves, taking his twin sister Aqlīmā with him (although in other versions he departs with his sister Ashūt). His progeny, it is added, become devotees of music, wine, fornication, and idolatry, until God makes them perish in the Flood.[10]

The moral is not immediately obvious. The immediate causes of Abel's death are Cain's intemperateness and spite, preceded by his disobedience of his father's and God's wish. Preceding this, in turn, is Cain's incestuous love for his twin sister. Perhaps 'incestuous', at this primordial pre-legal stage, is not the right word; the story suggests that Cain's preference was based on logic and an understandable preference of the beautiful to the ugly. Nevertheless, the story carries the strong implication, seen in retrospect, that incest lies at the root of murder and virtually all other major sins. To the pessimist al-Maʿarrī this first case of incest, though necessary, was enough to condemn all mankind. No matter that humans are not descended from Cain, for Seth also must have married within the forbidden degrees (although, as far as I can see, the sources are strangely silent on this delicate point; one source says that God revealed a new marriage law to Seth which abolished Adam's rule of marrying full siblings).[11] The primeval sin is sexual:

When we recall Adam and his deeds,
  how he married his daughters to his sons, indecently,
We know that mankind derives from fornication stock
  and that all people have their origin in fornication.[12]

The attempt, by the Shīᶜite authorities mentioned in the previous chapter, to eliminate the incest element from the story of Adam's sons may have a 'polemical anti-Zoroastrian point', as G. Vajda states,[13] although to me this is by no means necessary: it could simply be inspired to eliminate such a major sin from the ancestor of all mankind, including the Prophet and his family. It is true, however, that the story of the first humans was used by the Zoroastrians to justify close-kin marriage. As al-Masᶜūdī says,

> The Zoroastrians maintain that Adam did not arrange for cross-marriages, nor did he strive to do so. They have a hidden purpose with this, since they claim that this implies that it is a good thing to have a brother marry his sister or a mother her son.[14]

Zoroaster 'allowed marriage with sisters and daughters, justifying this with the fact that Adam married his sons to his daughters'.[15] This is confirmed by some Pahlavi texts.[16] According to the Christian Abū Qurra (d. *c.* 820), the Zoroastrians go back even further, to the beginning of creation, to justify next-of-kin marriage:

> Hormuzd (Ahuramazda) ... created the heaven and the earth and what was between them ... Only it was dark, without light. So he was sad and asked Satan for advice about this. Satan advised him to marry his mother. So he did; she became pregnant and gave birth to the sun, for the light of the day. And (he also advised him) to marry his sister. So he did; and she became pregnant and gave birth to the moon, for the light of night. Therefore the Magians marry their mothers, their sisters and their daughters, so that they may give birth to the likes of sun and moon, just as Hormuzd, their god.[17]

Arabic accounts of the Zoroastrian version of the first humans, perhaps surprisingly, do not put much emphasis on the incest theme. The first man is called Jayūmart (Gayōmart), therefore identical with Adam, although some say he is the son of Adam and Eve. His children, called Mīshī (or Mīshā, or Mashya) and Mīshāna (or Mashyāna, or Mashyani), marry and have a daughter, Siyāmī. The last-mentioned gives birth to eight children, sired by her father.[18] Thus father—daughter incest is added to sibling incest. A rather more prominent place is given to incest in an account of the Manichaean version of how the first humans managed to produce progeny, offered by Ibn al-Nadīm (*fl.* 377/987) in his *Fibrist*. Qābīl, here given his more original form Qāyin, prominently figures in a welter of incest in this story. The Manichaeans, or Manāniyya as Ibn al-Nadīm calls them, believe that Ādam and Ḥawwāʾ (Eve) were produced by the sexual congress of 'the archons,[19]

Rebuke,[20] Greed, Lust, and Sin', the archons Male and Female being particularly instrumental. Subsequently,

> the archon[21] returned to his daughter Eve and had intercourse with her through the lust that was in him. Thereupon she gave birth to a son with a distorted appearance, with blond hair, whose name was Cain, the Ruddy Man. Then this son had intercourse with his mother and made her give birth to a white son whom he called Abel, the White Man. Then Cain had again intercourse with his mother and made her give birth to two girls, one called Wise One of the Age[22] and the other Daughter of Greed. Cain took Daughter of Greed as his wife and gave Wise One of the Age to Abel, who took her as his wife.[23]

Here Cain is, as it were, an epicentre of incest: himself offspring of an incestuous union, he commits two forms of incest, one with his mother and the other with his daughter. He kills Abel, not because of a conflict over their twin-sisters but because he wrongly suspects him to have fathered the two daughters of his wife, who has in fact been impregnated by an angel. Cain ends up in hell, together with his mother Eve and his daughter/wife Daughter of Greed, but the other daughter is saved.[24] It is hard to imagine what Ibn al-Nadīm and his contemporaries could have made of all this. He himself, at any rate, refrains from any commentary.

It is difficult to tell the story of Cain and Abel without reference to sibling incest, even though an attempt was made to eliminate this, as we have seen. The Hebrew Bible offers several other stories involving close-kin unions or incest, by Muslim standards. Most of these are ignored, however, by our Muslim authors. Jacob's marriage to two sisters was acknowledged and justified by the fact that Moses had not yet brought the Law. More blatant examples are not mentioned, except in order to refute them as blasphemous lies about sinless patriarchs, even prophets. Abraham was not married to his half-sister, and Lot did of course not get his daughters with child. These daughters are mentioned in the Arabic tradition: we are told their names were Raythā and Raᶜziyā (or perhaps Rīthā and Raᶜrabā, or Raythā and Ghaythā),[25] but the scandalous origins of the Moabites and Ammonites are passed over in silence in books and chapters on the Tales of the Prophets. One only finds it mentioned by al-Masᶜūdī, in his account of the debate before Ibn Ṭūlūn, and by Ibn Ḥazm, in his refutation of the Hebrew Bible.[26]

Canaan/Kanᶜān and Nimrod/Namrūd

Nimrod, the mighty hunter of Genesis 10:9, is connected in Arabic lore with the story of Abraham/Ibrāhīm. His name, Namrūd in Arabic, was considered to be derived, in spite of its different origin in Assyrian, from the Hebrew and Arabic root *MRD* denoting rebelliousness, and occasionally linked with *namir* 'panther'. He is one of the great villainous rulers of Arabic lore. Al-Thaᶜlabī's *Qiṣaṣ al-anbiyā*ᵓ ('Tales of the Prophets') tells the story of a prediction made to Namrūd about a boy 'born in your region' who will be the cause of his destruction. This makes him have all newborn babies killed, in an act later to be out-Nimroded by Herod. Full of evil though the story may be, there are no hints of incest here. In other, less 'official' elaborations it is different. The *Tales of the Prophets* ascribed to al-Kisāᵓī (and which were probably not composed by the philologist of that name of the 2nd/8th century)[27] takes us back one generation, to Nimrod's father Canaan/Kanᶜān, who was likewise told that a newborn child would destroy him. This child, however, is his own son, by Shalkhāᵓ (or Sulkhāᶜ, or Salkhāᵓ) the shepherdess, whose husband he had killed. The mother, told to abandon the child and let it die of hunger and thirst, instead entrusts it to a shepherd who raises it and gives it the name of Nimrod. Then boy grows from a bully into a war-lord and tyrant; he wages war against his father, defeats him and has him beheaded, without knowing that he has killed his father.[28]

Nimrod 'takes possession of his [father's] kingdom': one may well conclude that this implies that he married his mother, in order to bring this Oedipus story to its proper improper conclusion, but the text does not say it. This step is taken, inevitably one might think, in a yet later elaboration, found in the introductory part of the very lengthy popular epic of ᶜAntar:[29]

> He fought against Kanᶜān, without knowing that he was his father, and killed him. He took possession of his kingdom, his treasures, palaces, slave-girls and concubines, among them Salkhāᵓ the shepherdess, giving her a special place and making her his favourite.[30]

The incest is stated plainly, but casually, without any comment or details and extremely briefly, especially when one considers the extraordinary length of the epic. There is no mention of any offspring. Rank calls this story 'a complete Arab Oedipus', but he has noticed the 'absence of those defenses or themes of repression that are so characteristic of the Greek legend.'[31] It is obvious that Oedipus, the tragic hero, and Nimrod, the villain, could hardly be more different.

Stories of Prophets

Al-Thaᶜlabī's *Tales of the Prophets*, with its elaborations of the stories ultimately based on Jewish and Christian material, explicitly deals with the incest motif in the story of Cain and Abel, which is not found in that form in the Hebrew Bible. In other cases, however, al-Thaᶜlabī and other Muslim accounts ignore the various incestuous incidents offered by the Old and New Testaments. As explained above, when Abraham says that Sarah is his sister, the Muslim commentators cannot accept this. They interpret this as a metaphor: Abraham was being deliberately ambiguous, but he really meant that she was his 'sister in religion', or 'sister in the Book of God', or 'sister in disposition (*ukhtī fī l-khilqa*)'.[32]

In another story the incest motif is adopted. In the New Testament (Mark 6:14-29, Matthew 14:1-12), St John the Baptist is beheaded after the unnamed daughter (later known as Salome) of Herodias, Herod's wife, dances her famous dance for her stepfather. Herodias is herself Herod's brother's wife, a relationship forbidden by John—hence Herodias's lethal grudge against him. The dance suggests an obvious erotic element, and Mark tells us that Herod was 'pleased' with it to the point of promising her 'unto half his kingdom'. Nevertheless, the king is not described as lusting after the girl or wanting to marry her; it is merely a jolly birthday celebration. It is different in the Arabic version. Oddly, al-Thaᶜlabī incorporates two versions of this story in his *Tales of the Prophets*, one of them anachronistically set in the time of Nebuchadnezzar.[33] The first[34] gives two opinions: the king wanted to marry either his stepdaughter, or the daughter of his sister; in both cases it concerns not Herodias, but her daughter, the girl conventionally called Salome (although she is not named in the Arabic). From a literary point of view this has the great advantage of linking the erotic dance with the forbidden, incestuous union that is desired. Al-Thaᶜlabī's second version[35] is told at its proper place, this time in several variations and including one in which incest plays no role. In one variation, Jesus, John the Baptist and the twelve disciples preach that marriage with one's niece is forbidden. The king, called Hayradūs, wants to marry his brother's daughter; John is killed (no dance is mentioned). In another version the king has an eye on his stepdaughter, a union also forbidden by John. Here, the girl, in fine clothes, seduces the king by means of wine and erotic display, with the well-known result.[36] Yet another variation is closer to the New Testament story, in that John's prohibition is directed at the union of the king with Hirdūyā/Herodias, his brother's wife; there is no mention of a dancing daughter here.[37]

The confusion about the precise nature of the forbidden union is caused partly, one imagines, by the ambiguous nature of the New Testament version, in which one forbidden relationship is mentioned (king with brother's wife) and another only hinted at (king with stepdaughter). At the same time, some of the Muslim versions seem to be eager to expose what is forbidden in Islam but allowed in Judaism: marriage with a niece. It remains to be said that later European versions, by Flaubert, Wilde and others, have greatly emphasized the incest element, in keeping with the apparently much greater obsession of modern European literature with the theme of incest.

Sisterly Love

Compared with the very rich harvest of incest-related stories offered by western literatures, especially if we include the Greek myths, Arabic literature is remarkably poor.[38] As is well-known, Freud based his ideas on incest on what has become known as the Oedipus complex, which takes it for granted that sons desire their mothers sexually. It has been suggested that this theory, if valid at all, should be adapted in the case of Arab culture. Hasan el-Shamy, a folklorist, has argued that the sexual attraction and concomitant jealousy between brother and sister is so strong that it takes the place of the western Oedipus conflict.[39] In the present study I am not concerned with the modern world, but strong bonds between brother and sister are often found in pre-modern texts, too. Classic examples are found among the women elegists, above all al-Khansāʾ (first half of 7th century), who composed numerous laments on her brothers Ṣakhr and Muʿāwiya.

Laments by sisters are virtually indistinguishable from laments by other related females, including wives and lovers. A lament on Yazīd ibn al-Ṭathriyya (d. 126/744) is, significantly, attributed to his sister Zaynab, or his mother, or the girl he loved, Waḥshiyya.[40] But one should not conclude that poems by sisters are therefore informed by incestuous feelings. Overt sexual feelings are not expressed, and proving that they are implicitly present is just as difficult as proving that they are not. In any case, love between brother and sister was often so strong that this love could be used to illustrate and emphasize the love between lovers. ʿAlī ibn Hishām (d. 217/832) said of his concubine, the *qayna* (singing-girl) Mutayyam: 'She used to love me with a strong love that surpassed the love of a sister for her brother',[41] implying of course that in normal circumstances the love between siblings is stronger than that between lovers. Tears are shed in very many Arabic love poems, but none more so than in women's laments on brothers. They protest that they will never stop crying; they wish to be dead, and even clearly hint at suicide: 'But for the many who cry around me for their brothers, I would kill myself'.[42] Suʿdā bint al-Shamardal, a pre-Islamic or early Islamic poet, says of her slain brother: 'At night, alone, I weep for Asʿad', as if to imply she would have spent the night with him if he were alive.[43] As Marlé Hammond writes, 'She thereby invites the thought of Asʿad into her bed ... And although this kind of fraternal longing, that is the kind of longing displayed in the *nasīb*s of Suʿdā and al-Khansāʾ, is not sexual in a carnal sense, it is highly sensual, in accordance with a desire for physical intimacy appropriate to a sibling relationship.'[44] In a lament for her brother, al-Fāriʿa bint Ṭarīf describes herself as distraught, 'seeking him in the sky, as a person whose nose has been cut off seeks his nose'.[45] The image, which may seem comical to us,[46] would no doubt be grist to the mill of the Freudians, to whom a nose is rarely if ever an organ for breathing and smelling: the woman is surely looking for her brother's penis.[47] Perhaps similar associations would spring to their minds when they see al-Khansāʾ describe her deceased brother Ṣakhr as 'a Rudaynite lance, his youth not spent; as if a bracelet were under the folds of his cloak'.[48] He was slim, tall and strong like a lance, his belly lean and white as a bracelet of gold or silver, as the ancient commentator explains. Is this imagery sexual? Whether the lance describes only the man's body or, in addition, part of his anatomy, one must admit that, fourteen centuries after their composition, such lines—for this one is not particularly exceptional—seem rather suggestive, in the sexual sense. But the very fact that such lines were produced publicly, transmitted and discussed by many anthologists and philologists, proves that a sexual interpretation was far at least from their minds and that of the poet. Unto the pure all things are pure, as St Paul said[49] (and Shelley, speaking of sibling incest, after him);[50] and the Saint added, 'unto them that are defiled and unbelieving is nothing pure'.

It is the strong bond between brother and sister that lies at the bottom of the widespread custom of spouses calling each other 'brother' and 'sister', found in Sumerian love lyrics and other Near-Eastern literatures (the Song of Songs is a well-known example): they are terms of endearment and have no sexual, incestuous meaning. Language should not be confused with reality.[51]

Lampoons and Insults

'Motherfucker' may be one of the commonest nouns in the spoken English of today. This deplorable fact may say something about North American civilization. The word and its use, however, are by no means restricted to contemporary English and the modern world. Medieval Arabic texts are a rich source of invective, in prose and especially in verse, and incestuous insinuations and imputations are not rare. In the chapter on the alleged Zoroastrian practices we have already come across some poetical insults, such as the line by the gifted and powerful vizier al-Ṣāḥib ibn ʿAbbād (d. 385/995): '... As for the Persians, all night their "snakes" slither into sister and mother.'[52] In a ninth-century list of beggars with odd nicknames a certain Saʿdawayh, a Persian judging by the tail end of his name, is given the epithet *nāʾik ummihi* ('Motherfucker').[53] In the seventh century, the poet Ziyād al-Aʿjam, possibly a Persian, was called 'An uncircumcised one, who prays after having fucked his mother' by Kaʿb al-Ashqarī.[54] One did not have to be of Persian origin to be thus insulted. 'He used to be called Motherfucker[55] / called thus among Bedouin and urban dwellers' is an anonymous verse lampooning the Bedouin poet Abū l-ʿUdhāfir Ward b. Saʿd, who had settled in Basra and later in Baghdad, in the time of Hārūn al-Rashīd.[56] Such insults are not only found in the urban and perhaps decadent milieus of the Abbasid period. In the seventh century a woman called Zaynab proved herself a true daughter of her father, the poet Aws ibn Maghrāʾ, who was notorious for his lampoons. When a certain Ḥuyayy ibn Hazzāl of the tribe of Tamīm insulted her with some obscene verses, she replied with three lines of *rajaz*, the short metre traditionally employed for extemporized invective exchanges:

Ḥuyayy has fucked his mother like a mare is fucked,
Four times, and five times. Then he sat down,
His lust spent, with panting breath.[57]

In *rajaz*, too, is the following three-liner by an unknown poet; it is not known from which period it dates, but it looks old:

You two men of Ḍabba, do not shrink back:
Come on, go to your mother, then screw
With a prick like the prick of Ibn Alghaz.[58]

The pre-Islamic poet ᶜAbīd ibn al-Abraṣ, as told above,[59] was lampooned as having had sex with his sister. The pre-Islamic al-Nuᶜmān ibn al-Mundhir (*reg. c.* 580-602), Arab king of al-Ḥīra, was accused of having tender feelings for his mother in a lampoon that describes him as

A king who fondles his mother and his slave(s),
His joints are flaccid, his penis the size of a kohl-needle.[60]

This lampoon is said to have been made by ᶜAbd al-Qays ibn Khufāf al-Tamīmī and Murra ibn Saᶜd ibn Qurayᶜ al-Saᶜdī, in a rare joint effort, but wickedly put into the mouth of their enemy, the great poet al-Nābigha al-Dhubyānī, who subsequently earned great fame with his ensuing apologetic odes. Others attribute this line to the poet al-Mutalammis, made on another pre-Islamic king of al-Ḥīra, ᶜAmr ibn Hind (d. 570).[61] Al-Ḥīra lay in the Persian sphere of influence, but there is no explicit reference to Zoroastrian practice in the poem.

The Umayyad period witnessed the heyday of ritualized invective, particularly in the protracted series of flytings between the greatest poets of the age, al-Akhṭal, al-Farazdaq and Jarīr. In order to insult one's opponent one may mention his personal shortcomings, real or imagined (particularly the latter); but since someone's honour is lodged as much in one's female relations as in one's person, it is equally or even more effective to vilify the sexual habits of the opponent's wife or sister, or, collectively, the women of the tribe or clan. For this is still poetry with a nomadic, tribal ethos. The poems of the great Umayyad poets were popular in the towns such as Damascus, Kufa and Basra, but the poets were, at most, fringe-urban, in that they were often active performing in town, whereas the steppe and desert were their true homes.

Jarīr (d. *c.* 111/729) described the clan of his (Christian) rival al-Akhṭal (d. *c.* 92/710) as follows:

I have been informed that Taghlib copulate with their own men
and that their women consider what is taboo as permitted.
They wed, when they are drunk, their daughters ...[62]

To his Muslim opponents such as al-Farazdaq (d. *c.* 110/728) and al-Baᶜīth he is even more explicit: 'if you fucked your mother ...',[63] 'I implore you, Baᶜīth, tell me: did you fuck your mother by night or by day?'[64] But Jarīr is outdone by al-Farazdaq in this respect. In addition to blunt four-letter words (which in Arabic are usually between two- and five-letter words), one finds more subtle insinuations. Some verses are distinctly odd:

A mother of the Jaᶜfar clan is not glad with a daughter
if she has a boy, his umbilical cord severed.
When he grows up he shies away from her when she calls him,
wishing to wash, for the sake of purifying himself.

According to the ancient commentator, this means that the mothers of the clan have sex with their sons, who flee from their mothers when they reach the age of puberty.[65] In another poem al-Farazdaq suggests that the sons are willing enough:

Whenever the spouse of a Jaᶜfarī woman dies,
her son, having reached puberty, visits her.
Their bodies know that the Jaᶜfar clan
are Magians, their cunts and their pricks.[66]

The commentator explains that 'the son takes the place of the spouse' and that the last phrase, synecdochically, stands for the women and the men. Another tribe, Bāhila, is attacked in these lines:

A man from Bāhila has ravished his female next-of-kin (*maḥārim*),
touching his sister's crotch at her belt.
O Bāhila, which judgement has made permissible
to you your sisters beneath their clothes?
Your arses ride their pudenda at night,
which are dyed in an unpleasant manner.[67]

The Banū Nahshal are lampooned with the following:

When the prick of a Nahshalī seems full-grown to his mother, at three spans, her religion is wearing thin.[68]

Few, if any, of these insults are meant to be taken wholly seriously (as is obvious from the wildly hyperbolical 'three spans'). To accuse someone of incest in earnest is a grave matter, which could lead to the penalties prescribed in Islamic law for fornication if proved, or for false accusation of fornication, if unproved. Poetry lifts the accusation out of the realm of reality, even though the shame that is imparted is real enough and not dependent on the truth of the allegation. One wonders, nevertheless, whether the smoke is always without a fire somewhere. It happens that a whole clan or tribe is lampooned collectively on the basis of one incident in the remote past, fondly remembered by rival clans. In the case of the tribes or clans of Jaᶜfar, Bāhila or Nahshal, however, no such incidents are known to me. One wonders if it is merely a coincidence that a man from Bāhila, named ᶜArjal, is attacked in a verse by Dhū l-Rumma (d. 117/735), the last great Bedouin poet:

... if ᶜArjal lets me make him hump
his mother, like a yearling white-streaked kid.[69]

The urban poets in the Abbasid age could not add much to this verbal violence, except in scale and, in some cases, in attitude. Abū Nuwās (d. *c.* 199/814), in one of his antinomian poems, does not attack merely one person or one tribe; instead of condemning fornication and incest he enjoins mankind to indulge in it:

Fuck all people on earth, do not spare your brother,
no, nor a noble guest who visits you.
Bugger your neighbour and do not forget your father,
and likewise a bad cousin, too.[70]

He was, in turn, addressed by his girlfriend ᶜInān:

Come on, fuck your mother, for she's an old hag.[71]

Normally, the incest motif continues to be used in an invective sense. Bashshār ibn Burd (d. 167/783), the first great Arabic poet of Persian descent, attacks another poet, Ḥammād ᶜAjrad:

ᶜAjrad jumps on his mother:
a sow giving suck to a sucker.[72]

On his part, Ḥammād said of Bashshār, casually throwing in an incestuous parenthesis:

You are called Burd's son, but you are another's.
But even if you were Burd's son (may you fuck your mother!), who is Burd?

We are told that Bashshār privately expressed his admiration of this line ('By God, well said by that son-of-a-bitch!').[73]

Of another poet, Bashshār says,

When he meets his mother, he turns her arse
and applies himself, with henna'ed prick, to sodomy.[74]

The plural may refer to more than one generation, on an opponent whom he has likened to a mule:

When his mothers neigh his prick yearns
for them; then a churning and skewering takes place.[75]

A mother may be replaced by an aunt: 'I have known a chief (?*ʿarīf*) who fucked his maternal aunt',[76] or by daughters: 'al-Khulayq has fucked his daughters and his sons have made their mother go barefoot, riding her',[77] or by sisters:

They live in(?) their mothers and their daughters,
being disrespectful to them, ...[78]
If you wish, you may meet one of their high-ranking males
on his sister, clinging like a tick.[79]

Bashshār is said to have lost his life on account of lampooning the caliph al-Mahdī—although some sources say that the verses were composed in his name by one of his enemies. One of the epigrams quoted in this connection is the following:

A caliph who fornicates with his paternal aunts
and who plays *dabbūq*[80] and polo:
May God give us another in his place
and may He shove Mūsā back into al-Khayzurān's cunt.[81]

In one source a variant of the first half of the second verse makes the poem even more obscene: 'May God make him suck his mother's clitoris ...'[82] This common expression will be discussed below.

Ibn al-Rūmī (d. 283/896), another great poet excelling in lampoons as well as in more lofty genres, uses the motif almost mechanically as an expletive: 'If my right hand will not cuff you, leaving you (humiliated as?) a deacon of the monastery, / Then may you fuck your mother, on my behalf, with the prick of Ezra's ass'.[83] A somewhat unclear instance is offered by Ibn Dāniyāl (d. 710/1310), in a long and racy poem in his *Ṭayf al-khayāl*. The Devil, Iblīs, speaks and, in one edition, seems to say 'My friend, I have fallen into my sister's cunt—how unpleasant!' (... *yā ṣāḥibī innanī / waqaʿtu fī kussi-khti*[84] *mā akrah*).[85] A recent study of this poem by Li Guo, however, prefers the variant reading '... *yā bi-abī anta qad / waqaʿta fī kussi-khti*' and translates it as 'Idiot! You are trapped in your sister's cunt',[86] This reading merely changes self-satire into invective. To complicate matters, Guo mentions yet another reading, of *yā bi-abī* as *yā Mānī*, 'You Manichaean'.[87] Even though this presents a metrical difficulty, it is tempting to see here an allusion to the Zoroastrian practice.

The womenfolk of one's opponent are the targets of lampoons in both Umayyad and Abbasid invective. There is, however, a difference. In the Umayyad period, and before, women in invective are generally described as being violated and raped against their will and in any case very much against the will of the husbands or other male relatives. In the later period, on the other hand, the dominant form is to describe one's opponent as a cuckold or a pimp, who willingly and knowingly lets his womenfolk be dishonoured, often with all parties involved enjoying it. Incest, in all periods, is mentioned as an occasional extra, and from the voluminous mass of 'sexual' invective one gets the impression that it is more shameful to be described as a cuckold, whether a consenting one or not, than as the perpetrator of incest. This is the result of the general attitude towards sex, at least in a secular, non-religious system of values based on honour and shame rather than virtuousness and sin: it is not shameful to penetrate, to be the active partner in sexual intercourse—no matter whether with a female or male partner; whereas it is shameful to be penetrated or (in the case of the cuckold and pimp) to have one's womenfolk penetrated by others. It is almost as if incest is used as an invective motif only for those who are outside the system of honour and shame: those ethnically and religiously outside the pale, such as the Zoroastrians, or those that are socially beneath contempt, such as the fellaheen, the Egyptian peasants lambasted in al-Shirbīnī's (fl. 1098/1687) exceptional monograph *Hazz al-quḥūf*:

Everyone of you copulates with aunts paternal
  and copulates with sisters and aunts maternal ,
And deems the act permissible, which makes him an unbeliever,
  whom to kill is patently lawful.[88]

In addition, there is another kind of invective poetry where honour and shame play no part: jesting, *hazl*, and this applies to a large proportion of lampooning verse. Banter may, of course, also be expressed in ordinary prose. When a *rāwiya* (transmitter) of the poet al-Farazdaq said, provocatively, 'I'll do anything to displease you', al-Farazdaq retorted, in prose: 'It would displease me if you fucked your mother'.[89] Many vile epigrams were made in jest, between friends. It is not always possible, in retrospect, to distinguish the serious from the jesting, and even the victims of jesting invective were not always able to do so, with sometimes unpleasant and unintended consequences. In general, it ought to be stressed again that the frequency of the theme of incest in insults bears no straightforward relation to reality. To assume such a relation is a mistake committed, for instance, by Otto Rank when he maintains that the poems of Catullus on Gellius and others, in which he accuses them of incest with their mothers, 'suggest how frequently incestuous relationships occurred, or can at least be presumed to have occurred'.[90] By this reasoning one might as well conclude, on the basis of the frequency of verbal insults, that mother—son incest was and is far more common in medieval Arab or present-day American society than father—daughter or brother—sister incest; but such a conclusion is obviously wrong.

There is one very common expression that, taken literally, refers to a form of incestuous sexual behaviour, and which was no doubt far more common as an expression than as an act performed in reality. It is, in a sense, the equivalent of the American English 'motherfucker', even though it is more properly interpreted as 'mothersucker'. To be precise, the Arabic idiom is *māṣṣ* (less often *ʿāḍḍ*) *baẓr ummihi*, 'sucker (or biter) of one's mother's clitoris', found in countless anecdotes, usually in prose and in the vocative or imperative mode: *yā māṣṣa baẓri ummika*, 'You mothersucker!', *umṣuṣ baẓra ummika*, 'Suck your mother's clitoris!'.[91] One also finds it in the form of an imprecation: 'May God make him suck his mother's clitoris!', as in the lampoon by Bashshār quoted above. Very often the context is jocular, as good-humoured banter rather than bitter invective; it is not limited to the lower classes, for it is often put in the mouth of caliphs in works of 'polite' literature. In marked contrast to sexual practice in the modern United States of America, there are very few references to oral sex, whether *fellatio* or *cunnilingus*, in medieval Arabic texts, which is obviously not the consequence of prudery but rather of a genuinely difference in taste.[92] This makes the Arabic idiom all the more striking. One might even conclude that the expression carries little implication of sexual activity as a variation on other, far more popular forms of intercourse, vaginal or anal. In fact, al-Jāḥiẓ, quoted by a later author, seems to have interpreted it in a non-sexual way: 'When one says *yā māṣṣ baẓr ummihi*, one means "You who eats up his mother's bridal gift from someone other than his father"'.[93] He refers to a widowed mother being married by her son to a new husband, which is often described as something rather shameful. I have found no evidence for the accuracy of al-

Jāḥiẓ's opinion—which, judging by the nature of his prodigious output, was not inspired by prudishness—and even if it is accurate, there is no hint of the alleged origin whenever the words are uttered as an expletive. Whatever its origin, it is certainly derogatory, but the main thrust may well have been, rather than any incestuous behaviour, the insinuation that one's mother has not been subjected to female circumcision or clitoridectomy, which was a major source of invective especially in poetry of the early Islamic and the Umayyad periods. I am not aware of any modern equivalent of the idiom; one gets the impression (although I have not taken the trouble to investigate the matter) that the obscenities commonly heard today such as *kuss ummak/ukhtak* '(up) your mother's/sister's cunt' do not carry overtones of incest, but rather fit in with the old tradition of taunting one's enemy's with their female relations' alleged lewd behaviour or with their having been enjoyed by the speaker. All sexual reference to mothers and sisters is *per se* shameful and insulting.

Metaphorical Incest

In Chapter Two we have seen a few examples of the Magian marriage motif being used by poets as a metaphor: for wine, mixed with water which is its 'father', or for the fire produced by the friction of two pieces of wood from the same tree. Here are a few more instances of the incest motif that do not directly refer to the Zoroastrians. Ibn al-Rūmī made a short poem for his patron Abū l-ʿAbbās ibn Thawāba, after the latter had been praised in verse by his own brother Abū l-Ḥusayn, who had emulated the poet in this respect:

> We found that he who is called Abū l-Ḥusayn,
> who matches you in proud nobility,
> Has praised you in verse with what is not permitted,
> O son of lofty mountain-like high deeds:
> Aren't rhymes a man's daughters,
> if the appearance of truth is not to be distorted?
> Therefore do not accept his panegyrics:
> One is forbidden to marry one's nieces.
> Accept this fatwa from a jealous friend ...![94]

This conceit is built, firstly, on the common metaphor of literary productions being the author's 'progeny', and, secondly, on the equally common comparison of beautiful panegyrical verses that contain hitherto untouched conceits to pretty maidens offered to the patron. Abū l-Ḥusayn, says the poet, is offering his own virgin daughters to his brother! Ibn al-Rūmī seems to complicate matters further by calling Abū l-ʿAbbās 'the son' of lofty deeds:

not the 'father', the one who produces them, but a son as if he were the product of his actions. These actions inspired, or 'fathered', one might say, the brother's verses; but Ibn al-Rūmī does not exploit this further opportunity for hinting at incestuous dealings.

Ibn al-Rūmī is jesting and he does not mean, of course, that accepting the poems in question would be an enormity on a par with the crime of incest. Far more serious is Abū l-Alāʾ al-Maʿarrī, in one of his characteristic epigrams in which he addresses mankind, in love with the world (*dunyā*, feminine in Arabic):

You have asked the World herself in marriage in your folly
  but are unable to behave decently:
Would a man in his senses marry his mother,
  even though she has become a whore among men?[95]

It cannot be said that incest, real or featuring in imagery, is a very common motif in poetry. A number of poems play with intricate imagined genealogies which by implication involve incest. An anonymous poet, probably ancient, boasts in the primitive metre *rajaz*:

I am night's paternal and maternal cousin;
When it is dark I don its cloak.
I am not like someone who is scared by his own image.[96]

The poet is merely embroidering on the expression 'son of the night', heroic epithet for someone who travels fearlessly at night.[97] Trying to outdo his predecessors, he may not immediately have been aware that his metaphorical genealogy would imply at least one case of incest between siblings.

Another, more self-conscious use of genealogical oddities is found in much later times. The poetry of the Mamluk and Ottoman periods is famous, or infamous in the eyes of many later critics, for its fondness for paronomasia and double-entendre. Perhaps the most notorious homonym in the Arabic lexicon is *khāl*, with its twenty-odd meanings, including 'mole (birthmark)' and 'maternal uncle'. As may be expected, poets could not resist punning on these and other meanings, to the point of making such a pun the point of an (untranslatable) epigram.

How dear to me, he who takes mankind captive with a face
  that puts the full moon to shame with its beauty!
His mole (*khāluhū*) spreads over him (*ʿammahū*), with novel beauty,
  and it is rare to see a paternal uncle (*ʿamm*) who is also a maternal uncle (*khāl*).[98]

On her right cheek
there is a spot of musk I'd like to smell.
I thought, when it appeared, it was her mole/maternal uncle
but I found that its beauty spread all over her/was her maternal uncle.[99]

The incestuous implications of these jests are very much in the background, and playing on words is all.

Genealogical Puzzles

To work out how a someone could be a *khāl* and an *ʿamm* simultaneously requires a little mental effort. Incest and inbreeding are admirably suited for making genealogical puzzles that might fascinate and challenge the curious. Rank, basing himself on a case of father—daughter incest that took place in Graz in 1907, demonstrates how it could be argued that a man may be his own father.[100] As could be expected, the medieval Arabs, with their interest in genealogy, produced similar challenges. They preferred poetry for this genre, but were not the first to do so: several Greek examples are known, as in the popular story of Apollonius of Tyre, which begins with an incestuous father, who sets a riddle that defeats all his daughter's suitors except Apollonius.[101] It has been said that 'Puzzles and riddles, like incest, bring together elements that ought to be kept apart.'[102] To puzzles and riddles, one should add puns; a pun or double entendre exploits the fact that a word or an expression may function in more than one way, just as incest implies that a person takes on more roles than is usual.[103] Ibn al-ʿAllāf (d. 318 or 319/930-931), a poet from Baghdad known for his poetic curiosities (such as a lengthy elegy on his cat), made the following mad riddle in verse:

Say to the son of the mother of my mother's mother-in-law:
I am the son of the brother of your sister's son: no mistake.
Suppose you married your sister to a brother of mine,
let her give birth to a boy who is my paternal uncle;
And my brother would be paternal uncle to that paternal uncle,
and the paternal uncle would be between my flesh and blood.
Now what am I to you, what are you to me?
Please advise, if your understanding is like mine.[104]

This poem is quoted by the tenth-century commentator of Abū Nuwās's poems, Ḥamza al-Iṣfahānī, who adds:

> I asked Abū Yūsuf al-Jabarī to explain it. He said: Call the person addressed ʿAmr, and the speaker Zayd. Let ʿAmr be the son of Khadīja,

and Khadīja the mother of Fāṭima. Let Fāṭima be the mother of ᶜAbd Allāh and Khālid. Let ᶜAbd Allāh be Zayd's father, while Jaᶜfar and Bakr are Zayd's brothers on his mother's side. Then let Jaᶜfar, Zayd's (half)brother, marry Fāṭima, the sister of ᶜAmr, and give birth to Aḥmad, who is the brother of ᶜAbd Allāh on his mother's side. He (Aḥmad) is Zayd's paternal uncle. Aḥmad is Zayd's paternal uncle[105] because he (Zayd) is the son of his (Aḥmad's) brother (i.e. ᶜAbd Allāh). Thus he is 'between his flesh and blood', as he says. And since Zayd is ᶜAbd Allāh's son, and he (ᶜAbd Allāh) is Khālid's brother, Zayd is the son of Khālid's brother. And since Khālid is Fāṭima's son and Fāṭima is ᶜAmr's sister, and since Khālid is the son of ᶜAmr's sister, and Zayd is the son of Khālid's brother, therefore Zayd is the son of the brother of the son of ᶜAmr's sister. Because Fāṭima is ᶜAbd Allāh's mother and ᶜAbd Allāh is Zayd's father, Fāṭima is the mother-in-law of Zayd's [unnamed] mother, since she is the mother of his father. And because ᶜAmr is Khadīja's son, and Khadīja is Fāṭima's mother, ᶜAmr is the son of the mother of the mother-in-law of Zayd. God knows best.[106]

The point of the expression 'between my flesh and blood', and of the whole exercise, seems to be that 'Zayd' and 'Aḥmad' are paternal uncle of each other, for Aḥmad is (half-)brother of Zayd's father ᶜAbd Allāh, and Zayd is (half-)brother of Aḥmad's father Jaᶜfar. It may sound intricate, but no incest is involved here, nor even any excessive inbreeding. The odd relationships are the result of an unusual marriage, of a women ('Fāṭima') with someone ('Jaᶜfar') who, in a 'normal' genealogical tree would be two steps below, or two generations younger, than herself, because 'Jaᶜfar' is a half-brother of 'Zayd', grandson of 'Fāṭima'. Such matters are particularly interesting to specialists in inheritance law, as Ḥamza al-Iṣfahānī makes clear in remarks on other, similar riddles that he quotes. He also cites, as 'an ancient riddle', the line on a she-camel by the pre-Islamic poet Aws b. Ḥajar, that was used by Kaᶜb b. Zuhayr in his more famous poem: 'A sturdy/lean one (*ḥarf*), her brother being her father, of good breed, her paternal uncle being her maternal uncle'.[107] Interestingly, and unlike the commentator of Kaᶜb's line, Ḥamza gives a solution in human terms:

This is to be solved by way of an analogy. A woman named Hind gives birth to a girl called Daᶜd. A man named Zayd marries Daᶜd and begets from her a son called Ḥamd. Then Zayd, Daᶜd's husband, marries Hind, Daᶜd's mother, and begets from her a son called Bishr, son of Zayd. Ḥamd, Zayd's son, marries Daᶜd, Hind's daughter, and begets from her a daughter called Ḥarf,[108] the one mentioned by the poet. Thus Ḥamd is Ḥarf's father as well as her brother, and Bishr is Ḥarf's paternal as well as her maternal uncle.[109]

It is to be noted that the names of fictitious individuals chosen for this pre-Islamic example are all pre-Islamic, unlike the previous case, where some of the names, though old, have clear 'Islamic' connotations (Khadīja, the Prophet's first wife, Fāṭima, his daughter, ᶜAbd Allāh 'God's servant'). This is appropriate, of course, but may also have been inspired by the impropriety of using Islamic names, since this case certainly involves incest and extreme inbreeding.

Ḍiyāᵓ al-Dīn ibn al-Athīr (d. 637/1239), author of important works on stylistics and literary criticism, mentions that a riddle poem was submitted to him:

I have a maternal aunt, and I am her maternal uncle;
  I have a paternal aunt and I am her paternal uncle.
As for the woman whose paternal uncle I am,
  the mother of my father is her mother [*sic*].
Her father is my brother, her brother is my father.
  and I have a maternal aunt who is thus described.
Where is the lawyer who has the various kinds
  of expertise and knowledge in this matter,
Who will explain to us her relationship clearly
  and reveal what worries our mind;
For we are no Zoroastrians or unbelievers:
  we follow the divine Law of Aḥmad (i.e. Muḥammad).[110]

Ibn al-Athīr tells proudly that he solved the problem quickly, 'without a mental stammer':

> Imagine a man who is married to two women, called ᶜĀᵓisha and Fāṭima. ᶜĀᵓisha bears him a daughter and Fāṭima bears him a son [the speaker in the poem]. Then he marries his daughter to his wife Fāṭima's father. A daughter is born (from this union). Then this daughter is the maternal aunt of his son, and the latter is her maternal uncle, since he is her mother's brother...

The other relationships are similarly explained. The oddities are, again, the result of oblique marriage relationship, across the generations, but there is nothing legally or morally amiss, as the poet himself makes clear, and 'Islamic' names are used to solve the matter. However, incest or at least close-kin marriage is involved in another example, a riddle poem incorporated, and to all appearances composed, by Ibn al-Ṣayqal (d. 701/1301), author of a collection of *Maqāmāt*, a tour de force of linguistic and stylistic virtuosity that makes al-Ḥarīrī's more famous collection look like a schoolboy's exercise.[111] The poem, said to have been written on a piece of paper, addresses a *faqīh*, legal scholar, asking his opinion on a case concerning a deceased father and his three daughters, who are described as chaste and above suspicion. One daughter has subsequently died, too, and the division of the inheritance looks odd: the scholar is asked to solve the problem. Since a proper understanding of the poem and the details depends on the intricacies of Islamic inheritance laws, and since the reader's puzzle-solving capacities may have been taxed enough by now, a translation of the poem is omitted here. The lawyer reads the poem and gives his opinion likewise in versified form; the narrator's amazement at the perspicuity of the man is matched by his admiration for his concision, since he has managed to give the solution in the same number or verses (ten) as that of the versified question, and with the same metre and rhyme at that. It turns out that one of the daughters was born out of wedlock, 'in fornication' (*min sifāḥ*), and was then legally married to her natural father. The two other daughters are in fact her own daughters as well as the father's. It will be remembered that the matter of such a marriage was discussed by the jurists and that al-Shāfiʿī had allowed it. The editor of the *Maqāmāt* points this out in a note,[112] but Ibn al-Ṣayqal himself—presumably a Shāfiʿite—as well as his fictional narrator and lawyer did not find it necessary to express any views on the legal and ethical aspects of the case.

This is obviously a fictitious case, taken from a work of fiction. Versified riddles of this kind are, however, not confined to literary works. Versification, after all, is omnipresent in medieval Arabic, and many a metrical and rhymed text is far removed from 'true' poetry, according to those medieval critics and philosophers who reject the strictly formal definition of *shiʿr*. The poems quoted in this section, though taken from literary works, are not particularly poetic. Ibn al-Ṣayqal's pair of poems are cast in the shape of a question posed to a Mufti and his fatwa, or answer. A very similar but shorter Q&A set is found in a serious and famous collection of fatwas by one of the most influential Islamic scholars, the *Fatāwī* by Ibn Taymiyya (d. 728/1328). It is presented as if it were a real, non-fictitious case. Yet it is rather suspect, not because it is put in doggerel verse[113] but because it seems intended merely as a problem to test the Mufti's acumen and not, as is usual, to ask for advice on how to act in a problematic case.[114]

Question.
My grandmother is his mother, and my father his grandfather.[115]
I am his paternal aunt and he is my maternal aunt:
Give us a fatwa, O Imam—May God have mercy on you
and protect you against Time's calamities.

The solution is given again in the same metre and rhyme, as the rules of the game require.

Answer.
A man who married his son to the mother of a girl,
and who legally married this girl.
She gave him a daughter, who made the verses,
and who calls the son of that woman 'my maternal aunt'.[116]

The answer looks more like another puzzle than a solution, which is why a paraphrase in prose is added:

> A man marries a woman; his son marries her mother. The man has a daughter and his son has a son. Then his daughter is the one speaking in the poem. Her grandmother is her mother's mother, and she (i.e. the speaker's grandmother) is the mother of the son's son, being the wife of the (man's) son. Her father is the grandfather of the son's son, and she is his paternal aunt, being his father's sister; while he is her maternal uncle, being her mother's brother. God knows best.

At first sight this looks improper: as if the first-mentioned son marries his own grandmother. But the words 'legally married' are chosen advisedly, for the father of the female speaker has in fact two wives, so the son has married the mother of his stepmother. In view of the strong aversion to marrying stepmothers, it may seem strange that marrying even more obliquely, to a preceding generation, should be legal. Technically, everything is in order, since one is forbidden to marry any wife of one's father and of his ascendants; a 'step-grandmother' falls outside this category.

Although of a rather different kind and provenance, one peculiar 'puzzle' is presented by a teknonym or agnomen of Fāṭima, daughter of the Prophet Muḥammad and ancestor of all his surviving progeny. Arabs are regularly called after their children, usually the first-born, as 'Father/Mother of X' (Abū/Umm X) and Fāṭima, mother of the two imams al-Ḥasan and al-Ḥusayn, could therefore be expected to be called Umm al-Ḥasan. In later centuries, among Shīᶜites, however, she is also called, bafflingly, Umm Abīhā, 'Her Father's Mother'. It would be difficult to design an incestuous genealogy where this designation would hold literally. Of course, no incest is intended here and the explanations are to be found in different levels of metaphor and esotericism, rife in extreme Shīᶜism. Fāṭima is said to have 'learned in a revelation that the name of her very last descendant would be Muḥammad, like that of her father',[117] which does not sound like a convincing origin but is obviously an explanation of an existing name. No doubt the name is connected with the idea of the 'Muḥammadan Light' and the pre-existence of the Prophet,[118] together with a very common honorific of Fāṭima: 'the Shining One' (al-Zahrāᵓ). In one version of this, Fāṭima's light is placed by God in Muḥammad's loins, which in a sense could make her 'her father's mother'.[119] Another of her names, Fāṭir ('Creator', strangely masculine), which sounds like a play on her real name, could also be connected with this.[120] The fact that to some extent she may be compared to Mary in Christianity has tempted L. Veccia Vaglieri to see the name as a counterpart of 'Mother of God';[121] and in Christianity we find a not dissimilar seemingly incestuous designation for Mary as *mater et filia* of Christ.[122]

More Stories and Legends:

—Taʾabbaṭa Sharran

The founding legend of incest in western literature is, of course, *Oedipus*, who was not known to the medieval Arabs. However, in legends from the pre-Islamic past and the 'stories of the Prophets' that were mentioned before, Arabic counterparts to Oedipus have been found, in the eyes of some scholars. The story of Nimrod has been discussed above; Suzanne Pinckney Stetkevych has drawn another parallel in a fascinating study, by explicitly comparing the pre-Islamic brigand poet Taʾabbaṭa Sharran to Oedipus, complete with Sphinx (the *ghūl*), deformed foot, and all.[123] Or rather not all, for any clear incest is absent from the story. What is 'Oedipal' to her in the story is 'not so much the elements that Freud emphasized—the male infant's desire to kill his father and sleep with his mother—but rather the perversion or confusion of the natural order that leads to extinction rather than the propagation of the line'.[124] However, Taʾabbaṭa Sharran's mother figures prominently in his story, from his birth until after his death. Not surprisingly Stetkevych sees a reference to incestuous intercourse in the episode in which the young boy offers his mother her leather bag ('a female emblem') filled with live vipers ('phallic'), which he had carried under his arm, an incident to which, according to one story at least, he owed his odd nickname (literally, 'He Carried Evil Under His Arm').[125] Stetkevych might, for that matter, have found something smacking vaguely of incest in the report that whenever the poet went out on a raid his mother would cast a spell to find out about her son, using his urine.[126]

Stetkevych does not, of course, suggest that the Oedipus story somehow drifted across to Arabia; if there are parallels, they are there because they are archetypes. What is clear is that overt incest, in this story, is either altogether absent or suppressed. Only a Freudian reading will see penises in snakes, a vagina in a leather bag, or semen in urine.

—*Luqmān*

Incest does happen in the story of the legendary sage of pre-Islamic Arabia, counterpart of the ancient Near-Eastern sage Aḥiqar. Luqmān,[127] associated with the legendary Arabian people of ᶜĀd, is mentioned in the Qur'an in the sura that is named after him as having been given wisdom by God (Q 31:12), and there follow some of his wise words addressed to his son; in later lore he became the author of Aesop-style fables. He is famous not only for his wisdom but for his longevity, too: he lived the lives of seven vultures, consecutively. His image is wholly positive in the Qur'an or, for instance, in al-Thaᶜlabī's *Tales of the Prophets*, but there is a darker side to him, involving murder and incest, not what one expects from a proverbial sage. It is possible that he is a conflation of at least two different figures.[128] He is described as unwittingly emulating Lot, not with a daughter but with his sister, and as killing a daughter (not to mention numerous wives). The following is a version given by al-Jāḥiẓ, who starts *in medias res*:[129]

> When Luqmān ibn ᶜĀd killed his daughter (she was Ṣuḥr, the sister of Luqaym) he said to her, at the moment he killed her, 'Aren't you a woman?!'. The reason was this. He had married numerous women, who had all of them betrayed him.[130] When he had killed the last one of them, he came down from the mountain. The first person he met was his daughter Ṣuḥr. He pounced upon her and killed her, saying, 'And you are a woman too!'. He had, moreover, been afflicted with his sister, who brought forth stupid children. She had said to one of Luqmān's wives, 'Tonight I am clean [after menstruation]. It is your turn tonight [to sleep with your husband], so let me sleep in your bed, for Luqmān is a man who begets noble children (*munjib*). Perhaps he will have intercourse with me so that I will bring forth a noble child!'. And thus he had intercourse with his sister and she became pregnant with Luqaym. This is what al-Namir ibn Tawlab[131] said:
>
> Luqaym: Luqmān's son from his daughter,
> so he was a nephew to him and a son.
> On nights when he was made stupid and she pretended
> to be chaste to him, but he was fooled in the dark.
> So a wise man made her pregnant
> and she gave birth to him (and he became) a wise man.

The story ends here and we are not told whether or not Luqmān ever found out the truth. Al-Jarīrī (d. 390/1000) mentions that someone concluded from this story that Luqmān was a Zoroastrian, but he rightly rejects this.[132] In a slightly different version of the story the reason for the bed-trick is childlessness, which makes the story more akin to that of Lot:

> It is also told that no children were born to Luqmān. Thus his wife said to his sister, 'What do you think? Luqmān, with all his strength and powerful physique, has no children!' She replied, 'So what can be done?' His wife said to his sister, 'You must put on my clothes, so that he will have intercourse with you in the dark.' So she did, he copulated with her and she bore a child by him, who was called Luqaym. He became one of the most astute of men.[133]

The poem by al-Namir ibn Tawlab highlights the paradox: the wise man is made stupid, either simply by letting himself be fooled in this manner, or, as an early authority, Muḥammad ibn Ḥabīb (d. 245/860), asserted, by letting himself be made drunk with wine,[134] thus providing yet another parallel with the story of Lot. The drunkenness, also mentioned in al-Maydānī's version, did not prevent Luqmān from noticing something odd: when his wife returned to his bed the following night, he is said to have exclaimed, 'This is a familiar cunt!', which became a proverbial expression.[135]

That Luqmān combines the traits originally belonging to more than one legendary person was already posited by al-Jāḥiẓ and other medieval scholars.[136] Al-Jāḥiẓ suggests, in a somewhat confused passage, that al-Namir ibn Tawlab's poem is an attempt to raise the status of the Arabian Luqmān, making him as wise as the Qur'anic one with his supposedly Hebrew or at least non-Arabian origin:

> The Arabs used to glorify Luqmān son of ᶜĀd, the Elder, and the Younger, Luqaym son of Luqmān, and their intelligence, status, knowledge, wisdom, eloquence and self-control. But these two are not the same as Luqmān, the wise man mentioned in the Qur'an, according to the exegetes. It is on account of his elevated status and great importance that al-Namir ibn Tawlab said, 'Luqaym, Luqmān's son from his daughter' (etc.).[137]

The passage is confused because 'his elevated status' seems to refer to the Qur'anic Luqmān, whereas the poem is about the Arabian one, who is obviously equated, in the third verse, with the wise man from the Qur'an. It is as if the sentence about the exegetes is an interpolation, and it may be that al-Jāḥiẓ himself did not hold their view. In any case, the considerations of these commentators were probably informed less by sober philology than by moral outrage. Unlike the many interesting ambivalent figures from the Hebrew Bible, almost all Muslim heroes and prophet-precursors of Muḥammad must be blameless. Needless to say, from the point of view of the western literary tradition, steeped as it is in flawed heroes since the Greek tragedies, it is far more interesting to have only one Luqmān.

—*A Bed-Trick with Compounded Incest in Baghdad*

There are only a few stories of any length in classical Arabic in which incest is the main theme. Two of them are told in a monograph on love by the theologian, preacher and historian Ibn al-Jawzī (d. 597/1200), *Dhamm al-hawā*. As its title indicates, this is a book on 'the condemnation of passionate love'—not love in general (*ḥubb*), but *hawā*, which is a stronger form. In addition to containing general discussions on love in all its forms, the work is a mine of anecdotes and stories of lovers. The stern theologian is by no means without sympathy for those who suffer from passion, but towards the end he devotes several chapters to the unfortunate results of excessive love, for which he now uses the even stronger term *ᶜishq*, 'love-passion': 'On those who became unbelievers because of *ᶜishq*', 'On those who killed because of *ᶜishq*', 'On those who killed their beloved', 'Those who were killed by *ᶜishq*', 'Those who killed themselves because of *ᶜishq*'. The series is headed, however, by 'Those whom *ᶜishq* drove to commit incest (literally, to fornicate with those of the forbidden degrees)'. It contains two stories, both of which will be presented here. Both are introduced with chains of transmitters, and both chains include al-Tanūkhī.

The great story-teller al-Tanūkhī (d. 384/994) is famous especially for his collection of tales with a happy ending, *al-Faraj baᶜd al-shidda* ('Relief After Distress', or 'All's Well That Ends Well'). More stories, anecdotes, poems and interesting titbits are contained, with little system, in another collection compiled by him, *Nishwār al-muḥāḍara* (roughly but aptly translated as 'Tabletalk'). The two incest stories, in view of their ending, could not have been incorporated in *al-Faraj*. They are not preserved in the existing text of the other collection, but the modern editor has included in his edition tales ascribed to al-Tanūkhī in later works. Al-Tanūkhī, too, gives his chain of transmitters, as he usually does. This, together with the plain and unadorned language and the 'realistic' details, gives his tales the appearance of veracity. In many cases his stories strongly suggest that they are fiction rather than fact, and sometimes they clothe folkloristic motifs in the garb of realism, as András Hámori and others have demonstrated in various studies. As for the present stories, the reader ought to judge, and since to my knowledge no English versions have yet appeared, I give a full translation.[138]

Muḥammad b. ᶜAbd al-Bāqī al-Bazzāz informed me: Abū l-Qāsim ᶜAlī b. al-Muḥassin al-Tanūkhī informed me, on the authority of his father, who said: Abū Isḥāq Ibrāhīm b. ᶜAlī b. Saᶜīd al-Naṣībī told me, saying: Abū l-Ḥasan b. Najīḥ told me, saying: A respectable man, who was a friend of mine, and who used to live near the al-Khayzurān cemetery in Baghdad, told me, saying:

One night I dreamed that I looked out of my house, towards the cemetery, as I usually do when I cannot sleep. And look! The tombs opened up, and their occupants came out, with dishevelled hair, dust-coloured, barefoot, and naked, and they gathered in one place there. In the end there was no tomb left occupied. They made a lot of noise, crying, praying, and beseeching God not to have that woman buried with them who was to be buried the following day. In my dream I asked one of them, and he said:

—That woman is one of the people of Hell! If she is buried with us we shall hear her being tortured and all that will happen to her. So we ask God to let her be buried elsewhere.

Then I woke up, greatly amazed about it all. After a long night, I asked the gravediggers in the morning if they had dug the grave of a woman. One of them pointed to a large vaulted tomb that belonged to a rich family of merchants. The wife of one of them had died and he wanted to bury her in the tomb. The grave had already been dug. Then I told my dream to the gravediggers. At that they filled in the grave immediately. I kept an eye on the matter of the woman.[139] Messengers of the family arrived, to ask about the grave. The gravediggers said,

—We cannot make a grave in this spot, because we hit upon a quagmire under the earth. A corpse would not be stable there.

They asked the owners of a number of other tombs to have a grave dug with them, but they refused. The news had spread among the gravediggers. So they went to another cemetery and dug a grave for the woman. I inquired about the place from where the funeral procession would come and I was told. Then I went there and escorted the bier with the others, an enormous crowd. The husband was obviously an important man.[140] Behind the bier I noticed a man, young but already bearded, with a handsome face. They said it was the woman's son. He and his father were being offered condolences, and both were distraught by their loss.

When the woman had been buried I went to them and said,

—I have had a dream about the deceased. If you like, I will tell you.

The old man, the deceased woman's husband, answered,

—I would rather not hear it.

The young man, however, turned to me and said,

—Please tell, if you will.

I said,

—In private!

He got up, and I said,

—It is an awful dream, so don't hold it against me.

—Tell me!

So I told him my dream and said,

—You should look into the matter, and find out why God has made the woman suffer as I told you, so that you may avoid doing the same! And if you could possibly let me know, if you please, I too may avoid the like!

—By God, he said, My friend, I know nothing about my mother that would have brought this about, apart from that she used to drink date-wine, listen to music and scandal-monger about(?)[141] other women; and this would not lead to these awful things. But there is an old woman in our house, some ninety years old, who was her nurse and maid. If you have the energy, you could come with me and we'll ask her. Perhaps she will tell us what has brought this upon her, so that we can avoid it.

So I went along with him to the house where the deceased had lived. He showed me into a room, and there sat a decrepit old woman. He spoke to her about what had happened and I told her my dream. She said,

—I ask God to forgive her! She was a terribly abandoned woman.

—Mother, said the young man, You mean apart from drinking, listening to music, and women?

—O yes, my dear boy. Were it not that I would hurt you, I could tell you what I know. What this man has seen in his dream is only a small portion of the many tortures that I fear are in store for her.

—I want you to tell me, said the young man.

I spoke kindly to the old woman and said,

—Please tell us, so that we may avoid it and be admonished by it.

—It would be a long story if I told you all I know about her and what I have gone through myself with her.

She wept, and continued,

—As for me, God knows that I have repented years ago. I hoped that she would repent too, but she didn't. But I shall tell you three instances of her deeds, which are in my view the worst of her sins.

—Speak!, we said.

She said to the young man,

—She was one of the lewdest people on earth. No day passed but she would bring one or two men into your father's house, without his knowledge, and they would have sex with her and leave. They would be smuggled in with all kinds of ruses, while your father was at the market. When you had grown up and reached puberty you looked extremely attractive. Then I saw her look at you lustfully. I was amazed. Then, one day she said to me:

—Mother, I am so badly in love with this son of mine. He must sleep with me!

—Child, fear God!, I said. Aren't the other men enough for you?

—It must happen.

—How could it? How could he come to you? He is a child! And you will become involved in a scandal, without even attaining your desire. So leave it, for God's sake!

—You must help me.

—Doing what?

—Go to So-and-so, the schoolteacher ...

He was a schoolteacher in our neighbourhood, an educated man, who used to write letters to her lovers and write replies on her behalf; she was devoted to him and gave him presents. She continued:

— ... and tell him to write a note to him, speaking of passion, heartfelt ardour, and love's ecstasy, and asking him for a meeting. Then you give him the letter, pretending it is from that girl. (She mentioned a young and pretty girl, one of the neighbours).

The old woman continued,

—So that is what I did. I took the letter and gave it to you. When you heard the name of that girl, your heart was set aflame; you wrote an answer to the letter asking her for a meeting at her place, pointing out that you did not have a suitable place. Then I gave your reply to your mother. She said,

—Write to him, in that girl's name, that she hasn't got a place either, and that the only way is to meet at his place. If he says he hasn't got a place, prepare such-and-such a room for him with rugs and cushions, and put perfume and fruit in it. Say to him: She is a young girl and she[142] will be embarrassed, but passion for you has prevailed and she will come here to meet you one night. Let there be no light with you, so that she will not be embarrassed, and your mother and your father will not find out, if they see a lamp burning in that room.—Now if he says he is willing, let me know!

The woman continued,

—So I did all that, and you said you were willing. The appointment was arranged for a certain night, and I told her. She dressed, applied incense to her clothes, put on perfume and scent, and went up to the room. You came, thinking that this girl was there. You fell on her and had sex with her until the morning. At daybreak I came, woke her up and took her down while you were still sleeping. She had gone up to you after your father had fallen asleep. After a number of days, she said to me,

—Mother, I am ... by God, I am pregnant from my son. What can I do?

—I don't know, I said.

—I know, she said.

After that she would meet you by means of the ruse that I told you about, until the time of birth was near. She told your father that she was ill, fearing for her life, and wanted to go to her mother's house so that she could recover there. He allowed her to go and she went. She told her mother that she was ill and she was given a room in the house; I was with her. We let a midwife come and when she had given birth she killed the child, took it outside and buried it secretly. After staying a few more days she returned to her home. Then, after a few days, she said to me,

—I want my son.

—Shame on you!, I said. Haven't you got enough already?

—I must, she said.

So I came to you again, using the same stratagem as before. The following morning she said to me,

—By God, I am pregnant again. This time, by God! it will be my death and I shall be exposed.

She kept meeting you, using the same ruse, until the delivery was near. She went to her mother and did as before, this time giving birth to a girl that was so pretty that she could not bring herself to kill her. One night I took the girl away from her and handed her to some poor people to whom a baby had been born. I gave them some money, a lot of dirhams, from your father's wealth, and arranged with them that they would suckle her and bring her up. I would give them a certain sum every month. The mother did indeed send this to them every month, doubling the amount. Thus the girl was pampered and sent soft clothes, and she grew up being spoilt and in comfort, while the mother saw her any day if she longed for her. Your father arranged a marriage for you and so you married your wife. This put an end to what went on between you and your mother, while she was still enamoured of you like no other and jealous of your wife. There was nothing she could do about it.

But then the young girl reached the age of nine. The mother passed her off as a slave-girl that she had bought, and brought her to her own house, so that she could see her all the time, because she was so fond of her. The girl was not aware that she was her mother. She gave her a name proper for slaves.[143] The girl grew up, having a very pretty face. The mother taught her to sing and play the lute, and she excelled in it. When she had reached the age of womanhood, the mother said to me one day,

—Mother, you see how deeply I love this girl of mine. You are the only one who knows that she is my daughter. I cannot disclose the matter to anyone. We have now reached the point that if I do not find a man for her, she will escape from my power and seek men herself, to be sold to them, for she thinks she is a slave-girl. If I prevent her, her life as well as mine will be misery. But if I sell her and am separated from her I shall die! Now I thought that I should unite her with my son.

—O you woman, fear God!, I said. What has happened should be enough for you.

—It must be.

—And how should it be done?

—Go and write a letter in which you mention love's passion and ardour, and take it to my son's wife. Tell her that it is from So-and-so the soldier, our neighbour ...

She mentioned a young man whose cheek-down had just sprouted, an extremely handsome lad with whom she was ardently in love, and he with her.

— ... and be nice to her, so that you manage to get her reply to him.

This I did; and I had to suffer humiliation, and contempt from your wife, who chased me away. But I kept coming to her and in the end she relented(?).[144] She read the letter and wrote a reply with her own hand. I gave the reply to your mother, who took it and showed it to your father. Thus she slandered[145] her and cast enmity between her and her parents and your father, with which we had to live for months. In the end your father demanded that you divorce your wife or else move out and leave him forever. He would pay the bridal money back from his own purse. You obeyed your parents[146] and divorced your wife, and your father paid out the bridal money. You were distraught, you cried and did not want to eat. Then your mother came to you and said,

—Why are you sad about that whore? I'll give you my slave-girl, the singer. She is prettier than the other, she is a virgin and a decent girl, whereas the other is no longer a maid, and an adulteress.[147] I'll arrange an unveiling for you such as is done with free women[148] and provide her with a trousseau from my own money and that of your father, better than the first one that you got.

When you heard that, your grief disappeared and you agreed with her proposal. She arranged the trousseau, had jewellery made, and unveiled her to you. She then gave birth to these children of yours and now lives in your house. Now this is *one* of the things I know about your mother. Another one is ...

She began to tell another story. But the young man said,

— Enough, enough! Stop! Don't say anything! God curse that woman and have no mercy on her!

He began to ask God's forgiveness and to cry, saying,

—By God, my house is ruined. I must be separated from the mother of my children.

He shook my hand and I stood up, with grief in my heart, since I had not heard the rest of what the old woman wanted to tell.

*

This lurid and sad story is told as if it really happened. There are reasons for doubt. It is rather typical of al-Tanūkhī's stories that the ultimate source, unlike all other chains in the transmission, is left anonymous. The narrator's dream vision is strikingly apt, but the rest of the story is devoid of supernatural or intrinsically impossible things. Nevertheless, quite a few matters are unlikely, such as the boy's continuing ignorance during the long-lasting affair in the dark with his mother, who even manages to hide her pregnancies from him and her husband. The double incest remains unknown to the victims (although the husband may have had his suspicions, witness his reluctance to hear the narrator's dream). Recognition is, of course, an extremely important narrative element in stories of incest committed unwittingly. Here the recognition is not effected in the main tale, but in the telling, afterwards, by an accomplice. The narrators in the story thereby acquire an extraordinary responsibility and importance. The old woman only tells her story after some prodding; although she is evidently an accessory to appalling crimes, she has at least repented. Very striking is the callous character of the male narrator, the 'respectable man' who lives near the cemetery. He rather cruelly tells his dream to the young man, ostensibly in order to learn a moral lesson and avoid committing similar sins, as he repeats several times. At the very end, however, when we expect him to stop at the words 'I stood up with grief in my heart', he adds a devilish clause that shows he is not grieving for the young man's plight, but only for having missed yet more lurid tales. It is clear that the narrator, or al-Tanūkhī if he recast and adapted his source, is mixing jest and earnest, giving a sardonic twist to a tragic tale. The black humour is apparent too when it turns out that the dark deeds described were only one out of three instances, and these apparently merely some of the numerous heinous deeds of the woman. It is difficult to think of anything that could match the list of adultery, incest, infanticide, marriage-wrecking and deceit found in this story alone. Unless one relishes black humour, the tale, told in a masterful fashion, is objectionable and not exactly morally uplifting, the more so because the mother is, apparently, neither exposed nor punished in this world, which runs counter to one's expectation of poetic justice. Until the end of her wicked life she preserves her reputation and she dies deeply mourned by the son and the husband (who remains very much in the background). This lack of morality, in addition to the unmentionable sin of incest, was perhaps among the reasons why the Egyptian Ministry of Culture and National Guidance, in their undated reprint of al-Nuwayrī's encyclopedia, decided to expurgate it. If the tale has a moral, it is one that fits in with the general misogynistic strand in medieval literature: women are bad. All in all, the story looks like very carefully composed fiction, an exercise in accumulating as many sins as possible in one lively narrative. Ibn al-Jawzī does not express any doubts about the truth of the story, but al-Nuwayrī (d. 732/1332) adds the following comment:[149]

> There are many stories of this kind. But I have only given this story, because I do not believe that it has actually happened, nor will its like ever happen, if God wills.

One supposes he is right. But if he is correct in asserting that there are 'many stories of this kind', then very few of them have survived in the sources; possibly many were never written down.

The story involves a bed-trick, a very common motif that is the subject of a recent scholarly and entertaining study by Wendy Doniger.[150] As Doniger says, there is 'close connection between incest and the bedtrick'.[151] Incest normally has to be hidden in the dark or behind a disguise. But what makes the story especially interesting is the fact that it presents a case of double incest. Writing on European medieval literature, and having discussed the story of Judas,[152] Elizabeth Archibald says that

> One of the most startling innovations of medieval writers is this double incest theme: intercourse between siblings or father and daughter who are well aware of their relationship is followed by the exposure of their illegitimate son, who later quite innocently marries his unrecognized mother-aunt-sister (or, much less frequently, a mother and son who know their relationship produce a daughter who later marries her father-brother). Such double incest stories do not seem to occur in classical literature.[153]

In al-Tanūkhī's tale, we have an example of what Archibald calls the less frequent variant, and an example that seems to predate the European ones. It is interesting to read that Otto Rank, who spoke of 'displeasing' medieval tales and 'voluptuous and torrid fantasies', believed that they were due to 'the great repression of drives expressed in Christianity', which 'could be maintained only at the cost of a fantasy life pouring forth to the most voluptuous degree'.[154] While it may be true that double incest stories (like incest stories in general) are more frequent in Christian medieval times than in the medieval Middle East, there is at least a possibility that the Arab Muslims, traditionally deemed less sexually 'repressed' than Christians, preceded them; but then, it would fit the 'voluptuousness' with which the 'orientals' have always been credited. Archibald is no doubt correct in seeking a more plausible explanation in the consideration of narrative interest:[155] double incest usefully compresses, condenses, complicates and intensifies the plot, and makes the story even more fit to point a moral, if desired.

In the west, the earliest double incest story is apparently the legend of Gregorius, first found in Old French in *c.* 1150. A brother rapes his sister; they continue their affair until she is pregnant. The baby boy is exposed, but survives and is baptized Gregorius. Later he marries his own mother, without either being aware of the truth. When they find out, they are horrified and do penance. He leaves her, and becomes an admirable Pope.[156] This story is obviously very different from the Tanūkhī story, as is the story of Albanus, who is the product of a father and his daughter and who marries his unrecognized mother. Here, too, penance follows, but the sinners relapse and are killed by their offspring, who becomes a holy hermit.[157]

The European story closest to al-Tanūkhī's tale, being about a mother falling in love with her son, mating with him in the dark, and producing a daughter who later marries the son-father, is found in the *Heptameron* by Marguerite de Navarre (d. 1549), with variations by Matteo Bandello (d. 1561) in his *Le Novelle*, and Martin Luther (d. 1546) in his *Lectures on Genesis*.[158] I am unable to say whether the Arabic story served as a model or whether both versions ultimately go back to an even older one; it would be difficult to think of plausible channels of transmission. There are some important differences in the French version: the mother is much less wicked. Falling in love in spite of herself and being filled with remorse afterwards, she sends the daughter away, and the subsequent marriage is not of her doing. When she finds out the truth, she is distraught and does penance for the remainder of her life. It is suggested, therefore, that she may escape eternal hellfire, unlike the lady from Baghdad. Both escape punishment in this world. This may not satisfy everybody's sense of justice. Thus, in another story, a wicked mother who chases away and replaces her son's wife, tricking him into bed, is burned by him when he finds out: this gruesome tale was told, in fairy-tale style and apparently to an audience including young children, by an Egyptian Bedouin woman and reported by Lila Abu-Lughod.[159]

—*The Lovers of Fatḥ Alley, Baghdad*

Like the story of the wicked woman of Baghdad, another story revolving around incest is found in Ibn al-Jawzī's *Dhamm al-hawā*. Al-Tanūkhī figures again in its chain of authorities, together with his immediate informant in the other story, Ibrāhīm al-Naṣībī. The narrator is identified as the father of a certain Abū ʿAlī ibn Fatḥ. These names give few clues, but if the last name is a mistake for Abū l-Ḥasan ʿAlī b. Fatḥ, he may perhaps be identified as a civil servant (*kātib*) called al-Muṭawwaq, who lived in the early tenth century.[160] In a shortened version found in a book by Mughulṭāy b. Qīlij (d. 762/1361), on lovers who died as 'martyrs' of their love, the name appears as 'al-Muhallab b. al-Fatḥ al-Baghdādī'. Again, here follows a full translation.[161]

> Muḥammad b. ʿAbd al-Bāqī al-Bazzāz informed me: Abū l-Qāsim ʿAlī b. al-Muḥassin al-Tanūkhī informed me: Ibrāhīm b. ʿAlī al-Naṣībī told me: Abū Bakr al-Naḥwī told me: Abū ʿAlī b. Fatḥ told me, he said: My father told me:

In a certain year I was sitting in my alley when a young man entered. He had a handsome face and appearance and showed signs of affluence. He asked if he could rent a house in the alley that was standing empty. Most of the alley belonged to me. I took him to a big and beautiful house, that was unoccupied and showed it to him. He liked it, paid me a month's rent, and took the key. The following morning he came back, together with a servant boy. They opened the door, the boy swept the floor and sprinkled it with water, the man sat down, the boy went off, and returned in the afternoon together with porters and a woman. They entered the house, the door was shut and we heard nothing more.

Before the evening prayer the boy came out and the man and the woman remained in the house. For some days they did not open the door. On the fourth day he came to see me. I asked,

—Well, what is the matter?

He pointed out that he was hiding because he was in debt and asked me to arrange that someone would come and buy for him his daily needs, all in one go (for a whole week). This I did. Once every week he came out, weighing out many dirhams and giving them to this servant whom I had appointed for him, so that he could buy for him bread, meat, fruit, date-wine and vegetables, and fill a large number of jars with water that he had put ready, all of which would last him for these [seven] days. He would not open the door, unless the provisions ran out.

This went on for a year. Nobody ever came to see him, nobody left. I did not see him, nor did anyone else. Then, one evening, at the time of the sunset prayer, he knocked on my door. I went out and asked,

—What do you want?

—You ought to know that my wife is about to give birth. Please help and send for a midwife.

Now there was a midwife who lived in my house, belonging to the mother of my children. I took her to him and she stayed with him that night. The following morning she came to me and told that the woman had given birth to a girl that night. She had seen to it that the baby was all right, but the mother was dying. She returned to her. At midday the girl[162] died. The midwife came and told us. The man said,

—O God, please let some woman come or let someone slap their face (in lamentation), or let one of the neighbours come to comfort me, or let a whole lot of people come.

This I did. I found him in a bad state, crying and sobbing. I brought a bier between sunset prayer and evening prayer; I had arranged for a grave to be dug at a nearby cemetery. The gravediggers left in the evening. The man had said he would see me after their departure, and had said: I do not want anyone to see me; you and I will carry the bier, if you would do me that favour, and if you want (God's) reward. Then I felt ashamed and said, I'll do it. When it was nearly dark I went to him and said,

—Time for the bier to leave?

—Please, could we first bring this girl to your house, on one condition.

—What is it?

—I cannot bear to stay longer in this house now that my lady[163] has gone, or even stay in town. I have a lot of money and household stuff. Please take it, and take the girl. Spend the money on her, from the price of the goods, until the girl has grown up. If she dies while there is some left, it is yours, with God's blessing. If she lives it will be enough for her until she reaches womanhood. Then arrange her affairs as you think fit. I shall go after the burial and leave town.

I lectured him, insisting that he should be firm and stay, but without success. So I took the girl to my house. He carried the bier while I was with him, assisting him. When we stood at the grave's edge he said to me,

—Be so kind and stand at a distance, for I want to say farewell and disclose her face, so that I can see her and then bury her.

I did. He unwrapped her face, bent over her and kissed her. Then he tied up her shroud and took her down in the grave. Then I heard a scream from the grave. Startled, I came near and looked down. He had drawn a sword that had been hanging under his clothes, unsheathed, while I was unaware of it. He had leaned on it so that it entered his heart and came out at his back, he had uttered that scream, and died—it was as if he had been dead a thousand years!

I was utterly astonished. I was afraid it would become known and turn into an unpleasant story. So I laid him down on top of her, in the grave niche, hiding them behind mud bricks, then pouring the earth back[164] and neatly putting the grave in order. I poured on it a few jarfuls of water that I had in that place.[165] I returned home and moved everything in that house to mine, storing it in a separate room which I locked and sealed. I said to myself: As likely as not, this won't be the end of the story. I must not touch any of that money or those goods. (It was a lot, though, worth thousands of dinars.) I'll do a good deed and pay for the baby myself. I shall consider it as a foundling found on the street, and I'll bring her up for God's reward.

And so I did. About a year passed after the death of the girl and the young man. One day I was sitting at my door when an old man passed by. He looked noble and affluent. He was riding a lively mule, a black servant was walking before him. He greeted me and stopped, asking,

—What is the name of this alley?

—Fatḥ Alley.

—Do you live here?

—Yes.

—How long have you lived here?

—Since I grew up. It is called after me and I own most of it.

The man bent his leg and dismounted. I got up and went to him, politely receiving him. He sat down opposite me and talked to me, saying,

—There's something I want.

—Speak.

—Do you know hereabout a person who arrived two years ago? A young man looking thus ...

He gave a description of the young man.

— ... and who rented a house here?

—Yes, I do.

—What did he do and what has happened to him?

—Who are you, that I should tell you?

—Tell me!

—I won't, unless you tell me the truth.

—I am his father.

Then I told him the story, as completely as I could. The man was on the verge of tears and said,

—The worst thing for me is that I cannot say 'God have mercy on him'.

I thought that he alluded to the suicide, so I said,

—Perhaps his mind was deranged and so he killed himself.

The man wept and said,

—That is not what I mean. Where is the girl?

—With me, she and all the goods.

—Please give me the girl.

—I won't, unless you tell me the true story.

—Please allow me not to!

—I swear by God, you must.

—My friend, the afflictions in this world are many. This is one of them. This son of mine grew up, I educated him and taught him. A sister grew up with him, there wasn't a prettier girl than she in Baghdad. She was younger than he. He fell in love with her and she with him, while we were unaware. Then their affair became known. I scolded them and rebuked them. But it ended with him deflowering her. When I learned that, I beat him and her with whips and kept the matter a secret so that I would not have a scandal on my hands. I separated them and kept them confined. Their mother was as firm with them as I was. But they managed to meet, using tricks, like two unrelated lovers. We heard about that, so I expelled the boy from home and put shackles on the girl. Many months went by. I had a slave who served me and was like a son to me. It was through him that my son was able to trick us, for the slave would act as a messenger between the two. They took a lot of money and household things from me and fled, two years ago. In order to take all that and to flee they employed a trick that would take too long to explain. I have not heard anything about them since. The loss of the money meant nothing to me, because they had gone. Good riddance!—Only I kept longing for them. Then I was told that the slave lived in a certain street, a few days ago. I raided his house, he fled to the roof. I said to him, 'I beseech you, for God's sake, how are my children? For I am killed by longing for them. You'll be safe.' He said to me, 'You ought to go to Fatḥ Alley, in West Side, and ask about them there.' Then he flung himself onto another roof and fled. I am known as So-and-so, a wealthy merchant from East Side.

He began to cry, and said,

—Please take me to the grave.

I took him to the edge of the grave. Then I made him enter my house and showed him the young girl. He began to cover her with kisses, crying. He took her up and was about to go.

—Wait, I said, take your belongings with you.

—They are yours, freely at your disposal.

I kept trying to convince him, I actually pulled him and said,

—Please take the money, and relieve me of the responsibility.

—On condition that we split it in two between us.

—By God, I will not be involved in one little bit of it.

—Then fetch some porters.

I brought them. He took up his inheritance and the girl and left.

*

This story is told in the same unadorned style as the preceding one. The narrator, however, is very unlike the callous narrator of the other story. He is compassionate, helpful, polite, and unselfish. It is possible that this is because the narrator, Fatḥ, though somewhat obscure, is at least known by name and the story reaches us through his son Abū ʿAlī (or perhaps ʿAlī), who may have ennobled his father's role. There are other differences between the two stories. Although neither dwells on erotic and sexual scenes (as a *Thousand and One Nights* version or a modern European version might have done), the first tale is more concerned with the mechanics of the affair. The ruses employed are described in considerable detail and are perhaps as important as the fact that the affair is incestuous. In the second tale the narrator, or a later embellisher, could have elaborated on the tricks employed by the two lovers. Instead, we are told that the trick is too long to be told. The emphasis is on the psychology of the lovers, the father and the narrator. Unlike the depraved mother who is in control of the dire events, if not of her own passion, the incestuous siblings are not depicted as bad. Their love is mutual, the sex obviously consensual, and they are not exploiting each other. It is not explained why brotherly love changes into sexual passion, it just happens. There is no psychological development; if there has been a struggle in the lovers' minds between resisting their urges and giving in to them, we are not told them. The lovers are not explicitly described as being very depraved. It is true that the father scolds them and punishes them, but he seems more concerned about a possible public scandal than about his children's souls being damned by sinning against the Islamic incest regulations (likewise the narrator, after the suicide, is more eager to protect his own reputation than to reveal the truth). Religion is mostly absent from the story. The father is torn between respect for decorum and paternal love ('Good riddance!—Only I kept longing for them'). In killing himself the brother is committing a grave sin according to Islamic ideas, but in a sense he is exonerated, as the narrator suggests, by being deranged by his love. He is a 'martyr' of love and his story is incorporated in Mughulṭāy's compilation on love's martyrs. It is unlikely, though, that he would have gone straight to Paradise as a hero dying in war for the sake of Islam, for a very famous (but somewhat suspect) saying of the Prophet promises Paradise only to those love-martyrs 'who keep their love hidden and are chaste'. The siblings tried to hide their love from others but not from each other, nor were they chaste. The brother is described not as a wicked sinner, however, but rather as one of the many unhappy lovers who died or even killed themselves, to be pitied rather than condemned by the reader. The girl's death in childbed is presented not as divine punishment but as something that often happens. An essential final difference with the first story is that there is no cheap horror with macabre dreams here, nor any black humour, and no narrative twists to undermine the tragedy. The narrative suspense is not, as often in incest stories, a matter of 'when will the incest be discovered', but rather of the question 'what is the solution of the riddle of the reclusive couple'.

Altogether, although the story may be fictional, it is far more realistic than the first one. Although I have not been able to find a reference to 'Fatḥ Alley' in Baghdad's West Side, it seems unlikely that al-Tanūkhī would have used a fictional place name for his Baghdadian audience.

—*ʿArūs al-ʿArāʾis*

The Thousand and One Nights is usually called 'popular literature': anonymous stories intended, at least in traditional Arab culture, for children and simple minds rather than the cultured elite, who despised it for its unpolished language as much as for its blatant and fantastic fiction. This is a simplification, because there are very close ties between the collection as we know it and 'polite' literature. Many shortish stories are found, with little change, in the *Nights* as well as in, for instance, al-Tanūkhī's collections. If there is a distinct difference, it is that 'polite' literature is averse to lengthy stories. The two stories translated above are on the long side, whereas the *Nights* is full of much longer stories. This is characteristic of other popular narratives, such as the epics of ᶜAntar or the Banū Hilāl, which were more truly 'popular' than the *Nights*.

The history of the *Thousand and One Nights* in Arabic goes back to early Abbasid times, judging by reports in books, but the text as known is late medieval. Older than it is a much smaller but interesting collection called *al-Ḥikāyāt al-ᶜajība wa-l-akhbār al-gharība* ('Wondrous Stories and Strange Reports'). Some of its stories are also found in the *Nights*. Among those that are not, the most striking is the story of a girl called ᶜArūs al-ᶜarāʾis ('Bride of Brides').[166] She is a paragon of depravity. Seeing that her crimes include murder, parricide, mutilation, deceit, arson and much fornication, the absence of incest is all the more striking because the motif occurs, briefly, twice in the story. Her tale is told in order to console a king for the loss of his daughter. The narrator of the enframed main story, who has many adventures with ᶜArūs al-ᶜarāʾis, has himself a criminal past and has once been apprehended for trying to rape his mother.[167] When, many pages later, he describes his homecoming, his mother is glad to see him:[168] like the reader or listener, she may have forgotten her son's earlier behaviour. In the course of the many events in the story the narrator and his wicked girlfriend come upon a strange people, barefoot and naked, with hairy tails like horses, who make a lot a noise. They are all descended from a black slave-girl, dumped on a peninsula by a king of the Jinn when it turned out she was pregnant by another partner. She gives birth to twins, a boy and a girl. When the boy reaches puberty he copulates with his sister and his mother; all the creatures are descended from them.[169]

This, taken by itself, is an interesting variation on the story of Adam, Eve, and their offspring. Cain and Abel behaved in a relatively restrained manner, being fully human, whereas the slave-girl and her children have fewer inhibitions. It is suggested that the brutal, animal nature of their descendants, who have turned into cannibals, is either a result of this behaviour or it might have been present in their origins, a black girl (the Zanj, from East Africa, were considered the lowest human race on earth) and an unknown father.

ᶜArūs al-ᶜarāʾis and her lover have no dealings with them and they are merely seen from a distance. It is one of the many loose ends in the story, elements that are left undeveloped and do not seem to add anything meaningful to the main story.

—The Cohabiting Bedouin Siblings

Otto Rank, who has no difficulty in finding countless stories of incest in western literature until the time of writing, a hundred years ago, says that in the *Thousand and One Nights* 'we encounter the theme of sibling love again and again'.[170] He is correct only if 'love' is understood to include non-incestuous brotherly and sisterly love. This is hardly likely in his case, and he therefore grossly exaggerates, unless one takes his 'again and again' literally as 'a couple of times'. His two examples, the 'Tale of the First Calender' and 'The Miraculous Tale of Omar Alnuman and His Sons Sharkan and Dhul Makan', virtually exhaust the theme as it appears in explicit terms.

Sibling love that would have counted for Rank as certainly incestuous, if only subliminally, is found in the story of Ḥammād the Bedouin,[171] which is embedded in the long tale of King ᶜUmar ibn al-Nuᶜmān. Ḥammād ibn al-Fazārī is another villainous narrator. A robber and kidnapper, he is captured and about to be executed. He hopes to be spared by telling a strange story, a stratagem that often works in the *Thousand and One Nights* and which, of course, is in fact the ploy of ploys in the collection as a whole. Here, for once, it misfires, because Ḥammād relates one of his own crimes.

During a hunting party he and his friends lose their way in the desert. They see a tent and are regaled on water, milk, dates and meat by a young man and his sister. Ḥammād asks the hand of the sister in marriage in blunt terms ('I want you to marry her to me, or else I'll kill you and carry her off'). Not wholly surprisingly, the brother (who later introduces himself as ᶜAbbād ibn Tamīm ibn Thaᶜlaba) refuses. Duels ensue, in which the young man kills Ḥammād's friends one after the other but spares the life of Ḥammād himself, treating him as an honoured guest. A few days later, Ḥammād treacherously kills his host in his sleep; the sister throws herself on a sword, killing herself. The Bedouin robs their goods and leaves.

Have the siblings been lovers? If even Richard Burton does not add a note on possible sexual meanings, then who should? One must admit that it is rather odd to find the two living together in a lone tent, away from their family. But this is medieval Arabic Disneyland, not reality, as is clear also from the fact that the food is served on a silver plate. The appearance of the couple is that of the stereotypical beautiful lovers in the Arabian Nights genre. Before the fighting starts, the anxious girl addresses her brother in verse, in which she says she cannot live without him; rather, 'I shall kill myself in my passionate love for you!' For 'love' she uses not only *ḥubb* but the rather stronger *hawā* as well. The brother answers in verse and prose, saying 'If I die, do not let anybody possess you!', at which she slaps her face: 'God forbid, brother!'. She is true to her word, but before killing herself she mourns her brother in the style of the old Bedouin women poets, not forgetting to mention how handsome he is even in death:

You lie felled to the ground,
  your face in its beauty resembling the round moon.

She claims that her brother had wanted to marry her to the robber, after all, in spite of his earlier protestations. The narrator is, of course, unreliable in deed and most likely in word, too. Although there are some superficial points of resemblance with the story of the couple in Fatḥ Alley (a sibling couple living together, a suicide with a sword that comes out of the back), there is only a whiff of a hint of improper love in this preposterous tale, which redeems itself by what Mia Gerhardt called its 'surprise effect'.[172]

—*Burning Love Between Siblings*

In the tale of the First Calender we have a true case of incestuous sibling love,[173] thrown in gratuitously, without a clear link with the context.[174] The story being easily accessible, only a summary is given here.

The 'calender' (or calandar, dervish, or mendicant), originally a prince, is told by his male cousin, the king's son, to escort a veiled lady to a tomb at a cemetery. The cousin arrives, too, with water, mortar and an adze. A tomb is broken open. Under an iron cover a staircase is disclosed, leading to a vault. The cousin and the woman descend; the narrator is told to put back the cover and the earth. The next day he feels he ought to return to the spot, but he has hidden it so well that he cannot find it. Later—after a digression in which he loses an eye and his father (also a king) is killed, but which will not detain us here—he tells his cousin's father what happened to his son. They go to the cemetery and now recognize the spot. They open the tomb and at the bottom of the stairs smoke rises. Undaunted, they proceed into the vault. Amid stores of food they find the couple, lying in an embrace on a bed, under a canopy, charred to a cinder. The uncle then spits in his son's face and cries, 'You deserved it, you evil creature! This is your punishment in this world. There remains the punishment in the hereafter, which will be worse and more lasting!' Then he slaps the corpse with his sandal. By now his shocked nephew would like to hear an explanation, which he gets:[175]

> Nephew, my son was in madly in love with his sister from early childhood. I would forbid him to see her. They are still very young, I said to myself. But when they grew older the ugly thing (*al-qabīḥ*) happened between them. I heard about this and could not believe it. But I scolded him in eloquent words and said to him, 'Beware of these ugly deeds which no-one has ever done before you and no-one will do after you; or else we shall live in shame and loss of reputation until we die, and the story will be spread by every caravan. Take care that these deeds will not be carried out by you, for I'll be very angry and kill you.'[176] Then I kept him away from her, and her from him, but the wicked girl was terribly in love with him. Satan had taken possession of her. When the boy saw that I had kept

> him away from her, he secretly prepared this subterranean place and brought food here, as you have seen. When I had gone out hunting he took the opportunity and came to this place. But God Almighty, praised be He, was jealous towards him and her, and burnt them.

The penultimate verbal phrase, *ghāra ʿalayhi wa-ʿalayhā* (not found in Mahdī's text) contains some subtle punning. The verb has to be connected with the root *GhYR* 'to be jealous, or zealous'; as in the Hebrew Bible, God is a jealous god. The Prophet is reported to have said, 'God is jealous and a believer is jealous. God's jealousy happens when a believer commits what has been forbidden to him'.[177] At the same time there may be an intended pun with the word *ghār*, 'cave'. A superficial but possible reading is to interpret the verb *ghāra* (more usually *aghāra*) *ʿalā* as 'to raid, attack', coming from the root *GhWR*.

There are some interesting parallels with al-Tanūkhī's story about the sibling lovers.[178] When the father scolds his son, he seems, again, more concerned about the family's reputation than the salvation of his children's souls. But whereas in al-Tanūkhī's story the father's feelings are mixed, for in spite of his 'good riddance' he keeps longing for his children, in the present story the father gloats about the terrible punishments, earthly and infernal, and indecorously abuses his son's corpse. This, together with the horror of cave and charred bodies, adds a cheap gruesomeness that is absent from al-Tanūkhī. The most striking parallel is the subterranean cave, which like the house in Fatḥ Alley is a confined 'fine and private place' where the lovers 'do ... embrace'. *Pace* Marvell's poem the lovers embrace in the tomb: their cave is a sepulchre. The Calender's story has conflated the two locations, house and tomb, of the other tale. Burning, or being struck by a thunderbolt, is the fate of many incestuous lovers in the classical and medieval European tradition.[179] It foreshadows the hell-fire that is in store for them, just as the wicked mother in al-Tanūkhī's story is to be burned in hell. The difference is that in the popular version of the *Nights* a popular demand for poetic justice is satisfied: the lovers also receive punishment on (or rather under) earth.

Even though the story belongs to the core of the *Thousand and One Nights* it has received relatively little attention. Burton, in his translation, comments in a note: 'Incest is now abominable everywhere except amongst the overcrowded poor of great and civilized cities', adding that 'such unions were common and lawful amongst ancient and highly cultivated peoples'.[180] He is being ironic, one supposes, when he uses the word 'civilized' here. The note has disappeared, understandably, from the edition 'prepared for household reading' by his widow, Lady Burton, in which the 'sister' has become a 'half-sister';[181] this has been adopted by Dawood in his post-Victorian translation. In a polygynous society, after all, the word *ukht* often means 'half-sister'. The translation by E. W. Lane, also made for a genteel reading public, transforms the sister into a foster-sister. In the notes, found only in the three-volume edition, he confesses that he has made 'a slight alteration', but 'it is one which does not in the least affect the consistency of the tale.'[182]

That this prudishness was not limited to the Victorian age is clear from Shelley's long poem *The Revolt of Islam* (published 1818), which has more to do with the French Revolution than with Islam. It deals with the love (sexually consummated in Canto VI) of Laon and Cythna, who were full siblings in the original version but had to be turned in brother and foster-sister on publication. Similarly, Byron, in his 'Turkish Tale', *The Bride of Abydos*, changes the lovers Zuleika and Selim, half-siblings in his first draft, into cousins.

—Blood that Yearns for Blood

The only remaining story in the *Nights* that is relevant is an episode in the very long tale (or romance, novel, epic, *geste*) of King ᶜUmar al-Nuᶜmān.[183] It is, 'first of all, a family saga set against the backdrop of the continuous struggle between the Muslims, the Byzantines, and the crusaders'.[184] ᶜUmar, king of Baghdad and surroundings including India and China, has one son, Sharkān, and 360 concubines, one of whom gives birth to twins, a boy called Ḍawᵓ al-Makān and a girl named Nuzhat al-Zamān. Years later, this girl is abducted and eventually sold as a slave to Sharkān, who is unaware that she is his half-sister. Having freed her, he marries her. A daughter is born, called Quḍiya fa-Kān. Recognizing an amulet the mother puts on the baby, Sharkān realizes that he has married his half-sister. Rather than keeping their knowledge a secret and save their marriage, they are filled with remorse. He divorces her, marries her to a chamberlain, and sends them off. Later, Quḍiya fa-Kān marries Kān Mā Kān, who is the son of Ḍawᵓ al-Makān and thus her mother's brother's son: perfectly legal by Islamic rules, although FZD[185] rather than the customary FBD.

Here we find, not the conscious incest of the preceding tales, but the common motif of incest committed unknowingly, brought about by Fate instead of human choice. Some of the names seem to reflect this: Quḍiya fa-Kān and Kān Mā Kān are fairy-tale names, not real ones, meaning roughly 'It Was Decreed So It Happened' and 'It Happened Once Upon A Time', respectively. Other names reinforce the fictional atmosphere: Nuzhat al-Zamān ('Entertainment of the Age'), Ḍawᵓ al-Makān ('Light of the Place'). The remaining relevant name, Sharkān, is something of a puzzle, for it has some negative associations. The name is not attested elsewhere, unlike e.g. the not uncommon early Arabic name Sharīk (literally, 'Partner'), and may have been formed as a variation, to rhyme with the several other names in *-ān*. In Islamic times, the name Sharīk lost much of its appeal, because the word became the standard term for 'partner' of God, the existence of which is emphatically denied by Islam, in which polytheism, called *shirk*, is the gravest sin imaginable. A different but equally negative connotation is inspired by the presence of the verb *kān* ('it was, it happened') in other names. Reinterpreting Sharkān as Sharr-Kān, one arrives at the meaning 'Evil That Happened'.[186] This may not be the original reading of the name, but it is one that is at least supported by the Arabic text itself, near the beginning of the story: ᶜUmar called (his son) Shar(r)kān 'because he grew up as a bane of Time's banes (*āfa min āfāt al-zamān*)...' This is not necessarily a bad reflection on the hero-to-be, for traditional male names in Arabic have negative or violent meanings (from ᶜAbbās 'Frowner' to Ṣaddām 'Collider'), denoting power and domination.

Shar(r)kān, like most of the other members of his family, is not a model hero without flaws, however, nor is Nuzhat al-Zamān, his half-sister and wife, a paragon of virtue. She has brought the misery upon herself by running off, before she has fully grown up, with Ḍawᵓ al-Makān, her full brother, in order to go on pilgrimage. Or at least that is what they and the narrator say. Although they live and travel together for a considerable time, there is no hint of sibling incest here; but the modern reader may raise an eyebrow. That nothing serious happened between them becomes obvious when, later, one is told that Sharkān takes her maidenhood.

The incest between Nuzhat al-Zamān and Sharkān is sinless, at least as long as they do not know. The girl is, needless to say, a dazzling beauty, and happens to be decked in her finery, straight from the bath, when her brother sees her for the first time after the long separation. In addition, she has shown herself adept in all the sciences and arts, able to quote Ibn al-Bayṭār and Avicenna. In any normal love story, this would be more than enough to make the two fall in love. Yet, there is something else: 'When king Sharkān saw her, blood yearned for blood (*ḥanna l-dam ilā l-dam*)'.[187] In other words, incestuous love is presented as something natural in this pre-Freudian statement. Immediately after this, the narrator emphasizes that this happened unconsciously: she had been separated from him since she was a young girl; indeed, he had never seen her[188] and only heard about her birth years after the event. In a Westermarckian interpretation, this would mean that love between them would not be hampered by the 'familiarity breeds contempt' mechanism, while the blood-yearning-for-blood is a mere fictional device.

Then, at the birth of 'It Was Decreed So It Happened', knowledge turns the sinless deed into a sin. Sharkān takes it badly. Staring at the amulet the truth begins to dawn upon him: 'his reason left him and he became very angry'. When he has grasped the facts, 'his heart trembled, his colour paled, he began to shudder, he hung his head, and realized that she was his sister, from his father's side. Then he lost consciousness.'[189] Soon after, having heard her story, he makes a decision and says to himself: 'How can I be married to my sister? I must marry her to one of my chamberlains. If anything transpires, I shall claim that I have divorced her before going in to her.' Nuzhat al-Zamān, too, is shocked by the knowledge: 'When she realized, she lost her right mind, cried, slapped her face and said "We have fallen into a grave sin! What should we do, and what do I say to my father and mother when they ask me: How did you get this daughter?"'

Unlike al-Tanūkhī's rebellious and antinomian lovers, the couple will not persist in their situation. In fact, they act not unlike the parents of sinners of the other stories, in showing themselves keen to protect their reputation and avoid a scandal. The woman speaks of a 'grave sin', but moral scruples seem to be in the background and there is no reference to Islamic law or to punishment on earth or in the hereafter. The whole affair, including its practical solution, is decreed by God, which is why they give the offspring of their union her very appropriate name. Thus they console each other, he kisses her head, and we hear nothing more about the love they may still have kept for each other.

It would be beyond the scope of this study to investigate how this episode functions in the larger framework of the epic tale. Suffice it to mention the opinion of Wen-chin Ouyang, who sees it as an introduction to the turning point in the tale, between disintegration of the family and re-aggregation and reunion.[190] Thus the incest seems to take the reunion one step too far, but it was a step in the right direction, at least.

—Father's Wives Again

There are a few stories in the *Thousand and One Nights* that hinge on the sexual rivalry, real or imagined, between father and son. The best known story of this type is known variously as The Wiles of Women, The Craft and Malice of Women, or The King, his Son, his Favourite and the Seven Viziers;[191] it is also known independently, as the *Book of Sindibad* (not to be confused with the teller of tall tales, the travelling merchant wrongly known as 'Sindbad the Sailor'). This is a collection of tales enframed by a story about a prince who is accosted by his father's favourite concubine. The story is widely known outside Arabic, in Middle-Eastern and European versions. The prince does not succumb to the temptation, and the woman then accuses him of indecent assault: the Potiphar theme, as Rank calls it,[192] or the Phaedra plot, as does Archibald.[193] It is, indeed, an old motif. A very similar tale is found in the ancient Egyptian story of *The Two Brothers*, where the wicked woman is not a father's concubine but an elder brother's wife who, in a sense, is a kind of mother-figure.[194] In Arabic the motif has an early antecedent in the report about the pre-Islamic poet-hero ᶜAntara ibn Shaddād.[195] There may be a connection with a line from his famous *Muᶜallaqa*, said to refer to the woman in question:

O wild ewe of the hunt: To whomever you are allowed,
you are forbidden to me (if only she were not!).[196]

It has been suggested[197] that the frame story of the Wiles of Women is derived from a late-classical Greek tale, the strongly misogynistic tale of Secundus the Silent (late 2nd-early 3rd century AD), which was very popular in the European Middle Ages and was translated into various languages, including Latin, Syriac, Armenian and Arabic.[198] However, the behaviour of the young prince in the 'Wiles of Women' story and that of Secundus could not be more different, and I cannot see any strong connection between the *Life of Secundus* and the *Book of Sindbad*, for which the traditionally held Pahlavi origin seems more convincing. This Secundus, eager to test his hypothesis that all women are whores, creeps into his mother's bed; in the dark he succeeds in tempting her for money, but he is careful to avoid actual consummation. Kissing her breasts 'with prolonged kisses', he argues that he does so because they have nourished him as a babe; it would not be right 'to approach that place whence I issued', a place like the Red Sea in which infidels perish, or like the fiery furnace of Babylon in which only the pious are preserved unharmed.[199] These comparisons seem to make the implication that Secundus is himself impious, with which a modern reader can only concur. The mother, greatly shocked and contrite, hangs herself, whereas her son becomes a celebrated, though silent, sage. In the series of questions and definitions that make up most of the remainder of the tale, Secundus defines 'Woman' as 'a poisonous serpent, ... a creeping thing that crawls along secretly ... Her garment is smooth like the skin of a serpent'.[200]

This Christian Arabic text did apparently not circulate widely in Muslim circles, for the lurid story is not known in sources written by Muslims. It is true that Secundus the Silent is briefly mentioned in al-Masʿūdī (as Sāqundus *al-faylasūf al-ṣāmit*, 'the Silent Philosopher') in the account of Emperor Hadrian,[201] and that his definitions or sentences are found in Muslim Arabic sources.[202] The incest motif, however, is not mentioned there. The story seems to have reached Arabic popular literature: in his motif classification of Arab folklore, Hasan El-Shamy gives under motifs T410-T428, dealing with incest, the subcategory T412.2 'Incognito son tempts mother to see whether all women are wicked'.[203] It concerns the final part of a rather fantastic and composite Egyptian tale. Clever Muḥammad, after a series of adventures in childhood, returns home and tests his mother (after having been killed by her and having been revived by his bride). The mother succumbs to his advances, but he kills her together with her illegitimate child. He lives happily ever after, it would seem.[204] This tale was recorded in 1970 from an Orthodox Copt: again in a Christian milieu.

In medieval Europe stories of incestuous stepmothers are very rare;[205] one supposes the greater frequency in Arabic is related to the polygyny allowed by traditional Islam, whereby, it will be remembered, a man is able to have four wives and as many concubines as he is able to maintain. Since popular stories deal, preferably, with kings rather than the lower classes, and kings can afford a larger harem than commoners, it is only to be expected that the affairs between sons and father's wives or concubines are relatively common. As El-Shamy points out, in connection with a widespread humorous tale, affairs with father's wives 'should not be viewed as oedipal, for both the stepmother and the stepson belong to the same age-group; the stepmother is thus not a maternal figure.'[206]

An alleged affair with one's father's wife makes for a good story or joke,[207] but the incest, if one can call it that, does not offer anything that could interest us here. A version of the tale to which El-Shamy refers, in the preceding quotation, is also contained in the so-called Wortley-Montagu Manuscript, with further stories of the *Thousand and One Nights*.[208] This is a *fabliau*, a funny bawdy tale of a son who seduces his father's wife, upon which the father divorces the woman and remarries; the story then repeats itself. After some humorous developments, the story ends on a serious note when the boy is beheaded and his latest two female accomplices strangled by the authorities: an ending absent from the modern version. Finally, 'The Loves of al-Hayfāʾ and Yūsuf',[209] also from the Wortley-Montagu manuscript, tells the adventures of prince Yūsuf, who has to flee from his father's wrath after he has raped one of the latter's concubines, even before his father could deflower her. Being as beautiful as his namesake Joseph, his crime, quickly told, seems quickly forgotten and remains unpunished: it is not much more than a narrative device to get him moving towards the equally beautiful princess al-Hayfāʾ, whom he happily marries in the end. In all these tales involving affairs with fathers' wives, the act is not really a matter of sinning against nature or religion, resulting in guilty feelings or psychological struggle. How little Islamic rules matter in fairyland is clear from the complete ease with which the hero is able to be married to full sisters simultaneously.[210] Sex with one or more of one's father's wives is a matter of crime against society and rebellion against the father. In a Freudian analysis, there is no real difference, since the father's wife is a surrogate mother. Non-Freudians, however, must distinguish between the 'real' incestuous unions, where 'blood yearns for blood', and other forbidden unions. The differences in narrative functions between the two types seems to give support to the distinction.

—*Popular Epics*

The Thousand and One Nights, though popular, is in fact a hybrid between 'polite literature' and the truly popular epics such as that of the Banū Hilāl. Admittedly, it is impossible to make clear-cut distinctions between, for example, the Stories of the Prophets, the *Nights*, and the popular epics. Thus a version of the story of Namrūd and his incestuous behaviour is found in *Sīrat ʿAntar*, as mentioned above. The popular epics, all anonymous and impossible to date with any precision, are vast, and I cannot claim any great familiarity with them. The useful survey and index by Lyons, on which I have relied much, reveals that they cannot be considered a very rich source for our topic: his entry 'incest motif' in the 'Comparative index' is extremely learned, ranging over a multitude of civilizations and languages,[211] but the actual references to the Arabic epics are relatively few in number.[212] The dominant kind is that of one-sided father—daughter love, or its more sinister variant, father—daughter rape. One instance has been mentioned above: the Arabic folk-version of Bahman and Humāy.[213] In the epic of Sayf ibn Dhī Yazan, set in Yemen before and during the coming of Islam, a girl called 'Morning Star' (Kawkab al-Ṣabāḥ) marries Marʿash, king of Jinn and a Muslim, after her father, the pagan king Azraq ('Blue'), had tried to seduce her.[214] Marriage with Jinn is deemed possible, not only in fairy-stories but in serious and scholarly Muslim treatises;[215] it would certainly be considered better than coupling with a father who is aptly named after an ill-omened colour. Azraq is killed by Marʿash; all those involved seem to be minor characters in the story.

The Arabic version of the epic of Ḥamza, a story about a heroic uncle of the Prophet Muḥammad, seems to be a translation from a Persian original. Here one again finds a father who is in love with his daughter, even though no seduction or worse takes place.[216] Ḥusn ('Beauty') is the daughter of king ʿAnīd ('Obdurate'), and he tells her that he loves her 'as a man loves the object of his worship'. She has, however, fallen in love with a young man whom she marries, only to be killed soon after by her lover's rival. The names of father and daughter are Arabic, but it seems they belong neither to the Arabs nor the Persians, the two opposing parties of the epic.

Certainly Persian is Sharwīn, who loves his own daughter in the epic of ʿAntar.[217] He pretends to agree to a marriage of the girl with the ruler of Isfahan, but has him murdered; nothing more is told about the relationship between father and daughter, both very minor characters in the vast epic.[218]

The redoubtable Crusader-fighting Mamluk sultan Baybars (reg. 658-676/1260-1277) became the hero of a popular epic where the enemies are mostly Christians instead of Persians. A Copt named Qabṭāwīl, a sorcerer in Upper Egypt, wants to marry his own daughter, Tāj Nās ('People's Crown').[219] The priests tell him that in their religion this is not permitted, although it might be sanctioned by Juwān (perhaps a corruption of Johannes), leader of the Christians and the arch-villain of the epic. Juwān agrees on condition that the father destroys the Muslims. The daughter, virtuous and converted to Islam, marries another Muslim called Shīḥa. There is question of apparent incest because he and Qabṭāwīl have magically been transformed into each other's shapes, but the daughter is saved and kills her father in a magical duel. In a later episode, another Christian father, Sāṭirīn, is in love with his daughter, Ward al-Masīḥ ('Christ's Rose').[220] Again, the daughter converts to Islam and marries a Muslim; her father, perhaps more from love than conviction, becomes a Muslim too. Both being on the good side, it is understood that nothing untoward happens. Judging by the father's name, we have here an echo of the old story of the king of Hatra, Sanatruk or Sāṭirūn, of whom it was said that he inclined towards the Zoroastrian custom of marrying daughters, and his daughter al-Naḍīra, who betrayed him.[221] Further on in the epic, the action moves briefly to China, the Emperor of which is in love with his daughter Zuhūr ('Flowers') and wishes to marry her.[222] When told by a Muslim suitor of the girl that this is in fact forbidden, the emperor goes to the other extreme and kills the girl. He soon regrets this deed and does penance by converting to Islam.

Wicked fathers and pure girls: there is hardly an exception. An earlier, Greek example is found in the story of Apollonius of Tyre, which became extremely popular (and was used by Shakespeare in his *Pericles*), a tale that 'might almost have been written to counteract the story of Myrrha as Ovid tells it',[223] or of other wicked daughters such as those of Lot. It has recently been argued by Dick Davis that the story of Apollonius is roughly contemporary with the Parthian tale retold in Persian as *Dārābnāma* by Ṭarsūsī (6th/12th century), where a similar father—daughter rape is found with some strikingly corresponding details, and that the two may somehow be connected in view of the widespread presence of Greek culture in the ancient Middle East since the time of Alexander the Great.[224] Father—daughter rape, which, as Davis has noticed, is not rarely used as 'a device of initiating a long and complex narrative',[225] is common, too, in European late medieval narratives;[226] and one has the impression, for once, that popular literature in this respect reflects the harsh facts of the real world, which are often obscured in much of the literature of higher status with its misogynistic tendencies. One difference with reality is that the wicked fathers in popular stories are almost invariably kings,[227] but this does of course not mean that incest was more rife in high circles. One girl, ᶜĀqiṣa, in the epic of Sayf ibn Dhī Yazan, rejects suitors and says that she only wants to marry a king like her father, a description that seems to suit only her brother Sayf, thus echoing the argument used by the mother of Wīs in Gurgānī's 'Parthian' romance.[228] Sayf replies, 'Have you ever heard of anyone marrying his sister?'[229] In the end she happily agrees to the marriage that her family had arranged for her. In the epic of Baybars, Fitnat al-Masīḥ ('Christ's Seduction'), the daughter of king of Rūm (Byzantium) asks a Muslim man to marry her, although he is already married to her sister and points out that in Islam one cannot marry two sisters simultaneously.[230] As we have seen, in other popular stories this Islamic rule is conveniently forgotten. Islamic regulations are sometimes projected back in pre-Islamic times: ᶜAntar recoils from his great love, ᶜAbla, when he is falsely told that she is his milk-sister.[231]

In general, it is striking, firstly, that incestuous love is strongly associated in these stories with non-Muslims and non-Arabs and, secondly, that virtually all the affairs remain chaste, without producing offspring from incestuous couplings. One of the rare exceptions, on both counts, is found in the epic of the Banū Hilāl, a wide-spread saga that deals with the migrations of Arab nomads to North Africa in the eleventh century. Among its countless characters is a person called ᶜAzīz ibn Khālih, which means 'ᶜAzīz, the son of his maternal uncle'. It is to be noted that in another version he is called ᶜAzīz ibn Khālid, and is thus given a respectable genealogy. Is this a later, cleaned-up version, or is it the original name, colloquially shortened until it seemed to suggest an incestuous birth? If the latter, then the story about him was made up as an explanation. One does not need to puzzle long over the name to realize that the said ᶜAzīz is the offspring of a brother and sister. The story involves another bed-trick, and even a bed-prick. Abū Zayd, the principal hero of the saga, was jealous of his own strength, to the extent of being unwilling to pass it on to offspring. He therefore makes a practice of *coitus interruptus*, much to the annoyance of his wife and his tribesmen. Just as had happened to Luqmān (whose story may have inspired the anonymous narrators), a sister of Abū Zayd offers her services to the community by taking the woman's place while he is unaware of the wife-swap. At the crucial moment, she thwarts his withdrawal method by driving a needle into his back. Thus ᶜAzīz is conceived.[232] As in the stories of Luqmān and Lot, or of Adam's children for that matter, incest is a means to a practical end here, and not the summation of a sinful unquenchable passion. It is, like inbreeding, a way of keeping it all in the family, whether it be wealth, progeny, or heritable physical and intellectual qualities.

Giovanni Canova, one of the foremost Banū Hilāl specialists, who briefly deals with the story of ᶜAzīz Uncleson, adds in a note that a similar story was recently collected in Bahrain and published by Hasan El-Shamy.[233] This category ('The Sister who Desires a Son Sired by her Brother Achieves her Goal') is indeed found in the great collection of motifs by El-Shamy in his *Folk Traditions of the Arab World*. There, under 'Incest' and 'Incestuous'[234] one finds numerous references. Although this may whet one's appetite, a thorough study of these stories is beyond the scope of the present study, which is concerned with 'classical' or 'medieval' literature and not with relatively recently collected tales, timeless though many of them may be.

It ought at least to be mentioned that the motif of the lecherous father who desires his daughter is found in Arabic variations of the 'Cinderella' story, and has been studied by Ibrahim Muhawi.[235] He argues that in the Arabic versions the matter is, more than in European versions, linked with the question of the ownership of the woman's body, religion and morals remaining in the background. Blood-relationship gives the father or brother a right of ownership, a right that may be confused with sexual entitlement. Finally, an interesting anthropological analysis of a complex of Sudanese folk tales is given by Ahmed Al-Shahi and F. C. T. Moore. In 'Fatima the Beautiful' a girl carrying water asks for help; but her family will not help her unless she marries her own brother. She escapes to the woods and semi-desert, consorting with a monstrous creature, and finally returns to sedentary life, finding a partner outside her own clan. As Al-Shahi and Moore point out, it is a story of an escape from in-marrying to out-marrying, associated with stability of land tenure and readjustment of it, respectively, expressed in extreme terms, from incest via unnatural out-marrying to an acceptable compromise.[236] Another Sudanese story is an example of the common motif of unwitting incest narrowly averted, when Wad el-Nimair marries his own daughter, who had survived being thrown into the river by her seven(!) wicked stepmothers. Wad el-Nimair is warned just in time, before the consummation of the marriage.[237]

Dreams

Dream interpretation in Islam comprises an extensive body of texts.[238] They offer an interesting mixture of indigenous and ancient, non-Arabic material, in the latter category notably the very popular Greek work by Artemidorus (second half of second century AD), the *Oneirocritica*, which was translated into Arabic. Much material in Arabic is ascribed to the famous Abū Bakr Muḥammad ibn Sīrīn (d. 110/728), the father of Arabic dream interpretation. This material, in turn, influenced Byzantine dream books, where Ibn Sīrīn, or at least his name, lived on as 'Achmet ibn Sereim'.[239] It should go without saying that the dream interpretations should be read with fresh eyes, not through Freudian glasses, darkly.[240] Incest, already in Artemidorus, is a very common topic.

The Arabic dream books are of various kinds, some offering true, or allegedly true, dreams as told by the dreamers who are then provided with an interpretation. Others—those I have relied on mostly—are classifications, in Artemidorus' manner, of all kinds of possible dreams or dream elements and motifs, arranged systematically or alphabetically; these may also include actually experienced dreams with their interpretations, given in anecdotal form. Very often, a dream of one particular object, concept or event is given a bewildering multitude of explanations. This may be explained partly by the compilatory nature of the texts consulted, but one likes to think that this would also facilitate the use of dream interpretation in daily life. Dreams were, after all, rightly or wrongly, considered as being highly significant, throwing light not so much into the repressed past and the darknesses of the subconscious as on the uncertain future, as a means for prognostication. A specialist, like a modern psychoanalyst, could choose from the many interpretations precisely the one that might suit the dreamer or the circumstances.

—*Dreams Denoting Incest*

In the Arabic texts consulted by me, incest is found both in the dreams and the interpretations. An instance of the latter is given by ᶜAbd al-Ghanī al-Nābulusī (d. 1143/1731) in his large compilation. Dreaming of irrigating an olive tree with olive oil stands for intercourse with one's mother; it is the same if one sprinkles vinegar on a vine, or, even more oddly, if one urinates earth onto the ground in one's dream.[241] The interpretation employs the natural metaphor of impregnation and reproduction or fruit-bearing, which is often helped by the concurrence, in Arabic, of grammatical gender and biological sex. Thus *shajara* 'tree' and *arḍ* 'earth' are both feminine, and while the word for 'vine' used here, *karm*, is masculine, one could in this case easily supply a feminine variant, *karma*. The olive-oil pouring motif is found as an actual dream in another work, ascribed to Ibn Sīrīn:

> It is told that a man came to him [*viz.* Ibn Sīrīn] and said,
> —I dreamt that I was pouring olive oil at the base of an olive tree.
> —Please tell me your story.
> —I was taken captive as a young boy. Then I was freed and I reached manhood.
> —Are you married?
> —No, but I have bought a slave-girl.[242]
> —Look into the matter and make sure she isn't your mother.
> The man went away and kept investigating the girl's background until in the end he found out that she was his mother.
> It is also told that a man came to him and said,
> —I dreamt that I went to the trunk of an olive tree. I pressed it and drank its sap.
> —Fear God! said Ibn Sīrīn. Your dream means that your wife is your milk-sister.
> The man investigated the matter and it was as he had said.[243]

The interpretation of the first dream is fairly straightforward. The tree/mother is irrigated/impregnated with the oil/semen of its/her own fruit/son. The dreamer himself is not strictly needed in the analogy: he merely serves as the instrument in the dream and the analogue in the interpretation. The second dream is slightly more complicated, for if one construes an analogy as in the preceding case one runs into difficulty. Here the dreamer drinks the sap/milk from the trunk/breast of the tree/foster-mother, but where does the sister fit in? She is obviously the fruit/offspring of the tree/mother, but that implies that the dreamer's consumption of the olive is equated with being married to the woman. The analogy of consumption and sexual consummation is by no means rare, but there remains a kind of asymmetry because the sister is metamorphosed, in the dream, into the vegetable realm whereas the brother/husband remains human throughout. Needless to say, dreams, like poetry, have their own kind of logic. Just as poetry has its poetic syllogism, as discussed by al-Fārābī (d. 339/950) and others who elaborated on Aristotle's *Poetics*, there is an oneiric syllogism. The two kinds of logic are similar in some ways, in spite of the harsh things the oneirocritics say about poetry being falsehood.[244] Both make use of metaphor and metonymy, based on resemblance or contiguity of concepts and objects, and the very common etymological or pseudo-etymological methods of dream interpretation are matched by paronomasia and other forms or wordplay in poetry.

The oneirocritical logic is usually not difficult to decipher. Dreaming that one urinates on bread also denotes incest,[245] apparently because bread may stand for one's mother, by whom one is fed and raised,[246] or for one's child.[247] Urinating into one's own nose, too, denotes incest:[248] a nose is said to stand not only for genitalia but also for one's relatives,[249] and urine for semen. Saᶜīd ibn al-Musayyab (d. 94/712 or 713), one of the 'seven jurists of Medina' and also known as an oneirocritic, was consulted about a dream in which a man urinated into his hand. He explained it as indicating an incestuous marriage; and sure enough, upon investigation, the man's wife was found to have a milk-relationship with him. Another man's dream of urinating on the trunk of an olive tree also revealed to Ibn al-Musayyab an unwittingly contracted forbidden marriage.[250] Urinating blood in one's dream, we are told, is a bad sign. It may stand for having intercourse with one's wife while she is menstruating (strongly disapproved) or that she will miscarry: here the blood stands for real blood. However, if the blood seems to burn or hurt the penis, it means having intercourse with a divorced woman (apparently meaning divorced by oneself, so that she would be forbidden) or a forbidden relative without knowing.[251] Here the blood is the 'genealogical' kind of blood which makes us speak of blood-relatives. If a man dreams of intercourse while he himself is menstruating (for in dreams everything is possible), it again means that he is committing incest.[252] Turning partly into a woman as an indication of incest is found in another anecdote about Ibn Sīrīn. There he explains the dream of a man who told him that he dreamed that he had an enormous breast. 'You are fornicating with a blood-relative (*maḥram*)', said Ibn Sīrīn, and the author explains: 'For the breast was from him and his skin, and that means a *maḥram*. The interpretation of this dream can only be forbidden intercourse.'[253] A female breast, in a man's dream, stands for his wife or his daughter, says al-Nābulusī; he, too, believes that the dream in question refers to incest. Bestiality in dreams is not necessarily bad, and even being the passive partner in sex with animals could denote unexpected benefits or good things coming from one's enemy, provided that the animal is tame and well-behaved in the dream, but 'it may also denote copulating with women of the forbidden degrees (...) if this is corroborated by other evidence'.[254] Blood and milk come together in the dream of sucking the former from one's index finger and the latter from one's thumb in a dream: this means intercourse with a woman and her sister (which, it will be remembered, is forbidden). Another authority thinks it is about sex with mother and daughter.[255] Dreaming of cream is a good sign, as is eating honey; but eating cream together with honey is not: some interpret it as incest with one's mother.[256] It is not that the combination is too rich to be good: the explanation has to be sought in the common association of honey with sex (even the Prophet is said to have used the word *ʿusayla* 'sweet little honey' as a euphemism for intercourse[257]), linked with the association of cream with milk and of milk with mother. Dreaming that one pierces a pearl with a wooden drill means incest:[258] piercing a pearl is a commonplace expression in Arabic for deflowering a girl and using a wooden drill seems to indicate the impropriety (rather than the impossibility) of the act. A trouser-cord or waistband denotes a woman for a male dreamer; if he sees one in his trousers in his dream, his wife is forbidden to him but she will bear him a son.[259] The explanation is not wholly transparent here, and does not necessarily involve incest since wives may be forbidden for other reasons. The dreams are sometimes bizarre. Dreaming of copulating with oneself (presumably buggering, but the mechanics are not explained) may denote several things such as worry, stinginess, divorcing one's wife or severe illness, but also, not illogically, incest with one's kin.[260]

Metaphorics are not always necessary. Dreaming of becoming a Zoroastrian means that one has rejected Islam by committing 'obscene deeds' (*fawāḥish*); a word that, in view of the opinions treated in Chapter Two, must refer to incest rather than, for instance, fire-worship.[261] Some dreams even stand precisely for what they picture. A man who dreamt that he slipped in the public bath is told by the interpreter to expect a mishap; and he duly slips in the bath, breaking a leg.[262] However, it is more rewarding for everyone concerned if things are not what they seem. Thus a public bath (*ḥammām*) may denote hell, because of the heat, the fire, the noise, and the smells. Normally, however, it stands for a woman, because it is associated with nakedness and one sweats in its dark rooms (standing for ejaculation). Consequently, dreaming of being in the bath with one's clothes on means that there is some matter, good or bad depending on the circumstances, involving a woman with whom there should be no sexual contact, including one's mother, daughter or sister.[263] A *ḥammām* could also stand for one's *ḥam*, or father-in-law, by the method of pseudo-etymological explanation. By the same token a vine (*karm*) may denote a magnanimous man (*karīm*), even though it is more often a woman on account of the grape's sweet taste, or the drunkenness that its fermented juice induces, similar to the intoxication of sex, as Ibn Sīrīn explains.[264] Dream interpretation is nothing if not flexible.

—Dreams About Incest

Dreaming about incestuous sex could mean precisely that, by dint of what was pointed out before. This, however, is not what the authorities say. Artemidorus' chapter on sexual intercourse in dreams begins with a long passage about fathers who bugger their sons from the age of five onwards, or having sex with their own daughters or mothers; it almost seems as if other, more normal forms of intercourse are treated as an afterthought.[265] His interpretations of heterosexual incestuous sex are often, but by no means always, negative. Much of Artemidorus' text found its way into the later Arabic treatises, which seem on the whole much less obsessed with incest. This has nothing to do with prudishness: sex is abundant, both in the dreams and their interpretations, and every imaginable form of it is found, in addition to some virtually unimaginable forms. In the great majority of cases, sexual dreams receive a non-sexual interpretation. Basically, being the active, penetrating partner is good, and it may denote power or material benefit, while being penetrated accordingly means humiliation or loss.

Artemidorus usually gives a negative explanation of incest dreams, but there are exceptions. It is the same with the Arabic dream books. Here are some dreams and their interpretations:

> He who dreams that he marries a woman from among his blood relations (*dhāt raḥim*) will rule his family.[266]

In a patriarchal society such domination is of course very desirable. Sex, or more precisely being the penetrating partner, is, as always, equated with power and dominance. However, just as exegetes and jurists had said when justifying the incest rules, sex implies aggression and is incompatible with true respect.

> If one dreams that one has intercourse with a woman of the forbidden degrees, then one has little love and sympathy for the person one does it with. Perhaps his affection for her will cease. If she is dead, it means that worries and grief will arise.[267]

It is added, however, that 'it is said that dreaming this is good for both the active and the passive partner'. The following gives the dream a positive twist by providing a happy ending:

> If one dreams, or is dreamed about (by someone else), that one has intercourse with one's mother, sister, or female blood-relative: this is only dreamt by someone who has broken with his relatives[268] and has been remiss in giving them their due; he will come back and tie the bonds of kinship again.[269]

This surprisingly positive interpretation is supported by a very similar passage:

> Sexual intercourse with a woman of the forbidden degrees means bonds[270] after despair, and gifts, especially in the case of the mother after one has broken with her, because it is a return to the place from which one came, with things to spend (*nafaqa*), turning to her after turning away. But if one (dreams that one) copulates with these women in the months of pilgrimage, or there are indications to that effect in the dream, then it means that one treads[271] with one's feet on the holy ground and one will attain what one desires there.[272]

The reference to pilgrimage may be partly based on the common designation of Mecca as 'Mother of Towns'. In addition, there is an obvious link between the words *maḥram* (woman of the forbidden degrees) and *muḥarram*, 'sacred'; the word *ḥaram* is used for the sacred area that comprises Mecca and Medina. The only reference to incest in the famous work on erotics, *The Perfumed Garden* by al-Nafzāwī (9th/15th century), found in a short digression on dreams, also explains dreaming of incest with mother or sister as a reference to treading on holy ground and going on pilgrimage.[273]—Such favourable explanations, while no doubt helpful in some situations, will not satisfy everyone. Dream books are not afraid of gross contradictions, and thus we also find a second opinion:

> It is told that a man came to Ibn Sīrīn and mentioned that he had had intercourse[274] with his mother; when he had done with her, he had intercourse with his sister. His right hand had been amputated. Then Ibn Sīrīn wrote his answer on a piece of paper, being too embarrassed to speak to the man: 'This man has no respect for his parents, breaks the bond with his kin, is stingy with favours, and behaves badly to his mother and sister.[275]

Dream interpreters are supposed to take the circumstances of the dream and the dreamer into account. The missing right hand provided an unmistakable clue: the man, apparently having been convicted of theft, is no good.[276] Another interpretation attempts to combine the positive and the negative:

> If one dreams of intercourse with one of his parents but without ejaculating, it means tying the bond with them; if he ejaculates, it means severing the bonds.[277]

The idea that incest with the mother denotes a return to one's origin is given a geographical interpretation by the same author:

> Sometimes intercourse of a man with his mother denotes that he will die in the town where he was born.[278]

Death is itself a kind of return (dust to dust), and therefore an incestuous dream with a deceased mother doubly points to death of the dreamer:

> If one dreams of intercourse with one's mother who is deceased, this means the end of his life's term, in view of God's word (Q 20:55), «From her we created you and we shall make you return into her, and from her we shall bring you forth another time.»[279]

Of course the writer knows that the feminine pronoun 'her' in the Qur'anic text refers not to a mother but to the earth, but such a simple and common metaphor is easily employed in dream interpretation. He continues by adding that according to another view incestuous dreams with a living mother means a return to her after absence. Incestuous dreams about dead kin are not invariably bad: it could mean a beneficent act towards the deceased, such as a prayer, or towards his offspring.[280] ᶜAbd al-Ghanī al-Nābulusī summarizes the views on sexual dreams involving the mother in a rich passage, beginning with straightforward Freud:

> If one dreams that one copulates with one's mother while she is still alive, this means enmity towards one's father; and if his father is ill, it means that he will die and the dreamer will become responsible for his mother's affairs and be like a spouse and a son to her at the same time. If he is hostile to his mother, it means that she will love him.
>
> If one is travelling, dreaming of intercourse with one's mother means one will return to her from one's travelling. If the man is poor or his mother wealthy, dreaming of intercourse with her means that he will get all he wants from her, or that she will die and he will inherit from her. If a sick person dreams of intercourse with his mother while he is ill, he will recover from his illness and it is an indication of the soundness of his nature, because Nature is the mother of all people. If the mother is dead,

this means that he will die, for the earth is called 'mother'. This dream is favourable for someone who is litigating over a piece of land, or intends to buy land. But for farmers it is a bad dream, because they will sow seeds in 'dead' earth in which nothing will grow. To a traveller this dream means that he will return to his town. If one is litigating over the property of one's parents[281] this dream means that one will be victorious.

If a man dreams that he copulates with his mother without lust, he will flee from his country, if he shows composure (*razāna*) after the act. If it is otherwise, he will leave his town of his own accord. If a man copulates with his mother while her face is turned away, it is a bad sign that means that the inhabitants of his mother's town will turn their affection away and hate him, or that the people of his own town or craft will turn away from him, or that what he wants will escape him.

If a man dreams of intercourse with his mother while he is asleep,[282] it means that sorrow and anxiety will occur to him. Dreaming of intercrural intercourse with one's mother is a bad sign that indicates great poverty. Dreaming of intercourse with one's mother while she is on top means that one will die, especially if one is ill, because the earth is a mother, and it is on top of the dead. But sometimes, for someone sound of body, this dream points to a decent[283] life for the rest of his lifetime.

If a man dreams that his mother is having sex with him[284] it means that children and wealth will perish, and that the dreamer will be ill.[285]

Many of these interpretations are logical in the light of what was said earlier. Others are not immediately obvious, but I shall not discuss them. Sex with one's daughter receives far less attention. Al-Nābulusī writes that dreaming about intercourse with a young daughter or son means illness for the child and harm to the dreamer; but if the girl is older, it has a positive explanation: she will be married off, receiving a neat trousseau from the dreamer. If the girl is already married, it means that she will leave her husband and return to her father.[286]

It is a moot point whether homosexual relations with one's kin can be called incest. The Arabic books have less of it than Artemidorus, but one finds the view, perhaps unexpected, that buggery with one's father means that one is respectful (*bārr*) of him. 'This dream is not dreamed by a disrespectful son', al-Nābulusī adds reassuringly.[287] The underlying idea is that intercourse means domination and subduing if it concerns an opponent or enemy, but benefit and respect if it is done with a friendly party. Elsewhere, however, the author explains that buggering one's father means driving him from his town or acting aggressively towards him.[288]

All in all, the dream interpreters are refreshingly down-to-earth and show a lack of moralistic prejudice. It would help neither their own profession nor their customers if they were scandalized by voluntary confessions of what by all accounts are shocking matters even if the acts are unreal. Dream books must have helped to give reassurance and possibly moral and practical guidance, for all their weirdness. Needless to say, the great variety of detailed dream fragments in the dream books does not prove that all these things were dreamed about regularly or even once: many of them must have their origin in the fantasies of the authors, thus being, as virtual dreams, even more remote from reality than real dreams. It may be significant that in the material I have consulted only one of the incestuous dreams (as opposed to dreams denoting incest) is given in the form of an anecdote—and there the interpreter is too embarrassed to answer the man to his face. To what extent the dreams, recorded or invented, reflect everyday realities it is difficult to say. Even though one must assume that in terms of reality father—daughter incest is by far the most common form, and in spite of the view of those who consider the strong bond between siblings as a kind of Middle Eastern equivalent of the oedipal bonds prevalent in western culture, it must be admitted that in the dream material here discussed it is the mother—son relationship that seems to come up most frequently. The rather lengthy passage in al-Nābulusī's work on mothers has no comparable counterparts for daughters or sisters, nor is there anything much on sex with fathers' wives, a topic that greatly stirred the imagination of storytellers and jurisprudents alike. Milk-relationship is also conspicuously absent.

Was Freud right, after all? Or have father—daughter incest and sibling incest been repressed in Freudian manner? Alternatively, the influence of Artemidorus may be detected here, for he begins his chapter on mothers[289] by saying that it is a subject with many ramifications, parts and subdivisions. Several of Artemidorus' interpretations are echoed very closely in al-Nābulusī's text translated above: intercourse with one's mother denoting hostility to the father or the father's death, the son acting as the mother's guardian; the idea of one's craft or the favour of one's fellow citizens being a kind of mother; the return to one's home town; the earth as 'mother'; the mother's wealth reverting to the dreamer; the intercrural sex; the mother on top; the 'decent' living: all this comes straight from Artemidorus,[290] who adds that 'the noun "intercourse" corresponds to the noun "love"'.[291] This equation does not work very well in Arabic, where words for intercourse (*mujāmaʿa, muwāqaʿa, muḍājaʿa, waṭʾ, nikāḥ, ghashayān*, etc., to mention some non-obscene terms) are never included in the long list of words for love and passion. In other words, al-Nābulusī's passage may reflect Greek rather than Arab ideas, and it is an open question to what extent translation and paraphrase of ideas have led to their assimilation and adoption.

Epilogue

It is impossible, and possibly undesirable, to take up all the different strands of the preceding chapters, and weave them into a clear pattern. I have started out without aiming to prove or disprove grand theories or to test broad hypotheses, and this final section is called 'Epilogue' advisedly, rather than 'Conclusions'. My primary aim has been to bring together as much as possible of the material relating to incest and inbreeding that could be found, and to shed some light on these topics that have, for obvious reasons, remained rather in the dark until now. Discussing and questioning taboos are rather fashionable these days, and it is possible to write about them, at least in the West, even though they are still in many ways taboos. I am by no means certain that this book could have been written by a Muslim and published in a Muslim country without problems, which is an additional reason why it is written by someone who is neither an Arab nor a Muslim and who still calls himself, almost defiantly, a Western orientalist. I have not tried to suppress my own feelings on incest completely, occasionally using emotive expressions that could have been omitted in a purely scholarly and detached discourse, when I myself have qualified certain acts as horrid, abhorrent, lurid, or perverse, although the frequency with which my sources do this has relieved me from doing this often. It is likely that in a short time some of my own prejudices will be out of fashion, for several taboos relating to sexuality, gender, race or colour have disappeared in the course of the last decades, and new ones have come into being, both in enlightened and reactionary circles.

Incest and inbreeding are not often discussed in the sources, with the exception of Qur'an commentaries and works of jurisprudence. In the present study, therefore, I have attempted to be, if not exhaustive, then at least relatively thorough in including what I have found. Only in the case of the vast corpus of juridical texts have I ignored the intricacies and innumerable theoretical case-studies of the legists, not being myself sufficiently competent in this difficult field. Furthermore, I have no doubt missed many interesting stories, opinions and allusions hidden in the vast mass of classical Arabic texts: historiographical and annalistic works, the many grand-scale compilations of biographies and prosopographies, the paraenetic, homiletic and moralistic works, commentaries on the Qur'an, medical and philosophical works, and the immense quantity of poetry. My reading has been fairly broad but necessarily desultory.

One should generally be wary of broad generalizations that contrast 'Islam' or 'the Arabs' with 'Christendom' or 'the Europeans', especially when one deals with a time span of many centuries and with complex sets of behaviour and cultural or literary expression. If I venture to sketch, in the following or in what preceded, some broad distinctions between these vague entities called

'East' and 'West', the reader is encouraged not to take them too seriously. Reading the fascinating works of Otto Rank of nearly a century ago and that of Elizabeth Archibald published very recently, one is struck by the frequency of the incest theme in the western tradition, from the ancient Greeks and Romans through the Middle Ages with their Latin and vernacular heritage, via the early modern world to the beginning of the twentieth century. Since the publication Otto Rank's book the theme has far from disappeared from the literary scene; there is a clear distinction between taboos in real life and literary taboos, a distinction that certainly exists now but has probably always existed in cultures where 'literature' and 'fiction' overlap to a considerable extent. It is rather different in pre-modern Arabic literature and Arab culture, even though there, too, many taboos may freely be celebrated in literary texts. One thinks of drinking wine, love affairs adulterous or homosexual, or pornography: all this is found in enormous quantities, especially in poetry, in an abundance that often embarrasses and scandalizes Arabs alive today. Incest, on the other hand, is a marginal theme. The books on sex and eroticism, such as *al-Rawḍ al-ʿāṭir (The Perfumed Garden)* by al-Nafzāwī,[1] al-Tijānī's *Tuḥfat al-ʿarūs wa-mutʿat al-nufūs* ('The Bride's Treasure and the Souls' Pleasure'), al-Tīfāshī's *Nuzhat al-albāb fīmā lā yūjad fī kitāb* ('The Diversion of the Mind: or What in Books you will not Find'), or the highly pornographic stories at the end of al-Tīfāshī's *Rujūʿ al-shaykh ilā ṣibāh fī l-quwwa ʿalā l-bāh* ('The Old Man's Rejuvenation in his Powers of Copulation') describe almost every imaginable kind of sex with all and sundry, young or old, heterosexual, homosexual and bestial, but as far as I can see they are not interested in incestuous sex. Perhaps this is because, in a purely physical, technical sense, incestuous sex is not different from ordinary sex. These books are more interested in techniques than in the psychological, ethical and religious sides. Nevertheless, in view of their obvious eagerness to be outrageous, it is surprising that they do not make occasional use of the incest motif as an additional shocker. Why this difference between Europe and the Arab world? Is it a matter of the selectiveness of the sources or is there a more basic reason?

The large number of incest stories in medieval Europe, compared with the relative scarcity in medieval Arabic, may be a result of the exposure of Europe to the Latin and Greek heritage with all its myths and legends that abound in incest.[2] True, the ancient Near East had its share of incestuous myths. A well-known case is Egypt, where gods often come in triads consisting of father, mother and son, the son being a kind of father reborn, and behaving accordingly. The Sumerian god Enki deserves special mention for his activities in this field. He impregnates successively the goddess Ninkhursag, his daughter, his granddaughter, and cohabits with his great-granddaughter apparently without further offspring.[3] However, such ancient Near Eastern myths disappeared almost without trace together with the knowledge of the relevant languages: ancient Egyptian, Sumerian, Akkadian, and did not contribute to the repertory of Arab lore and literature. Arabic literature is relatively poor in myths and many authoritative handbooks and encyclopedias on classical Arabic literature altogether lack entries for 'myth', 'mythology', or '*usṭūra*', the modern Arabic term for 'myth'. Nor were the Arabs aware of the non-mythical instances of close-kin marriage in the Near East apart from that of the Zoroastrians. There was no memory of the Ptolemaic Greek practices in Egypt, let alone of the far more remote practices of others such as the Elamites in Iran in the second millennium BC, among whom the highest ranking son of a king was the one whose mother was the king's sister.[4]

Perhaps 'Christianity', with its less than relaxed attitude towards sex, was more obsessed with incest than 'Islam' (I use inverted commas to signal my reluctance to speak in such generalizing terms); the extremely strict incest rules of Christian canon law seem to suggest this. These rules would result in greater dangers and greater fear, although, as said before, it could be the other way round, a greater obsession with incest and fear of inbreeding lying at the root of the stricter marriage laws. In practice the two, legislation and attitudes, would have influenced one another mutually and would have grown together. An essential difference between Islamic and Christian society is the frequency of polygyny and concubinage in the former, together with the ease of the wife's divorce by the husband and the frequency of remarriage, often with much younger wives. This, with all its objectionable aspects, would greatly have reduced the number of situations where desperate and unscrupulous men might seek recourse to incest with next-of-kin.

At the same time it must be said that the proliferation of incest stories in medieval Europe is to some extent a result of the flowering of vernacular languages there, each of which tended to develop its own literary versions and variants of old stories, whereas Arabic, unlike Latin in the West, virtually reigned supreme as a literary language in the medieval Middle East, rivalled only by Persian.

Aristotle already knew that kinship is a powerful factor in making a story more interesting. Tragedy and violence are always fascinating to most people. 'Whenever the tragic deed, however, is done among friends—when murder or the like is done or meditated by brother on brother, by son on father, by mother on son, or son on mother—these are the situations the poet should seek after.'[5] That 'the like' in this quotation refers to incest is obvious since the story of Oedipus serves as one of Aristotle's paradigmatic tales.

Incest is a powerful literary topic that tightens a narrative plot by economically combining what are probably the two strongest ties between humans, those of family and sexual love, and by providing a tension between the reader's sympathy for the protagonist and his abhorrence of the near-universal taboo. Family ties, sex, and sin intertwined: it is the narrative fruitfulness of this triad, one presumes, that Shelley had in mind when he said that 'incest is, like many other incorrect things, a very poetical circumstance'.[6] This bon mot does not easily translate into classical Arabic. Shelley said it in connection with one of the many early modern European plays that deal with incest (one by Calderón) and thus referred to fictional narrative in general. Serious drama, in the form of tragedy, comedy or tragi-comedy, is absent from classical Arabic literature (an absence that is often found odd, whereas one ought, rather, to consider its presence in the western tradition an oddity). Overt fiction has a low status in medieval Arabic literature, where, moreover, poetry and narrative have an uneasy relationship; their marriage was considered, not incestuous, too close for comfort, but, on the contrary, as somewhat vulgar, too far removed in status from serious literature. It is different in Persian literature, where the long narrative poem, epic or romantic, very much belonged to high-status literature. There, too, however, incest is a rare theme as far as I can judge. A notable exception is the Persian courtly romance *Vis and Ramin*, written soon after 441/1050 by Fakhr al-Dīn Gurgānī.[7] In this story Wīs (most Persianists prefer Vīs), a princess, is married to her full brother Wīrū (or Vīrū) by her mother, who argues that no other husband is worthy of her. The girl is willing but the marriage is not consummated (the chapter-heading says that 'their desire was not attained').[8] In fact the girl has been promised by her mother to king Mōbad or Mawbad (whose name means 'Zoroastrian priest') and she is duly married to him, this marriage remaining unconsummated, too. In the end, Wīs, widowed, is united with her lover Rāmīn, Mōbad's brother. Rāmīn, however, is Wīs's milk-brother, so the story is utterly un-Islamic in its marital arrangements. On the basis of the names of persons and places Minorsky concluded that the story may go back to the time of the Parthian Arsacid dynasty, before the Sasanids. The story is thus set in pre-Islamic times, and it was apparently known in versions predating Gurgānī's: the Arabic poet Abū Nuwās (d. *c.* 198/813) mentions 'Rāmīn and Wīs' in a poem full of Persian words and references.[9] Gurgānī tells the story without any comment, neither justifying the marriages historically nor condemning them as a good Muslim, and the story 'retains a strong Zoroastrian flavour'.[10] Some modern students of the story tend to gloss over the incestuous elements; if they condemn it, it is often because of the lovers' 'flagrant, and successful adultery',[11] celebrated in erotic scenes. Julie Meisami, in a chapter on the moral dimensions of character in Persian romance, finds '[t]he aging king Mawbad ... an inappropriate (not to say unnatural) partner for Vīs', even though marriages of old male and young female have always been frequent, and she accepts with the girl's mother that Wīrū 'by virtue of both kinship and station is her most worthy partner'.[12] That this kinship amounts to full siblingship the reader must remember from a passing remark made some forty pages before;[13] the milk-relationship between Wīs and Rāmīn is not discussed at all. Of the three men, Mōbad is not merely the most appropriate partner, but the only possible one, from a legalistic Muslim point of view. This indifference to the incestuous element in the romance is perhaps justified, for Gurgānī himself shows no concern for it. By presenting next-of-kin marriage as normal and legal, unconnected with crime, sin or guilt, he fails to exploit the potential of incest as it is found in Islamic or Christian contexts. Claude-Claire Kappler, however, far from glossing over it, sees the matter as central in the story. If it contains immorality, the main culprit is old king Mōbad, who breaks up a *khwētōdas* marriage of brother and sister, a great sin according the old Pahlavi texts. In the end, the just cause triumphs, since the girl marries her milk-brother who therefore is in fact her brother.[14] Kappler does not explain how this provocative reading could be acceptable to a Muslim readership. She juxtaposes her interpretation with that of Clarisse Herrenschmidt, who reads the romance as the successful attempt of a girl to escape from in-marrying to out-marrying, the nurse being the link between the two domains of family and strangers.[15]

Literature is never a true mirror of society and reality. The relative paucity of the incest theme in medieval Arabic literature does not mean that it played no role in real life. An example of the difference between literature and real life is the matter of milk-relationship: problems and dilemmas caused by milk-kinship are a common topic in law manuals and fatwa collections, the latter category of which especially reflect everyday concerns, but they are virtually absent from narrative literature, where it cannot provide the same *frisson* as a lurid father—daughter rape or sex between siblings. In spite of the near-equation of milk-relationship and consanguinity in Islamic law, the former is considerably less shameful and more likely to be discussed openly in everyday life. It is useful to keep in mind that there are two different kinds of taboo in any society: the taboo of *committing* incest, which has been found to be a universal or near-universal of human culture, and the taboo of *speaking* of incest. Both kinds are wide-spread; but if one is stronger or weaker in a particular society, the other is not necessarily stronger or weaker in the same proportion. Nor is the taboo on discussing incest equally strong in every kind of discourse: legal texts, dream interpretation, and invective or jesting poetry tend to be more explicit than story-telling. It goes without saying that in speaking about the Other, such as Zoroastrians or barbaric peoples in foreign parts there are no qualms about discussing incest. Ultimately the taboo of speaking, or writing, determines what we know about the other taboo. A study of a past society, such as undertaken in this book, is dependent on the written sources, in which the two kinds of taboo are intimately and closely related.

Notes

Notes to the Introduction

1. Ruth Perry, on Ellen Pollak, *Incest and the English Novel, 1684-1814*, Baltimore, Md., 2003, in an advertizement in the *Times Literary Supplement*, July 25, 2003, p. 10.

2. Tillion, *The Republic of Cousins*, p. 37.

3. '*xwêtôdas* (...) a symboliquement obsédé l'Iran musulman': Herrenschmidt, 'Le xwêtôdas ou mariage «incestueux» en Iran ancien', p. 117 note 6.

4. Van der Post, 'Incest en inteelt in de Arabische wereld'.

5. 'Décrié par le Coran, le forfait de l'inceste est banni des mœurs locales des Arabes et des musulmans': Malek Chebel, *Encyclopédie de l'amour en Islam*, entry 'inceste', pp. 338-39 (my translation).

6. Con Coughlin, *Saddam: The Secret Life*, London, 2002, p. 122.

7. On Saddam Husein's family relationships see Amatzia Baram, 'La «maison» de Ṣaddâm Ḥusayn'.

8. Doniach, *The Oxford English-Arabic Dictionary of Current Usage*; Schregle, *Deutsch-arabisches Wörterbuch*, offers for 'Inzest' *ghashayān al-maḥārim, zinā dhawī l-qurbā*, and for 'Inzucht' (inbreeding) *tanāsul dākhil nawᶜ wāḥid, zawāj al-aqārib, tazāwuj afrād al-usra fīmā baynahum* 'procreation within one species [*sic*], marriage of relatives, intermarriage of family members'.

9. Karmi, *Manār*, and Karmi, *Al-Mughni Al-Akbar*, both *s.v.* 'incest'.

10. al-Jawharī, *Ṣiḥāḥ*, *s.v.* RHQ, quoting al-Aṣmaᶜī as his authority; similarly Ibn Manẓūr, *Lisān al-ᶜArab.*

11. The verse is quoted in Ibn Manẓūr, *Lisān al-ᶜArab*, together with a verse by al-Aᶜshā that is equally unconvincing.

12. Wehr, *A Dictionary of Modern Written Arabic.*

13. Rather surprisingly, the incest motif is not mentioned in J. Christoph Bürgel, 'Zoroastrianism as Viewed in Medieval Islamic Sources', in Jacques Waardenburg (ed.), *Muslim Perceptions of Other Religions: A Historical Survey*, pp. 202-212.

14. e.g. Archibald, *Incest and the Medieval Imagination.*

Notes to Chapter One

1. Stricker, *Camephis*, see esp. pp. 26-49, 73-76.

2. *Camephis*, p. 35 (my translation).

3. *Camephis*, p. 37 (my translation).

4. See e.g. Goody, *The Oriental, the Ancient and the Primitive*, pp. 128, 275, 319-20, Ridley, *The Red Queen*, pp. 274-77, Wilson, *Consilience*, pp. 191-99, 348, each of whom gives further references.

5. e.g. Wilson, *Consilience: The Unity of Knowledge*, pp. 191-99, 241-42; William H. Durham, *Coevolution*, ch. 6 'Enhancement: the Cultural Evolution of Incest Taboos', pp. 286-360), Fox, *The Red Lamp of Incest*, Shepher, *Incest: A Biosocial View.*

6. See e.g. Durham, *Coevolution*, pp. 307-9.

7. Hopkins, 'Brother-sister marriage in Roman Egypt', Shaw, 'Explaining incest', Goody, *The Oriental, the Ancient and the Primitive*, chapter 'The abominations of the Egyptians', pp. 319-41.

8. Goody, *The Oriental, the Ancient and the Primitive*, p. 381, referring to an unpublished study by A.C. Lee, 'Close-kin marriage in Late Roman Mesopotamia' (1988).

9. See e.g. Brown, *Human Universals*, ch. 5 'Incest Avoidance' (pp. 118-29), where he speaks of 'apparent universality, or near-universality' (p. 118). Also Sidler, *Zur Universalität des Inzesttabu.*

10. For a recent survey of data and an analysis, see Pierre Bonte, 'Manière de dire ou manière de faire : Peut-on parler d'un mariage «arabe» ?', in Pierre Bonte (ed.), *Épouser au plus proche*, pp. 371-98, and see, in the same collection pp. 453-73, Élisabeth Copet-Rougier, 'Le mariage «arabe» : Une approche théorique'.

11. Ridley, *The Red Queen*, p. 274.

12. Richard Dawkins, *The Selfish Gene*, p. 99: 'Incest taboos testify to the great kinship-consciousness of man, although the genetical advantage of an incest taboo is nothing to do with altruism; it is presumably concerned with the injurious effects of recessive genes which appear with inbreeding (For some reason many anthropologists do not like this explanation).' See also pp. 293-94.

13. Durkheim, *Incest*, p. 61.

14. Aberle *et al.*, 'The incest taboo', p. 349.

15. *Aristotle's Masterpiece*, London, 1670, p. 177, a reference I owe to Susan J. Wiseman, '*'Tis Pity She's a Whore*: Representing the Incestuous Body', pp. 184 and 271 n.14. See also Archibald, *Incest and the Medieval Imagination*, pp. 50-52.

16. Archibald, *Incest and the Medieval Imagination*, p. 50; cf. p. 237.

17. Burton, *The Anatomy of Melancholy*, i, 212 (the parenthesized translation is the editor's).

18. Sachau, *Syrische Rechtsbücher*, iii, 36-37; he uses the word *ḥegīrūthā*, from the root *ḤGR* 'to halt, limp, be crippled, lame, weak'.

19. William H. Durham, *Coevolution*, pp. 345-57 and see Table 6.1 in Appendix A, pp. 512-14.

20. Xenophon, *Memorabilia*, IV, iv, 19-23 (tr. E. C. Marchant, pp. 320-23), makes Socrates say that transgressing the laws through parent—child couplings means 'begetting them badly' which is the offenders' 'great penalty'; but there is no clear mention of bodily or mental deficiencies. See Archibald, *Incest and the Medieval Imagination*, p. 12.

21. This is the usual rendering of the word *Jāhiliyya*, used by Muslim Arabs to refer to the pre-Islamic period.

22. Ignaz Goldziher, as early as 1880, identified some key texts and passages, in his one-page article 'Polyandry and Exogamy among the Arabs'.

23. *History of Animals*, vi, 22 (576[a]): 'Horses will cover mares from which they have been foaled and mares which they have begotten; and indeed, a troop of horses is considered perfect when they mount their own progeny' (tr. d'A. W. Thompson, in Aristotle, *The Complete Works*, ed. Jonathan Barnes, p. 903). For animals' aversion to incest, see below, pp. 41, 47-48.

24. al-Jāḥiẓ, *Bayān*, i, 185, [al-Aṣmaʿī], *Ibil*, 80 (with *istaghribū* instead of *ightaribū*, with the same meaning), Ibn Qutayba, *Maʿānī*, p. 503, Ibn Qutayba, *ʿUyūn*, ii, 67, Ibn ʿAbd Rabbih, *ʿIqd*, vi, 117, Ibn Durayd, *Jamhara*, p. 913 (with *istaghribū*), al-Khālidiyyān, *Ashbāh*, i, 229, al-Tawḥīdī, *Imtāʿ*, i, 94, al-Nahshalī, *Mumtiʿ*, p. 204, al-Rāghib al-Iṣbahānī, *Muḥāḍarāt*, i, 207, al-Maydānī, *Majmaʿ*, ii, 404, al-Bakrī, *Tanbīh*, p. 124, al-Bakrī, *Simṭ*, p. 871, al-Māwardī, *Adab*, p. 161, Ibn al-Athīr, *Nihāya*, *s.v.* *ḌWY*, al-Zamakhsharī, *Asās*, *s.v.* *ḌWY*, Ibn Manẓūr, *Lisān al-ʿArab*, *s.v.* *ḌWY*, al-Tijānī, *Tuḥfa*, pp. 75, 175, al-Baghdādī, *Ḥāshiya ʿalā sharḥ Bānat Suʿād*, II, i, 477-78. It is not found in the 'canonical' Hadith collections used for the *Concordance* by Wensinck *et al.*

25. For more instances of the verb *ightaraba* meaning 'to marry among strangers', mostly taken from the early genealogical work by Ibn Saʿd (d. 230/845) on the Prophet's contemporaries, see Gertrude H. Stern, *Marriage in Early Islam*, pp. 67-68.

26. al-Khalīl, *ʿAyn*, vii, 73 (supplied by the editor from al-Azharī's *Tahdhīb al-luhga*).

27. [al-Aṣmaʿī], *Ibil*, p. 80 (speaking of camels).

28. Ibn Durayd, *Jamhara*, p. 242 (cf. p. 913).

29. al-Tawḥīdī, *Imtāʿ*, iii, 27.

30. Ruʾba, *Dīwān*, p. 16 (incorrectly *uḍwī*), Ibn Fāris, *Mujmal*, *s.v.* *ḌWY* (which has *kayfa aḍwā*, 'How could I be a weakling', as in his *Maqāyīs al-lugha*, iii, 376).

31. al-Jāḥiẓ, *Tarbīʿ* ed. Pellat, p. 32 (§ 52).

32. al-Khalīl, *ʿAyn*, vii, 74, Ibn Fāris, *Mujmal*, *s.v.* *ḌWY*.

33. al-ᶜĀmilī, *Kashkūl*, p. 748. Another metaphoric use is found in *aḍwā ḥaqqahu*, 'to infringe s.o.'s right' (Ibn Manẓūr, *Lisān al-ᶜArab*, *s.v.* ḌWY).

34. The Aramaic and Syriac verb *ṣwē* or *ṣwā* 'to contract, to be hot, dry up, wither' (Jastrow, *Dictionary s.v.* ṢWY, with the example *ū-ṣwū karᶜēh* 'his legs shrivelled', Payne Smith, *Thesaurus*, col. 3370-71) is related to Arabic *ṣawiya* 'to dry up, wither', rather than to *ḍawiya*.

35. Ibn Qutayba, *ᶜUyūn*, ii, 66, iv, 3, Ibn ᶜAbd Rabbih, *ᶜIqd*, vi, 117, al-Māwardī, *Adab*, p. 161, al-Zamakhsharī, *Rabīᶜ*, iv, 299, Ibn Manẓūr, *Lisān al-ᶜArab*, *s.v.* NZᶜ, al-Baghdādī, *Ḥāshiya*, II, i, 478; also in *Gharīb al-Ḥadīth* (by whichever author) on the authority of Ibrāhīm al-Ḥarbī, as quoted in Zayn al-Dīn ᶜAbd al-Raḥīm b. al-Ḥusayn al-ᶜIrāqī's commentary on the *aḥādīth* of al-Ghazālī's *Iḥyāᵓ* (ii, 41, *in margine*).

36. As translated in Robertson Smith, *Kinship and Marriage*, p. 91 (first parenthesis added by me). See Ḥātim al-Ṭāᵓī, *Dīwān*, ed. F. Schultess, Leipzig, 1897, p. 47, German translation pp. 71-72), Ibn ᶜAbd Rabbih, *ᶜIqd*, vi, 130-31, and see Hoyland, *Arabia and the Arabs*, p. 128.—The word *nazīᶜ* is also used for horses or camels, see *Naqāᵓiḍ Jarīr wa-l-Farazdaq*, p. 303, Ibn Manẓūr, *Lisān al-ᶜArab s.v.* NZᶜ.

37. al-Rāghib al-Iṣbahānī, *Muḥāḍarāt*, i, 207.

38. Attributed to ᶜAbd al-ᶜĀṣ b. Thaᶜlaba al-Tanūkhī (pre-Islamic) in Ibn Ḥabīb, *Asmāᵓ al-mughtālīn*, p. 128, (reading *walīd* instead of *radīd*). The line has also been attributed to the famous pre-Islamic poet al-Nābigha al-Dhubyānī (*Dīwān* ed. Ahlwardt, p. 164 and see Yāqūt, *Muᶜjam al-buldān*, i, 588). See also al-Jāḥiẓ, *Burṣān*, p. 24, Ibn Qutayba, *Maᶜānī*, p. 503 (with *radīm*, literally 'worn out', instead of *radīd*), al-Khālidiyyān, *Ashbāh*, i, 229 (with *salīl*, 'offspring'), al-Tawḥīdī, *Imtāᶜ*, i, 94, al-Maydānī, *Majmaᶜ*, ii, 404, al-Bakrī, *Tanbīh*, p. 124, al-Bakrī, *Simṭ*, p. 871, al-Rāghib al-Iṣbahānī, *Muḥāḍarāt*, i, 207 (with *walīd*), al-Zamakhsharī, *Asās*, *s.v.* ḌWY, Ibn Manẓūr, *Lisān al-ᶜArab*, *s.v.* ḌWY, al-Tijānī, *Tuḥfa*, p. 75, al-Baghdādī, *Ḥāshiya*, II, i, 479.

39. al-Ghazālī, *Iḥyāᵓ*, ii, 41. In the commentary on the Traditions of this work, printed in the margin, an authority (Ibn al-Ṣalāḥ) is quoted as having said on this saying, 'I have not found a reliable source for this'. Also Ibn al-Athīr, *Nihāya*, *s.v.* ḌWY, al-Tijānī, *Tuḥfa*, p. 74, Ibn Manẓūr, *Lisān al-ᶜArab*, *s.v.* ḌWY.

40. al-Jāḥiẓ, *Bayān*, i, 185.

41. al-Iṣfahānī, *Aghānī*, xxii, 81, ᶜAbīd ibn al-Abraṣ, *Dīwān*, p. 1, Ibn al-Shajarī, *Mukhtārāt*, p. 311, Ibn Manẓūr, *Lisān al-ᶜArab*, *s.v.* ḌWY.

42. al-Jāḥiẓ, *Ḥayawān*, iii, 213.

43. [al-Aṣmaᶜī], *Ibil*, p. 80. 'Distantly related': it is taken for granted that no two persons are wholly unrelated, if one goes back sufficiently far.

44. All this in Ibn Manẓūr, *Lisān al-ᶜArab*, *s.v.* ḌWY; many other old dictionaries could be quoted in support.

45. al-Dīnawarī, *Nabāt*, pp. 129-30.

46. al-Tawḥīdī, *Imtāᶜ*, i, 94.

47. al-Hamadhānī, *Maqāmāt*, p. 166.

48. Ibn Manẓūr, *Lisān al-ᶜArab*, *s.v.* ḌWY, cf. Ibn al-Kalbī, *Nasab al-khayl*, p. 69.

49. Ibn Manẓūr, *Lisān al-ᶜArab*; cf. Dhū l-Rumma, *Dīwān* ed. Abū Ṣāliḥ, p. 1381. One may compare Aᶜwaj ('Crooked'), a noble horse of Kinda, very often mentioned: Abū ᶜUbayda, *Khayl*, p. 178, Ibn al-Kalbī, *Nasab al-khayl*, pp. 30-31, *Naqāʾiḍ Jarīr wa-l-Farazdaq*, p. 303, etc.

50. Its full title is, in translation, *The Leprous, the Lame, the Blind, and the Squinting*, which does not exhaust the contents.

51. On the paradox in the sense of beautifying the bad or ugly and the reverse, see Van Gelder, 'Beautifying the Ugly'.

52. The edition wrongly has a *ḍamma* on the final *mīm*.

53. See above, p. 13 and note 38.

54. Literally perhaps 'that ripple like waves' (*tamūju*), therefore 'are crooked' (cf. the line quoted below, p. 16).

55. I am not sure if *khālid* is used here as a personal name, nor if it is relevant that of two famous members of Asad, called 'the two Khālids (al-Khālidān)', one, Khālid b. Naḍla, was nicknamed al-Mahzūl ('the Skinny'); see Ibn Manẓūr, *Lisān al-ᶜArab*, *s.v.* KhLD and Caskel, *Ǧamhara*, Index, *s.v.* H̱ālid b. Naḍla. I have not found any succession of generations called Khālid, so perhaps *khālid* means 'vigorous old man' here.

56. This practice, usually called *shighār*, whereby brides were exchanged without bridal money, thus keeping property in the family, was forbidden in Islam; see references to the Ḥadīth in Wensinck *et al.*, *Concordance*, *s.v. shighār*.—The verses are repeated in *al-Burṣān* on p. 379 and the first two lines in al-Tawḥīdī, *Imtāᶜ*, i, 94.

57. al-Jāḥiẓ, *Burṣān*, pp. 23-25.

58. al-Marzūqī, *Sharḥ Ḥamāsat Abī Tammām*, p. 270.

59. Quoted by al-Marzūqī in the commentary on the previous line; cf. Muslim ibn al-Walīd, *Dīwān*, p. 311.

60. al-Jāḥiẓ, *Bayān*, ii, 97-98; see also Ibn Durayd, *Jamhara*, pp. 760 and 1162 (*s.v.* QRQM), al-Qālī, *Amālī*, ii, 246, al-Bakrī, *Tanbīh*, p. 123-24, al-Bakrī, *Simṭ*, p. 871, Ibn Manẓūr, *Lisān al-ᶜArab*, *s.v.* QRQM, Ibn Sīda, *Mukhaṣṣaṣ*, i, 29 (var. *al-ḥasab* for *al-karam*).

61. Ibn ᶜAbd Rabbih, *ᶜIqd*, iii, 475, Ibn Sīda, *Mukhaṣṣaṣ*, i, 29, Ibn Manẓūr, *Lisān al-ᶜArab*, *s.v.* QRQM, SMLQ (which offers various other interpretations of *samlaq*, here translated as 'evil-tempered' following Ibn ᶜAbd Rabbih).

62. Ibn Manẓūr, *Lisān al-ᶜArab*, *s.v.* QRQM; cf. Ibn Sīda, *Mukhaṣṣaṣ*, i, 29.

63. Ibn Manẓūr, *Lisān al-ᶜArab*, *s.v.* ḌWY.

64. I follow Goody, *The Oriental, the Ancient and the Primitive*, p. 488 (ch. 1 note 1) in reserving the terms endogamy and exogamy for systems where all members are generally obliged to marry inside or outside the group, respectively.

65. Anonymously in al-Jāḥiẓ, *Ḥayawān*, i, 346, al-Khālidiyyān, *Ashbāh*, ii, 237, al-Ābī, *Nathr al-durr*, vi, 478, al-Baghdādī, *Khizānat al-adab*, i, 444 (and several other works on syntax).

66. Anonymously in Ibn Qutayba, *Maᶜānī*, p. 502. I do not quite understand *ka-ᶜuryāni l-nujūm*.

67. Jarīr, *Dīwān*, p. 677; Ibn Qutayba, *ᶜUyūn*, ii, 67, Ibn Qutayba, *Maᶜānī*, p. 503, al-Qālī, *Amālī*, iii, 50, al-Khālidiyyān, *Ashbāh*, i, 228, al-Bakrī, *Tanbīh*, p. 125, al-Bakrī, *Simṭ*, p. 872, Kaᶜb b. Zuhayr, *Dīwān*, p. 40, al-Baghdādī, *Ḥāshiya*, ii, 478, al-Tījānī, *Tuḥfa*, p. 75.

68. al-Khālidiyyān, *Ashbāh*, i, 229. The saying that 'strange women produce better offspring' is ascribed variously to 'the (Bedouin) Arabs', to a man quoted by al-Aṣmaᶜī, and to al-Aṣmaᶜī himself, see Ibn Qutayba, *ᶜUyūn*, ii, 67 and iv, 3, Ibn ᶜAbd Rabbih, *ᶜIqd*, vi, 103, 117, al-Tawḥīdī, *Imtāᶜ*, i, 94, al-Zamakhsharī, *Rabīᶜ*, iv, 299, al-Zamakhsharī, *Mustaqṣā*, i, 353, al-Ibshīhī, *Mustaṭraf*, ii, 254, al-Tījānī, *Tuḥfa*, p. 174.

69. Jarīr, *Dīwān*, p. 662, al-Khālidiyyān, *Ashbāh*, i, 229.

70. al-Marzūqī, *Sharḥ Dīwān al-ḥamāsa*, p. 1760.

71. al-Jāḥiẓ, *Bayān*, iii, 99, Ibn Qutayba, *ᶜUyūn*, ii, 67, Ibn Qutayba, *Maᶜānī*, p. 503, al-Nahshalī, *Mumtiᶜ*, p. 201, al-Bakrī, *Tanbīh*, p. 125, al-Bakrī, *Simṭ*, p. 872, al-Rāghib al-Iṣbahānī, *Muḥāḍarāt*, i, 207, al-Thaᶜālibī, *Thimār al-qulūb*, p. 345, Ibn Manẓūr, *Lisān al-ᶜArab*, *s.v.* ḌWY, al-Tījānī, *Tuḥfa*, p. 75. The first word is variously read as *tanakhkhabtuhā*, *tanajjabtuhā*, *tanaḥḥaytuhā*, or *takhayyartuhā*.

72. al-Khālidiyyān, *Ashbāh*, i, 229, al-Baghdādī, *Ḥāshiya*, II, i, 479.

73. al-Māwardī, *Adab*, p. 161.

74. al-Tawḥīdī, *Imtāᶜ*, i, 94, al-Khālidiyyān, *Ashbāh*, i, 229 (vss. 1-2), al-Rāghib al-Iṣbahānī, *Muḥāḍarāt*, i, 207 (vss. 1-3), al-Maᶜarrī, *Fuṣūl*, p. 161 (vss. 1-3).

75. al-Khālidiyyān, *Ashbāh*, i, 230, al-Rāghib al-Iṣbahānī, *Muḥāḍarāt*, i, 207, in both sources attributed to al-ᶜUtbī (i.e. probably Muḥammad b. ᶜUbayd Allāh al-ᶜUtbī, d. 228/843).

76. al-Iṣfahānī, *Aghānī*, xxi, 118, where Zabbān is misspelled Zayyān; al-Tījānī, *Tuḥfat al-ᶜarūs*, pp. 76-77.

77. Ibn Qutayba, *Maᶜārif*, p. 112, al-Iṣfahānī, *Aghānī*, xii, 194-95.

78. The verb is derived from *baḍᶜ* or *biḍāᶜ*, 'copulation', or from *buḍᶜ*, the several meanings of which include 'copulation' and 'vulva'.

79. al-Bukhārī, *Ṣaḥīḥ*, ch. *Nikāḥ*, no. 36; also Abū Dāwūd, *Sunan*, ii, 486-87 (ch. *Ṭalāq*, no. 33); and see the lexicons such as Ibn al-Athīr, *Nihāya*, and Ibn Manẓūr, *Lisān al-ᶜArab*, *s.v.* BḌᶜ. For another English translation, together with its context and a discussion, see Watt, *Muhammad at Medina*, pp. 378-85. The four types of pre-Islamic *nikāḥ* described in an obviously related passage quoted by al-Shahrastānī, *Milal*, ii, 246 and attributed to Muḥammad ibn al-Sāʾib al-Kalbī, are not identical and do not include *nikāḥ al-istibḍāᶜ*.

80. Serjeant, 'Zinā, Some Forms of Marriage and Allied Topics in Western Arabia', p. 22. The Sabaic text was discussed in A. F. L. Beeston, 'Temporary Marriage in Pre-Islamic South Arabia'; *pace* Serjeant (p. 150), Beeston does not identify this practice with the *istibḍāᶜ* described in al-Bukhārī.

81. Wilken, *Das Matriarchat*, pp. 26-29.

82. See e.g. Wilken, *Das Matriarchat*, Smith, *Kinship and Marriage*, pp. 132-33, 139.

83. See Watt, *Muhammad at Medina*, pp. 378-85.

84. Ibn Ḥajar, *Fatḥ al-bārī*, ix, 146.

85. Lane, *An Arabic-English Lexicon*, *s.v.* BḌᶜ: 'from a desire of obtaining generous offspring', Hoyland, *Arabia*, p. 132: 'to acquire a child sired by a man distinguished for bravery and generosity'.

86. Discussed in ch. IV.

87. al-Tarmānīnī, *al-Zawāj ᶜinda l-ᶜArab*, p. 19.

88. reading *ᶜāmūd* 'chief, head of a family; base' instead of *ᶜāmūr*.

89. To give an idea: in traditional Arab genealogy there are some eighteen generations between Muḍar (brother of Rabīᶜa) and the Prophet Muḥammad (who lived more than three centuries before al-Masᶜūdī).

90. al-Masᶜūdī, *Murūj al-dhahab*, i, 162-63.

91. See e.g. al-Tarmānīnī, *al-Zawāj ᶜinda l-ᶜArab*, p. 18.

92. al-Khalīl b. Aḥmad, *al-ᶜAyn*, iii, 234, Ibn Manẓūr, *Lisān al-ᶜArab*, *s.v.* FḤL, al-Fīrūzābādī, *Qāmūs*, *s.v.* FḤL. According to many scholars, ancient and modern, the true author of *al-ᶜAyn* is al-Layth b. al-Muẓaffar (d. before 187/800).

93. Yāqūt, *Muᶜjam al-buldān*, iii, 449, al-Qazwīnī, *Āthār al-bilād*, p. 584.

94. Ibn al-Mujāwir, *Taʾrīkh al-mustabṣir*, i, 53 (I thank Dr Paul Dresch for drawing my attention to this source).

95. Ibn Manẓūr, *Lisān al-ᶜArab*, *s.v.* QRQM.

96. *fa-inna dhālika yuqallil*: Farah translates 'as that weakens desire'.

97. al-Ghazālī, *Iḥyāʾ*, ii, 41. For another English translation, see al-Ghazālī, *Marriage and Sexuality in Islam*, p. 91.

98. Murtaḍā l-Zabīdī, *Itḥāf*, v, 348-49.

99. Al-Qazwīnī (end of 6th/12th century), *Mufīd al-ᶜulūm*, pp. 130-31, which instead of *ḍāwiyyan* has *niḍwan*, 'jaded, emaciated', obviously a corruption even though it more or less suits the context. The anonymous Persian counterpart of *Mufīd al-ᶜulūm* entitled *Baḥr al-fawāʾid* has the same passage, see Meisami's translation, Anon., *The Sea of Precious Virtues*, p. 162.

100. al-Tijānī, *Tuḥfat al-ᶜarūs*, p. 76, quoting an unnamed authority.

101. al-Ābī, *Nathr al-durr*, vi, 514.

102. al-Maydānī, *Majmaᶜ al-amthāl*, ii, 387.

103. *yaqbiḍu l-nafs ᶜan inbisāṭihā*: the antonymous pair *QBḌ* and *BSṬ* are associated with clenching/constriction/anguish and unfolding/relaxation/happiness, respectively.

104. *fa-yatakhayyalu l-insān annahu yankiḥu baᶜḍahu*: this I find rather unclear.

105. *al-fuḍūl al-muʾdhiya*: he is still speaking of sperm!

106. Ibn al-Jawzī, *Ṣayd al-khāṭir*, pp. 69-70.

107. Wolf, *Sexual Attraction and Childhood Association: A Chinese Brief for Edward Westermarck*; see also Wilson, *Consilience*, pp. 193-94.

108. Westermarck, *The History of Human Marriage*, chapters xiv-xv, 'Prohibition of Marriage Between Kindred' (pp. 290-355); see p. 320: 'What I maintain is, that there is an innate aversion to sexual intercourse between persons living very closely together from early youth, and that, as such persons are in most cases related, this feeling displays itself chiefly as a horror of intercourse between near kin.'

109. The attempt of Robin Fox, in his very readable *The Red Lamp of Incest*, to reconcile sociobiological views with Freud's theories resembles, to me, the attempts of those who desire to reconcile science with religion (or perhaps science with fiction).

110. See Roscoe, 'Amity and aggression: A symbolic theory of incest'.

111. On the role of milk in kinship and incest rules, see Chapter Three.

112. Ibn Ḥazm, *Rasāʾil*, i, 370.

113. Ibn al-Jawzī, *Dhamm al-hawā*, p. 232.

114. Quoted by Ḥamza al-Iṣfahānī in Abū Nuwās, *Dīwān*, iv, 141-42.

115. Ikhwān al-Ṣafāʾ, *Rasāʾil*, iii, 277.

116. (1) by al-Majnūn (Ibn Qutayba, *Shiᶜr*, p. 564), (2) by al-Mukhtār ibn Wahb (al-Hajarī, *Taᶜlīqāt*, i, 123), (3) by ᶜUrwa ibn Ḥizām (Ibn Dāwūd al-Iṣbahānī, *Zahra*, p. 439), (4) by Jamīl (al-Iṣfahānī, *Aghānī*, ii, 390, 392, viii, 103), (5) by Kuthayyir (Ibn Dāwūd al-Iṣbahānī, *Zahra*, p. 437), (6) by ᶜUrwa ibn Udhayna (al-Iṣfahānī, *Aghānī*, v, 400), (7) by Dāwūd ibn Salm (al-Iṣfahānī, *Aghānī*, vi, 8, 12).

117. al-Iṣfahānī, *Aghānī*, vii, 299.

118. Goody, *The Oriental, the Ancient and the Primitive*, p. 275, referring to a study by G.T. Kurian, 'Child marriage—a case study in Kerala', in D. Narain (ed.), *Explorations in the Family and Other Essays*, Bombay, 1975.

119. Goody, *The Oriental, the Ancient and the Primitive*, p. 275.

120. Wolf, *Sexual Attraction and Childhood Association*; see Wilson, *Consilience*, pp. 193-94.

121. Durham, *Coevolution*, pp. 313-14.

122. Ibn al-Jawzī, *Adhkiyāʾ*, p. 143.

123. al-Khālidiyyān, *Ashbāh*, i, 229.

124. al-Iṣfahānī, *Aghānī*, xi, 60, cf. Goldziher, "Polyandry and Exogamy among the Arabs", also in his *Gesammelte Schriften*, ii, 76.

125. al-Ābī, *Nathr al-durr*, vi, 409 and Ibn Abī l-Ḥadīd, Sharḥ *Nahj al-balāgha*, v, 58: '*Zawwijū banāt al-ʿamm banī l-ʿamm fa-in taʿaddaytum bihinna ilā l-ghurabāʾ fa-lā taʾlū bihinna ʿan al-akfāʾ*.'

126. al-Māwardī, *Adab*, p. 155.

127. al-Nahshalī, *Mumtiʿ*, p. 204. Robertson Smith (*Kinship and Marriage*), p. 195 gives a similar Talmudic saying provided by I(gnaz) G(oldziher): *Rov banīm dōmīn le-aḥē ha-ēm* 'children on the whole resemble the brothers of the mother' (Babylonian Talmud, *Bābā Bathrā*, 110a).

128. al-Thaʿālibī, *Thimār al-qulūb*, pp. 343-46.

129. al-Maydānī, *Majmaʿ*, ii, 404.

130. Murtaḍā l-Zabīdī, *Itḥāf*, v, 349.

131. al-Iṣfahānī, *Aghānī*, ix, 182.

132. al-Khālidiyyān, *Ashbāh*, i, 228-30, al-Rāghib al-Iṣbahānī, *Muḥāḍarāt*, i, 207, 'The stuntedness of children from father's brother's daughters (*ḍawāyat al-walad min banāt al-ʿamm*)', in a chapter on family relationships.

133. [al-Aṣmaʿī], *Ibil*, p. 80.

134. The word *ḥarf* has been interpreted as 'big, solid, sturdy', or as 'mountain-top', which led Suzanne Stetkevych in her translation of the poem to opt for 'Huge as a mountain' ('Pre-Islamic Panegyric', p. 26, *The Poetics of Islamic Legitimacy*, p. 56); but also as 'lean, slender', though never implying stuntedness. Sells ('*Bānat Suʿād*', p. 150) has 'worn to an edge', which aptly exploits another meaning of the word ('edge, side').

135. Kaʿb b. Zuhayr, *Diwān*, p. 6. Instead of the appropriate horsy words ('sire', 'dam') used for camels by most English translators, I prefer ordinary words, like the Arabic.

136. al-Baghdādī, *Ḥāshiya*, II, i, 468.

137. al-Baghdādī, *Ḥāshiya*, II, i, 468-69.

138. al-Bakrī, *Tanbīh*, p. 125, al-Bakrī, *Simṭ*, p. 871.

139. al-Bakrī, *Tanbīh*, p. 125, al-Bakrī, *Simṭ*, p. 871.

140. Quoted in al-Baghdādī, *Ḥāshiya*, II, i, 469, also al-Damīrī, *Ḥayāt*, i, 15.

141. Ibn Maymūn, *Muntahā l-ṭalab*, i, 138, Abū Nuwās, *Dīwān*, iv, 87, al-Baṣrī, *al-Ḥamāsa al-Baṣriyya*, ii, 327, al-Baghdādī, *Ḥāshiya*, II, i, 465; nearly identical, anonymously, in al-Ushnāndānī, *Maᶜānī*, p. 104. See below, pp. 139-40 for a solution of the genealogical puzzle in 'human' terms.

142. al-Ushnāndānī, *Maᶜānī*, p. 104. For the 'signs' (*shuhūd*), see the dictionaries, e.g. Ibn Manẓūr, *Lisān al-ᶜArab*: 'the *shuhūd* are the membranes on the head of the calf; the *shuhūd* of the she-camel are what is left at the place of delivery, such as afterbirth and blood'.

143. See e.g. Ibn al-Kalbī, *Nasab al-khayl*, p. 30, Ibn al-Aᶜrābī, *Asmāᵓ khayl al-ᶜArab*, p. 35, al-Shimshāṭī, *Anwār*, i, 270, 272, 276, al-Nuwayrī, *Nihāya*, x, 39. The name also appears as Zād al-Rākib.

144. See Q 38:30-33.

145. Ibn al-Aᶜrābī, *Asmāᵓ khayl al-ᶜArab*, p. 49, al-Marzūqī, *Sharḥ Ḥamāsat Abī Tammām*, p. 210, Ibn Hudhayl, *Ḥilyat al-fursān*, p. 181.

146. Ibn Ḥuṣn, about whom little is known (*fl. c.* 1865), quoted and translated by Marcel Kurpershoek, *Oral Poetry and Narratives from Central Arabia*, iv, 348-49.

147. Ibn Rashīq, *ᶜUmda*, ii, 190-98, 234-36.

148. Abū ᶜUbayda, *Khayl*, p. 175. I note in passing that the root of the word *hujna/hajna*, here rendered as 'base admixture', also produces the word *muhajjana* that is found in Kaᶜb's line and has been translated as 'of good breed'. See the dictionaries on these confusing words and their cognates *hajīn* ('half-noble, with non-Arab mother, mongrel') and *hijān* ('of good breed').

149. Abū ᶜUbayda, *Khayl*, p. 176, *Dīwān* (Ahlwardt), p. 113.

150. Abū ᶜUbayda, *Khayl*, p. 182.

151. Ibn al-Kalbī, *Nasab al-khayl*, p. 34, Ibn Manẓūr, *Lisān al-ᶜArab*, *s.v.* ḤNF, al-Iṣfahānī, *Aghānī*, xvii, 187-88, Ibn Rashīq, *ᶜUmda*, ii, 234-35. In Abū ᶜUbayda, *Ayyām al-ᶜArab*, ii, 181, al-Ghabrāᵓ is said to be the daughter of Dāḥis.

152. al-Iṣfahānī, *Aghānī*, vi, 1-2.

153. *ᶜAmmuhā khāluhā wa-in ᶜudda yawman / kāna khālan lahā idhā ᶜudda ᶜammā*; ᶜUmar b. Abī Rabīᶜa, *Dīwān*, i, 76, al-Baghdādī, *Ḥāshiya*, II, i, 468.

154. On another line by ᶜUmar mentioning Qurayba, see al-Iṣfahānī, *Aghānī*, i, 293, 304; in the *Dīwān* (p. 205) the name appears as Sukayna.

155. al-Sukkarī, *Sharḥ ashᶜār al-Hudhaliyyīn*, p. 1114.

156. al-Jāḥiẓ, *Ḥayawān*, i, 137-38, id., *al-Bighāl*, pp. 75-76.

157. al-Jāḥiẓ, *Ḥayawān*, i, 138.

158. al-Jāḥiẓ, *Ḥayawān*, i, 156.

159. al-Jāḥiẓ, *Ḥayawān*, i, 148.

160. The dictionaries define *Bayāsira* (sg. *baysarī*) as 'a people in Sind' who may be hired by seafarers for protection against enemies. See also J. C. Wilkinson, 'Bayāsirah and Bayādīr', 74-85 (where the passage by al-Jāḥiẓ is not mentioned).

161. al-Jāḥiẓ, *Ḥayawān*, i, 157.

162. On interracial intermarriage, see Lewis, *Race and Slavery in the Middle East*, esp. pp. 23-25, 31, 35, 38-40, 84-91, 101.

163. The lengthy monograph on medieval Islamic embryology and heredity, Weisser, *Zeugung, Vererbung und pränatale Entwicklung*, contains nothing on inbreeding, incest, or their consequences.

164. al-Ṭabarī, *Firdaws*, p. 578.

165. al-Rāzī, *Ḥāwī*, xxiii/1, 264.

166. al-Rāzī, *Ḥāwī*, xxiii/1, 266-68.

167. Quoted by al-Tawḥīdī, *Imtāʿ*, iii, 27, on the authority of Ibn al-Aʿrābī.

168. al-Ṭabarī, *Firdaws*, p. 36.

169. Ibn al-Rūmī, *Dīwān*, (i,) 104.

170. Ibn Rabbih, *ʿIqd*, vi, 373-76, al-Tawḥīdī, *Baṣāʾir*, v, 49-51, Ibn Abī Uṣaybiʿa, *ʿUyūn al-anbāʾ*, pp. 162-65.

Notes to Chapter Two

1. I thank Professor Charles Burnett for this reference and for supplying copies of the relevant texts.

2. Ibn Riḍwān, *Commentary on Ptolemy's* Tetrabiblos, MS Tehran, Majlis 191, fol. 44a. See Ptolemy, *Tetrabiblos*, pp. 154-55. Elsewhere, Ptolemy says of the inhabitants of western and southern Asia, which includes Parthia, Media, Babylonia, Mesopotamia and Assyria, that 'they beget children by their own mothers' (*Tetrabiblos*, pp. 140-41). Ibn Riḍwān comments: 'This was found in ancient religions; perhaps it occurred only rarely' (*Commentary*, fol. 41b-42a); he does not mention the Zoroastrians.

3. Ibn Riḍwān, *Commentary*, fol. 44b. In both cases the MS seems to read *ikhwān*, 'brothers', rather than *akhawāt*, 'sisters', a difference of merely one diacritical dot. Ptolemy has 'sisters'.

4. Ibn Qutayba, *ᶜUyūn*, i, 7, al-Masᶜūdī, *Murūj*, i, 290 (which has *aqrab li-l-nasab*), Ibn ᶜAbd Rabbih, *ᶜIqd*, i, 41, al-Ḥuṣrī, *Zahr al-ādāb*, ii, 189 (repr. Beirut 1972, p. 545). It is not found in the lengthy 'testament' (*ᶜahd*) of Ardashīr to his successors given in al-Ābī, *Nathr*, vii, 84-107, but ascribed there to Kisrā/Chosroes (vii, 74). See also ᶜAbbās, *ᶜAhd Ardashīr*, p. 88.

5. And *khvēdhvagdas, khvētvadas, khvētūdād, khᵛētōdāt, khetyōdath, khēdyōdath* (among others). Macrons often appear as circumflexes, and instead of *kh* one may expect *x*.

6. Morony, entry 'Madjūs' in *EI²* (v, 1110b); cf. Spooner, 'Iranian Kinship and Marriage', pp. 52-56, Stricker, *Camephis*, pp. 26-40, 48, Sidler, *Zur Universalität des Inzesttabu*, pp. 86-149 (with many references to Greek, Latin and Iranian but no Muslim Arabic sources), Slotkin, 'On a possible lack of incest regulations in Old Iran', Christensen, *L'Iran sous les Sassanides*, pp. 322-24, Yarshater (ed.), *Cambridge History of Iran* vol. 3, pp. 471-72, 644, 938, Shaki, 'The Sassanian Matrimonial Relations', pp. 335-36, Choksy, *Evil, Good, and Gender*, pp. 90-91, 129, Herrenschmidt, 'Le *xwêtôdas* ou mariage «incestueux» en Iran ancien'.

7. They are vols 5, 18, 24, 37 and 47 of the series. See West, *Pahlavi Texts*, i, 212-13, 307, 387-89, ii, 105, 199-200, 225, iii, 26, 71, 73-74, v, 6, 51, 52. 166; and see West's appendix, 'The meaning of Khvêtûk-das or Khvêtûdâd', in iii, 389-430, with references to other, including some older, texts. His article is 'still fundamental, but all the translations from the Pahlavi are in need of revision' (Herrenschmidt, 'Le *xwētōdas* ou mariage «incestueux»', p. 119 [my translation]).

8. West, *Pahlavi Texts*, i, 213 (from *Bahman Yasht* ii, 57-61).

9. West, *Pahlavi Texts*, i, 307 (from *Shāyast Lā-shāyast*, viii, 18).

10. West, *Pahlavi Texts*, iii, 26 (from *Dīnā-ī Maīnōg-ī Khiradh*, iv, 3-4).

11. West, *Pahlavi Texts*, iii, 71 (from *Dīnā-ī Maīnōg-ī Khiradh*, xxxvi).

12. West, *Pahlavi Texts*, v, 51 (from *Dīnkard*, VII, ix, 5).

13. West, *Pahlavi Texts*, v, 166-67 (from *Zād-Sparam*, xxiii, 13).

14. West, *Pahlavi Texts*, ii, 399-410.

15. West, *Pahlavi Texts*, ii, 416.

16. Stricker, *Camephis*, p. 34 (my translation).

17. Spooner, 'Iranian Kinship and Marriage', p. 56.

18. Sidler, *Zur Universalität des Inzesttabu*, pp. 138-49.

19. Brosius, *Women in Ancient Persia, 559-331 BC*, pp. 45-46.

20. Brosius, *Women in Ancient Persia*, pp. 66, 69. For some more cases, see Herrenschmidt, 'Le *xwêtôdas* ou mariage «incestueux»', pp. 114-18.

21. Boyce, *A History of Zoroastrianism*, i, 254, eadem, *Zoroastrians*, pp. 53-54, 97, 110-11, 137-38.

22. Nöldeke, *Aufsätze zur persischen Geschichte*, p. 106 (no source is given).

23. See Rank, *The Incest Theme*, p. 304, quoting Heinrich Lessmann, *Aufgaben und Ziele der vergleichenden Mythenforschung*, p. 40 (Lessmann does not provide a source for this 'Iranian tradition').

24. See below, p. 182.

25. Catullus, poem 90, in *The Poems of Catullus*, tr. James Mitchie, pp. 202-3 (Latin and English).

26. Athenaeus, *Deipnosophists*, ii, 496-99. See also v, 416-17: Alcibiades and a friend marry the same bride of Abydos, producing a daughter of uncertain fatherhood. Later, they both cohabit with the daughter, each claiming that the other is the father. Incidentally, Byron's *Bride of Abydos*, though an unrelated tale, also deals with incest, an earlier draft of half-sibling incest being replaced by an affair between cousins who at first believed they were brother and sister (see also below, p. 164).

27. See e.g. Boyce & Grenet, *A History of Zoroastrianism, III*, pp. 277-78, 303, 437, 520-21, 545.

28. Abū Qurra, *Maymar fī wujūd al-khāliq wa-l-dīn al-qawīm*, p. 202; cf. below, p. 124.

29. On the Shuʿūbiyya, see Enderwitz, entry 'Shuʿūbiyya' in EI^2, which gives all the important further references.

30. See A. Melvinger, entry 'al-Madjūs' in EI^2, v, 1181-21.

31. Ibn Diḥya, *al-Muṭrib*, pp. 140-41; cf. El-Hajji, *Andalusian Diplomatic Relations*, p. 173.

32. al-Tawḥīdī, *Imtāʿ*, i, 70-96. To my knowledge this essay has never been translated in full. A summary is given in Margoliouth, 'Some Extracts', pp. 388-90 (nothing on the theme of incest). The beginning of the session (not on incest) is translated in Lewis, *Race and Slavery*, pp. 143-45 and, by John Damis, in Lichtenstaedter, *Introduction to Classical Arabic Literature*, pp. 353-57. Shortened translations of the session as a whole

are given by Bergé, 'Mérites respectifs des nations' and by myself (in Dutch), in Vrolijk (ed.), *De Taal der engelen*, pp. 161-70.

33. For a variant of the Ibn al-Muqaffaʿ story, see Ibn ʿAbd Rabbih, *ʿIqd*, iii, 324-25.

34. See Ch. Pellat, entry 'al-Djayhānī' in EI^2, Supplement, Ducène, 'Al-Ǧayhānī: fragments'.

35. On Abū Ḥāmid Aḥmad ibn ʿĀmir al-Marwarrūdhī, see al-Subkī, *Ṭabaqāt al-Shāfiʿiyya*, ii, 82-83, Ibn Khallikān, *Wafayāt*, i, 69, 396-97.

36. al-Tawḥīdī, *Baṣāʾir*, ii, 11.

37. al-Tawḥīdī, *Baṣāʾir*, vi, 150.

38. al-Tawḥīdī, *Baṣāʾir*, i, 147-48, Ibn Khallikān, *Wafayāt*, i, 69.

39. Yāqūt, *Muʿjam al-udabāʾ*, xv, 5: '*Shīrāzī al-aṣl wa-qīla Nīsābūrī*'.

40. Ibn Abī l-Ḥadīd, *Sharḥ Nahj al-balāgha*, iii, 261.

41. The syntax of the original has to be amended: for *la-kāna lā yanbaghī an yadhkurū ... wa-an yakhrasū ...*, read e.g. *la-kāna yanbaghī allā yadhkurū ... wa-an yakhrasū* (thanks to Donald Richards for noticing this).

42. I do not understand *ḍaʿīf bi-l-samāʿ* and have translated it as if the first word should be read *maʿīf*.

43. *i.e.* Jews and Christians.

44. An old syncretistic group of 'astrolators' in Ḥarrān (Carrhae), tolerated though pagan, and barely surviving at the time of the debate; see T. Fahd, entry 'Ṣābiʾa' in EI^2.

45. Some words supplied to make the text coherent.

46. A saying meaning 'they went from bad to worse'.

47. *Ghayra* is the mixture of appropriate sexual jealousy and sense of honour that men are supposed to have with regard to their female kin.

48. I omit a short passage in which it is argued that the revolutionary religious movement led by Mazdak was crushed by a strong Sasanid ruler in AD 528 or 529, whereas Zoroaster found a weak king, willing to elevate and support him.

49. I am not certain of the meaning of *farāghuhum* here; the context seems to suggest 'being (temporarily) free from lust'.

50. Burying infant girls (*waʾd al-banāt*), forbidden in Islam, was practised by some pre-Islamic tribes. See Leemhuis, entry 'waʾd al-banāt' in EI^2.

51. The editors, unable to identify him, suggest reading al-Anṭākī, and think ʿAlī ibn Aḥmad al-Anṭākī could be meant, who died in Baghdad in 376/986-7. However, a certain Abū l-Ḥasan ibn Kaʿb al-Anṣārī is quoted several times by al-Tawḥīdī as one of his contemporaries and described as a Muʿtazilite *adīb* and theologian (*Baṣāʾir*, ii,

26). He is mentioned together with al-Marwarrūdhī in *Baṣā'ir*, i, 236 (see also editor's note).

52. The Prophet Muḥammad.

53. See above, p. 38.

54. See above, p. 18.

55. Compare the different version, above, p. 15. The text has *sirr* 'secret' instead of the correct *shibr* 'span'. In its closest possible form, the equation (probably a poetic exaggeration) implies a marriage between a man and his niece (or sister's daughter); his brother serves as the offspring's paternal uncle and mother's maternal uncle.

56. Cf. Q 3:128, 8:51, 22:10, 41:46, 50:29.

57. See e.g. Morony, entry 'Madjūs' in *EI²*, Boyce, *Zoroastrianism*, pp. 149-62 (chapter eight: 'The Faith under Islamic Rule'). Spooner, 'Iranian Kinship and Marriage', p. 53, also remarks that all early Muslim invectives are directed against past rather than contemporary practice.

58. Boyce, *Zoroastrians*, p. 54.

59. Spuler, *Iran in frühislamischer Zeit*, pp. 377-78.

60. al-Muqaddasī, *Aḥsan al-taqāsīm*, p. 368-69, tr. Collins in al-Muqaddasī, *The Best Divisions*, p. 299.

61. Ibn Khallikān, *Wafayāt*, ii, 75.

62. Yāqūt, *Muʿjam al-buldān*, iii, 446-47, al-Qazwīnī, *Āthār al-bilād*, p. 582. For the Chigil or Čigil Turks, see P.B. Golden, in the entry 'Turks', *EI²*, x, 689; Yāqūt, *Muʿjam al-buldān*, *s.v.* 'Jikil', ii, 95.

63. Yāqūt, *Muʿjam al-buldān*, iii, 449. This and the preceding report are by the tenth-century traveller Abū Dulaf Misʿar ibn Muhalhil.

64. al-Nawbakhtī, *Firaq al-shīʿa*, p. 25, see Watt, *The Formative Period*, pp. 46, 330, van Ess, *Theologie und Gesellschaft*, i, 284, 455, iv, 742.

65. Watt, *The Formative Period of Islamic Thought*, p. 46; Ḥamza is mentioned by name on pp. 48-49 and 51.

66. al-Muqaddasī, *Aḥsan al-taqāsīm*, pp. 421, 429, and see 441; tr. Collins, pp. 344, 349, and 358, respectively.

67. cf. al-Muqaddasī, *Aḥsan al-taqāsīm*, p. 441, tr. Collins p. 357.

68. Reading uncertain, not found elsewhere.

69. [Ibn Iyās], *Badāʾiʿ*, p. 156.

70. al-Maʿarrī, *Luzūmiyyāt*, ii, 27.

71. See below, pp. 76-77.

72. Translation by R.A. Nicholson, in his *Studies in Islamic Poetry*, p. 104, Arabic text ibid. p. 239 and al-Maᶜarrī, *Luzūmiyyāt*, i, 172.

73. Traditionally, he is said to have lived in the sixth century B.C. It has been argued that this is a fiction dating from the time of Alexander the Great and that the 'real' Zoroaster lived as early as between 1400 and 1000 B.C. (Boyce, *A History of Zoroastrianism. I: The Early Period*, p. 190), or even between 1700 and 1500 B.C. (Boyce, *Zoroastrians*, pp. 2, 18, 93). See also Kellens, 'Zoroastre dans l'histoire ou dans le mythe ?'.

74. Ibn ᶜAbd Rabbih, *ᶜIqd*, vi, 236.

75. al-Damīrī, *Ḥayāt al-Ḥayawān al-kubrā*, i, 15 and see al-Tawḥīdī, *Imtāᶜ*, ii, 31, where instead of 'he bit off his yard' (*qaṭaᶜa dhakarahu*) one finds the less drastic 'he did not complete the act and stopped' (*lam yutimm wa-qaṭaᶜa*), which is closer to Aristotle.

76. Aristotle, *History of Animals*, ix, 47 = 630^b-631^a, tr. by d'A. W. Thompson, in Aristotle, *The Complete Works*, ed. by Jonathan Barnes, p. 980. See also the pseudo-Aristotelian *On Marvellous Things Heard* (830^{b}5), tr. by L. D. Dowdall in Aristotle, *The Complete Works*, p. 1272.

77. al-Tawḥīdī, *Imtāᶜ*, ii, 31.

78. *al-sāḥil*: since al-Awzāᶜī lived in Damascus and died (in 157/774) in Beirut, I suppose the Mediterranean coast may be intended.

79. Ibn al-Kalbī, *Nasab al-khayl*, p. 27.

80. al-Qazwīnī, *Mufīd al-ᶜulūm*, p. 425.

81. Wilson, *Sociobiology*, p. 38., idem, *Consilience*, pp. 192-93.

82. Both versions in al-Iṣfahānī, *Aghānī*, iv, 411-12. For another translation, see Rosenthal, *Humor in Early Islam*, p. 110.

83. See M. J. Kister, entry 'Ḳays b. ᶜĀṣim' in *EI*², iv, 832-33.

84. al-Iṣfahānī, *Aghānī*, xiv, 69-70 gives a particularly gruesome story of his behaviour.

85. al-Iṣfahānī, *Aghānī*, xiv, 84, al-ᶜAskarī, *Awāʾil*, p. 31, al-Raqīq al-Qayrawānī, *Quṭb al-surūr*, p. 419.

86. C. Pellat in Ashtiany *et al.* (eds), *ᶜAbbasid Belles-Lettres*, pp. 96, 108.

87. al-Thaᶜālibī, *Yatīma*, iii, 269, al-Ṣāḥib ibn ᶜAbbād, *Dīwān*, p. 286.

88. Goody, *The Oriental, the Ancient and the Primitive*, Part II: India (pp. 155-312).

89. Sachau, *Alberuni's India*, ii, 155; Arabic text in al-Bīrūnī, *Akhbār al-Hind*, p. 278.

90. West, Pahlavi Texts,v, 389-90 (note 4; from *Shāyast lā shāyast*, xviii, 4).

91. From a Pahlavi *Riwāyat*, West, *Pahlavi Texts*, ii, 416, 423.

92. See D. Sourdel, entry 'Bihʾāfrīd b. Farwardīn' in *EI*², i, 1209, W. Madelung, entry 'Ustādhsīs' in *EI*², x, 926-27.

93. al-Khwārazmī, *Mafātīḥ*, [p. 26] p. 38. Ibn al-Nadīm, *Fihrist*, p. 344 calls him 'a Magian who performed the five prayers without prostration', but does not mention anything about his views on marriage. See also al-Baghdādī, *Farq*, p. 347.

94. al-Bīrūnī, *al-Āthār al-bāqiya*, pp. 210-11 (tr. by Sachau, *The Chronology of Ancient Nations*, p. 193), al-Shahrastānī, *Milal*, i, 238 (tr. by Gimaret and Monnot, i, 637).

95. Fück, 'Sechs Ergänzungen zu al-Bīrūnī', p. 75. For Marzubān ibn Rustam, see J. T. P. de Bruijn, entry 'Marzbān-nāma' in *EI*², v, 632.

96. Strabo, *Geography*, tr. by Horace Leonard Jones, vii, 364-65 (= 16.4.25).

97. Strabo, *Geography*, vii, 366-67. See also Sidler, *Zur Universalität des Inzesttabu*, pp. 40-43. An echo of this story seems to be heard in the report of Ibn al-Mujāwir (d. 690/1291) that in Qalhāt (in Oman) every seven men would buy a slavegirl, each visiting her in turn and leaving his sandals at the door to indicate that she was occupied (*Taʾrīkh al-mustabṣir*, ii, 283).

98. On him see M. J. Kister, entry 'Ḥājib ibn Zurāra' in *EI*², iii, 49.

99. Reading, with Abū Ḥātim al-Rāzī, *aḥashtu ... sawʾatan* which is obviously better than *ajashshat ... sawʾatun* found in the edition of *al-ʿArab*.

100. Ibn Qutayba, *ʿArab*, p. 372, cf. Abū Ḥātim al-Rāzī, *Zīna*, i, 148-49, where the daughter is called Dukhtanūs, apparently confusing her with the daughter of Ḥājib's brother Laqīṭ (see below).

101. See e.g. Ibn ʿAbd Rabbih, *ʿIqd*, ii, 9-20.

102. Ibn Qutayba, *Maʿārif*, 621.

103. On al-Aqraʿ ibn Ḥābis see e.g. Caskel, *Ǧamhara*, Tab. 61, Register, p. 191, on Abū Sūd ibn Kalb, see Tab. 71, Register, p. 515. On the link between Tamīm and Zoroastrianism, see also al-Maqdisī, *Badʾ*, iv, 31.

104. See C. Pellat, entry 'Laḳīṭ b. Zurāra' in *EI*², v, 640, Sezgin, *Geschichte*, ii, 194.

105. Maʿarrī, *Ṣāhil*, p. 634.

106. Sezgin, *Geschichte*, ii, 225.

107. The name, from a root associated with farting, sneezing or generally being inarticulate, sounds hardly auspicious. In Ibn Ḥabīb's version she is called al-F.qāṭa (reading uncertain, and root unknown, possibly a corruption of al-Q.fāṭa).

108. al-Iṣfahānī, *Aghānī*, xiv, 11; cf. Ibn Saʿīd, *Nashwat al-ṭarab*, i, 234, al-Raqīq al-Qayrawānī, *Quṭb al-surūr*, p. 420.

109. al-Iṣfahānī, *Aghānī*, xiv, 12-13.

110. *Innī la-asmaʿu shakhkhah, lā budda min an azukhkhahā zakhkhah*. For the meaning of the verb *zakhkha* see e.g. al-Zamakhsharī, *Asās al-balāgha*, *s.v.* or the larger lexicons.

111. Ibn Ḥabīb, *al-Muḥabbar*, pp. 471-72; the two lines by al-Ḥusayn are also quoted, with 'sand' instead of 'skirt'.

112. The two versions of the story are rather at odds with the report that al-Burj was one of the '*mu*ʿ*ammarūn*', implying that he lived to an exceptionally (or incredibly) great age (al-Qālī, *Amālī*, ii, 289).

113. al-Thaʿlabī, *Qiṣaṣ*, p. 395, tr. Brinner, pp. 731-32, Ṭabarī, *Tafsīr*, xii, 523 al-Zamakhsharī, *Kashshāf*, vi, 222 (ad Q 85:4), Loth, 'Ṭabarī's Korancommentar', pp. 610-12.

114. See R. Paret, entry 'Aṣḥāb al-ukhdūd', *EI*[2], i, 692, C. E. Bosworth's annotated translation of al-Ṭabarī, *The History*, v, 192-205 (cf. al-Ṭabarī, *Tārīkh*, ed. Leiden, i, 922-25), Loth, 'Ṭabarī's Korancommentar', pp. 610-22.

115. See also Marzolph, *Arabia ridens*, ii, 31 (no. 113).

116. al-Yaʿqūbī, *Tārīkh*, i, 174.

117. al-Yaʿqūbī, *Tārīkh*, i, 159.

118. Calling al-Yaʿqūbī an 'Arab historian' (Muhammad Qasim Zaman, entry 'al-Yaʿḳūbī' in *EI*[2], xi, 257) is misleading.

119. al-Masʿūdī, *Murūj*, i, 260-327, idem, *Tanbīh*, pp. 85-111.

120. Ṣāʿid al-Andalusī, *Ṭabaqāt al-umam*, pp. 59-65.

121. Ṣāʿid al-Andalusī, *Ṭabaqāt al-umam*, pp. 64-65, 116.

122. The name also appears as Ḥumānā/Ḥumānī, Ḥumāya, Humāʾ, and, more often, Humāy (see C. Huart and H. Massé, entry 'Humāʾ' in *EI*[2], iii, 572).

123. al-Dīnawarī, *al-Akhbār al-ṭiwāl*, pp. 29-30. cf. al-Maqdisī, *Bad*ʾ, iii, 150 (where the daughter/wife is called Humāy); cf. Abū l-Fidāʾ, *Mukhtaṣar*, i, 52.

124. al-Thaʿālibī al-Marghanī, *Ghurar*, pp. 389-99.

125. al-Masʿūdī, *Tanbīh*, pp. 94, 106, *Murūj*, i, 268, 272-73.

126. al-Thaʿālibī al-Marghanī, p. 389, says, 'Khumāy was also called Jihrāzād'. In al-Yaʿqūbī, *Tārīkh*, i, 158, Khumānī is called 'the daughter of Jihrazād'; al-Masʿūdī, *Murūj*, i, 279 also mentions Dīnāzād, wife of Bukhtnaṣṣar, as related to Ḥumāya. It is all rather confused. For the connection with Shahrazād and *The Thousand and One Nights*, see Ibn al-Nadīm, *Fihrist*, p. 304: 'It is said that this book was composed for Ḥumānā/Ḥumānī, the daughter of Bahman'. See also Sallis, *Sheherazade Through the Looking Glass*, p. 24.

127. Ṭabarī, *Tārīkh* ed. de Goeje i, 689 (ed. Hārūn i, 569), as translated by Moshe Perlmann, al-Ṭabarī, *The History*, iv, 83.

128. Ibn al-Balkhī, *Fārs-nāma*, p. 54; on Bahman and Khumānī, see also p. 15.

129. al-Maqdisī, *Bad*ʾ, iii, 150.

130. al-Maqdisī, *Bad*ʾ, iii, 150-52.

131. Lyons, *The Arabian Epics, Volume 2: Analysis*, p. 212, and *Volume 3: Texts*, p. 505.

132. Firdawsī, *Shāhnāma*, v, 483-84, Ferdowsi, *The Epic of the Kings* (tr. Reuben Levy), pp. 219-28.

133. al-Maqdisī, *Badʾ*, iv, 26-30.

134. al-Maqdisī, *Badʾ*, iv, 26.

135. al-Maqdisī, *Badʾ*, iv, 29.

136. al-Maqdisī, *Badʾ*, iv, 31.

137. al-Tawḥīdī, *Baṣāʾir*, ix, 153.

138. Quoted in al-Shahrastānī, *Milāl*, ii, 245.

139. Ibn Qutayba, *ʿArab*, p. 372.

140. reading *ajlāf* instead of *aḥlāf*.

141. Yāqūt, *Muʿjam al-buldān*, iv, 620.

142. al-Ābī, *Nathr al-durr*, ii, 200; cf. Marzolph, *Arabia ridens*, ii, 174 (no. 738).

143. al-Jāḥiẓ, *Bayān*, ii, 260, cf. Ibn Qutayba, *ʿUyūn*, ii, 45; Ibn ʿAbd Rabbih, *ʿIqd*, vi, 158, al-Ābī, *Nathr al-durr*, vii, 356, Ibn ʿAbd al-Barr, *Bahjat al-majālis*, i, 550, al-Māwardī, *Adab*, p. 32, al-Ḥamdūnī, *Tadhkira*, iii, 288. In some versions the sum is 10,000 dirhams. See also Marzolph, *Arabia ridens*, ii, 8 (no. 28).

144. See M. Guidi & M. Morony, entry 'Mōbadh' in *EI*², vii, 213-16. Supposedly, he was the renowned Ādhurfarnbag Farrukhzādān (also spelled Āturfarnbag-i Farrukhzātān); see Boyce, *Zoroastrians*, p. 153, Guidi/Morony in *EI*², vii, 214, Morony in *EI*², v, 1112.

145. al-Rāghib al-Iṣbahānī, *Muḥāḍarāt*, ii, 243. For the formulaic expression *ḥattā faḥaṣa bi-rijlihi* see Müller, *'Und der Kalif lachte'*, pp. 334-42.

146. al-Tawḥīdī, *Baṣāʾir*, vii, 79; cf. Marzolph, *Arabia ridens*, ii, 168 (no. 706).

147. Muslim polemics missed a chance, it seems, in not pouncing on the 'holy incest' implied by widespread medieval ideas on Mary as *mater et filia*, both mother and daughter of God, in addition to being her son's bride. See Archibald, *Incest and the Medieval Imagination*, pp. 238-44; and see below, p. 142-43 on Fāṭima being called 'her Father's Mother'.

148. He uses the vulgar word *nayk*.

149. al-Rāghib al-Iṣbahānī, *Muḥāḍarāt*, ii, 241.

150. See pp. 76.

151. al-Jāḥiẓ, *al-Radd ʿalā l-Naṣārā*, in his *Rasāʾil*, iii, 316; other English translations in Finkel, 'A Risāla', p. 328, and al-Jāḥiẓ, *The Life and Works of Jāḥiẓ* (tr. Hawke), p. 88, French tr. in Allouche, 'Un traité polémique', p. 135, German tr. in (al-Jāḥiẓ), *Arabische Geisteswelt*, p. 143 (tr. Müller).

152. See the exegetes on Q 2:65, 5:60, 7:166; Ch. Pellat, entry 'Maskh' in *EI*[2] vi, 736-38, Traini, 'La métamorphose des êtres humains', Rubin, 'Apes, Pigs, and the Islamic Identity'.

153. See e.g. al-Jāḥiẓ, *al-Tarbīʿ wa-l-tadwīr*, in his *Rasāʾil*, iii, 66, 82, 92, 100, ed. Pellat, pp. 22, 55, 64, 72; *Fakhr al-sūdān*, in *Rasāʾil*, i, 224, *Ḥayawān*, i, 242, ii, 50, 333, iv, 58. v, 566.

154. al-Masʿūdī, *Murūj al-dhahab*, ii, 82.

155. See e.g. *Encyclopaedia Judaica*, entry 'Levirate Marriage and Ḥalizah' (xi, 122-31). The relevant O.T. texts are Gen. 38:9, Deut. 25:5-6 and Ruth 3:12-13.

156. al-Masʿūdī, *Murūj al-dhahab*, ii, 83. For the Jewish regulations concerning consanguineous marriages, see Lev. 18:6-18 and Deut. 23:20-23; cf. also *Encyclopaedia Judaica*, entry 'Incest' (viii, 1316-18), Ricks, 'Kinship Bars to Marriage in Jewish and Islamic Law'. In this context, it ought to be mentioned that the relevant passages from the Hebrew Bible, in which the forbidden degrees are listed (principally Lev. 18 and 20, with scattered rules in Deut. 23 and 27), oddly fail to mention explicitly one's daughter, an omission not exploited by Muslim polemicists, as far as I know.

157. al-Masʿūdī, *Murūj al-dhahab*, ii, 82-83.

158. Ibn Ḥazm, *Faṣl*, i, 133.

159. Ibn Ḥazm, *Faṣl*, i, 134. For an eighth-century Christian defence of Lot and his daughters, see Īshōʿbokht in Sachau, *Syrische Rechtsbücher*, iii, 40-41 (Syriac and German translation).

160. Ibn Ḥazm, *Faṣl*, i, 135.

161. Ibn Qayyim al-Jawziyya, *Ighāthat al-lahfān*, ii, 342-43.

162. Ibn Ḥazm, *Faṣl*, i, 143.

163. Ibn Ḥazm, *Faṣl*, i, 146-47.

164. Ibn Ḥazm, *Faṣl*, i, 147.

165. See Gen. 38: Tamar is married first to Judah's son Er, then to the latter's brother Onan, who is unwilling to consummate the marriage and is therefore killed by God. Disgruntled about not being allowed to wed a third brother, Shelah, Tamar then seduces Judah, disguised as a harlot.

166. Compare Joshua 6 (where it is said that Joshua saved Rahab's life, not that he married her).

167. Ex. 7:20, Num. 26:59.

168. al-Iṣfahānī, *Aghānī*, vii, 61; much shortened in al-Ābī, *Nathr al-durr*, iii, 67: 'It is said that he assaulted a *jāriya* (daughter? slave-girl?) of his and deflowered her'.

169. Ibn al-Ṭiqṭaqā, *Fakhrī*, p. 182 (*intihāk ḥurumāt Allāh*), al-Damīrī, *Ḥayāt al-ḥayawān*, i, 72 (*qad intahaka maḥārim Allāh*), al-Suyūṭī, *Tārīkh al-khulafāʾ*, p. 300 (*muntahikan ḥurumāt Allāh*).

170. Ibn al-ʿIbrī, *Tārīkh*, p. 118, al-Suyūṭī, *Tārīkh al-khulafāʾ*, p. 300.

171. For a translation of two lines and references, see below, p. 79.

172. On Fukayha bt Qatāda, of the tribe Qays b. Thaʿlaba, see Ibn Ḥabīb, *Muḥabbar*, pp. 433-34.

173. Jarīr, *Dīwān*, p. 899, *Naqāʾid Jarīr wa-l-Farazdaq*, p. 342.

174. Ibn al-Muʿtazz (d. 296/908), on a Zoroastrian, puts it more directly: 'He takes his father's place with his mother, not tying up his trousers for her' (Abū Khaḍra, *Ibn al-Muʿtazz*, p. 244, not found in the *Dīwān* editions I have consulted).

175. *Naqāʾiḍ Jarīr wa-l-Farazdaq*, p. 536 (adopting the variant *aḥrāḥuhā* for the second *ajsāduhā*). Not found in the bowdlerized *Dīwān*.

176. *Naqāʾiḍ Jarīr wa-l-Farazdaq*, p. 604, al-Farazdaq, *Dīwān*, ii, 170.

177. See on the equivocal sources van Gelder, '*Mawālī* and Arabic Poetry'.

178. al-Iṣfahānī, *Aghānī*, xiv, 295, a variant version xv, 393.

179. Ibn al-Muʿtazz, *Ṭabaqāt*, p. 23, al-Ḥuṣrī, *Zahr al-ādāb*, p. 475, idem, *Jamʿ al-jawāhir*, p. 343, al-Mutanabbī, *Dīwān* (al-ʿUkbarī), iv, 122, idem, *Dīwān* (al-Wāḥidī), p. 340.

180. al-Tawḥīdī, *Baṣāʾir*, i, 111.

181. Yāqūt, *Muʿjam al-udabāʾ*, xvii, 85-86.

182. *Qaḍāhā raḍāʿa l-thadyi minhu bi-ayrihī / fa-farra lahā farjan wa-farrat lahū famā.* It looks as if *fellatio* is meant, but the line is not without problems. The translation of *qaḍāhā* follows a suggestion of Everett Rowson (personal information); or perhaps one ought to read *fa-ḍāhā* (implying that he 'matches' being suckled as a child with being sucked). The rare meaning 'to open, disclose' of the verb *farra* is suggested by the editor; Rowson suggests reading *qarra* and *qarrat*.

183. The 'knocking' is present in the Arabic: *ṭuriqat bi-l-ḥaml.*

184. 'Muttering' (*zamzama*) is often mentioned in descriptions of the Zoroastrians during devotions or meals.

185. See below, p. 78.

186. Abū Tammām, *Dīwān*, iv, 214.

187. al-Ṣafadī, *Wāfī*, xvi, 605.

188. al-Mutanabbī, *Dīwān* (al-ʿUkbarī), iv, 123, idem, *Dīwān* (al-Wāḥidī), p. 340.

189. al-Mutanabbī, *Dīwān* (al-ʿUkbarī), iv, 122, idem, *Dīwān* (al-Wāḥidī), p. 340, al-Ḥuṣrī, *Zahr al-ādāb*, p. 475, idem, *Jamʿ al-jawāhir*, p. 343.

190. Muslim ibn al-Walīd, *Dīwān*, p. 47.

191. al-Shayzarī, *Jamharat al-Islām*, p. 75.

192. Muslim ibn al-Walīd, *Dīwān*, p. 56.

193. Ibn Saʿīd, *Mughrib*, ii, 213.

194. Dhū l-Rumma, *Dīwān* (Macartney), p. 175, (Abū Ṣāliḥ), pp. 1431-32, al-Dīnawarī, *Nabāt*, pp. 128-29, Ibn Durayd, *Jamhara*, pp. 242, 913, Ibn Fāris, *Maqāyīs al-lugha*, iii, 376, Ibn Manẓūr, *Lisān al-ʿArab*, *s.v.* ḌWY.

195. ed. Macartney p. 175, ed. Abū Ṣāliḥ, which has a different order of lines, p. 1426.

196. See C. Pellat, entry 'al-Maḳṣūra' in *EI*², vi, 195-96.

197. Ibn Durayd, *Maqṣūra*, pp. 204 (lines 218-21).

198. Ḥāzim al-Qarṭājannī, *Dīwān*, p. 48 (line 581).

199. Ibn Qutayba, *Adab al-kātib*, p. 22, idem, *al-Maʿānī*, pp. 563, 637, al-Jurjānī, *Muntakhab*, p. 381, Ibn Manẓūr, *Lisān al-ʿArab*, *s.v.* NML, Ibn Abī l-Ḥadīd, *Sharḥ Nahj al-balāgha*, v, 505-6. The reading *naḥuttu* instead of *nakhuttu*, preferred by Ibn al-Aʿrābī (who thinks of real ants), is mentioned and rejected by Ibn al-Anbārī, *Nuzha*, p. 122; cf. also al-Baṭalyawsī, *Iqtiḍāb*, iii, 12-14.

200. See e.g. Ibn Sīnā, *Qānūn*, iii, 117.

201. al-Rāzī, *Tafsīr*, ii, 400, *ad* Q 4:23.

202. See T. Fahd, entry 'Ṣābiʾa' in *EI*², viii, 675-78.

203. Arberry's translation.

204. For references to the collections of al-Bukhārī and Ibn Ḥanbal, see Wensinck *et al.*, *Concordance*, vi, 174, *s.v.* MJS.

205. pseudo-Masʿūdī, *Akhbār al-zamān*, p. 78. Satan is also involved in another story concerning the Zoroastrian practice, see below, p. 124.

206. Said to be a mountain near Ardabīl in Ādharbayjān, see al-Qazwīnī, *ʿAjāʾib al-makhlūqāt*, i, 268-69.

207. Ibn al-Jawzī, *Talbīs Iblīs*, pp. 57-58; cf. al-Rāghib al-Iṣbahānī, quoted above, p. 62 and note 149.

208. al-Jāḥiẓ, *Ḥayawān*, v, 67.

209. Ibn al-Jawzī, *Talbīs Iblīs*, p. 69.

210. Ibn al-Jawzī, *Talbīs Iblīs*, p. 69. See also M. Guidi & M. Morony, entry 'Mazdak' in *EI*², vi, 949-52, Niẓām al-Mulk, *Siyar al-mulūk*, chapter 44, pp. 257-78), id., *The Book of Government*, tr. Darke, pp. 190-206.

211. See the entries 'Mazdak' and 'Zindīḳ' in *EI*².

212. al-Ṭabarī, *Tārīkh* (de Goeje), III, i, 549-51, tr. Williams, ii, 141-42, tr. Bosworth, xxx, 13-14. See also Chokr, *Zandaqa et zindīqs en Islam*, pp. 77-80.

213. The dictionary meanings of *ru^{c}būb* ('coward; restless [camel])' and *ru^{c}būba* ('delicate [girl]; piece of a camel's hump') are unhelpful. Here a connection with *ru^{c}b* 'terror' is obvious (cf. Williams's translation: 'The Terrorizer'). Bosworth suggests it is a club.

214. Presumably Abū ^{c}Alī al-Ḥusayn ibn ^{c}Alī al-Karābīsī, who died around 245/859, see C. Brockelmann, entry 'al-Karābīsī' in *EI^{2}*, iv, 596.

215. al-Ash^{c}arī, *Maqālāt al-islāmiyyīn*, i, 95.

216. I read *tamaḥḥaḍa* instead of the syntactically odd *al-maḥḍ*.

217. al-Baghdādī, *al-Farq bayn al-firaq*, pp. 264-65 (for shorter references to the Maymūniyya and incest, see pp. 11, 18, 75, 350). For another English translation, by A. S. Halkin, see al-Baghdādī, *Moslem Schisms and Sects*, pp. 105-6.

218. Watt, *The Formative Period of Islamic Thought*, p. 34.

219. al-Isfarāyīnī, *Tabṣīr*, p. 123 'Maymūn ... then chose from the Zoroastrian religion the permissibility of marriage with daughters of daughters and with sons of sons. He allowed his followers to marry them. He also allowed them to marry daughters of brothers and sisters'; ibid. p. 125-26: 'Those who designed the religion of the Bāṭinites (Esotericists) were descended from the Zoroastrians and they inclined towards the religion of their forefathers... So they allowed all pleasures and lusts, they allowed marriage with daughters and sisters'. See also ibid. p. 54.

220. al-Baghdādī, *al-Farq bayn al-firaq*, p. 270.

221. al-Baghdādī, *al-Farq bayn al-firaq*, p. 281.

222. The South Arabians; Muḥammad was a North Arabian.

223. al-Ma^{c}arrī, *Ghufrān*, pp. 438-39. On Manṣūr al-Yaman, see W. Madelung, *EI^{2}*, *s.v.*

224. Muḥammad b. Mālik, *Kashf asrār al-Bāṭiniyya*, pp. 209-10.

225. Mackintosh-Smith, *Travels with a Tangerine*, p. 200; a story heard by the author in Sur in Oman.

226. Muhawi, 'Gender and Disguise in the Arabic *Cinderella*', p. 268; the author refers also to the Qur'anic description of woman as 'tilth' for the husband (Q 2:223).

227. Bouhdiba, *Sexuality in Islam*, p. 114.—In a sexual but non-genetic, non-incestuous sense, the motif is used by the Seville poet Ibn Sahl (d. 648 /1251), on a pretty boy: 'My ministrations make roses bloom / When surreptitiously I glance at him, / And so I wonder what makes illicit / The plucking of these roses by their grower.' (tr. by Pierre Cachia, in his *Arabic Literature: An Overview*, p. 94, Arabic text and translation in Monroe, *Hispano-Arabic Poetry*, pp. 306-7).

228. Quoted in the chapter on marriage by the Shāfi^{c}ite scholar al-Bayjūrī (or al-Bājūrī, d. 1276/1860) in his *Ḥāshiya* (glosses on Ibn Qāsim al-Ghazzī's *Fatḥ al-qarīb*), ii, 117.

Notes to Chapter Three

1. George P. Murdock, 'The Common Denominator of Cultures', in Ralph Linton (ed.), *The Science of Man in the World Crisis*, New York, 1945; see Wilson, *Consilience*, pp. 162 and 345.

2. Bouhdiba, *Sexuality in Islam*, p. 16.

3. seventh degree canonical, corresponding to what in Roman and civil law would be called the fourteenth degree.

4. Archibald, *Incest and the Medieval Imagination*, pp. 29-30, 34. She points out that this was theory and was not adhered to all too strictly in practice (pp. 34, 42).

5. See the reports of al-Masʿūdī and al-Bīrūnī, above, pp. 20-21 and 51.

6. *yatazawwajūna ... lā min al-qarīb al-qarāba*: Ibn al-Nadīm, *Fihrist*, p. 319. Chwolsohn, *Die Ssabier und der Ssabismus*, ii, 115-17, has a long and learned note on this passage, in which he gives many, mostly ancient Greek and Latin sources on incest laws and customs among Persians, Egyptians, Greeks, and Romans, but says nothing about the Ṣābiʾans.

7. Aws ibn Ḥajar, *Dīwān*, p. 75. The first line in Ibn Qutayba, *Maʿānī*, p. 521, Ibn Durayd, *Jamhara*, pp. 813 (with more references), 1170, Ibn Manẓūr, *Lisān al-ʿArab*, *s.v.* ḌZN. On the word *ḍayzan* see below. The last phrase literally reads 'with arrogance in its axillae'. A giraffe is considered stupid (al-Jāḥiẓ, *Ḥayawān*, vii, 38).

8. Ibn al-Kalbī, quoted in al-Shahrastānī, *Milal*, ii, 245, French translation in Shahrastani, *Livre des religions*, ii, 515-16. The passage about the claim by throwing one's cloak is found in several other sources, including al-Farrāʾ, *Maʿānī l-Qurʾān*, i, 259, al-Ṭabarī, *Tafsīr*, iv, 193 (on Q 4:19), and al-Wāḥidī, *Asbāb al-nuzūl*, p. 108.

9. Muḥammad ibn Ḥabīb, *Muḥabbar*, pp. 325-26.

10. Ibn Ḥabīb, *Muḥabbar*, pp. 326-27.

11. See above, p. 19.

12. Ibn Qutayba, *Maʿārif*, pp. 112-13.

13. See also al-Iṣfahānī, *Aghānī*, i, 17.

14. Ibn Qutayba, *Maʿārif*, p. 113, al-Iṣfahānī, *Aghānī*, iii, 123; on Zayd, see M. Lecker, entry 'Zayd b. ʿAmr', in *EI*[2], xi, 474-75.

15. Ibn Ḥabīb, *Muḥabbar*, pp. 326-27.

16. Smith's translation, in *Kinship and Marriage*, p. 107 note 1, from Abū l-Fidāʾ, *Mukhtaṣar*, i, 99. On *ḍayzan*, see also al-Tarmānīnī, *al-Zawāj ʿinda l-ʿArab*, pp. 32-36.

17. See C. Pellat, entry 'al-Ḥaḍr' in *EI*[2], iii, 50-51, cf. Ibn Hishām, *Sīra*, i, 71-73 (tr. Guillaume, pp. 699-701, al-Ḥamdūnī, *Tadhkira*, iii, 32-33, al-Bayhaqī, *Maḥāsin*, p. 564, al-Masʿūdī, *Murūj*, ii, 402-4.

18. al-Akhfash, *Ikhtiyārayn*, p. 710.

19. In addition to the sources given before, see Ibn Hishām, *Sīra*, i, 71-73 (tr. Guillaume, pp. 699-701), al-Akhfash, *Ikhtiyārayn*, pp. 710-11, Ibn Qutayba, *ʿUyūn al-akhbār*, iv, 119-20, al-Iṣfahānī, *Aghānī*, ii, 140-44, al-Ḥamdūnī, *Tadhkira*, iii, 32-33; see Christensen, 'La princesse sur la feuille de myrte', Zakeri, 'Arabic reports on the fall of Hatra', with more references. One may speculate that her betrayal of her father was prompted by his incestuous views or even acts, but the incest motif is found in only one source.

20. See p. 60.

21. Ibn al-Nadīm, *Fihrist*, p. 102, Yāqūt, *Muʿjam al-udabāʾ*, xiv, 133.

22. Smith, *Kinship and Marriage*, pp. 191-92.

23. or al-Shafāʾ, al-Shaffāʾ?

24. ʿAwf's genealogy is ʿAwf b. ʿAbd ʿAwf b. al-Ḥārith (e.g. Ibn Qutayba, *Maʿārif*, p. 235) or ʿAwf b. ʿAbd ʿAwf b. ʿAbd b. al-Ḥārith (e.g. Caskel, *Ǧamharat an-nasab*, Tab. 20, Index p. 128, Ibn Ḥajar, *Iṣāba*, iv, 176), while that of his wife is given as al-Shifāʾ bt ʿAwf b. ʿAbd b. al-Ḥārith (Caskel, *Ǧamharat an-nasab*, Index p. 128, al-Balādhurī, *Ansāb*, v, 101, Ibn Saʿd, *Ṭabaqāt*, viii, 247-48, al-Ṣāfadī, *Wāfī*, xvi, 168-69; see also Ibn Hishām, *Sīra*, i, 251 note 1). It is not clear how her father ʿAwf fits in. Robertson Smith would no doubt claim that the confusion was deliberately made by the Muslim genealogists to mask the incestuous nature of the union.

25. *Kinship and Marriage*, p. 194.

26. Smith, *Kinship and Marriage*, p. 192.

27. Ibn Ḥabīb, *Muḥabbar*, pp. 8-9.

28. Ibn Ḥabīb, *Muḥabbar*, pp. 12-18.

29. I use the numbering customary today among most Muslims and Islamologists; Arberry follows a slightly different system.

30. Bell translates the perfect form *kāna* as 'it has become', as if to stress that in pre-Islamic times it was not; but this is to ignore the pre-Classical Qur'anic use of *kāna*.

31. On him, see e.g. G. C. Anawati, entry 'Fakhr al-Dīn al-Rāzī', in *EI^2*, ii, 751-55.

32. For a survey of the rules in English, see Laleh Bakhtiar, *Encyclopedia of Islamic Law: A Compendium of the Major Schools*, Section 10.6, 'The Prohibited Degrees of Female Relatives', pp. 408-23; a French survey in Linant de Bellefonds, *Traité de droit musulman comparé*, ii, 105-51. For a modern survey in Arabic, see e.g. the chapter 'al-Muḥarramāt min al-nisāʾ' in al-Tarmānīnī, *al-Zawāj ʿinda l-ʿArab*, pp. 96-118.

33. The phrase, in various forms, occurs several times in the Qur'an (e.g. 3:104, 110, 7:157, 9:67, 71, 112, 22:41, 31:17).

34. Michael Cook, *Commanding Right and Forbidding Wrong in Islamic Thought*.

35. For the sake of convenience I shall adopt the Muslim idiom of Qur'anic passages, God's literal words having been 'revealed' to the Prophet Muḥammad by the angel Gabriel.

36. al-Bukhārī, *Ṣaḥīḥ*, chapter *Tafsīr* on sura 4. [vi, 57].

37. Bell (tr.), *The Qurʾān*, i, 70.

38. See e.g. al-Zamakhsharī, *Tafsīr*, on Q 4:19.

39. See e.g. al-Suyūṭī, *Lubāb al-nuqūl*, pp. 217-18 (ad Q 4:19).

40. Abū Qays's *ism* was Ṣayfī, that of al-Aslat was ᶜĀmir; they belonged to the tribe of Aws (see Ibn al-Kalbī, *Ǧamhara*, Tab. 184).

41. al-Ṭabarī, *Tafsīr*, iv, 205, cf. al-Wāḥidī, *Asbāb al-nuzūl*, pp. 108-9.

42. Ibn Ḥabīb, *Muḥabbar*, pp. 326-27.

43. al-Zamakhsharī, *Tafsīr*, ad 4:22.

44. Conte, 'Choisir ses parents dans la société arabe', p. 170, also believes that the expression is not pre-Islamic.

45. Abū ᶜUbayda, *Majāz al-Qurʾān*, i, 121.

46. See e.g. Ibn Manẓūr, *Lisān al-ᶜArab*, *s.v.* QTW.

47. al-Rāzī, *Tafsīr*, ii, 398, *ad* Q 4:22.

48. Ibn al-ᶜArabī, *Aḥkām al-Qurʾān*, i, 371.

49. e.g. Ibn al-Humām, *Sharḥ Fatḥ al-qadīr*, iii, 213.

50. Spectorsky, *Chapters on Marriage and Divorce*, p. 106.

51. e.g. Ibn al-Humām, *Sharḥ Fatḥ al-qadīr*, iii, 213.

52. II Samuel 16:20-23.

53. al-Jāḥiẓ, *Qiyān*, in his *Rasāʾil*, ii, 155, ed. Beeston, p. 8, his translation (used here) p. 18 and see his note, p. 48, where he defends the interpretation of *qaḍīb* as penis rather than rod or sceptre. Colville (al-Jahiz, *Sobriety and Mirth*, p. 188) goes too far when he translates 'proceeded to copulate with her'.

54. al-Tawḥīdī, *Baṣāʾir*, iv, 77.

55. al-Rāghib al-Iṣbahānī, *Muḥāḍarāt*, ii, 129-30, cf. al-Yaᶜqūbī, *Tārīkh*, p. 172. For the Persian versions, see the entry 'Farhād wa-Shīrīn' by H. Massé in *EI*^{2}. For the trick with the poison, see al-Ābī, *Nathr al-durr*, iv, 135-36, al-Ḥamdūnī, *Tadhkira*, viii, 213.

56. Fox, *Kinship and Marriage*, pp. 57-58.

57. Conte, 'Choisir ses parents dans la société arabe', pp. 170-71 (my translation).

58. Héritier, *Two Sisters and Their Mother*.

59. Héritier, *Two Sisters and Their Mother*, pp. 267-68.

60. al-Rāzī, *Tafsīr*, ii, 398, *ad* Q 4:22.

61. Summarized at some length in al-Rāzī, *Tafsīr*, ad Q 4:22.

62. *Aghānī*, xxi, 73: '*Nākanī minhum thamāniya*', Ibn Ḥazm, *Naqṭ al-ᶜarūs*, p. 70: '*Dakhala lī* [var. *rakibanī*] *sabᶜat khulafāʾ*'.

63. al-Rāzī, *Tafsīr*, ii, 399, *ad* Q 4:23; al-Suyūṭī, *Itqān*, iii, 63 (in chapter 46, on *mujmal* and *mubayyan*).

64. Abū Ḥayyān, *Baḥr*, iii, 209.

65. See al-Suyūṭī, *Itqān*, iii, 59.

66. There are almost no references to incest with a grandmother. A joke about a man who beds his father's mother (he argues to his protesting father: 'You do it to my mother; why shouldn't I do it to yours?') goes back to an ancient Greek original (Marzolph, 'Philogelos arabikos', pp. 205-6).

67. Ibn Ḥazm, *Muḥallā*, ix, 521.

68. Conte, 'Choisir ses parents dans la société arabe', p. 172.

69. Archibald, *Incest and the Medieval Imagination*, p. 29.

70. The difference between *zinā* and *sifāḥ* seems to be that the former is any forbidden sexual intercourse, and the latter 'illegal cohabitation' rather than casual adultery. See e.g. Ibn Manẓūr, *Lisān al-ᶜArab*, *s.v.* SFḤ: *al-musāfaḥatu l-zinā wa-l-fujūr ... wa-huwa an tuqīma mraʾatun maᶜa rajulin ᶜalā fujūrin min ghayri tazwījin ṣaḥīḥ*.

71. al-Kāsānī, *Badāʾiᶜ al-ṣanāʾiᶜ*, ii, 257, cf. vii, 35-36. See also e.g. Ibn al-Humām, *Sharḥ Fatḥ al-qadīr*, iii, 200.

72. tr. Spectorsky, in *Chapters on Marriage and Divorce*, p. 102.

73. On the tension between law and morality in Islamic law, see Coulson, *Conflicts and Tensions in Islamic Jurisprudence*, ch. 5: 'Law and Morality' (pp. 77-95).

74. He uses the he technical term *ṭard wa-ᶜaks*, approximately 'chasing to and fro': arguing a case from two opposite but mutually corroborating and complementing sides.

75. al-Rāzī, *Tafsīr*, ii, 401.

76. See Linant de Bellefonds, *Traité de droit musulman comparé*, ii, 111-12.

77. Ibn Qudāma, *Mughnī*, ix, 529-30.

78. This, at least is the most likely scenario; other possibilities can be imagined (a woman A, while married to B, has a daughter C from another man D; C is then legally B's daughter; A, divorced or widowed, marries E and has a son F. Then F is C's uterine sister, even though legally they are not related).

79. Schacht, *Introduction to Islamic Law*, p. 129: 'The slave becomes free by law if he becomes the property of a person who is his *maḥram*, i.e. related to him within the forbidden degrees.'

80. This refers to an incident described in Hadith and law books in connection with *liᶜān* (a special oath whereby a husband denies paternity or affirms his wife's adultery; see Schacht, *Introduction*, index).

81. Ibn Qudāma, *Mughnī*, ix, 529-30.—On the matter of marrying daughters born from fornication, see also Landau-Tasseron, 'Adoption, acknowledgement of paternity and false genealogical claims in Arabian and Islamic societies', pp. 179-80, where a few other sources are discussed; Bakhtiar, *Encyclopedia of Islamic Law*, pp. 463-65.

82. Ibn Qayyim al-Jawziyya, *Iᶜlām al-muwaqqiᶜīn ᶜan Rabb al-ᶜālamīn*, ii, 102.

83. For a summary of the legal rules on this see Linant de Bellefonds, *Traité de droit musulman comparé*, ii, 114-20.

84. Entry 'Raḍāᶜ or Riḍāᶜ, 2. In Arabian society', in *EI*^{2}, viii, 362.

85. Giladi, *Infants, Parents and Wet Nurses*, p. 21.

86. Giladi, *Infants, Parents and Wet Nurses*, pp. 21, 25-26.

87. Bouhdiba, *Sexuality in Islam*, p. 17.

88. Chelhod, entry 'Raḍāᶜ or Riḍāᶜ' in *EI*^{2}, viii, 362.

89. Schacht & Burton, entry 'Raḍāᶜ or Riḍāᶜ', in *EI*^{2}, viii, 361.

90. al-Sarakhsī, *Mabsūṭ*, xxx, 288.

91. Giladi, *Infants, Parents and Wet Nurses*. pp. 25-26, 77-78.

92. Watt, *Muhammad at Medina*, p. 281 and cf. p. 383.

93. 'le lait vient de l'homme', Françoise Héritier-Augé, 'Identité de substance et parenté de lait dans le monde arabe', esp. pp. 152, 158, 161, 163-64; eadem, *Two Sisters and their Mother*, pp. 271-72, Édouard Conte, 'Choisir ses parents dans la société arabe', pp. 167-68; idem, 'Filiations prophétiques' (see the section 'Le Prophète allaitant', pp. 70-75).

94. Giladi, *Infants, Parents and Wet Nurses*, pp. 68-114.

95. Giladi, *Infant, Parents and Wet Nurses*, pp. 21-22. On milk-relationship, see also Françoise Héritier-Augé, 'Identité de substance et parenté de lait dans le monde arabe'.

96. Françoise Héritier-Augé, 'Identité de substance et parenté de lait dans le monde arabe', eadem, *Two Sisters and Their Mother*, pp. 269-82.

97. Benkheira, 'Donner le sein, 'est *comme* donner le jour: la doctrine de l'allaitement dans le sunnisme médiéval'.

98. Benkheira, 'Donner le sein', pp. 47-48, my translation.

99. Giladi, *Infants, Parents and Wet Nurses*, p. 22; cf. al-Rāzī, *Tafsīr*, ii, 401.

100. There are several variants, such as *al-raḍāʿa tuḥarrimu mā tuḥarrimu l-wilāda* 'suckling makes forbidden (the same) that birth makes forbidden', see the Hadith compilations and law books.

101. See e.g. Abū Ḥayyān, *al-Baḥr al-muḥīṭ*, iii, 210, Giladi, *Infants, Parents and Wet Nurses*, p. 78.

102. Giladi, *Infants, Parent and Wet Nurses*, p. 71. One is reminded of the girl in Naguib Mahfouz's novel *Zuqāq al-midaqq (Midaq Alley*, set in 20th-century Cairo) who asks half-seriously whether her milk-brother might be a suitable partner for her if it turned out that each has sucked from a different breast (Najīb Maḥfūẓ, *Zuqāq al-midaqq*, Cairo, n.d., p. 30, Naguib Mahfouz, *Midaq Alley*, tr. Trevor Le Gassick, London, 1975, p. 23).

103. See Linant de Bellefonds, *Traité de droit musulman comparé*, ii, 118-19.

104. al-Jāḥiẓ, *Ḥayawān*, v, 305.

105. Giladi, *Infants, Parents and wet Nurses*, p. 69, quoting al-Sarakhsī, *al-Mabsūṭ*, xxx, 297.

106. Fox, *Kinship and Marriage*, p. 195.

107. On the affair, see the entries 'Zayd b. Ḥāri<u>th</u>a' and 'Zaynab bt. <u>D</u>jaḥ<u>sh</u>' in *EI*[2], x, 475, 484-85, Ibn Ḥabīb, *Muḥabbar*, pp. 85-86 and the Qur'anic commentaries *ad* Q 33:37 ff., e.g. al-Farrāʾ, *Maʿānī l-Qurʾān*, ii, 343-44, al-Zamakhsharī, *Kashshāf*, v, 43-46.

108. see e.g. al-Māwardī, *Ḥāwī*, ix, 209.

109. Ibn Manẓūr, *Lisān al-ʿArab*, *s.v.* BHM.

110. See, for instance, al-Zarkashī, *Burhān*, i, 155-63, al-Suyūṭī, *Itqān*, iv, 93-118.

111. al-Maqdisī, *Badʾ*, iii, 66.

112. al-Thaʿlabī, *Qiṣaṣ al-anbiyāʾ*, p. 89, tr. Brinner, p. 172; cf. Lev. 18:18.

113. See, for instance, the 'Story of the Forty Girls' (*Ḥadīth al-arbaʿīn al-jāriya*) in *al-Ḥikāyāt al-ʿajība*, with the marginal and partly illegible remark by a copyist (p. 121): 'Combining two sisters is [not allo]wed in the [reli]gion of Islam [...] perhaps [the story is set?] before Islam'.

114. al-Sarakhsī, *Mabsūṭ*, iv, 196.

115. Compare Hebrew *ṣārā* 'associate wife', related, or perceived as related, to *ṣārā* 'anguish, distress'.

116. e.g. al-Ghazālī, *Iḥyāʾ*, ii, 37, al-Kāsānī, *Badāʾiʿ*, ii, 262, Ibn al-Humām, *Sharḥ Fatḥ al-qadīr*, iii, 208, Ibn Rushd, *Bidāya*, ii, 36, al-Ḥalabī, *Multaqā l-abḥur*, i, 240, Linant de Bellefonds, *Traité de droit musulman comparé*, ii, 139.

117. Conte, 'Choisir ses parents dans la société arabe', p. 172 (my translation).

118. Not identified.

119. al-Tawḥīdī, *Baṣāʾir*, i, 126.

120. Ibn al-Jawzī, *Akhbār al-ḥamqā wa-l-mughaffalīn*, p. 173 (which has al-Faḍl b. ʿAbd Allāh); see also Marzolph, *Arabia ridens*, ii, 136 (no. 542).

121. al-Farrāʾ, *Maʿānī l-Qurʾān*, ii, 270.

122. See e.g. Ibn Manẓūr, *Lisān al-ʿArab*, *s.v.* *ṢHR*.

123. Ibn Qudāma, *Mughnī*, ix, 513 (a Ḥanbalite scholar).

124. Ibn Rushd, *Muqaddima*, ii, 24 (a Mālikite scholar).

125. R. Peters, entry 'zinā' in *EI*[2] (xi, 509).

126. On him, see J. Schacht, entry 'al-Ḥalabī, Burhān al-Dīn Ibrāhīm' in *EI*[2], iii, 90.

127. al-Ḥalabī, *Multaqā l-abḥur*, i, 239-41.

128. al-Wansharīshī (d. 914/1508), *Miʿyār*, iii, 255. I have not been able to identify this Abū Muḥammad.

129. Spectorsky, *Chapters on Marriage and Divorce*, p. 156.

130. Spectorsky, *Chapter on Marriage and Divorce*, p. 105.

131. Ibn Bābawayh, *Man lā yaḥḍuruhu l-faqīh*, iii, 259. Another qualifies this: the midwife is only forbidden to him if she also helped to raise him (ibid.).

132. Ibn Bābawayh, *Man lā yaḥḍuruhu l-faqīh*, iii, 275.

133. Boswell, *Kindness of Strangers*, p. 3; on incest see pp. 107-9, 157-60, 373-78.

134. See on them below, ch. IV.

135. Boswell, *Kindness of Strangers*, p. 392.

136. Boswell, *Kindness of Strangers*, p. 151.

137. On foundlings in Islamic law, see Erich Pritsch & Otto Spies, 'Das Findelkind im islamischen Recht nach al-Kāsānī', *Zeitschr. für vergleich. Rechtswiss.* 57 (1954) 74-101.

138. See R. Peters, entry 'Zinā' in *EI*[2], x, 509-10.

139. Ibn al-Jawzī, *Dhamm al-hawā*, p. 157.

140. al-Dhahabī, *Kabāʾir*, p. 63.

141. Ibn Qayyim al-Jawziyya, *Rawḍat al-muḥibbīn*, p. 376, also given, according to an editorial note, by al-Ṭabarānī (d. 360/971) in *al-Muʿjam al-kabīr* and by Abū Nuʿaym (d. 430/1038) in *Ḥilyat al-awliyāʾ*.

142. al-Maqdisī, *al-Badʾ wa-l-tārīkh*, iv, 40.

143. See the entry 'incest' in the *Encyclopaedia Judaica*, viii, 1316-1318.

144. Archibald, *Incest and the Medieval Imagination*, p. 46.

145. See p. 74.

146. R. Peters, entry 'Zinā', *EI*[2], x, 510.

147. Ibn Taymiyya, *Fatāwī*, ii, 191-92.

148. Ibn Māja, *Sunan* (*ḥudūd*), ii, 68, Abū Dāwūd, *Sunan* (*ḥudūd*), iv, 390-91 (two versions), al-Nasāʾī, *Sunan* (*nikāḥ*), iii, 307-8, al-Dārimī, *Sunan* (*nikāḥ*), ii, 153, Ibn Ḥanbal, *Musnad*, iv, 292. See also e.g. Ibn al-Qayyim, *Rawḍat al-muḥibbīn*, pp. 374-75, and numerous legal handbooks.

149. See e.g. Spectorsky (ed.), *Chapters on Marriage and Divorce*, p. 119.

150. Spectorsky (ed.), *Chapters on Marriage and Divorce*, pp. 156-57.

151. Ibn Qudāma, *Mughnī*, xii, 341-43.

152. Ibn Shaddād, *Dalāʾil al-aḥkām*, ii, 400-1.

153. al-Māwardī, *Ḥāwī*, ix, 197 (chapter on the prohibited degrees), xiii, 217-18 (chapter on prescribed punishments).

154. al-Manbijī, *Lubāb*, ii, 749-53. In Brockelmann's *Geschichte* (Suppl. i, 660) his name appears as al-Manīḥī, al-Musabbiḥī (Suppl. ii, 950) and al-Manbijī (Suppl. ii, 958).

155. Spectorsky, *Chapters on Marriage and Divorce*, p. 119.

156. Ibn Taymiyya, *al-Ikhtiyārāt al-fiqhiyya min (al-)fatāwī*, p. 210.

157. al-Kāsānī, *Badāʾiʿ al-ṣanāʾiʿ*, vii, 35.

158. See also e.g. the Ḥanafite scholar al-Marghīnānī (d. 593/1196), *al-Hidāya, sharḥ Bidāyat al-mubtadiʾ*, ii, 102.

159. The technical term is *ishtibāh*, 'ambiguity', related to *shubha* 'resemblance', implying the presumption of *bona fides* in the accused. See E. K. Rowson, entry 'shubha' in *EI*[2], ix, 492-93.

160. al-Māwardī, *Ḥāwī*, xiii, 217-18, quoting (disapprovingly) Abū Ḥanīfa.

161. Ibn Qudāma, *Mughnī*, xii, 343.

162. Ibn Qayyim al-Jawziyya, *Rawḍat al-muḥibbīn*, p. 375.

163. Ibn Ḥajar, *Iṣāba*, iv, 131.

164. Bousquet, *L'Éthique sexuelle de l'Islam*, p. 81.

165. In medieval Middle Eastern society it is taken for granted that a homoerotic or homosexual relationship involves an age difference; affairs between coevals do occur but are rare, or at least rarely mentioned.

166. Ibn Qudāma, *Mughnī*, ix, 528-29.

167. al-Manbijī, *Lubāb*, ii, 752-53.

168. e.g. al-Bukhārī, *Ṣaḥiḥ*, ch. *Nikāḥ* no. 111.

169. Héritier, *Two Sisters and Their Mother*, pp. 278-79, on customs in Saudi Arabia, using research by Soraya Altorki.

170. Oddly, sister, niece and paternal aunt are not mentioned.

171. Ibn Qayyim al-Jawziyya, *Ighāthat al-lahfān*, ii, 145.

172. Ibn al-Qayyim, *Rawḍat al-muḥibbīn*, pp. 375-76.

173. Ibn al-Qayyim, *Rawḍa*, p. 376.

174. Saḥnūn, *Mudawwana*, xvi, 9.

175. al-Qaffāl al-Shāshī, *Ḥilyat al-ʿulamāʾ*, viii, 15.

176. An unusual alternative, apparently, to *dhāt maḥram*, forbidden female relative.

177. *milk yamīn*: the phrase refers to Q 4:24 «what your right hands possess», meaning slaves used as concubines.

178. Ibn Ḥazm, *Muḥallā*, xi, 253-54.

179. Ibn Ḥazm, *Muḥallā*, xi, 256-57.

180. al-Qāḍī Nuʿmān, *Daʿāʾim*, ii, 454.

181. al-Suyūrī al-Ḥillī (fl. 800/1397), *Tanqīḥ*, iv, 335 (a commentary on a work by al-Ḥillī al-Muḥaqqiq al-Awwal, d. 676/1277).

182. Friedmann, *Tolerance and Coercion in Islam*, pp. 184-86, cf. pp. 107-8.

183. Ibn Qayyim al-Jawziyya, *Aḥkām ahl al-dhimma*, i, 391-96. See also e.g. al-Shāfiʿī, *al-Umm*, v, 50, Fattal, *Le statut légal des non-Musulmans en pays d'Islam*, p. 128.

184. al-Shāfiʿī, *al-Umm*, v, 50.

185. See Friedmann, *Tolerance and Coercion in Islam*, p. 73, quoting al-Shāfiʿī's *al-Umm*.

186. Ibn Qayyim al-Jawziyya, *Aḥkām ahl al-dhimma*, i, 395-96. The verb 'to confirm' (*aqarra*) is the technical term for conditionally tolerating non-Islamic practices of the protected communities.

187. See Wensinck, *Concordance et Indices*, v, 129 (*Wa-farriqū bayna kull dhī maḥram min al-Majūs*, 'And separate those Zoroastrians married within a forbidden degree').

188. al-Sarakhsī, *Mabsūṭ*, v, 39.

189. al-Jazīrī, *al-Fiqh ʿalā l-madhāhib al-arbaʿa*, iv, 199.

190. Linant de Bellefonds, *Traité de droit musulman comparé*, ii, 105-120 ('Empêchements au mariage, section I: empêchements permanents'); Bakhtiar, *Encyclopedia of Islamic Law*, pp. 408-23.

191. See above, pp. 40, 93, 108.

192. Translation by M. Perlmann, in *Ibn Kammūna's Examination of the Three Faiths*, p. 147; Arabic text in Ibn Kammūna, *Tanqīḥ al-abḥāth*, p. 101.

193. al-Rāghib al-Iṣbahānī, *Tafṣīl al-nashʾatayn*, p. 142.

194. al-Qushayrī, *Laṭāʾif al-ishārāt*, ii, 19. The editor, in a note, begs to disagree.

195. Beeston's translation; al-Jāḥiẓ, *Qiyān*, ed. Beeston, pp. 3-4, transl. p. 15; the parentheses in square brackets are Beeston's. The expression 'tillage ground' is taken from Q 2:223. For a less accurate translation, see al-Jahiz, *Sobriety and Mirth*, p. 183.

196. Durham, *Coevolution*, pp. 316 ff.

197. al-Sarakhsī, *Mabsūṭ*, xxx, 288.

198. al-Rāzī, *Tafsīr*, ii, 400.

199. Ibn Qudāma (*Mughnī*, ix, 512) even speaks of 'enmity' (*ʿadāwa*) in a similar context.

200. al-Kāsānī, *Badāʾiʿ al-ṣanāʾiʿ*, ii, 257.

201. al-Shāfiʿī, *Umm*, v, 22.

202. al-Qushayrī, *Laṭāʾif al-ishārāt*, ii, 18.

203. al-Kiyā al-Harrāsī, *Aḥkām al-Qurʾān*, ii, 217.

204. Ibn ʿAbd Rabbih, *ʿIqd*, vi, 82, Ibn ʿAbd al-Barr, *Bahjat al-majālis*, ii, 46, al-Ghazālī, *Iḥyāʾ*, ii, 41.

205. Ibn ʿAbd Rabbih, *ʿIqd*, vi, 117, al-Ibshīhī, *Mustaṭraf*, ii, 256.

206. al-Zamakhsharī, *Rabīʿ*, iv, 282-82, al-Ibshīhī, *Mustaṭraf*, ii, 255; the poem without the anecdote in Ibn Qutayba, *ʿUyūn*, iv, 45, al-Tijānī, *Tuḥfa*, 147-48.

207. Ibn Abī Ṭāhir Ṭayfūr, *Balāghāt al-nisāʾ*, p. 227 (where the girl is wrongly called Ḥāritha and the father Aws ibn Laʾm).

208. al-Iṣfahānī, *Aghānī*, x, 295-96.

209. A. S. Bazmee Ansari, entry 'al-Dihlawī, S͟hāh Walī Allāh', *EI²*, ii, 254-55.

210. Walī Allāh al-Dihlawī, *Ḥujja*, ii, 131-34.

211. Shāh Walī Allāh, *Ḥujjat Allāh al-bāligha*, ii, 132.

212. al-Ghazālī, *Iḥyāʾ*, ii, 37.

213. e.g. his *al-Wajīz fī fiqh madhhab al-imām al-Shāfiʿī*, ii, 2.

214. al-Qalyūbī (d. 1069/1659), *Ḥawāshī ʿalā sharḥ al-Maḥallī ʿalā Minhāj al-ṭālibīn [li-l-Nawawī]*, ii, 197, al-Ramlī (d. 1006/1596), *Nihāyat al-muḥtāj ilā sharḥ al-Minhāj*, vi, 181.

215. Ibn Qudāma, *Mughnī*, ix, 512.

216. Not identified.

217. al-Shirbīnī (d. 977/1569), *Mughnī l-muḥtāj ilā maʿānī alfāẓ al-Minhāj*, iii, 120.

218. al-Ibshīhī, *Mustaṭraf*, ii, 249.

219. See e.g. Ibn Manẓūr, *Lisān al-ᶜArab*, *s.v.* ẒHR (vi, 201).

220. J. Schacht, entry 'Nikāḥ', *EI*[2] viii, 28 speaks of *īlāᵓ* and *ẓihār* as 'vows of continence', although in his *Introduction* (p. 165) he speaks of 'repudiation'.

221. Thus e.g. al-Tahānawī, *Kashshāf*, *s.v.* *ẓihār* (p. 931).

222. J. Pedersen & Y. Linant de Bellefonds, entry 'Ḳasam', *EI*[2] iv, 690.

223. Ibn Rushd, *The Distinguished Jurist's Primer (Bidāyat al-Mujtahid)*, ii, 127.

224. Arberry's translation.

225. Schacht, *Introduction*, p. 165. Every legal textbook has a section on *ẓihār*, incorporated in the chapter on *ṭalāq*, repudiation or divorce.

226. Ibn Manẓūr, *Lisān al-ᶜArab*, *s.v.* ẒHR (vi, 201).

227. al-Ḥalabī, *Multaqā l-abḥur*, i, 282-83.

228. For example, in the responses by Ibn Ḥanbal and others translated by Spectorsky (*Chapters on Marriage and Divorce*), the matter is discussed or mentioned on pp. 71-72, 76-77, 112, 126, 131-32, 139, 164, 168, 175, 183, 185-86, 201, 203, 206, 227-28, 233-35 (and see the translator's introduction, pp. 31, 39-42).

229. Smith, *Kinship and Marriage*, p. 193.

230. See e.g. al-Farrāᵓ, *Maᶜānī l-Qurᵓān*, iii, 138.

231. *i.e.* slaves.

232. According to the traditional definitions, a man's pudendum stretches from his navel to his knees, that of a woman is all of her body except face, hands and feet.

233. al-Bayḍāwī, *Tafsīr*, p. 468 (*ad loc.*).

234. Abū Ḥayyān, *Baḥr*, iii, 209.

235. As may be expected, commentators speak of and argue for the 'wonderful arrangement' of the relevant Qur'anic texts (e.g. al-Kiyā al-Harrāsī, *Aḥkām al-Qur'ān*, ii, 231).

236. Ibn al-Jawzī, *Talbīs Iblīs*, p. 65.

237. al-Rāzī, *Tafsīr*, ii, 400.

238. al-Yaᶜqūbī, *Tārīkh*, i, 6.

239. Ibn Bābawayh al-Ṣadūq, *Man lā yaḥḍuruhu l-faqīh*, iii, 240-41. Compare e.g. the version given in al-Thaᶜlabī, *Qiṣaṣ al-anbiyāᵓ*, p. 38, where the Shīᶜite imam Jaᶜfar al-Ṣādiq is given as the source.

Notes to Chapter Four

1. See Stillman, 'The Story of Cain and Abel', p. 241, Bork-Qaysieh, *Die Geschichte von Kain und Abel*, p. 11, G. Vajda in the entry 'Hābīl wa Ḳābīl' in *EI^2*, and W. M. Thackston in al-Kisāʾī, *The Tales of the Prophets*, pp. 346-47.

2. e.g. Ibn Qutayba, *Maʿārif*, p. 11, al-Maqdisī, *al-Badʾ wa-l-taʾrīkh*, ii, 86, al-Thaʿlabi, *Qiṣas al-anbiyāʾ*, p. 25.

3. See G. Vajda, entry 'Hābīl wa Ḳābīl', *EI^2* i, 13-14 for a summary and some of the many sources; also J. Eisenberg, entry 'Hābīl and Ḳābīl', *Shorter Encyclopaedia of Islam*, p. 115, Stillman, 'The Story of Cain and Abel', and Bork-Qaysieh, *Die Geschichte von Kain und Abel*. For an English translation of one of the major sources, see al-Thaʿlabī, *ʿArāʾis* tr. Brinner, pp. 73-80 (= al-Thaʿlabī, *Qiṣaṣ al-anbiyāʾ*, pp. 37-41). See also e.g. Ibn Hishām, *Tījān*, pp. 23, 27, Ibn Qutayba, *Maʿārif*, p. 17, al-Ṭabarī, *Tārīkh* (Leiden) i, 137-47, (Cairo) i, 137-46, id., *The History*, i, 308-17 (tr. Franz Rosenthal), [al-Masʿūdī], *Akhbār al-zamān*, p. 51, Ibn al-Athīr, *al-Kāmil*, i, 42-43, Ibn Kathīr, *Bidāya*, i, 92.

4. al-Masʿūdī, *Murūj*, i, 37 has Iqlīmiyā.

5. The last-mentioned form in [Ibn Iyās], *Badāʾiʿ al-zuhūr*, p. 46. Al-Yaʿqūbī, *Tārīkh*, i, 6 has Lūbadhā (or Lūbidhā, as vowelled by the editor), al-Masʿūdī, *Murūj*, i, 37 has Lūbadā, al-Ṭabarī, *Tārīkh*, (Leiden) i, 146, (Cairo) i, 145 has Layūdhā. Byron, no stranger to incest, borrowed the names of Lamech's wives Adah and Zillah for his 'mystery' play *Cain*, written in 1821. He did not use the motif of sibling rivalry over twin-sisters; Adah's love for her twin-brother Cain is not yet a sin, though, as Lucifer says: 'It one day will be in your children' (I.i).

6. The twins are of different sex and therefore cannot be identical twins, so that genetically they are no closer than any full brother and sister.

7. al-Masʿūdī, *Murūj al-dhahab*, i, 38.

8. Explicitly in Ibn Qutayba, *Maʿārif*, p. 17 (quoting Wahb ibn Munabbih).

9. al-Thaʿlabī, *Qiṣaṣ al-anbiyāʾ*, pp. 38-39.

10. al-Thaʿlabī, *Qiṣaṣ al-anbiyāʾ*, pp. 40-41.

11. Ibn Hishām, *Tījān*, p. 27.

12. Yāqūt, *Muʿjam al-udabāʾ*, iii, 165. The rhyme would lead one to seek the epigram in al-Maʿarrī's *Luzūmiyyāt*, but it is not found there. Al-Maʿarrī uses the related terms *zinya* and *zinā* here, both customarily translated as fornication or adultery.

13. *EI^2*, entry 'Hābīl wa Ḳābīl'.

14. al-Masʿūdī, *Murūj al-dhahab*, i, 38.

15. al-Thaʿālibī al-Marghanī, *Ghurar akhbār mulūk al-Furs*, pp. 259-60.

16. West, *Pahlavi Texts*, ii, 105, 199-200 (from *Dādistān-ī Dīnīk*, xxxvii, 82 and lxv), v, 6 (from *Dīnkard*, VII, i, 10).

17. Abū Qurra, *Maymar fī wujūd al-khāliq wa-l-dīn al-qawīm*, p. 202.

18. al-Ṭabarī, *Tārīkh* (Leiden) i, 147-48, 154, (Cairo) i, 146, 153, tr. Rosenthal, pp. 318-19, 325; Ibn al-Athīr, *Kāmil*, i, 45, 48; al-Maqdisī, *Badʾ*, iii, 138-39, etc. See Stricker, *Camephis*, pp. 31-32, for the idea that Gayōmart engendered his children posthumously by impregnating the earth, his 'mother'. The children's names appear in many forms (cf. West, *Pahlavi Texts*, ii, 105: Marhayâ, Marhîyôîh, ii, 200: Mashyâîh, Mashyâyôîh, v, 6: Masyâ, Masyâôî). See also Herrenschmidt, 'Le *xwētōdas* ou mariage «incestueux»', pp. 120-23.

19. *al-arākina*: plural of *urkūn* or *arkūn* 'chief', from Greek *archon*, here some elemental beings or principalities. One wonders if there was some interference of *al-arkān* (pl. or *rukn*) 'the elements'.

20. *zajr*; or read *rijz* 'filth, idolatry, punishment'?

21. Not specified but presumably the Male principality.

22. *ḥakīmat al-dahr*: the word *dahr* may also mean 'timeless eternity' or 'Fate'.

23. Ibn al-Nadīm, *Fihrist*, p. 331. For a slightly different rendering, see Dodge's translation, p. 784. Instead of 'Greed', Dodge has 'Corruption' (reading *ḥaraḍ* rather than *ḥirṣ*?).

24. Ibn al-Nadīm, *Fihrist*, p. 332.

25. al-Ṭabarī, *Tārīkh* (Leiden) i, 334, (Cairo) i, 299, tr. (William M. Brinner) ii, 118, al-Thaᶜlabī, *Qiṣaṣ*, p. 91, tr. Brinner, p. 176 (who has Rayhā and Ghaythā).

26. See above, Ch. II.

27. But see W. M. Brinner, entry 'al-Kisāʾī, Muḥammad ibn ᶜAbd Allāh' in Meisami and Starkey (eds), *Encyclopedia*, p. 453.

28. al-Kisāʾī, *Qiṣaṣ al-anbiyāʾ*, pp. 122-24 , tr. Thackston pp. 129-31; B. Heller, entry 'Namrūd', *EI²*, vii, 952-53 with more references.

29. *Sīrat ᶜAntar* i, 4-34, Schützinger, *Ursprung und Entwicklung der arabischen Abraham-Nimrod-Legende*, pp. 66-69, Heath, *The Thirsty Sword*, pp. 170-71.

30. *Sīrat ᶜAntar*, i, 7.

31. Rank, *The Incest Theme*, pp. 348-49.

32. al-Thaᶜlabī, *Qiṣaṣ al-anbiyāʾ*, p. 69, tr. Brinner, p. 136, [al-Masᶜūdī], *Akhbār al-zamān*, p. 200, [Ibn Iyās], *Badāʾiᶜ*, p. 80. See also Firestone, 'Prophethood, Marriageable Consanguinity, and Text'.

33. The probable cause is a confusion of the Zechariah of the Old Testament with the father of John/Yaḥyā, see A. Rippin, entry 'Yaḥyā b. Zakariyyāʾ' in *EI²*, xi, 249.

34. al-Thaᶜlabī, *Qiṣaṣ*, pp. 301-2, tr. Brinner, pp. 564-66.

35. al-Thaᶜlabī, *Qiṣaṣ*, pp. 340-41, tr. Brinner pp. 634-37.

36. See also [Ibn Iyās], *Badāʾiᶜ*, p. 181.

37. See also e.g. al-Yaᶜqūbī, *Tārīkh*, p. 71, al-Maqdisī, *Badʾ*, iii, 117-18, al-Ṭabarī, *Tārīkh* (Leiden) i, 719.—Hirdūyā is an obvious mistake for Hīrūd(h)iyā.

38. In addition to the general works mentioned before, see Ion Taloş, 'Inzest', in *Enzyklopädie des Märchens*, vii, col. 229-41, Richard Fabrizio, 'Incest', in Seigneuret (ed.), *Dictionary of Literary Themes and Motifs*, i, 649-65.

39. El-Shamy, 'The Brother-Sister Syndrome in Arab Family Life'; cf. Malti-Douglas, *Woman's Body*, p. 74 note 29 and Canova, 'Remarques sur l'histoire de ᶜAzīz ben H̲āleh', p. 191 note 55. See also El-Shamy, 'Siblings in *Alf laylah wa-laylah*'.

40. al-Iṣfahānī, *Aghānī*, viii, 182. Mostly, Zaynab is considered to be the author (e.g. al-Marzūqī, *Sharḥ Dīwān al-Ḥamāsa*, pp. 1046).

41. al-Iṣfahānī, *Aghānī*, vii, 299, cf. above, p. 26.

42. al-Khansāʾ, *Dīwān* (ᶜAwaḍayn), p. 252, (Abū Suwaylim), p. 326.

43. *al-Aṣmaᶜiyyāt*, p. 102.

44. Hammond, 'The Poetics of S/exclusion', p. 138.

45. Cheikho, *Anīs*, p. 174, al-Iṣfahānī, *Aghānī*, xii, 100, Ibn Khallikān, *Wafayāt*, vi, 33.

46. cf. Borg, *Mit Poesie vertreibe ich den Kummer meines Herzen*, p. 132.

47. See e.g. Rank, *The Incest Theme*, p. 238. It must be admitted that, in Arabic dream interpretation, a nose may stand for a penis, amidst a host of other things (see below, section on dreams).

48. al-Khansāʾ, *Dīwān* (ᶜAwaḍayn) p. 307, (Abū Suwaylim) p. 388.

49. *Epistle to Titus*, 1. 15.

50. *The Revolt of Islam*, Canto VI, 30.

51. See Joan Goodnick Westenholz, 'Love Lyrics from the Ancient Near East', in Sasson (ed.)[*q.v.*], *Civilizations of the Ancient Near East*, (iv,) 2474, 2479, 2480.

52. See above, p. 50.

53. al-Jāḥiẓ, *Bukhalāʾ*, p. 46, translated by Serjeant (*The Book of Misers*, p. 37) as 'Fornicator with his Mother' (I prefer to render *nāʾik* and similar obscenities in the appropriate register).

54. See above, p. 67.

55. *bāʾik-ummih* (which is not necessarily a scribal error for *nāʾik*, because the verb *bāka yabūku* has the same meaning, though it is primarily used for donkeys.)

56. Ibn al-Jarrāḥ, *al-Waraqa*, p. 4.

57. al-Balādhurī, *Ansāb* (Beirut) IV, i, 230, (Jerusalem) IVa, 200.

58. al-Nuwayrī, *Nihāyat al-arab*, ii (Cairo, 1924) 99. Ḍabba is probably the tribe of that name; Ibn Alghaz is only known from proverbial sayings referring to the size of his penis or his sexual prowess (see e.g. Ḥamza al-Iṣbahānī, *al-Durra al-fākhira*, p. 403, al-Maydānī, *Majmaᶜ al-amthāl*, ii, 409, al-Thaᶜālibī, *Thimār al-qulūb*, p. 142).

59. See p. 13.

60. Translation by S.P. Stetkevych, *The Poetics of Islamic Legitimacy*, p. 43; see Ibn Qutayba, *Shiᶜr*, p. 165, al-Iṣfahānī, *Aghānī*, xi, 13.

61. al-Iṣfahānī, Aghānī (ed. al-Abyārī), xxix, 9806, al-Baghdādī, *Khizānat al-adab*, vi, 351, al-ᶜAbbāsī, *Maᶜāhid al-tanṣīṣ*, i, 248, al-Mutalammis, *Dīwān*, p. 38.

62. *Naqāʾiḍ Jarīr wa-l-Akhṭal*, p. 87. The first line is lacking from the versions in al-Qurashī, *Jamhara*, p. 323 and Jarīr, *Dīwān*, p. 52.

63. *Naqāʾiḍ Jarīr wa-l-Farazdaq*, p. 226, Jarīr, *Dīwān*, p. 943.

64. *Naqāʾiḍ Jarīr wa-l-Farazdaq*, p. 252, *Dīwān*, p. 888.

65. *Naqāʾiḍ Jarīr wa-l-Farazdaq*, p. 915.

66. *Naqāʾiḍ Jarīr wa-l-Farazdaq*, p. 536, adopting the variant *aḥrāḥ* instead of *ajsād*.

67. *Naqāʾiḍ Jarīr wa-l-Farazdaq*, p. 1019. The last phrase is not wholly clear; it may refer to the blood of defloration.

68. *Naqāʾiḍ Jarīr wa-l-Farazdaq*, p. 1049. The verse does not explicitly mention incest, but the words 'to his mother' and what follows leave no doubt as to the intended meaning.

69. Dhū l-Rumma, *Dīwān* (Abū Ṣāliḥ), p. 1594, (Macartney) p. 626. The word *muzallam* has many meanings; I have chosen the one also used by al-Muraqqish al-Akbar, according to the commentary, in *al-Mufaḍḍaliyyāt*, no. 54 verse 10.

70. Abū Nuwās, *al-Nuṣūṣ al-muḥarrama*, pp. 185-86.

71. Abū Nuwās, *Dīwān*, i, 80, al-Iṣfahānī, *Imāʾ*, p. 38, Ibn Manẓūr, *Akhbār Abī Nuwās*, i, 36. The word for 'old hag', *kandabīra* (or perhaps *kandabayra* since in some versions this is required by the rhyme), is the Persian *ganda-pīr*.

72. Bashshār, *Dīwān*, ii, 48; cf. Julia Ashtiany's translation in J. Ashtiany *et al.* (eds), *ᶜAbbasid Belles-Lettres*, p. 279. The mother is mentioned later in the poem (ii, 49) in obviously obscene but rather obscure lines (not translated by Ashtiany) and I am not certain that incestuous sex is being described.

73. al-Iṣfahānī, *Aghānī*, xiv, 327.

74. Bashshār, *Dīwān*, i, 380.

75. Bashshār, *Dīwān*, iii, 105.

76. Bashshār, *Dīwān*, i, 286.

77. Bashshār, *Dīwān*, i, 378.

78. *yaᶜīshūna fī ummātihim wa-banātihim* is rather unclear to me, nor do I understand *ᶜan rāʾidin wa-marāḍi(n).*

79. Bashshār, *Dīwān*, iii, 86.

80. Irritatingly defined by the lexicographers as 'a well-known children's game'; its nature is unknown.—The syntax suggests '*while* playing ...', which seems unlikely, unless the two games should be taken metaphorically (*ṣawlajān* means 'mallet').

81. al-Iṣfahānī, *Aghānī*, iii, 243, Bashshār, *Dīwān*, iv, 229, al-Azdī, *Badāʾih al-badāʾiᶜ*, p. 36. Mūsā was al-Mahdī's son (later briefly to rule as al-Hādī) by his favourite wife al-Khayzurān. I do not know if it is a coincidence that 'al-Dabbūqī' is given as Mūsā l-Hādī's nickname (Murtaḍā l-Zabīdī, *Tāj al-ᶜarūs*, *s.v.* DBQ).

82. al-Tujībī, *al-Mukhtār min shiᶜr Bashshār*, p. 113.

83. Ibn al-Rūmī, *Dīwān*, p. 972. For Ezra's ass (here a wild ass for the sake of the internal rhyme: *bi-ayri ᶜayri l-ᶜUzayrī*), which like his master miraculously survived being dead for a century, see e.g. al-Thaᶜlabī, *Qiṣaṣ*, p. 308 (tr. Brinner, pp. 378-79), based on Q 2:259 (an echo of Ezekiel 37).

84. A licence for *kussi ukhtī*; the metre is *sarīᶜ*.

85. Ibn Dāniyāl, *Ṭayf al-khayāl*, p. 11.

86. Guo, 'The Devil's Advocate', pp. 203 and 181, respectively.

87. Guo, 'The Devil's Advocate', p. 208.

88. al-Shirbīnī, *Hazz al-quḥūf*, p. 87.

89. Ibn Abī ᶜAwn, *Ajwiba*, p. 218, al-Tawḥīdī, *Baṣāʾir*, vii, 79. Al-Farazdaq had several transmitters, six of whom are known by name (Sezgin, *Geschichte*, ii, 361).

90. Rank, *The Incest Theme*, p. 347.

91. al-Zamakhsharī, *Asās al-balāgha*, *s.v.* BẒR; there is even a special denominative verb *baẓrama*, meaning 'to say "*amaṣṣahu llāhu baẓra ummihi*"'.

92. On the rarity of oral sex and its bad odour, metaphorically speaking, see e.g. J. W. Wright, 'Masculine Allusion and the Structure of Satire', pp. 16, 23 note 73. *Pace* Chebel, *Encyclopédie de l'amour en Islam*, pp. 181-82, 241-42, references to heterosexual *cunnilingus* and *fellatio* are found in the written sources (e.g. al-Tīfāshī, *Rujūᶜ al-shaykh*, pp. 76, 79, 98-99; and see the poem by al-Ṣābiʾ, above, p. 68). The oneirocritical books, too, offer some material.

93. al-Rāghib al-Iṣbahānī, *Muḥāḍarāt al-udabāʾ*, ii, 124.

94. Ibn al-Rūmī, *Dīwān*, 577, vss. 3-4 also in al-Ḥuṣrī, *Zahr*, p. 432.

95. al-Maᶜarrī, *Luzūmiyyāt*, ii, 155-56. The word *muwaffaq* 'having been granted success (by God)' I have loosely rendered as 'in his senses' here.

96. al-Baghdādī, *Khizāna*, viii, 203, quoting Ibn Jinnī (d. 392/1002).

97. It is used in the famous and very early elegy in rhymed prose attributed to the mother of Taʾabbaṭa Sharrā, al-Iṣfahānī, *Aghānī*, xxi, 171 etc.

98. al-Ṣafadī (d. 764/1363), quoted in Shihāb al-Dīn, *Safīnat al-mulk*, p. 363.

99. By Taqiyy al-Dīn al-Sarūjī, in Ibn Ḥijja, *Khizāna*, p. 297.

100. Rank, *The Incest Theme*, p. 336.

101. See Doody, *The True Story of the Novel*, pp. 84, 497.

102. I am quoting Margaret Ann Doody, *The True Story of the Novel*, p. 88, who quotes Frank Kermode (*The Art of Telling: Essays on Fiction*, Cambridge, Mass., 1983, p. 79), who paraphrases Lévi-Strauss.

103. It is no coincidence that in Vladimir Nabokov's novel *Ada, or Ardor: A Family Chronicle* (1969) is a rich mixture with puns, puzzles and incestuous love as basic ingredients.

104. In Abū Nuwās, *Dīwān*, iv, 86.

105. Because Aḥmad and Zayd's father ʿAbd Allāh are half-brothers, sons of Fāṭima.

106. Abū Nuwās, *Dīwān*, iv, 86-87.

107. See above, pp. 29-30.

108. In the poem, *ḥarf* ('lean/sturdy', said of a riding animal, as in the poems by Aws and Kaʿb) is not a name. To my knowledge, it does not occur as a name.

109. Abū Nuwās, *Dīwān*, iv, 87-88.

110. Ibn al-Athīr, *al-Mathal al-sāʾir*, iii, 88-89.

111. Ibn al-Ṣayqal, *al-Maqāmāt al-Zayniyya*, pp. 535-36.

112. See also his introduction, p. 45.

113. For another versified question, see e.g. Ibn Taymiyya, *Fatāwī*, iv, 49 (it deals with inheritance law).

114. Ibn Taymiyya, *Fatāwī*, iv, 65.

115. The line would scan only if *wa-abī* were read *wa-abbī*!

116. In order to make sense and scansion right, *bi-bintin* should be *bi-bnatin* and *shuʿarāʾ* is to be emended to *shiʿr*.

117. See L. Veccia Vaglieri, entry 'Fāṭima' in *EI2*, ii, 845, 847, 848.

118. See I. Poonawala, entry 'Nūr Muḥammad', in *EI*², viii, 125.

119. L. Veccia Vaglieri, 'Fāṭima', *EI*², ii, 847.

120. 'Fāṭima', *EI*², ii, 848.

121. 'Fāṭima', *EI*², ii, 845.

122. See Chapter Two, note 147.

123. First, briefly, in her 'The Ṣuʿlūk and his Poem' (1984) pp. 665-71 (section 'Taʾabbaṭa Sharran and Oedipus'); also 'The rithāʾ of Taʾabbaṭa Sharran: A study of blood-vengeance in early Arabic poetry' (1986), see p. 38, and in her *The Mute Immortals Speak* (1993), ch. 3: 'Taʾabbaṭa Sharran and Oedipus: A Paradigm of Passage Manqué' (pp. 87-118), which is a revised version of her 1984 article. The foot parallel seems rather lame (see *The Mute Immortals Speak*, p. 101): the feet do not belong to Taʾabbaṭa Sharran but to the ghoulish female demon (*ghūl*) killed by him.

124. 'The Ṣuʿlūk and his poem', p. 666, almost identical in *The Mute Immortals*, p. 95.

125. For the story, see al-Iṣfahānī, *Aghānī*, xxi, 127-73.

126. Ibn Qutayba, *Shiʿr*, p. 312.

127. See on Luqmān e.g. H. T. Norris, 'Fables and Legends', pp. 378-81, B. Heller and N. A. Stillman, entry 'Luḳmān', EI^2 (v, 811-13).

128. See e.g. Norris, 'Fables and Legends', p. 379.

129. al-Jāḥiẓ, *Ḥayawān*, i, 21-22; cf. his *al-Bayān wa-l-tabyīn*, i, 184-85, al-Maydānī, *Majmaʿ al-amthāl*, ii, 460-61, al-Sharīshī, *Sharḥ Maqāmāt al-Ḥarīrī*, iv, 144, al-Ṣafadī, *al-Ghayth al-musajjam*, i, 132, al-Jarīrī, *Jalīs*, iv, 215-18, al-Baghdādī, *Khizāna*, xi, 107-8.

130. For more details, see the version in al-Jarīrī, *Jalīs*, iv, 215-16.

131. Poet, said to have died before 23/644 at an unlikely great age.

132. al-Jarīrī, *Jalīs*, iv, 218.

133. al-Baghdādī, *Khizāna*, xi, 108.

134. Quoted in al-Baghdādī, *Khizāna*, xi, 108.

135. al-Maydānī, *Majmaʿ al-amthāl*, ii, 460-61, al-Ābī, *Nathr al-durr*, vi, 158.

136. al-Jāḥiẓ, *Bayān*, i, 184, al-Baghdādī, *Khizāna*, xi, 107-8.

137. al-Jāḥiẓ, *Bayān*, i, 184.

138. For the first story, see Ibn al-Jawzī, *Dhamm al-hawā*, pp. 340-43, al-Tanūkhī, *Nishwār al-muḥāḍara*, v, 122-28, al-Nuwayrī, *Nihāyat al-arab*, ii, 183-88, expurgated from the later Cairo edition, in the Turāthunā ('Our Heritage') series, published by the Ministry of Culture and National Guidance (this explains the bowdlerization). For a German translation see Weisweiler, *Arabesken der Liebe*, pp. 295-301. The three nearly identical versions are indicated by IJ, T, and N, respectively, in my notes.

139. *rāʿaytu amra l-marʾati*; N has *rāʿahum amru l-marʾati* 'they were shocked by the matter of the woman'.

140. This sentence is lacking in N.

141. Weisweiler interprets it as '*with* (other) women (mit den Frauen)'. Instead of *tarmī bi-l-nisāʾ* the editor of IJ reads *turmā bi-l-nisāʾ* 'she was accused (of having sexual affairs?) with other women', which seems possible in the light of the words of the nurse, below.

142. Reading *wa-hiya tastaḥī* with N, instead of *wa-huwa dhā tastaḥī* (T) or *wa-huwa dhā nastaḥī* (IJ).

143. In Abbasid times male and female slaves, unlike free people, were often given names denoting precious objects ('Pearl') or abstract qualities ('Virtue').

144. *darra matnuhā* (T, IJ), meaning uncertain. N has *ramaytuhā*, which Weisweiler renders as '[ich] schmähte sie' (I reviled her), rather unlikely in this context.

145. *shannaʿat* (T, IJ) and *saʿat* (N) have the same meaning.

146. N has 'you obeyed him'.

147. The last clause is lacking in N.

148. Referring to the *jilwa*, 'unveiling (of a bride to her groom)'.

149. *Nihāyat al-arab*, ii, 188.

150. Wendy Doniger, *The Bedtrick: Tales of Sex and Masquerade*; see ch. 9 (pp. 383-95), 'Incest'.

151. Doniger, *The Bedtrick*, p. 383.

152. See Jacobus de Voragine (d. 1298), *The Golden Legend*, tr. William Granger Ryan, i, 167-68.

153. Archibald, *Incest and the Medieval Imagination*, p. 110.

154. Rank, *The Incest Theme*, p. 271, cf. Archibald, *Incest and the Medieval Imagination*, pp. 110, 232.

155. Archibald, *Incest and the Medieval Imagination*, pp. 110-111. On European double incest stories, see pp. 110-25, 135-37, 139, 140-41, 218, 238, Rank, *The Incest Theme*, pp. 285-86, 289-92, 296-98.

156. Archibald, *Incest and the Medieval Imagination*, pp. 111-21, Boswell, *Kindness of Strangers*, pp. 373-75, Rank, *The Incest Theme*, pp. 285-89.

157. Archibald, *Incest and the Medieval Imagination*, pp. 120-22 and index *s.v.* 'Albanus'; Rank, *The Incest Theme*, pp. 290-94, Boswell, *Kindness of Strangers*, pp. 375-77.

158. Marguerite de Navarre, *Heptameron*, Day 3, story 30, English translation by P. A. Chilton, pp. 317-21; for the other sources see the references in Archibald, *Incest and the Medieval Imagination*, pp. 141-43; also Doniger, *The Bedtrick*, pp. 388-89.

159. Abu-Lughod, *Veiled Sentiments*, pp. 138-42; Doniger, *The Bedtrick*, pp. 155-58.

160. See al-Tanūkhī, *Faraj*, ii, 94, 172; Ibn al-Nadīm, *Fihrist*, p. 129.

161. al-Tanūkhī, *Nishwār al-muḥāḍara*, v, 129-34, Ibn al-Jawzī, *Dhamm al-hawā*, pp. 344-46, Mughulṭāy, *al-Wāḍiḥ al-mubīn*, pp. 291-93. No other translations are known to me. For a study and a comparison with the story discussed below as 'Burning Love Between Siblings', see Hámori, 'The House of Brotherly Love' and its French version, 'La maison de l'amour incestueux'.

162. The mother is meant. The word used is *jāriya*, which could mean 'girl, slave-girl, concubine', but does not usually refer to a married woman.

163. He uses the word *ṣāḥiba*, '(female) companion, lady'.

164. In an Islamic burial no coffin is used. The earth is not poured straight onto the body, which is laid in a niche at the side at the bottom of the grave.

165. As a blessing.

166. *al-Ḥikāyāt al-ʿajība*, pp. 147-202, German tr. by Hans Wehr in Marzolph (ed.), *Das Buch der wundersamen Geschichten*, pp. 193-263 (first publ. in H. Wehr, *Wunderbare Erlebnisse—Seltsame Begebnisse*, Hartingen, 1959, pp. 7-111); another German tr. in M. Weisweiler, *Arabische Märchen*, Düsseldorf/Cologne, 1965, pp. 121-90. See Marzolph, 'As Woman as Can Be', Lyons, 'Qiṣṣat ʿArūs al-ʿarāʾis'.

167. *al-Ḥikāyāt al-ʿajība*, p. 149.

168. *al-Ḥikāyāt al-ʿajība*, p. 187.

169. *al-Ḥikāyāt al-ʿajība*, p. 183.

170. Rank, *The Incest Theme*, p. 376.

171. *Alf layla wa-layla* (Ṣubayḥ), ii, 16-20, English tr. by Burton, *The Book of the Thousand Nights and a Night*, ii, 327-35, German tr. Littmann, *Erzählungen*, ii, 211-21.

172. Gerhardt, *The Art of Story-Telling*, p. 393.

173. *Alf layla wa-layla* (Ṣubayḥ), i, 39-42, (Mahdī), pp. 148-53; English translations in Haddawy (tr.) *The Arabian Nights* (i), 86-92, Burton, *The Book of the Thousand Nights and a Night*, i, 96-104, Lane, *The Thousand and One Nights*, i, 134-39, Dawood, *Tales from the Thousand and One Nights*, pp. 258-62; German tr. in Littmann, *Erzählungen*, i, 121-31.

174. 'sans lien organique' (Claude Bremond, in Bencheikh *et al.*, *Mille et un contes de la nuit*, p. 111), 'somewhat disconnectedly' (Gerhardt, *The Art of Story-Telling*, p. 410).

175. *Alf layla wa-layla* (Ṣubayḥ), i, 42. There are some slight differences between this text and the one used by Haddawy (i, 90-91). Haddawy uses the edition by Muḥsin Mahdī (pp. 152-53), which is sometimes more wordy and funnier (without invariably raising the literary qualities, however).

176. Mahdī/Haddawy add 'for this girl is your sister, and God has forbidden her to you' (as if the boy or the audience did not know this already).

177. See Wensinck *et al.*, *Concordance*, v, 31-32 for this and similar sayings.

178. See also Hámori, 'The House of Brotherly Love' and 'La maison de l'amour incestueux'.

179. See Archibald, *Incest and the Medieval Imagination*, pp. 94, 147, 186 n. 85, 226-27, 231.

180. Burton, *The Book of the Thousand Nights and a Night*, i, 102.

181. Burton, *The Arabian Nights*, i, 96.

182. Lane, *The Thousand and One Nights*, i, 206.

183. *Alf layla wa-layla* (Ṣubayḥ), i, 162-320, ii, 2-21, Burton, *The Book of the Thousand Nights and a Night*, i, 398-416, ii, 1-337, Littmann, *Erzählungen*, i, 500-766, ii, 7-244. The king's name also appears as ᶜUmar ibn al-Nuᶜmān.

184. Marzolph & van Leeuwen, *The Arabian Nights Encyclopedia*, entry 'ᶜUmar ibn al-Nuᶜmân' in the section 'Stories', p. 435.

185. Note that in anthropological notation, Z is used for sister, S for son.

186. This is done, e.g. by Burton, *The Book of the Thousand Nights and a Night*, i, 399 and Marzolph & van Leeuwen, *The Arabian Nights Encyclopedia*, p. 430 ff.

187. *Alf layla wa-layla* (Ṣubayḥ), i, 199.

188. This is not accurate, for he has seen his father fondle her and her brother, which made him so jealous as to contemplate murdering them.

189. *Alf layla wa-layla* (Ṣubayḥ), i, 208.

190. Ouyang, 'Romancing the Epic', p. 15.

191. *Alf layla wa-layla* (Ṣubayḥ), iii, 138-77, Burton, *The Book of Thousand Nights and a Night*, v, 36-121, Lane, *The Thousand and One Nights*, iii, 145-67, Littmann, *Erzählungen*, iv, 259-371. See also Irwin, *The Arabian Nights*, pp. 75-76, Pinault, *Story-Telling Techniques*, pp. 56-59, Gerhardt, *The Art of Story-Telling*, pp. 400-1.

192. Rank, *The Incest Theme*, pp. 127-28.

193. Archibald, *Incest and the Medieval Imagination*, p. 221.

194. Pritchard, *Ancient Near Eastern Texts*, pp. 23-25; see Hollis, 'Tales of Magic and Wonder from Ancient Egypt', in Sasson (ed.), *Civilizations of the Near East*, (iv,) 2258-59.

195. al-Iṣfahānī, *Aghānī*, viii, 237-38, [al-Jāḥiẓ], *Maḥāsin*, pp. 290-91.

196. al-Anbārī, *Sharḥ al-qaṣāʾid al-sabᶜ al-ṭiwāl*, p. 353. Some say that the woman meant here was forbidden because she belonged to an enemy tribe.

197. Doniger, *The Bedtrick*, pp. 387-88.

198. Perry, *Secundus the Silent*; Arabic text in Appendix III (74 pp.), English tr. pp. 119-60; see also Archibald, *Incest and the Medieval Imagination*, p. 65.

199. Arabic text p. 11, tr. pp. 125-26.

200. Perry, *Secundus the Silent*, Arabic text p. 38, English tr. pp. 144-45.

201. al-Masʿūdī, *Tanbīh*, p. 128.

202. By Abū Sulaymān al-Manṭiqī al-Sijistānī, *Ṣiwān al-ḥikma*, pp. 244 (corrupted to Thiyāfandūs) and 259 (as Saqundās), and Ibn Hindū, *al-Kalim al-rūḥāniyya*, pp. 120-23 (as Siyāfīdūs). The identifications were made by Franz Rosenthal.

203. El-Shamy, *Folk Traditions of the Arab World*, i, 359.

204. El-Shamy, *Folktales of Egypt*, pp. 14-24 (for the testing episode, see pp. 23-24).

205. Archibald, *Incest and the Medieval Imagination*, p. 221.

206. El-Shamy, *Egyptian Folk Tales*, p. 222.

207. As in the story of the young man who lies down upon his father's concubine in the dark. She says, 'Who are you?' and he answers, 'Shut up, I'm my father.' See al-Tawḥīdī, *Baṣāʾir*, v, 166, al-Ābī, *Nathr al-durr*, v, 31, al-Zamakhsharī, *Rabīʿ al-abrār*, iv, 172; more references in Marzolph, *Arabia ridens*, ii, 143 (no. 577).

208. Burton, *The Book of the Thousand Nights and a Night*, xi, 457-63, German tr. by Tauer, *Neue Erzählungen aus den Tausendundein Nächten*, pp. 696-704; El-Shamy, *Folktales of Egypt*, pp. 222-23, 299-300 (a modern version recorded in 1969). See also al-Shirbīnī, *Hazz al-quḥūf*, p. 208.

209. Burton, *The Book of the Thousand Nights and a Night*, xi, 243-313, Tauer, *Neue Erzählungen*, pp. 429-98.

210. See above, p. 98 and note 113.

211. Lyons, *The Arabian Epic, Volume 2: Analysis*, p. 410.

212. ibid., p. 294.

213. See above, pp. 56-57.

214. Lyons, *The Arabian Epic*, ii, 250, iii, 608.

215. See e.g. Edward Badeen & Birgit Krawietz, 'Eheschliessung mit Dschinnen nach Badr al-Dīn al-Šiblī'.

216. Lyons, *The Arabian Epic*, ii, 233, iii, 569-70.

217. Lyons, *The Arabic Epic*, ii, 41, iii, 69.

218. In his sixty-page summary of the epic, Heath does not even mention the daughter but only the father (Heath, *The Thirsty Sword*, pp. 220-21).

219. Lyons, *The Arabian Epic*, ii, 84-85, iii, 169-70.

220. Lyons, *The Arabian Epic*, ii, 92, iii, 183.

221. See above, p. 80.

222. Lyons, *The Arabian Epic*, ii, 110, iii, 218-19.

223. Doody, *The True Story of the Novel*, p. 85. On *Apollonius of Tyre*, see e.g. Doody, pp. 82-89 and see index; Archibald, *Incest and the Medieval Imagination*, pp. 93-101.

224. Davis, *Panthea's Children*, p. 24; see pp. 21-26 on father—daughter rape.

225. Davis, *Panthea's Children*, p. 21.

226. Archibald, *Incest and the Medieval Imagination*, p. 190: 'Whether consummated or merely threatened, father—daughter incest seems to have been the most common literary form of incest in the later Middle Ages, at least in extended narratives; mother—son incest is the most common form in brief *exempla*.'

227. The same is valid for European medieval literature. The Appendix with synopses of 'Flight from Incestuous Father Stories' in Archibald, *Incest and the Medieval Imagination*, pp. 245-56, only offers emperors, kings, dukes or counts.

228. See below, Epilogue.

229. Lyons, *The Arabian Epic*, iii, 624 and see i, 41.

230. Lyons, *The Arabian Epic*, ii, 95, iii, 190-91.

231. Lyons, *The Arabian Epic*, ii, 26, iii, 35.

232. See Canova, 'Banū Hilāl Tales from Southern Arabia', p. 42; idem, 'Remarques sur l'histoire de 'Azīz ben H̲āleh du cycle épique hilalien', pp. 184-85 and 191 note 55.

233. Canova, 'Banū Hilāl Tales from Southern Arabia', p. 48. note 3.

234. El-Shamy, *Folk Traditions of the Arab World*, i, 359-60, ii, 253-54.

235. Muhawi, 'Gender and Disguise in the Arabic *Cinderella*', pp. 266-78.

236. Al-Shahi & More, *Wisdom from the Nile*; for the story, see pp. 110-25, for the analysis see the Introduction, pp. 1-60, *passim*.

237. Al-Shahi & Moore, pp. 61-63.

238. See Fahd, *La Divination Arabe*, pp. 246-367, where some 130 authors are listed. Only a handful have been edited. For a short survey, see idem, entry 'Ruʾyā, 1. In the meaning of dream', in *EI*[2]; see also John C. Lamoreaux, *The Early Muslim Tradition of Dream Interpretation* (New York, 2002).

239. See Oberhelman, 'Hierarchies of Gender, Ideology, and Power' and Mavroudi, *A Byzantine Book on Dream Interpretation*.

240. See also the similar warning on the Artemidorian material quoted by Archibald, *Incest and the Medieval Imagination*, p. 2.

241. al-Nābulusī, *Taʿṭīr*, i, 262.

242. A slave-girl may be used as a concubine in traditional Islam. The Arabic *jāriya*, often 'girl', may also be used for older servant women for whom the English 'girl' sounds inappropriate.

243. [Ibn Sīrīn], *Tafsīr al-aḥlām*, pp. 309-10; the work has been said to be a compilation made by al-Ḥusayn al-Khalīlī al-Dārī (early 9th/15th century), but appears to be in fact by Abū Sa^{c}d al-Wā^{c}iẓ al-Kharkūshī (d. 407/1016-17), see Weststeijn, 'Abū Da^{c}d al-Wā^{c}iẓ al-Ḫarkūšī's *al-bišāra wa-n-nid̲āra*'. The work is also printed in al-Nābulusī, *Ta^{c}ṭīr* (see i, 226 for the story).

244. See e.g. [Ibn Sīrīn], *Tafsīr*, p. 378, al-Nābulusī, *Ta^{c}ṭīr*, ii, 8.

245. [Ibn Sīrīn], *Tafsīr*, p. 167 (= al-Nābulusī, *Ta^{c}ṭīr*, i, 124), al-Nābulusī, *Ta^{c}ṭīr*, i, 185.

246. Thus [Ibn Sīrīn], as well as al-Nābulusī, *Ta^{c}ṭīr*, i, 184.

247. As in al-Nābulusī, *Ta^{c}ṭīr*, i, 186.

248. [Ibn Sīrīn], *Tafsīr*, p. 107 (also printed in al-Nābulusī, *Ta^{c}ṭīr*, i, 80), al-Nābulusī, *Ta^{c}ṭīr*, i, 40.

249. al-Nābulusī, *Ta^{c}ṭīr*, i, 16.

250. Ibn Sa^{c}d, *Ṭabaqāt*, v, 92.

251. [Ibn Sīrīn], *Tafsīr*, p. 106 (also in al-Nābulusī, *Ta^{c}ṭīr*, i, 80).

252. [Ibn Sīrīn], *Tafsīr*, p. 361 (= *Ta^{c}ṭīr*, i, 263).

253. [Ibn Sīrīn], *Tafsīr*, p. 93 (also in al-Nābulusī, *Ta^{c}ṭīr*, i, 71), and al-Nābulusī, *Ta^{c}ṭīr*, i, 94. In pseudo-Ibn Sīrīn the breast is said to be 'extremely' big (*ilā l-ghāya*), whereas in al-Nābulusī reads 'reaching to the pubic region' (*ilā l-^{c}āna*): a matter of a few dots in the Arabic script.

254. [Ibn Sīrīn], *Tafsīr*, p. 362 (= *Ta^{c}ṭir*, i, 264). The text has *al-muḥarramāt min al-ināth wa-l-dhukrān* 'women of the forbidden degrees, both females and males", which is obviously'contradictory.

255. Ibn Shāhīn, *Ishārāt*, p. 84, [Ibn Sīrīn], *Tafsīr*, p. 91 (= *Ta^{c}ṭīr*, i, 69), al-Nābulusī, *Ta^{c}ṭīr*, i, 18.

256. Ibn Sīrīn, *Tafsīr*, 131 (= *Ta^{c}ṭīr*, i, 98), Ibn Shāhīn, *Ishārāt*, p. 212, al-Nābulusī, *Ta^{c}ṭīr*, ii, 20.

257. See van Gelder, *Of Dishes and Discourse*, pp. 92, 116, 153 note 42.

258. [Ibn Sīrīn], *Tafsīr*, p. 282 (also in *Ta^{c}ṭīr*, i, 208), al-Nābulusī, *Ta^{c}ṭīr*, ii, 197.

259. al-Nābulusī, *Ta^{c}ṭīr*, i, 83.

260. al-Nābulusī, *Ta^{c}ṭīr*, ii, 236.

261. [Ibn Sīrīn], *Tafsīr*, p. 332, also printed in al-Nābulusī, *Ta^{c}ṭīr*, i, 243.

262. [Ibn Sīrīn], *Tafsīr al-aḥlām*, pp. 259-60, also printed in al-Nābulusī, *Ta^{c}ṭir*, i, 191.

263. [Ibn Sīrīn], *Tafsīr*, p. 258 (= al-Nābulusī, *Ta^{c}ṭīr*, i, 190-91), al-Nābulusī, *Ta^{c}ṭīr*, i, 158, Ibn Shāhīn, p. 163.

264. [Ibn Sīrīn], *Tafsīr*, p. 308 (also in al-Nābulusī, *Ta^{c}ṭīr*, i, 226).

265. Artemidorus, *Taʿbīr al-ruʾyā*, pp. 160-72.

266. Ibn Shāhīn (d. 872/1468), *Ishārāt*, p. 129, al-Nābulusī, *Taʿṭīr*, i, 270.

267. Ibn Shāhīn, *Ishārāt*, p. 130.

268. The Arabic idiom is 'has cut the womb (*qaṭaʿa l-raḥim*)'.

269. [Ibn Sīrīn], *Tafsīr*, p. 360 (= *Taʿṭīr*, i, 262); cf. al-Nābulusī, *Taʿṭīr*, i, 270.

270. The word used, *ṣilāt*, also means 'presents'.

271. The verb *waṭaʾa* means 'to tread' and 'to copulate'.

272. [Ibn Sīrīn], *Tafsīr*, p. 362 (= *Taʿṭīr*, i, 264); cf. al-Nābulusī, *Taʿṭīr*, ii, 294.

273. al-Nafzāwī, *al-Rawḍ al-ʿāṭir*, p. 107, tr. Burton, *The Perfumed Garden*, p. 183.

274. There is nothing in the text that says that the man is relating his dreams; but in the context it can hardly have been otherwise.

275. [Ibn Sīrīn], *Tafsīr*, pp. 363-64 (= *Taʿṭīr*, i, 265).

276. The text of the *Tafsīr* has *kaʾanna yamīnahu quṭiʿat*, 'it was as if his right hand was cut off'—apparently in the dream. I have preferred the reading in *Taʿṭīr*: *kāna yamīnuhu quṭiʿat* (the lack of concord of *kāna* is quite normal in classical Arabic).

277. Ibn Shāhīn, *Ishārāt*, p. 131.

278. Ibn Shāhīn, *Ishārāt*, p. 131.

279. Ibn Shāhīn, *Ishārāt*, p. 131; cf. al-Nābulusī, *Taʿṭīr*, ii, 294.

280. al-Nābulusī, *Taʿṭīr*, ii, 283.

281. I read *wālidayhi* instead of the obviously incorrect *waladayhi* 'his two children'.

282. I suppose this is a case of dreaming that one is dreaming.

283. The word *ṣāliḥ* could mean 'upright, virtuous' as well as 'adequate, comfortable'.

284. The point seems to be that the mother (subject of the transitive verb *jāmaʿa*) here is the more active partner.

285. al-Nābulusī, *Taʿṭīr*, ii, 236-37.

286. al-Nābulusī, *Taʿṭīr*, ii, 236.

287. al-Nābulusī, *Taʿṭīr*, ii, 294.

288. al-Nābulusī, *Taʿṭīr*, ii, 236.

289. Arabic tr. pp. 167-76.

290. Artemidorus, *Taʿbīr al-ruʾyā*, pp. 168-72.

291. Artemidorus, *Taʿbīr al-ruʾyā*, p. 169.

Notes to the Epilogue

1. To this one may wish to add the English text that was published in 1975 as *The Glory of the Perfumed Garden: The Missing Flowers*. The status of this text, however, seems to be as shadowy as the identity of the translator, who signs his Introduction as 'H. E. J.'; see also Ulrich Marzolph in his German translation of al-Nafzāwī, p. 147.

2. See Archibald, *Incest and the Medieval Imagination*, pp. 53 ff.

3. Pritchard, *Ancient Near Eastern Texts*, pp. 37-41. On incest in the ancient Near East, see also Hoffner, 'Incest, Sodomy and Bestiality' (which is concerned more with legislation, mostly Hittite, than with myth) and Petschow, 'Inzest'.

4. François Vallat, 'Susa and Susians in Second-Millennium Iran', in Sasson (*q.v.*), *Civilizations of the Ancient Near East*, (ii,) 1028-29.

5. Aristotle, *Poetics*, 1453b, tr. I. Bywater in Aristotle, *The Complete Works*, p. 2326.

6. Praz, *The Romantic Agony*, p. 118, quoting Shelley's *Prose Works*, ed. H. Buxton Forman, iv, 143.

7. See Minorsky, 'Vīs u Rāmīn, a Parthian Romance', H. Massé, entry 'Gurgānī' in *EI*^{2}, ii, 1142-43 (publ. 1965), F. C. de Blois, entry 'Wīs u Rāmīn' in *EI*^{2}, xi, 210 (publ. 2001), Davis, *Panthea's Children*, pp. 40-43, 49-52, 55-58, 67-72, Gurgānī, *Vis and Ramin*, tr. by George Morrison.

8. Gurgānī, *Wīs u Rāmīn*, pp. 32-33, tr. Morrison, pp. 29-30.

9. Abū Nuwās, *al-Nuṣūṣ al-muḥarrama*, p. 145; cf. Wagner, *Abū Nuwās*, p. 138, Minorsky, 'Vīs u Rāmīn', p. 197.

10. de Blois, 'Wīs u Rāmīn'.

11. Meisami, *Medieval Persian Court Poetry*, p. 138.

12. Meisami, *Medieval Persian Court Poetry*, p. 138; cf. p. 184.

13. Meisami, *Medieval Persian Court Poetry*, p. 97.

14. Kappler, '*Vîs et Râmîn*, ou comment aimer un autre que son frère ?', p. 68.

15. Kappler, '*Vîs et Râmîn*', p. 74.

Bibliography

The Arabic definite article *(a)l-*, in its various forms, in any position, is ignored in the alphabetical order. An Islamic date (marked with AH) is given only if no other date is given in the publication. The publisher's name is given only in the case of undated Arabic publications, so as to make it easier to identify the edition. Brackets are used for authors of pseudepigraphia.

It is customary in works such as this to divide the bibliography into sections on sources and secondary works. This convention has not been followed here, for practical as well as ideological reasons. An undivided list seems more friendly and time-saving to non-specialists, who may have problems in determining whether a certain name is medieval or modern. Moreover, separating medieval authors (mostly Arabs) from modern ones (mostly non-Arabs) would suggest an 'orientalist' attitude (in the Saidian sense) in strictly distinguishing between objects and observers. Both medieval and modern authorities have said many sensible as well as some rather silly things about incest and inbreeding; they all take part in the ongoing discourse on the topics.

ᶜAbbās, Iḥsān (ed.), *ᶜAhd Ardashīr*, Beirut, 1967.

al-ᶜAbbāsī, ᶜAbd al-Raḥīm b. ᶜAbd al-Raḥmān, *Maᶜāhid al-tanṣīṣ*, Cairo, AH 1316.

Aberle, D. T. *et al.*, 'The Incest Taboo and the Mating Patterns of Animals', in Nelson Graburn (ed.), *Readings in Kinship and Social Culture*, New York, 1971, pp. 346-55, first publ. in *American Anthropologist*, 65 (1963) 253-64.

al-Ābī, Abū Saᶜīd Manṣūr b. al-Ḥusayn, *Nathr al-durr*, ed. Muḥammad ᶜAlī Qurana *et al.*, Cairo, 1980-1990.

ᶜAbīd b. al-Abraṣ, *Dīwān*, ed. Charles Lyall, in *The Dīwāns of ᶜAbīd ibn al-Abraṣ, of Asad, and ᶜĀmir ibn aṭ-Ṭufail, of ᶜĀmir ibn Ṣaᶜṣaᶜah*, Cambridge, 1913.

Abū Dāwūd, *al-Sunan*, ed. ᶜIzzat ᶜUbayd al-Daᶜᶜās and ᶜĀdil al-Sayyid, Beirut, 1997.

Abū l-Fidāᵓ, *al-Mukhtaṣar fī akhbār al-bashar*, Cairo, AH 1325.

Abū Ḥātim Aḥmad b. Ḥamdān al-Rāzī, *al-Zīna fī l-kalimāt al-islāmiyya wa-l-ᶜarabiyya*, ed. Ḥusayn Fayḍ Allāh al-Hamdānī al-Yaᶜburī al-Ḥirāzī, Cairo, 1957-1958.

Abū Ḥayyān al-Gharnāṭī, *al-Baḥr al-muḥīṭ*, Cairo, AH 1329.

Abū Khaḍra, Fahd, *Ibn al-Muᶜtazz: al-rajul wa-intājuhu l-adabī*, ᶜAkkā (Acre), 1981.

Abu-Lughod, Lila, *Veiled Sentiments: Honor and Poetry in a Bedouin Society*, Berkeley & Los Angeles, 1986.

Abū Nuwās, *Dīwān*, ed. Ewald Wagner and Gregor Schoeler, Wiesbaden, 1958- .

———, *al-Nuṣūṣ al-muḥarrama*, ed. Jamāl Jumaᶜa, Beirut, 1998.

Abū Qurra, Thāwudhūrus (Theodore), *Maymar fī wujūd al-khāliq wa-l-dīn al-qawīm*, ed. Ignace Dik, Jounieh (Lebanon), 1982.

Abū ᶜUbayda, *Ayyām al-ᶜArab qabl al-Islām*, ed. ᶜAdil Jāsim al-Bayātī, Beirut, 1987.

———, *al-Khayl*, ed. Muḥammad ᶜAbd al-Qādir Aḥmad, Cairo, 1986.

———, *Majāz al-Qurʾān*, ed. Fuat Sezgin, Cairo, 1955-1962.

al-Akhfash al-Aṣghar, *Kitāb al-ikhtiyārayn*, ed. Fakhr al-Dīn Qabāwa, Damascus, 1974.

Al-Shahi *see* Shahi, Al-

Alf layla wa-layla, Cairo: Maktabat Muḥammad ᶜAlī Ṣubayḥ, n.d.

———, ed. Muḥsin Mahdī, Leiden, 1984.

Allouche, I. S., 'Un traité de polémique christiano-musulmane au IXᵉ siècle', *Hespéris*, 26 (1939) 123-55.

ᶜAlqama, *Dīwān*, in W. Ahlwardt (ed.), *The Divans of the Six Ancient Arabic Poets*, London, 1870.

al-ᶜĀmilī, Bahāʾ al-Dīn Muḥammad, *al-Kashkūl*, Beirut, 1983.

al-Anbārī, Abū Bakr Muḥammad b. al-Qāsim, *Sharḥ al-qaṣāʾid al-sabᶜ al-ṭiwāl al-jāhiliyyāt*, ed. ᶜAbd al-Salām Muḥammad Hārūn, Cairo, 1969.

Anon., *The Sea of Precious Virtues* (Baḥr al-Favāʾid)*: A Medieval Islamic Mirror for Princes*, tr. from the Persian, ed. and annotated by Julie Scott Meisami, Salt Lake City, Utah, 1991.

Arberry *see* Qur'an.

Archibald, Elizabeth, *Incest and the Medieval Imagination*, Oxford, 2001.

Aristotle, *The Complete Works of —: The Revised Oxford Translation*, ed. Jonathan Barnes, Princeton, NJ, 1995.

Artemidorus: Artémidore d'Éphèse, *Le livre des songes / Kitāb taʿbīr al-ruʾyā*, traduit du Grec en Arabe par Ḥunayn b. Isḥāq (mort en 260/873), ed. Toufic Fahd, Damascus, 1964.

al-Ashʿarī, *Maqālāt al-islāmiyyīn wa-khtilāf al-muṣallīn*, ed. H. Ritter, Istanbul, 1929-1930.

Ashtiany, Julia *et al.* (eds), *ʿAbbasid Belles-Lettres*, Cambridge, 1990 (The Cambridge History of Arabic Literature).

al-ʿAskarī, Abū Hilāl, *al-Awāʾil*, Beirut, 1987.

[al-Aṣmaʿī], *al-Ibil*, in August Haffner (ed.), *Texte zur arabischen Lexikographie*, Leipzig, 1905, pp. 60-158.

al-Aṣmaʿiyyāt, ed. Aḥmad Muḥammad Shākir and ʿAbd al-Salām Muḥammad Hārūn, Cairo, 1979.

Athenaeus, *The Deipnosophists*, (ed.) with an English tr. by Charles Burton Gulick, Cambridge, Mass., 1967.

Aws b. Ḥajar, *Dīwān*, ed. Muḥammad Yūsuf Najm, Beirut, 1979.

Badeen, Edward, and Birgit Krawietz, 'Eheschliessung mit Dschinnen nach Badr al-Dīn al-Šiblī', *Wiener Zeitschrift für die Kunde des Morgenlandes*, 92 (2002) 33-51.

al-Baghdādī, ʿAbd al-Qādir, *Ḥāshiya ʿalā sharḥ Bānat Suʿād*, ed. Nazif Hoca, Wiesbaden, 1980-1990.

———, *Khizānat al-adab wa-lubb lubāb lisān al-ʿarab*, ed. ʿAbd al-Salām Muḥammad Hārūn, Cairo, 1967-1986.

al-Baghdādī, Abū Manṣūr ʿAbd-al-Ḳāhir b. Ṭāhir, *al-Farq bayn al-firaq*, ed. Muḥammad Badr, Cairo, 1910.

———, *Moslem Schisms and Sects (Al-Farḳ Bain al-Firaḳ)*, Part II, tr. by Abraham S. Halkin, Tel-Aviv, 1935.

al-Bājūrī *see* al-Bayjūrī

Bakhtiar, Laleh, *Encyclopedia of Islamic Law: A Compendium of the Major Schools*, Chicago, Ill. 1996.

al-Bakrī, Abū ʿUbayd, *Simṭ al-laʾālī fī sharḥ Amālī al-Qālī*, ed. ʿAbd al-ʿAzīz al-Maymanī, Cairo, 1936.

———, *al-Tanbīh ʿalā awhām Abī ʿAlī fī Amālīh*, ed. together with al-Qālī, *al-Amālī* [*q.v.*].

al-Balādhurī, *Ansāb al-ashrāf*, ed. ʿAbd al-ʿAzīz al-Dūrī *et al.*, Beirut, 1978- .

———, *Ansāb al-ashrāf*, vol. IVa, ed. M. Schloessinger, Jerusalem, 1971.

Baram, Amatzia, 'La «maison» de Ṣaddâm Ḥusayn', in P. Bonte *et al.* (eds), *Émirs et présidents* [*q.v.*], pp. 301-29.

al-Baṣrī, Ṣadr al-Dīn b. Abī l-Faraj, *al-Ḥamāsa al-baṣriyya*, ed. Mukhtār al-Dīn Aḥmad, Hyderabad, 1964.

al-Baṭalyawsī, *al-Iqtiḍāb fī sharḥ Adab al-kātib*, ed. Muṣṭafā al-Saqqā and Ḥāmid ʿAbd al-Majīd, Cairo, 1981-1983.

al-Bayḍāwī, *Tafsīr al-Qurʾān*, Cairo, AH 1305.

al-Bayhaqī, Ibrāhīm b. Muḥammad, *al-Maḥāsin wa-l-masāwiʾ*, Beirut, 1970.

al-Bayjūrī (or Bājūrī), Ibrāhīm, *Ḥāshiya ʿalā sharḥ Ibn Qāsim al-Ghazzī ʿalā matn Abī Shujāʿ fī madhhab al-imām al-Shāfiʿī*, Bulaq, AH 1285.

Beeston, A. F. L. *et al.* (eds), *Arabic Literature to the end of the Umayyad period*, Cambridge, 1983 (The Cambridge History of Arabic Literature).

Beeston, A. F. L., 'Temporary Marriage in Pre-Islamic South Arabia', *Arabian Studies*, 4 (1978) 21-25.

Bell *see* Qur'an

Bencheikh, Jamel Eddine, Claude Bremond, André Miquel, *Mille et un contes de la nuit*, Paris, 1991.

Benkheira, Mohammed Hocine, 'Donner le sein, c'est *comme* donner le jour : la doctrine de l'allaitement dans le sunnisme médiéval', *Studia Islamica*, 92 (2001) 5-52.

Bergé, Marc, 'Mérites respectifs des nations selon le *Kitāb al-Imtāʿ wa-l-muʾānasa* d'Abū Ḥayyān al-Tawḥīdī (m. en 141/1023)', *Arabica*, 19 (1972) 165-76.

al-Bīrūnī, *Tārīkh al-Hind*, ed. Edward Sachau, London, 1887.

———, *Alberuni's India*, *see* Sachau, C. Edward, *Alberuni's India*.

———, *al-Āthār al-bāqiya ʿan al-qurūn al-khāliya (Chronologie orientalischer Völker)*, ed. C. Edward Sachau, Leipzig, 1878.

———, *The Chronologie of Ancient Nations: An English version of the Arabic text of the* Athâr [*sic*]-ul-bâkiya *of Albîrûnî, or 'Vestiges of the Past'*, tr. by C. Edward Sachau, London, 1879.

Bonte, Pierre, Éduard Conte, Paul Dresch (eds), *Émirs et présidents : Figures de la parenté et du politique dans le monde arabe*, Paris, 2001.

Bonte, Pierre (ed.), *Épouser au plus proche : Incest, prohibitions et stratégies matrimoniales autour de la Méditerranée*, Paris, 1994.

———, 'Manière de dire ou manière de faire : Peut-on parler d'un mariage «arabe» ?', in Pierre Bonte (ed.), *Épouser au plus proche* [*q.v.*], pp. 371-98.

Borg, Gert, *Mit Poesie vertreibe ich den Kummer meines Herzens: Eine Studie zur altarabischen Trauerklage der Frau*, Istanbul/Leiden, 1997.

Bork-Qaysieh, Waltraud, *Die Geschichte von Kain und Abel (Hābīl wa-Qābīl) in der sunnitisch-islamitischen Überlieferung: Untersuchung von Beispielen aus verschiedenen Literaturwerken unter Berücksichtigung ihres Einflusses auf den Volksglauben*, Berlin, 1993 (Islamkundliche Untersuchungen, 169).

Boswell, John, *Kindness of Strangers: The Abandonment of Children in Western Europe from Late Antiquity to the Renaissance*, London, 1988.

Bouhdiba, Abdelwahab, *Sexuality in Islam*, tr. from the French by Alan Sheridan, London, 1998.

Bousquet, G.-H., *L'Éthique sexuelle de l'Islam*, Paris, 1966.

Boyce, Mary, *A History of Zoroastrianism. I: The Early Period*, Leiden, 1975.

——— and Franz Grenet, *History of Zoroastrianism. III: Zoroastrianism under Macedonian and Roman Rule*, Leiden, 1991.

———, *Zoroastrianism: Its Antiquity and Constant Vigour*, Costa Meza, California, 1992.

———, *Zoroastrians: Their Religious Beliefs and Practices*, London, 1979.

Brockelmann, Carl, *Geschichte der arabischen Litteratur*, I-II, Leiden, 1943, 1949; Suppl. I-III, Leiden, 1937-1942.

Brosius, Maria, *Women in Ancient Persia, 559-331 BC*, Oxford, 1996.

Brown, Donald E., *Human Universals*, New York, 1991.

al-Bukhārī, *al-Ṣaḥīḥ*, Cairo: Dār al-Shaᶜb, n.d.

Bürgel, J. Christoph, 'Zoroastrianism as Viewed in Medieval Islamic Sources', in Jacques Waardenburg (ed.), *Muslim Perceptions of Other Religions: A Historical Survey*, New York & Oxford, 1999, pp. 202-12.

Burton, R.F. (tr.), *The Book of the Thousand Nights and a Night*, London, 1897.

———, *The Arabian Nights*, Prepared for Household Reading by Lady Burton, London, 1886.

Burton, Robert, *The Anatomy of Melancholy*, ed. Holbrook Jackson, London, 1972.

Cachia, Pierre, *Arabic Literature: An Overview*, London, 2002.

Canova, Giovanni, 'Banū Hilāl Tales from Southern Arabia', in *Proceedings of an International Conference on Middle Eastern Popular Culture, Magdalen College, Oxford, 17-21 September 2000*, [Oxford,] 2001, pp. 41-50.

———, 'Remarques sur l'histoire de 'Azīz ben H̲āleh du cycle épique hilalien', in *Proceedings of the 14th Congress of the Union Européenne des Arabisants et Islamisants, Budapest, 1988 = The Arabist*, 13-14 (1995) 173-91.

Caskel, Werner, *Ǧamharat an-nasab: Das genealogische Werk des Hišām ibn Muḥammad al-Kalbī*, I: Tafeln, II: Register, Leiden, 1966.

Catullus, *The Poems of Catullus*, tr. by James Mitchie, London, 1972.

Chebel, Malek, *Encyclopédie de l'amour en Islam : Érotisme, beauté et sexualité dans le monde arabe, en Perse et en Turquie*, Paris, 1995.

Cheikho, Louis, *Anīs al-julasāʾ fī dīwān al-Khansāʾ*, Beirut, 1988.

Chelhod, J., entry 'Raḍāᶜ or Riḍāᶜ, 2: In Arabian society', in *EI²*, viii, 362.

Chokr, Melhem, *Zandaqa et zindīqs en Islam au second siècle de l'hégire*, Damascus, 1993.

Choksy, Jamsheed K., *Evil, Good, and Gender: Facets of the Feminine in Zoroastrian Religious History*, New York, 2002 (Toronto Studies in Religion, 28).

Christensen, Arthur, *L'Iran sous les Sassanides*, 2me éd., Copenhagen, 1944.

———, 'La princesse sur la feuille de myrte et la princesse sur le pois', *Acta Orientalia*, 14 (1936) 241-57.

Conte, Édouard, 'Choisir ses parents dans la société arabe : La situation à l'avènement de l'islam', in Bonte, Pierre (ed.), *Épouser au plus proche* [*q.v.*], pp. 165-87.

Conte, Édouard, 'Filiations prophétiques : Réflexions sur la personne de Muḥammad', in P. Bonte *et al.* (eds), *Émirs et présidents* [*q.v.*], pp. 55-77.

Cook, Michael, *Commanding Right and Forbidding Wrong in Islamic Thought*, Cambridge, 2000.

Coulson, Noel J., *Conflicts and Tensions in Islamic Jurisprudence*, Chicago & London, 1969.

al-Damīrī, *Ḥayāt al-ḥayawān al-kubrā*, Cairo: al-Maktaba al-tijāriyya al-kubrā, n.d.

al-Dārimī, *al-Sunan*, Damascus, AH 1349.

Darmesteter, J., 'Le Hvaētvadatha ou le mariage entre consanguins chez les Parsis', *Revue de l'Histoire des Religions*, 24 (1891) 366-75.

Davis, Dick, *Panthea's Children: Hellenistic Novels and Medieval Persian Romances*, New York, 2002.

Dawkins, Richard, *The Selfish Gene*, Oxford, 1989.

Dawood, N. J. (tr.), *Tales from the Thousand and One Nights*, Harmondsworth, 1961.

de Blois, F. C., entry 'Wīs u Rāmīn', in *EI²*, xi, 210 (publ. 2001).

al-Dhahabī, Shams al-Dīn Abū ʿAbd Allāh Muḥammad b. Aḥmad, *al-Kabāʾir*, ed. Muḥammad ʿAlī Quṭb, Beirut, 1987.

Dhū l-Rumma, *Dīwān*, ed. ʿAbd al-Quddūs Abū Ṣāliḥ, Beirut, 1982.

———, *Dīwān*, ed. C. H. H. Macartney, Cambridge, 1919.

al-Dīnawarī, Abū Ḥanīfa, *al-Akhbār al-ṭiwāl*, ed. Vladimir Guirgass, Leiden, 1888 (with *Preface, Variantes et Index* by Ignace Kratchkovsky, Leiden, 1918),

———, *al-Nabāt: al-juzʾ al-thālith wa-l-nisf al-awwal min al-juzʾ al-khāmis*, ed. Bernhard Levin, Wiesbaden, 1974.

Doniach, N. S., *The Oxford English-Arabic Dictionary of Current Usage*, Oxford, 1987.

Doniger, Wendy, *The Bedtrick: Tales of Sex and Masquerade*, Chicago, 2000.

Doody, Margaret Anne, *The True Story of the Novel*, London, 1998.

Ducène, Jean-Charles, 'Al-Ǧayhānī : fragments (extraits du *K. al-masālik wa l-mamālik* d'al-Bakrī)', *Der Islam*, 75 (1998) 259-82.

Durham, William H., *Coevolution: Genes, Culture and Human Diversity*, Stanford, 1991.

Durkheim, E., *Incest: the Nature and Origin*, New York, 1963.

EI² see *Encyclopaedia of Islam*, New edition.

El-Hajji, Abdurrahman Ali, *see* el-Hajji.

El-Shamy, Hasan M., *see* Shamy, El-.

Encyclopaedia Judaica, Jerusalem, 1971-1972.

Encyclopaedia of Islam, New [= Second] Edition, vols i-xi, Leiden, 1960-2002.

Enderwitz, Susanne, entry 'al-Shuᶜūbiyya', in *EI²*, ix, 513-16 (1996).

Fabrizio, Richard, 'Incest', in Jean-Claude Seigneuret (ed.), *Dictionary of Literary Themes and Motifs*, New York, 1988, (i,) 649-65.

Fahd, T., entry 'Ṣābiʾa', in *EI²*, viii, 675-78 (1994).

al-Farazdaq, *Dīwān*, ed. Beirut: Dār Ṣādir, n.d.

al-Farrāʾ, *Maᶜānī l-Qurʾān*, ed. Aḥmad Yūsuf Najātī *et al.*, Cairo, 1955-1972.

Fattal, Antoine, *Le Statut légal des non-Musulmans en pays d'Islam*, Beyrouth, 1958.

Ferdowsi, *The Epic of the Kings: Shah-Nama, the National Epic of the Persians*, tr. by Reuben Levy, rev. by Amin Banani, London, 1990.

Finkel, Joshua, 'A Risāla of al-Jāḥiẓ', *Journal of the American Oriental Society*, 47 (1927) 311-34.

Firdawsī, *Shāhnāma*, ed. Jalāl Khāliqī Muṭlaq Ferdowsi, vol. 5, Costa Meza, Calif., 1997.

Firestone, Reuven, 'Prophethood, Marriageable Consanguinity, and Text: The Problem of Abraham and Sarah's Kinship Relationship and the Response of Jewish and Islamic Exegesis', *The Jewish Quarterly Review*, 83 (1992-1993) 331-47.

al-Fīrūzābādī, *al-Qāmūs al-muḥīṭ*, Cairo, 1952.

Fox, Robin, *Kinship and Marriage: An Anthropological Perspective*, Cambridge, 1983.

———, *The Red Lamp of Incest*, London, 1980.

Friedmann, Johanan, *Tolerance and Coercion in Islam: Interfaith Relations in the Muslim Tradition*, Cambridge, 2003.

Frye, Richard N., 'Zoroastrian Incest', in G. Gnoli and L. Lanciotti (eds), *Orientalia Iosephi Tucci memoriae dicata*, Roma, 1985-88, pp. 445-55.

Fück, Johann, 'Sechs Ergänzungen zu Sachaus Ausgabe von al-Bīrūnīs "Chronologie Orientalischer Völker"', in *Documenta Islamica Inedita*, ed. by Johann Fück, Berlin, 1952, pp. 69-98.

Gerhardt, Mia I., *The Art of Story-Telling: A Literary Study of the Thousand and One Nights*, Leiden, 1963.

al-Ghazālī, *Iḥyāʾ ʿulūm al-dīn*, Cairo: Maktabat al-Mashhad al-Ḥusaynī, n.d.

———, *Marriage and Sexuality in Islam: A Translation of al-Ghazālī's Book on the Etiquette of Marriage from the* Iḥyāʾ, by Madelaine Farah, Salt Lake City, Utah, 1984.

———, *al-Wajīz fī fiqh madhhab al-imām al-Shāfiʿī*, Cairo, AH 1318.

Giladi, Avner, *Infants, Parents and Wet Nurses: Medieval Islamic Views on Breastfeeding and Their Social Implications*, Leiden, 1999.

Goldziher, Ignaz, *Gesammelte Schriften*, ed. Joseph Desomogyi, Hildesheim, 1967.

———, 'Polyandry and Exogamy among the Arabs', in Ignaz Goldziher, *Gesammelte Schriften* [*q.v.*], ii, 76 [orig. publ. in *The Academy*, London, 18 (1880), p. 26].

Goody, Jack, *The Oriental, the Ancient and the Primitive: Systems of Marriage and the Family in the pre-Industrial Societies of Eurasia*, Cambridge, 1990.

Guo, Li, 'The Devil's Advocate: Ibn Dāniyāl's Art of Parody in His *Qaṣīdah* No. 71', *Mamlūk Studies Review*, 7 (2003) 177-209.

Gurgānī, Fakhr al-Dīn, *Vis and Ramin*, tr. from the Persian by George Morrison, New York, 1972.

———, *Wīs u Rāmīn*, ed. Mihr Jaʿfar Maḥjūb, Tehran, 1959.

al-Hajarī, Hārūn b. Zakariyyā, *al-Taʿlīqāt wa-l-nawādir*, ed. Ḥammūd ʿAbd al-Amīr al-Ḥammādī, Baghdad, 1980-81.

el-Hajji, Abdurrahman Ali, *Andalusian Diplomatic Relations with Western Europe during the Umayyad Period (A.H. 138-366/A.D. 755-976): An Historical Survey*, Beirut, 1970.

al-Ḥalabī, Ibrāhīm, *Multaqā l-abḥur*, ed. and comm. Wahbī Sulaymān Ghāwijī al-Albānī, Beirut, 1989.

al-Hamadhānī, Badī[c] al-Zamān, *al-Maqāmāt*, with comm. by Muḥammad [c]Abduh, Beirut, 1973.

al-Ḥamdūnī, *al-Tadhkira al-Ḥamdūniyya*, ed. Iḥsān [c]Abbās and Bakr [c]Abbās, 1996.

Hammond, Martha Latané, 'The Poetics of S/exclusion: Women, Gender and the Classical Arabic Canon', Ph.D. thesis, New York, Columbia University, 2003.

Hámori, András, 'The House of Brotherly Love: A Story in *al-Tanūḫī* and *The Thousand and One Nights*', in Miklós Maróth (ed.), *Problems in Arabic Literature*, Piliscsaba, 2004, pp. 15-26.

———, 'La maison de l'amour incestueux', in Aboubakr Chraïbi (ed.), *Les Mille et Une Nuits en partage*, Paris, 2004, pp. 199-215.

Ḥamza al-Iṣbahānī, *al-Durra al-fākhira fī l-amthāl al-sā'ira*, ed. [c]Abd al-Majīd Quṭāmish, Cairo, 1971-1972.

Ḥātim al-Ṭā'ī, *Dīwān*, ed. F. Schulthess, Leipzig, 1897.

Ḥāzim al-Qarṭājannī, *Dīwān*, ed. Muḥammad al-Ḥabīb b. al-Khūja (Belkhodja), Tunis, 1972.

Heath, Peter, *The Thirsty Sword:* Sīrat [c]Antar *and the Arabic Popular Epic*, Salt Lake City, Utah, 1996.

Héritier-Augé, Françoise, 'Identité de substance et parenté de lait dans le monde arabe', in Bonte, Pierre (ed), *Épouser au plus proche* [*q.v.*], pp. 149-64.

Héritier, Françoise, *Two Sisters and Their Mother: The Anthropology of Incest*, tr. Jeanine Herman, New York, 2002 [originally published as *Les Deux soeurs et leur mère : Anthropologie de l'incest*, 1994].

Herrenschmidt, Clarisse, 'Le *xwêtôdas* ou mariage «incestueux» en Iran ancien', in Bonte, Pierre (ed.), *Épouser au plus proche* [*q.v.*], pp. 113-25.

al-Ḥikāyāt al-[c]ajība wa-l-akhbār al-gharība/Das Buch der wunderbaren Erzählungen und seltsamen Geschichten, ed. Hans Wehr, Wiesbaden/Damascus, 1956.

Hoffner Jr., Harry A., 'Incest, Sodomy, and Bestiality in the Ancient Near East', in Harry A. Hoffner Jr. (ed.), *Orient and Occident: Essays Presented to Cyrus H. Gordon on the Occasion of his Sixty-fifth Birthday*, Kevelaer, 1973, pp. 81-90.

Hollis, Susan Tower, 'Tales of Magic and Wonder from Ancient Egypt', in Jack M. Sasson [*q.v.*], *Civilizations of the Ancient Near East*, (iv,) 2255-64.

Hopkins, K., 'Brother-Sister Marriage in Roman Egypt', *Comparative Studies in Society and History*, 22 (1980) 303-54.

Hoyland, Robert, *Arabia and the Arabs: From the Bronze Age to the Coming of Islam*, London, 2001.

al-Ḥuṣrī, *Zahr al-ādāb*, ed. Zakī Mubārak, Cairo, 1925 [date of preface]; repr. Beirut, 1972 (with different pagination).

Ibn ᶜAbd al-Barr, *Bahjat al-majālis*, ed. Maḥmūd Mursī al-Khūlī, Beirut, 1982.

Ibn ᶜAbd Rabbih, *al-ᶜIqd al-farīd*, ed. Aḥmad Amīn *et al.*, Cairo, 1948-1953.

Ibn Abī ᶜAwn, *al-Ajwiba al-muskita / Das Buch der schlagfertigen Antworten von Ibn Abī ᶜAwn. Ein Werk der klassisch-arabischen Adab-Literatur*, ed. May A. Yousef, Berlin, 1988.

Ibn Abī l-Ḥadīd, *Sharḥ Nahj al-balāgha*, ed. Ḥusayn al-Aᶜlamī, Beirut, 1995.

Ibn Abī Ṭāhir Ṭayfūr, *Balāghāt al-nisāᵓ*, Beirut, 1987.

Ibn Abī Uṣaybiᶜa, *ᶜUyūn al-anbāᵓ fī ṭabaqāt al-aṭibbāᵓ*, ed. Nizār Riḍā, Beirut: Dār Maktabat al-Ḥayāt, n.d.

Ibn al-Anbārī, Abū l-Barakāt, *Nuzhat al-alibbāᵓ fī ṭabaqāt al-udabāᵓ*, ed. Ibrāhīm al-Sāmarrāᵓī, Beirut, 1985.

Ibn al-ᶜArabī, Abū Bakr Muḥammad b. ᶜAbd Allāh, *Aḥkām al-Qurᵓān*, ed. ᶜAlī Muḥammad al-Bijāwī, Cairo, 1957-1958.

Ibn al-Aᶜrābī, *Asmāᵓ khayl al-ᶜArab wa-fursānihā*, riwāyat Abī Manṣūr al-Jawālīqī, ed. Nūrī Ḥammūdī al-Qaysī and Ḥātim Ṣāliḥ al-Ḍāmin, Beirut, 1987.

Ibn al-Athīr, Ḍiyāᵓ al-Dīn, *al-Mathal al-sāᵓir fī adab al-kātib wa-l-shāᶜir*, ed. Aḥmad al-Ḥūfī and Badawī Ṭabāna, Cairo, 1959-1973.

Ibn al-Athīr, ᶜIzz al-Dīn, *al-Kāmil fī l-tārīkh*, repr. Beirut, 1965-1967.

Ibn al-Athīr, Majd al-Dīn, *al-Nihāya fī gharīb al-ḥadīth wa-l-athar*, Cairo, A.H. 1311.

Ibn Bābawayh al-Ṣadūq, *Man lā yaḥḍuruhu l-faqīh*, ed. al-Sayyid Ḥasan al-Mūsawī al-Kharsān, Beirut, 1981.

Ibn al-Balkhī, *Fārs-nāma / The Fársnáma of Ibnu 'l-Balkhi*, ed. G. Lestrange and R.A. Nicholson, London - Cambridge, 1921.

Ibn Dāniyāl, Muḥammad, *Ṭayf al-khayāl: thalāth bābāt min khayāl al-ẓill / Three Shadow Plays*, ed. Paul Kahle, with a critical apparatus by Derek Hopwood, prepared for publication by Derek Hopwood and Mustafa Badawi, Cambridge, 1992.

Ibn Dāwūd al-Iṣbahānī, *al-Zahra*, ed. Ibrāhīm al-Sāmarrāʾi, Beirut, 1985.

Ibn Diḥya, *al-Muṭrib min ashʿār ahl al-Maghrib*, ed. Ibrāhīm al-Abyārī *et al.*, Cairo, 1954.

Ibn Durayd, *Jamharat al-lugha*, ed. Ramzī Munīr al-Baʿlabakkī, Beirut, 1987-1988.

———, *al-Maqṣūra* (with commentary by al-Tibrīzī), ed. ʿAbd Allāh Ismāʿīl al-Ṣāwī, Damascus, 1961.

Ibn Fāris, *Maqāyīs al-lugha*, ed. ʿAbd al-Salām Muḥammad Hārūn, Cairo, AH 1366-1371.

———, *Mujmal al-lugha*, ed. Zuhayr ʿAbd al-Muḥsin Sulṭān, Beirut, 1984.

Ibn Ḥabīb, Muḥammad, *Asmāʾ al-mughtālīn min al-ashrāf fī l-jāhiliyya wa-l-Islām*, in *Nawādir al-makhṭūṭāt* [*q.v.*], ii, 105-278.

———, *al-Muḥabbar*, ed. Ilse Lichtenstädter, Hyderabad, 1942.

Ibn Ḥajar al-ʿAsqalānī, *Fatḥ al-bārī*, Cairo, AH 1325.

———, *al-Iṣāba fī tamyīz al-ṣaḥāba*, Cairo, 1905-1907.

Ibn Ḥanbal, Aḥmad, *al-Musnad*, Cairo, AH 1313.

Ibn Ḥazm, *al-Faṣl* [usually but erroneously *al-Fiṣal*] *fī l-milal wa-l-ahwāʾ wa-l-niḥal*, Cairo, AH 1317-1321.

———, *al-Muḥallā*, Cairo, AH 1347-1351.

———, *Naqṭ al-ʿarūs fī tawārīkh al-khulafāʾ*, ed. Shawqī Ḍayf, *Majallat Kulliyyat al-ādāb* (Cairo), 13:2 (1951) 41-89.

———, *Rasāʾil*, ed. Iḥsān ʿAbbas, Beirut, 1987.

Ibn Ḥijja al-Ḥamawī, *Khizānat al-adab*, Bulaq, AH 1291.

Ibn Hindū, Abū l-Faraj, *al-Kalim al-rūḥāniyya fī l-ḥikam al-yūnāniyya*, ed. Muṣṭafā al-Qabbānī, Cairo, 1900.

Ibn Hishām, *al-Sīra al-nabawiyya*, ed. Muṣṭafā al-Saqqā *et al.*, Cairo, 1955.

———, *The Life of Muhammad: A Translation of Isḥāq's [sic]* Sīrat Rasūl Allāh, with an introd. and notes by A. Guillaume, Karachi, 1978.

———, *al-Tījān fī mulūk Ḥimyar*, Sanaa, [1979 (date of preface)].

Ibn Hudhayl, *Ḥilyat al-fursān wa-shiʿār al-shujʿān*, ed. Muḥammad ʿAbd al-Ghanī Ḥasan, Cairo, 1951.

Ibn al-Humām, Kamāl al-Dīn Muḥammad b. ʿAbd al-Wāḥid al-Ḥanafī, *Sharḥ Fatḥ al-qadīr ʿalā l-Hidāya sharḥ Bidāyat al-mubtadiʾ*, ed. ʿAbd al-Razzāq Ghālib al-Mahdī, Beirut, 1995.

Ibn al-ʿIbrī (Barhebraeus), *Tārīkh mukhtaṣar al-duwal*, ed. Anṭūn Ṣāliḥānī, Beirut, 1958.

Ibn Isḥāq *see* Ibn Hishām.

[Ibn Iyās], *Badāʾiʿ al-zuhūr fī waqāʾiʿ al-duhūr*, Cairo: ʿĪsā l-Bābī al-Ḥalabī, n.d. [not identical with the history of that name by Ibn Iyās].

Ibn al-Jarrāḥ, Muḥammad b. Dāwūd, *al-Waraqa*, ed. ʿAbd al-Wahhāb ʿAzzām and ʿAbd al-Sattār Aḥmad Farrāj, *ṭabʿa* 2, Cairo: Dār al-Maʿārif, n.d.

Ibn al-Jawzī, *al-Adhkiyāʾ*, ed. Muḥammad ʿAbd al-Raḥmān ʿAwaḍ, Beirut, 1986.

———, *Akhbār al-ḥamqā wa-l-mughaffalīn*, Beirut, 1988.

———, *Dhamm al-hawā*, ed. Aḥmad ʿAbd al-Salām ʿAṭā, Beirut, 1987.

———, *Ṣayd al-khāṭir*, ed. Nājī al-Ṭanṭāwī and ʿAlī al-Ṭanṭāwī, Beirut, 1979.

———, *Talbīs Iblīs*, Beirut, 1994.

Ibn al-Kalbī, Hishām b. Muḥammad, *Jamharat al-nasab*, *see* Caskel.

———, *Nasab al-khayl*, ed. Nūrī Ḥammūdī al-Qaysī and Ḥātim Ṣāliḥ al-Ḍāmin, Beirut, 1987.

[Ibn Kamāl Bāshā, Aḥmad b. Sulaymān], *Rujūʿ al-shaykh ilā ṣibāh fī l-quwwa ʿalā l-bāh*, Bulaq, AH 1309 [the author is Aḥmad b. Yūsuf al-Tīfāshī].

Ibn Kammūna, *Tanqīḥ al-abḥāth li-l-milal al-thalāth*, ed. M. Perlmann, Berkeley & Los Angeles, 1967.

———, *Ibn Kammūna's Examination of the Three Faiths*, tr. M. Perlmann, Berkeley & Los Angeles, 1971.

Ibn Kathīr, *al-Bidāya wa-l-nihāya*, Cairo, 1932- .

Ibn Khallikān, *Wafayāt al-aʿyān*, ed. Iḥsān ʿAbbās, Beirut, 1968-72.

Ibn Māja, *al-Sunan*, Cairo: al-Maṭbaʿa al-ʿilmiyya, AH 1313.

Ibn Manẓūr, *Akhbār Abī Nuwās*, ed. ʿAbbās al-Shirbīnī and Muḥammad ʿAbd al-Rasūl Ibrāhīm, Cairo, 1924.

———, *Lisān al-ʿArab*, Bulaq, AH 1308.

Ibn Maymūn, *Muntahā l-ṭalab min ashʿār al-ʿArab*, facs. ed. by Fuat Sezgin, Frankfurt am Main, 1986-93.

Ibn al-Mujāwir, *Taʾrīkh al-mustabṣir*, ed. Oscar Löfgren, Leiden, 1951, 1954.

Ibn al-Nadīm, *al-Fihrist*, ed. Gustav Flügel *et al.*, Leipzig, 1871-1872.

———, *The Fihrist of al-Nadīm: A Tenth-Century Survey of Muslim Culture*, tr. by Bayard Dodge, New York & London, 1970.

Ibn Qayyim al-Jawziyya, *Aḥkām ahl al-dhimma*, ed. Ṣubḥī al-Ṣāliḥ, Beirut, 1961.

———, *Ighāthat al-lahfān min maṣāyid al-shayṭān*, ed. Muḥammad Ḥāmid al-Faqī, Cairo, 1939 [date of afterword].

———, *Iʿlām al-muwaqqiʿīn ʿan Rabb al-ʿālamīn*, ed. Muḥammad ʿAbd al-Salām Ibrāhīm, Beirut, 1991.

———, *Rawḍat al-muḥibbīn wa-nuzhat al-mushtāqīn*, repr. Beirut, Dār al-kutub al-ʿilmiyya, n.d.

Ibn Qudāma, *al-Mughnī*, ed. ʿAbd al-Fattāḥ Muḥammad al-Ḥulw and ʿAbd Allāh b. ʿAbd al-Muḥsin al-Turkī, Cairo, 1986-1990.

Ibn Qutayba, *Adab al-kātib*, ed. Max Grünert, Leiden, 1900.

———, *al-ʿArab*, in Muḥammad Kurd ʿAlī (ed.), *Rasāʾil al-bulaghāʾ*, Cairo, 1954, pp. 344-77.

———, *Kitāb al-maʿānī l-kabīr*, Hyderabad, 1949.

———, *al-Maʿārif*, ed. Tharwat ʿUkāsha, Cairo, 1981.

———, *al-Shiʿr wa-l-shuʿarāʾ*, ed. Aḥmad Muḥammad Shākir, Cairo, 1966.

———, *ʿUyūn al-akhbār*, Cairo, 1925-1930.

Ibn Rashīq, *al-ᶜUmda fī maḥāsin al-shiᶜr wa-ādābihi wa-naqdihi*, ed. Muḥammad Muḥyī l-Dīn ᶜAbd al-Ḥamīd, repr. Beirut, 1972.

Ibn Riḍwān, ᶜAlī, *Commentary on Ptolemy's* Tetrabiblos *(Sharḥ al-maqālāt al-arbaᶜ li-Baṭlamiyūs)*, MS Tehran, Majlis 191.

Ibn al-Rūmī, *Dīwān*, ed. Ḥusayn Naṣṣār, Cairo, 1973-1981.

Ibn Rushd, Abū l-Walīd Muḥammad b. Aḥmad, *Bidāyat al-mujtahid wa-nihāyat al-muqtaṣid*, Cairo, AH 1339.

———, *The Distinguished Jurist's Primer (Bidāyat al-Mujtahid)*, tr. by Imran Ahsan Khan Nyazee, rev. by Mohammad Abdul Rauf, Reading, 1994-1996.

———, *Muqaddimāt*, in Saḥnūn [*q.v.*], *al-Mudawwana*.

Ibn Saᶜd, *Kitāb al-Ṭabaqāt al-kabīr*, ed. Eduard Sachau *et al.*, Leiden, 1904-1940.

Ibn Saᶜīd al-Maghribī, *al-Muṭrib fī ḥulā l-Maghrib*, ed. Shawqī Ḍayf, Cairo, 1980.

———, *Nashwat al-ṭarab fī tārīkh jāhiliyyat al-ᶜArab*, ed. Nuṣrat ᶜAbd al-Raḥmān, ᶜAmmān, 1982.

Ibn al-Ṣayqal al-Jazarī, Maᶜadd b. Naṣr Allāh b. Rajab al-Baghdādī, *al-Maqāmāt al-Zayniyya*, ed. ᶜAbbās Muṣṭafā al-Ṣāliḥī, [Baghdad], 1980.

Ibn Shaddād, Bahāᵓ al-Dīn, *Dalāᵓil al-aḥkām*, ed. Muḥammad b. Yaḥyā b. Ḥasan al-Nujaymī, Beirut, 1991.

Ibn Shāhīn al-Ẓāhirī, Khalīl, *al-Ishārāt fī ᶜilm al-ᶜibārāt*, printed in vol. ii of al-Nābulusī, *Taᶜṭīr al-anām* [*q.v.*].

Ibn al-Shajarī, *Mukhtārāt shuᶜarāᵓ al-ᶜArab*, ed. ᶜAlī Muḥammad al-Bijāwī, Cairo, 1975.

Ibn Sīda, *al-Mukhaṣṣaṣ*, Bulaq, AH 1316.

Ibn Sīnā, *al-Qānūn fī l-ṭibb*, Bulaq, AH 1294.

[Ibn Sīrīn, Muḥammad], *Tafsīr al-aḥlām al-musammā Muntakhab al-kalām fī tafsīr al-aḥlām*, Beirut, n.d.; also printed in al-Nābulusī [*q.v.*], *Taᶜṭīr al-anām*, vol. i.

Ibn Taymiyya, *al-Fatāwī*, Cairo, AH 1326-1329.

———, *al-Ikhtiyārāt al-fiqhiyya min fatāwī Ibn Taymiyya*, ikhtārahā ᶜAlāᵓ al-Dīn Abū l-Ḥasan ᶜAlī b. Muḥammad b. ᶜAbbās al-Baᶜlī al-Dimashqī, ed. Muḥammad Ḥāmid al-Faqī, Beirut: Dār al-maᶜrifa, n.d.

Ibn al-Ṭiqṭaqā, *al-Fakhrī*, ed. Hartwig Derenbourg, Paris, 1895.

al-Ibshīhī, *al-Mustaṭraf fī kull fann mustaẓraf*, Cairo, 1952.

Ikhwān al-Ṣafāʾ, *Rasāʾil*, Beirut, 1957.

Irwin, Robert, *The Arabian Nights: A Companion*, London, 1994.

al-Iṣfahānī, Abū l-Faraj, *al-Aghānī*, Cairo, 1927-1974.

——, *al-Aghānī*, ed. Ibrāhīm al-Abyārī, Cairo, 1969-1982.

———, *al-Imāʾ al-shawāʿir*, ed. Jalīl al-ʿAṭiyya, Beirut, 1998.

al-Isfarāyīnī, Abū l-Muẓaffar, *al-Tabṣīr fī l-dīn*, ed. Muḥammad Zāhid al-Kawtharī, Cairo, 1955.

Jacobus de Voragine, *The Golden Legend: Readings on the Saints*, tr. by William Granger Ryan, Princeton, NJ, 1993.

al-Jāḥiẓ, *Arabische Geisteswelt: Ausgewählte und übersetzte Texte von al-Ǧāḥiẓ (777-869)* [texts selected by] Charles Pellat, [tr. from the French by] Walter W. Müller, Zürich & Stuttgart, 1967.

———, *al-Bayān wa-l-tabyīn*, ed. ʿAbd al-Salām Muḥammad Hārūn, Cairo, 1968.

———, *al-Bighāl*, in his *Rasāʾil* [*q.v.*], ii, 211-378 (see also al-Jāḥiẓ, *al-Qawl fī l-bighāl*).

———, *The Book of Misers (Al-Bukhalāʾ)*, tr. by R. B. Serjeant, reviewed by Ezzeddin Ibrahim, Reading, 1997.

———, *al-Bukhalāʾ*, ed. Ṭāhā l-Ḥājirī, Cairo, n.d.

———, *al-Burṣān wa-l-ʿurjān wa-l-ʿumyān wa-l-ḥūlān*, ed. ʿAbd al-Salām Muḥammad Hārūn, Baghdad-Beirut, 1982.

———, *al-Ḥayawān*, ed. ʿAbd al-Salām Muḥammad Hārūn, Cairo, 1965-1969.

———, *The Life and Works of Jāḥiẓ: Translations of Selected Texts*, by Charles Pellat, tr. from the French by D.M. Hawke, London, 1969.

———, *al-Qawl fī l-bighāl*, ed. Charles Pellat, Cairo, 1955 (see also al-Jāḥiẓ, *al-Bighāl*).

———, *al-Qiyān: The Epistle on Singing-Girls of Jāḥiẓ*, ed. with tr. and comm. by A. F. L. Beeston, Warminster, Wilts, 1980.

———, *al-Rasāʾil*, ed. ʿAbd al-Salām Muḥammad Hārūn, Cairo, 1964-1979.

———, *Sobriety and Mirth: A Selection of the Shorter Writings of al-Jahiz*, tr. by Jim Colville, London, 2002.

———, *al-Tarbīʿ wa-l-tadwīr*, in his *Rasāʾil* [*q.v.*], iii, 53-109.

———, *al-Tarbīʿ wa-l-tadwīr*, ed. Charles Pellat, Damascus, 1955.

Jarīr, *Dīwān, bi-sharḥ Muḥammad b. Ḥabīb*, ed. Nuʿmān Muḥammad Amīn Ṭāhā, Cairo, 1986.

al-Jarīrī, al-Muʿāfā b. Zakariyyā, *al-Jalīs al-ṣāliḥ al-kāfī wa-l-anīs al-nāṣiḥ al-shāfī*, ed. Muḥammad Mursī al-Khūlī and Iḥsān ʿAbbās, Beirut, 1993.

Jastrow, Marcus, *A Dictionary of the Targumim, the Talmud Babli and Yerushalmi, and the Midrashic Literature*, New York, 1950.

al-Jazīrī, ʿAbd al-Raḥmān, *al-Fiqh ʿalā l-madhāhib al-arbaʿa*, vol. iv, 2nd. ed., Cairo, 1938 [date of preface].

Kaʿb b. Zuhayr, *Dīwān*, ed. Tadeusz Kowalski, Kraków, 1950.

Kappler, Claude-Claire, '*Vîs et Râmîn*, ou comment aimer un autre que son frère ...?', *Luqmān*, 7:2 (1991) 55-80.

Karmi, Hasan S., *Al-Manar: An English-Arabic Dictionary*, Beirut, 1970.

———, *Al-Mughni Al-Akbar: A Dictionary of Classical and Contemporary Arabic, English-Arabic*, Beirut, 1988.

al-Kāsānī, ʿAlāʾ al-Dīn Abū Bakr b. Masʿūd, *Badāʾiʿ al-ṣanāʾiʿ fī tartīb al-sharāʾiʿ*, Cairo, AH 1327-1328.

Kellens, J., 'Zoroastre dans l'histoire ou dans le mythe ? À propos du dernier livre de Gherardo Gnoli', *Journal Asiatique* 289 (2001) 171-84.

al-Khālidiyyān [Abū Bakr Muḥammad and Abū ʿUthmān Saʿīd ibnā Hāshim], *al-Ashbāh wa-l-naẓāʾir min ashʿār al-mutaqaddimīn wa-l-jāhiliyya wa-l-mukhaḍramīn*, ed. al-Sayyid Muḥammad Yūsuf, Cairo, 1958, 1965.

al-Khalīl b. Aḥmad, *al-ʿAyn*, ed. Mahdī al-Makhzūmī and Ibrāhīm al-Sāmarrāʾī, Baghdad, 1980-1985.

al-Khansāʾ, *Dīwān*, ed. Ibrāhīm ʿAwaḍayn, Cairo, 1985.

———, *Dīwān*, ed. Anwar Abū Suwaylim, Beirut, 1988.

al-Khwārazmī, Abū ʿAbd Allāh, *Mafātīḥ al-ʿulūm*, ed. G. van Vloten, Leiden, 1895.

al-Kisāʾī, Muḥammad b. ʿAbd Allāh, *Qiṣaṣ al-anbiyāʾ*, ed. Isaac Eisenberg, Leiden, 1922-1923.

al-Kisāʾī, *The Tales of the Prophets of al-Kisa'i*, tr. from the Arabic with notes by W. M. Thackston, Jr., Boston, 1978.

al-Kiyā al-Harrāsī, ʿImād al-Dīn ʿAlī b. Muḥammad, *Aḥkām al-Qurʾān*, ed. Mūsā Muḥammad ʿAlī and ʿIzzat ʿAlī ʿĪd ʿAṭiyya, Cairo, 1974.

Kurpershoek, P. Marcel, *Oral Poetry and Narratives from Central Arabia, IV: A Saudi Tribal History. Honour and Faith in the Tradition of the Dawāsir*, Leiden, 2002.

Landau-Tasseron, Ella, 'Adoption, acknowledgement of paternity and false genealogical claims in Arabian and Islamic societies', *Bulletin of the School of Oriental and African Studies*, 66 (2003) 169-92.

Lane, Edward William, *An Arabic-English Lexicon*, London, 1863-1877.

——— (tr.), *The Thousand and One Nights, commonly called, in England, The Arabian Nights' Entertainments*, London, 1859.

Lessmann, Heinrich, *Aufgaben und Ziele der vergleichenden Mythenforschung*, Leipzig, 1908.

Lewis, Bernard, *Race and Slavery in the Middle East: An Historical Enquiry*, Oxford, 1990.

Lichtenstaedter, Ilse, *Introduction to Classical Arabic Literature, With Selections from Representative Works in English Translation*, New York, 1974.

Linant de Bellefonds, Y., *Traité de droit musulman comparé*, Paris — The Hague, 1965-1973.

Littmann, Enno, (tr.) *Die Erzählungen aus den tausendundein Nächten*, Wiesbaden, 1966.

Loth, O., 'Ṭabarī's Korancommentar', *Zeitschrift der Deutschen Morgenländischen Gesellschaft*, 35 (1881) 588-628.

Lyons, M. C., *The Arabian Epic: Heroic and Oral Story-Telling*, Cambridge, 1995.

———, 'Qiṣṣat ʿArūd al-ʿarāʾis@, *Oriente Moderno*, 83 (2003) 559-73.

al-Maʿarrī, Abū l-ʿAlāʾ, *al-Fuṣūl wa-l-ghāyāt*, ed. Maḥmūd Ḥasan Zanātī, Cairo, 1938.

———, *al-Luzūmiyyāt*, ed. Amīn ʿAbd al-ʿAzīz al-Khānjī, Cairo, AH 1342.

———, *Risālat al-Ghufrān*, ed. ᶜĀ᾽isha ᶜAbd al-Raḥmān Bint al-Shāṭi᾽, *ṭabᶜa* 4, Cairo: Dār al-Maᶜārif, n.d.

———, *al-Ṣāhil wa-l-shāḥij*, ed. ᶜĀ᾽isha ᶜAbd al-Raḥmān, Cairo, 1984.

Mackintosh-Smith, Tim, *Travels with a Tangerine: A Journey in the Footnotes of Ibn Battuta*, London, 2001.

Malti-Douglas, Fedwa, *Woman's Body, Woman's World: Gender and Discourse in Arabo-Islamic Writings*, Princeton, 1992.

al-Manbijī, Abū Muḥammad ᶜAlī b. Zakariyyā, *al-Lubāb fī l-jamᶜ bayna l-Sunna wa-l-Kitāb*, ed. Muḥammad Faḍl ᶜAbd al-ᶜAzīz al-Murād, Beirut, 1983.

al-Marghīnānī, Burhān al-dīn ᶜAlī b. Abī Bakr, *al-Hidāya, sharḥ Bidāyat al-mubtadi᾽*, Cairo: Muṣṭafā l-Bābī al-Ḥalabī, n.d.

Margoliouth, D. S., 'Some Extracts from the *Kitāb al-imtāᶜ wal-mu᾽ānasah* of Abū Ḥayyān Tauḥīdī', *Islamica*, 2 (1926-27) 380-90.

Marguerite de Navarre, *The Heptameron*, tr. with an introd. by P. A. Chilton, Harmondsworth, 1984.

Marzolph, Ulrich, *Arabia ridens. Die humoristische Kurzprosa der frühen adab-Literatur im internationalen Traditionsgeflecht*, Frankfurt am Main, 1992.

———, 'As Woman as Can Be: The Gendered Subversiveness of an Arabic Folktale Heroine', *Edebiyât*, 10 (1999) 199-218.

———, and Richard van Leeuwen, *The Arabian Nights Encyclopedia*, Santa Barbara, CA, 2004.

———, (ed.), *Das Buch der wundersamen Geschichten. Erzählungen aus der Welt von Tausendundeine Nacht*. Munich, 1999.

———, 'Philogelos arabikos. Zum Nachleben der antiken Witzesammlung in der mittelalterlichen arabischen Literatur', *Der Islam*, 64 (1987) 185-230.

al-Marzūqī, *Sharḥ Dīwān al-ḥamāsa*, ed. Aḥmad Amīn and ᶜAbd al-Salām Hārūn, Beirut, 1991.

[al-Masᶜūdī], *Akhbār al-zamān wa-man abādahu l-ḥidthān*, Cairo, 1938.

al-Masᶜūdī, *Murūj al-dhahab*, ed. C. Pellat, Beirut, 1966-1979.

———, *al-Tanbīh wa-l-ishrāf*, ed. M. J. de Goeje, Leiden, 1893.

Mavroudi, Maria, *A Byzantine Book on Dream Interpretation: The* Oneirocriticon of Achmet *and Its Arabic Sources*, Leiden, 2002.

al-Māwardī, *Adab al-dunyā wa-l-dīn*, ed. Muṣṭafā al-Saqqā, Beirut: al-Maktaba al-thaqāfiyya, n.d.

———, *al-Ḥāwī l-kabīr fī fiqh madhhab al-imām al-Shāfiʿī*, ed. ʿAlī Muḥammad Muʿawwiḍ and ʿĀdil Aḥmad ʿAbd al-Mawjūd, Beirut, 1994-1996.

al-Maydānī, *Majmaʿ al-amthāl*, ed. Naʿīm Zarzūr, Beirut, 1988.

Meisami, Julie Scott, and Paul Starkey (eds), *Encyclopedia of Arabic Literature*, London, 1998.

Meisami, Julie Scott, *Medieval Persian Court Poetry*, Princeton, NJ, 1987.

Minorsky, V., 'Vīs u Rāmīn: A Parthian Romance', in his *Iranica: Twenty Articles*, Tehran, 1964, pp. 150-199.

Monroe, James T., *Hispano-Arabic Poetry: A Student Anthology*, Berkeley & Los Angeles, 1974.

Morony, M., entry 'Madjūs', in *EI²* iv, 1110-18 (1985).

Mughulṭāy, al-Ḥāfiz [Abū ʿAbd Allāh Nāṣir al-Dīn], *al-Wāḍiḥ al-mubīn fī dhikr man ustushhida min al-muḥibbīn*, Beirut, 1997.

Muḥammad b. Mālik al-Ḥammādī al-Yamānī, *Kashf asrār al-Bāṭiniyya wa-akhbār al-Qarāmiṭa*, ed. Muḥammad Zāhid al-Kawtharī, Cairo, 1955 (in al-Isfarāyīnī, *al-Tabṣīr fī l-dīn* [*q.v.*], pp. 179-221).

Muhawi, Ibrahim, 'Gender and Disguise in the Arabic *Cinderella*', *Fabula*, 42:3-4 (2001) 262-83.

Müller, Kathrin, *'Und der Kalif lachte, bis er auf den Rücken fiel'. Ein Beitrag zur Phraseologie und Stilkunde des klassischen Arabisch*, München, 1993.

al-Muqaddasī, *Aḥsan al-taqāsīm fī maʿrifat al-aqālīm*, ed. M. J. de Goeje, Leiden, 1906.

———, *The Best Divisions for Knowledge of the Regions*, tr. Basil Collins, Reading, 2001.

Murtaḍā l-Zabīdī, Muḥammad, *Itḥāf al-sāda al-muttaqīn bi-sharḥ Iḥyāʾ ʿulūm al-dīn*, Cairo, AH 1311.

———, *Tāj al-ʿarūs min jawāhir al-Qāmūs*, Kuweit, 1965- .

Muslim b. al-Walīd, *Dīwān*, ed. Sāmī al-Dahhān, Cairo, 1985.

al-Mutalammis, *Dīwān (Die Gedichte des Mutalammis)*, ed. K. Vollers, Leipzig, 1903.

al-Mutanabbī, *Dīwān* (with commentary attributed to al-ᶜUkbarī), ed. Muṣṭafā al-Saqqā *et al.*, Cairo, 1936-1938.

———, *Dīwān* (with commentary by al-Wāḥidī), ed. F. Dieterici, Berlin, 1861.

al-Nābigha al-Dhubyānī, *Dīwān*, in W. Ahlwardt (ed.), *The Divans of the six ancient Arabic poets*, London, 1870.

al-Nābulusī, ᶜAbd al-Ghanī, *Taᶜṭīr al-anām fī tafsīr al-aḥlām*, Cairo: ᶜĪsā l-Bābī al-Ḥalabī, n.d.

al-Nafzāwī, *Der duftende Garten zur Erbauung des Gemüts. Ein arabisches Liebeshandbuch*, tr. Ulrich Marzolph, Munich, 2002.

[al-Nafzāwī (attr. to)], *The Glory of the Perfumed Garden: The Missing Flowers*. An English Translation [by 'H. E. J.'] from the Arabic of the Second and Hitherto Unpublished Part of Shaykh Nafzawi's *Perfumed Garden*, London, 1972.

al-Nafzāwī, *The Perfumed Garden of the Shaykh Nefzawi*, tr. by Richard Burton and ed. with an Introd. and Additional Notes by Alan Hull Walton, London, 1963.

al-Nafzāwī, *al-Rawḍ al-ᶜāṭir fī nuzhat al-khāṭir*, ed. Jamāl Jumᶜa, London, 1993.

al-Nahshalī, ᶜAbd al-Karīm, *al-Mumtiᶜ fī ṣanᶜat al-shiᶜr*, ed. ᶜAbbās ᶜAbd al-Sattār and Nuᶜaym Zarzūr, Beirut, 1983.

Naqāʾiḍ Jarīr wa-l-Akhṭal, ed. Anṭūn Ṣāliḥānī (A. Salhani), Beirut, 1922.

Naqāʾiḍ Jarīr wa-l-Farazdaq, ed. A. A. Bevan, London, 1905-1912.

al-Nasāʾī, *al-Sunan al-kubrā*, ed. ᶜAbd al-Ghaffār Sulaymān al-Bundārī and Sayyid Kisrawī Ḥasan, Beirut, 1991-1992.

Nawādir al-makhṭūṭāt, ed. ᶜAbd al-Salām Hārūn, Cairo, 1972-1973.

al-Nawbakhtī, Abū Muḥammad al-Ḥasan b. Mūsā, *Firaq al-shīᶜa*, ed. H. Ritter, Leipzig, 1931.

Nicholson, Reynold Alleyne, *Studies in Islamic Poetry*, Cambridge, 1921.

Niẓām al-Mulk, *The Book of Government, or Rules for Kings: The Siyar al-Muluk or Siyasat-nama*, tr. from the Persian by Hubert Darke, London, 1978.

———, *Siyar al-mulūk (Siyāsat-nāma)*, ed. Hubert Darke, Tehran, 1962.

Nöldeke, Th., *Aufsätze zur persischen Geschichte*, Leipzig, 1887.

Norris, H.T., 'Fables and legends in pre-Islamic and early Islamic times', in Beeston [*q.v.*] *et al.* (eds), *Arabic Literature to the end of the Umayyad period*, pp. 374-86.

al-Nuwayrī, *Nihāyat al-arab fī funūn al-adab*, Cairo, 1923- .

Oberhelman, Steven M., 'Hierarchies of Gender, Ideology, and Power in Ancient and Medieval Greek and Arabic Dream Literature', in J. W. Wright Jr. and Everett K. Rowson (eds), *Homoeroticism in Classical Arabic Literature*, New York, 1997, pp. 55-93.

Ouyang, Wen-chin, 'Romancing the Epic: *ʿUmar al-Nuʿmān* as Narrative of Empowerment', *Arabic and Middle Eastern Literatures*, 3 (2000), 5-18.

Perry, Ben Edwin (ed.), *Secundus the Silent Philosopher: The Greek Life of Secundus, critically edited (...) together with translations of the Greek and Oriental Versions, the Latin and Oriental Texts, and a Study of the Tradition*, Ithaca, New York, 1964.

Petschow, H. P. H., 'Inzest', in *Reallexikon der Assyriologie*, Berlin, 1928- , Bd. v (1976-1980), pp. 144-50.

Pinault, David, *Story-Telling Techniques in the Arabian Nights*, Leiden, 1992.

Praz, Mario, *The Romantic Agony*, tr. from the Italian by Angus Davidson, 2nd ed. Oxford, 1970.

Pritchard, James B., *Ancient Near Eastern Texts Relating to the Old Testament*, 2nd ed., Princeton, 1955.

Pritsch, Erich, and Otto Spies, 'Das Findelkind im islamischen Recht nach al-Kāsānī', *Zeitschrift für vergleichende Rechtswissenschaft*, 57 (1954) 74-101.

Ptolemy, *Tetrabiblos*, ed. with an English tr. F. E. Robbins, London, 1940 (Loeb Classical Library).

Q: *see* Qur'an.

al-Qāḍī Nuʿmān, *Daʿāʾim al-Islām*, ed. Āṣāf b. ʿAlī Aṣghar Fayḍī, Cairo, 1960-1963.

al-Qaffāl al-Shāshī, *Ḥilyat al-ʿulamāʾ fī maʿrifat madhāhib al-fuqahāʾ*, ed. Yāsīn Aḥmad Ibrāhīm Darādika, Amman, 1988.

al-Qālī, Abū ʿAlī, *al-Amālī*, Cairo, 1926.

al-Qalyūbī, Aḥmad b. Aḥmad, *Ḥawāshī ʿalā sharḥ al-Maḥallī ʿalā Minhāj al-ṭālibīn [li-l-Nawawī]*, Cairo, AH 1306.

al-Qazwīnī, [Jamāl al-Dīn,] *Mufīd al-ʿulūm wa-mubīd al-humūm*, ed. Muḥammad ʿAbd al-Qādir ʿAṭā, Beirut, 1985 [where the author's name is incorrectly given as Zakariyyā b. Muḥammad al-Qazwīnī].

al-Qazwīnī, Zakariyyā b. Muḥammad, *ʿAjāʾib al-makhlūqāt*, printed in margin of al-Damīrī, *Ḥayāt al-ḥayawānāt al-kubrā* [*q.v.*].

———, *Āthār al-bilād*, Beirut, 1979.

Qur'an: text and numbering of the Egyptian State edition of 1344/1924 have been followed.

———, Arthur J. Arberry, *The Koran Interpreted*, London, 1964.

———, Richard Bell, *The Qurʾān: Translated, with a Critical Re-arrangement of the Surahs*, Edinburgh, 1937.

al-Qurashī, Abū Zayd Muḥammad b. Abī l-Khaṭṭāb, *Jamharat ashʿār al-ʿArab*, Beirut, 1963.

al-Qushayrī, *Laṭāʾif al-ishārāt: Tafsīr ṣūfī kāmil li-l-Qurʾān al-karīm*, ed. Ibrāhīm Basyūnī, Cairo, [1968]-1971.

al-Rāghib al-Iṣbahānī, *Muḥāḍarāt al-udabāʾ*, Bulaq, AH 1287.

———, *Tafṣīl al-nashʾatayn wa-taḥṣīl al-saʿādatayn*, ed. ʿAbd al-Majīd al-Najjār, Beirut, 1988.

al-Ramlī, Shams al-Dīn Muḥammad b. Aḥmad, *Nihāyat al-muḥtāj ilā sharḥ al-Minhāj [li-l-Nawawī]*, Cairo, 1938.

Rank, Otto, *The Incest Theme in Literature and Legend: Fundamentals of a Psychology of Literary Creation*, tr. by Gregory C. Richter, Baltimore, 1992 [orig. title *Das Inzest-Motiv in Dichtung und Sage*, Leipzig & Vienna, 1912].

al-Raqīq al-Qayrawānī, *Quṭb al-surūr fī awṣāf al-khumūr*, ed. Aḥmad al-Jundī, Damascus, 1969 [date of preface].

al-Rāzī, Abū Bakr, *al-Ḥāwī fī l-ṭibb*, Hyderabad, 1955-69.

al-Rāzī, Fakhr al-Dīn, *al-Tafsīr al-kabīr (Mafātīḥ al-ghayb)*, Bulaq, 1278.

Ricks, Stephen D., 'Kinship Bars to Marriage in Jewish and Islamic Law', in William M. Brinner and Stephen D. Ricks (eds), *Studies in Islamic and Judaic Traditions*, Atlanta, Georgia, 1986, i, 123-41.

Ridley, Matt, *The Red Queen: Sex and the Evolution of Human Nature*, Harmondsworth, 1994.

Roscoe, Paul B., 'Amity and Aggression: A Symbolic Theory of Incest', *Man*, 29:1 (1994) 49-76.

Rosenthal, Franz, *Humor in Early Islam*, Westport, Connecticut, 1956.

Ruʾba b. al-ʿAjjāj, *Dīwān*, ed. W. Ahlwardt, Berlin, 1903.

Rubin, Uri, 'Apes, Pigs, and the Islamic Identity', *Israel Oriental Studies*, 17 (1997) 89-105.

Sachau, Edward C., *Alberuni's India*, an English edition, with notes and indices, London, 1910.

——— (Ed. and tr.), *Syrische Rechtsbücher. Dritter Band: Corpus juris des persischen Erzbischofs Jesubocht (...)*, Berlin, 1914.

al-Ṣafadī, *al-Ghayth al-musajjam fī sharḥ Lāmiyyat al-ʿajam*, Beirut, 1975.

———, *al-Wāfī bi-l-Wafayāt*, Wiesbaden, 1932- .

al-Ṣāḥib b. ʿAbbād, *Dīwān*, ed. Muḥammad Ḥasan Āl Yāsīn, Beirut, 1974.

Saḥnūn, *al-Mudawwana*, Cairo, AH 1324-1325.

Ṣāʿid al-Andalusī, *Ṭabaqāt al-umam*, ed. Ḥayāt Bū ʿAlwān, Beirut, 1985.

Sallis, Eva, *Sheherazade Through the Looking Glass: The Metamorphosis of the* Thousand and One Nights, Richmond, Surrey, 1999.

al-Sarakhsī, Shams al-Dīn Muḥammad b. al-Ḥasan, *al-Mabsūṭ*, Cairo, AH 1324.

Sasson, Jack M. (ed. in chief), *Civilizations of the Ancient Near East*, New York, 1995.

Schacht, Joseph, *An Introduction to Islamic Law*, Oxford, 1964.

———, and J. Burton, entry 'Raḍāʿ or Riḍāʿ, 1: Legal aspects', in *EI²*, viii, 361-62.

Schregle, G., *Deutsch-arabisches Wörterbuch*, Wiesbaden, 1974.

Schützinger, Heinrich, *Ursprung und Entwicklung der arabischen Abraham-Nimrod-Legende*, Bonn, 1961 (Bonner Orientalistische Studien, N. S., 11).

Sells, Michael, '*Bānat Suʿād*: Translation and Introduction', *Journal of Arabic Literature*, 21 (1990) 140-54.

Serjeant, R. B., 'Zinā, Some Forms of Marriage and Allied Topics in Western Arabia', in Johann Heiss *et al.* (eds), *Studies in Oriental Culture and History: Festschrift for Walter Dostal*, Frankfurt am Main, 1993, pp. 145-59.

Sezgin, Fuat, *Geschichte des arabischen Schrifttums. II: Poesie bis ca. 430 H.*, Leiden, 1975.

al-Shāfiʿī, *al-Umm*, Bulaq, AH 1321-1325.

Shāh Walī Allāh al-Dihlawī, *Ḥujjat Allāh al-bāligha*, Cairo, AH 1352, 1355.

Shahi, Ahmed Al-, and F. C. T. Moore, *Wisdom from the Nile: A Collection of Folk-Stories from Northern and Central Sudan*, tr. with an introd., Oxford, 1978.

al-Shahrastānī, *Livre des religions et des sectes*, tr. avec introd. et notes par Daniel Gimaret et Guy Monnot, [Louvain,] 1986.

———, *al-Milal wa-l-niḥal*, ed. Muḥammad Sayyid Kīlānī, Cairo, 1976.

Shaki, Mansour, 'The Sassanian Matrimonial Relations', *Archiv Orientální*, 39 (1971) 322-45.

Shamy, Hasan M. El-, 'The Brother-Sister Syndrome in Arab Family Life, Socio-Cultural Factors in Arab Psychiatry: A Critical Review', *International Journal of Sociology*, 11 (1981) 313-23.

———, *Folktales of Egypt: Collected, Translated and Annotated with Middle Eastern and African Parallels*, Chicago, 1980.

———, *Folk Traditions of the Arab World: A Guide to Motif Classification*, Bloomington, 1995.

———, 'Siblings in *Alf laylah wa-laylah*', Marvels & Tales, 18:2 (2004) 170-86.

Shaw, Brent D., 'Explaining Incest: Brother-Sister Marriage in Graeco-Roman Egypt', *Man*, 27 (1992) 267-99.

al-Shayzarī, Muslim b. Maḥmūd, *Jamharat al-Islām*, facs. ed. Fuat Sezgin, Frankfurt am Main, 1986.

Shepher, Joseph, *Incest: A Biosocial View*, New York, 1983.

Shihāb al-Dīn Muḥammad b. Ismāʿīl, *Safīnat al-mulk*, Cairo, AH 1309.

al-Shimshāṭī, *al-Anwār wa-maḥāsin al-ashʿār*, ed. al-Sayyid Muḥammad Yūsuf and ʿAbd al-Sattār Aḥmad Farrāj, al-Kuwayt, 1977-1978.

al-Shirbīnī, Muḥammad, *Mughnī l-muḥtāj ilā maʿrifat maʿānī alfāẓ al-Minhāj [li-l-Nawawī]*, Cairo, AH 1308.

al-Shirbīnī, Yūsuf b. Muḥammad, *Hazz al-quḥūf fī sharḥ qaṣīd Abī Shādūf*, Cairo, AH 1308.

Sidler, Nikolaus, *Zur Universalität des Inzesttabu. Eine kritische Untersuchung der These und der Einwände*, Stuttgart, 1971.

al-Sijistānī, Abū Sulaymān al-Manṭiqī, *Ṣiwān al-ḥikma*, ed. ʿAbd al-Raḥmān Badawī, Tehran, 1974.

Sīrat ʿAntar, Cairo, AH 1306.

Slotkin, J. S., 'On a possible lack of incest regulations in Old Iran', *American Anthropologist*, 49 (1947) 634-47 [see reply by Ward H. Goodenough, 'Comments on the question of incestuous marriages in Old Iran', 51 (1949) 326-28, and rejoinder by Slotkin, 51 (1949) 531-32].

Smith, R. Payne *et al.*, *Thesaurus syriacus*, Oxford, 1879, 1901.

Smith, W. Robertson, *Kinship and Marriage in Early Arabia*, new ed. by Stanley A. Cook, London, 1903.

Spectorsky, Susan A. (tr.), *Chapters on Marriage and Divorce: Responses of Ibn Ḥanbal and Ibn Rāhwayh*, translated with introduction and notes, Austin, Texas, 1993.

Spooner, Brian, 'Iranian Kinship and Marriage', *Iran: Journal of the British Institute of Persian Studies*, 4 (1966) 51-59.

Spuler, Bertold, *Iran in frühislamischer Zeit. Politik, Kultur, Verwaltung und öffentliches Leben zwischen der arabischen und der seldschukischen Eroberung, 633 bis 1055*, Wiesbaden, 1952.

Stern, Gertrude H., *Marriage in Early Islam*, London, 1939.

Stetkevych, Suzanne Pinckney, *The Mute Immortals Speak: Pre-Islamic Poetry and the Poetics of Ritual*, Ithaca, 1993.

———, *The Poetics of Islamic Legitimacy: Myth, Gender, and Ceremony in the Classical Arabic Ode*, Bloomington, IN, 2002.

———, 'Pre-Islamic Panegyric and the Poetics of Redemption: *Mufaḍḍalīyah 119* of ʿAlqamah and *Bānat Suʿād* of Kaʿb ibn Zuhayr', in Suzanne Pinckney Stetkevych (ed.), *Reorientations / Arabic and Persian Poetry*, Bloomington, 1994, pp. 1-57.

———, 'The rithāʾ of Taʾabbaṭa Sharran: A study of blood-vengeance in early Arabic poetry', *Journal of Semitic Studies*, 31 (1986) 27-45.

———, 'The Ṣuʿlūk and his Poem: A paradigm of passage manqué', *Journal of the American Oriental Society*, 104 (1984), 661-78.

Stillman, Norman A., 'The Story of Cain and Abel in the Qur'an and the Muslim Commentators: Some Observations', *Journal of Semitic Studies*, 19 (1974) 231-39.

Strabo, *The Geography*, ed. with an English tr. by Horace Leonard Jones, London, 1917-1932 (Loeb Classical Library).

Stricker, B. H., *Camephis*, Amsterdam, 1975 (Medelingen der Koninklijke Nederlandse Akademie van Wetenschappen, afdeling Letterkunde, Nieuwe reeks, 38 no. 3).

al-Subkī, Tāj al-Dīn, *Ṭabaqāt al-Shāfiʿiyya*, Cairo, AH 1324.

al-Sukkarī, *Sharḥ ashʿār al-Hudhaliyyīn*, ed. ʿAbd al-Sattār Farrāj and Maḥmūd Muḥammad Shākir, Cairo, [1965].

al-Suyūrī al-Ḥillī, Miqdād b. ʿAbd Allāh, *al-Tanqīḥ al-rāʾiʿ li-Mukhtaṣar al-sharāʾiʿ*, ed. al-Sayyid ʿAbd al-Laṭīf al-Ḥusaynī al-Kūh-kamari, Qum, AH 1404.

al-Suyūṭī, *al-Itqān fī ʿulūm al-Qurʾān*, ed. Muḥammad Abū l-Faḍl Ibrāhīm, Cairo, 1975.

———, *Lubāb al-nuqūl fī asbāb al-nuzūl*, printed in al-Suyūṭī and al-Maḥallī, *Tafsīr* [*q.v.*].

———, *Tārīkh al-khulafāʾ*, ed. Muḥammad Muḥyī l-Dīn ʿAbd al-Ḥamīd, Beirut, 1988.

———, and Jalāl al-Dīn al-Maḥallī, *Tafsīr*, Beirut, 1995.

al-Ṭabarī, ʿAlī b. Rabban, *Firdaws al-ḥikma*, ed. M. Z. Siddiqi, Berlin, 1928.

al-Ṭabarī, Muḥammad b. Jarīr, *The Early ʿAbbāsī Empire, vol. 2: The sons and grandsons of al-Manṣūr, the reigns of al-Mahdī, al-Hādī and Hārūn al-Rashīd*, tr. by John Alden Williams, Cambridge, 1989.

———, *The History of al-Ṭabarī (Taʾrīkh al-rusul waʾl-mulūk): An Annotated Translation* (general editor Ehsan Yar-Shater), New York, 1985-1998.

———, *Tafsīr (Jāmiʿ al-bayān fī taʾwīl al-Qurʾān)*, Beirut, 1999.

———, *Tārīkh al-rusul wa-l-mulūk*, ed. M. J. de Goeje *et al.*, Leiden, 1879-1898.

———, *Tārīkh al-rusul wa-l-mulūk*, ed. Muḥammad Abū l-Faḍl Ibrāhīm, Cairo, 1960-1969.

al-Tahānawī, *Kashshāf iṣṭilāḥāt al-funūn*, ed. W. Nassau Lees *et al.*, Calcutta, 1862.

Taloş, Ion, 'Inzest', in *Enzyklopädie des Märchens*, Berlin, 1977- , vii (1993), col. 229-41.

al-Tanūkhī, al-Muḥassin b. ᶜAlī, *al-Faraj baᶜd al-shidda*, ed. ᶜAbbūd al-Shāljī, Beirut, 1978.

———, *Nishwār al-muḥāḍara*, ed. ᶜAbbūd al-Shāljī, Beirut, 1971-1973.

al-Tarmānīnī, ᶜAbd al-Salām, *al-Zawāj ᶜinda l-ᶜArab fī l-jāhiliyya wa-l-Islām: Dirāsa muqārina*, Kuwait, 1984.

Tauer, Felix, *Neue Erzählungen aus den Tausendundein Nächten*, Frankfurt am Main, 1995.

al-Tawḥīdī, Abū Ḥayyān, *al-Baṣāʾir wa-l-dhakhāʾir*, ed. Wadād al-Qāḍī, Beirut, 1988.

———, *al-Imtāᶜ wa-l-muʾānasa*, ed. Aḥmad Amīn and Aḥmad al-Zayn, Cairo, 1939-1953.

al-Thaᶜālibī, *Thimār al-qulūb fī l-muḍāf wa-l-mansūb*, ed. Muḥammad Abū l-Faḍl Ibrāhīm, Cairo, 1985.

———, *Yatīmat al-dahr*, ed. Muḥammad Muḥyī l-Dīn ᶜAbd al-Ḥamīd, Cairo, 1947.

al-Thaᶜālibī al-Marghanī, *Ghurar akhbār mulūk al-Furs*, ed. H. Zotenberg, Paris, 1900.

al-Thaᶜlabī, Abū Isḥāq Aḥmad b. Muḥammad, *ᶜArāʾis al-majālis fī qiṣaṣ al-anbiyāʾ or 'Lives of the Prophets'*, tr. and annotated by William M. Brinner, Leiden, 2002.

———, *Qiṣaṣ al-anbiyāʾ, al-musammā ᶜArūs al-majālis*, Cairo, n.d.

al-Tīfāshī, Shihāb al-Dīn Aḥmad, *Nuzhat al-albāb fīmā lā yūjad fī kitāb*, ed. Jamāl Jumᶜa, London, 1992.

———, *Rujūᶜ al-shaykh ilā ṣibāh* see Ibn Kamāl Bāshā.

al-Tijānī, *Tuḥfat al-ᶜarūs wa-mutᶜat al-nufūs*, ed. Jalīl al-ᶜAṭiyya, London, 1992.

Tillion, Germaine, *The Republic of Cousins: Women's Oppression in Mediterranean Society*, tr. by Quinin Hoare, London, 1983 [original title *Le harem et les cousins*, Paris, 1966].

Traini, R., 'La métamorphose des êtres humains en brutes d'après quelques textes arabes', in F. de Jong (ed.), *Miscellanea arabica et islamica: Dissertationes in Academia Ultratrajectina prolatae anno MCMXC*, Leuven, 1993, pp. 90-134.

al-Tujībī, Abū Ṭāhir Ismāʿil b. Aḥmad, *al-Mukhtār min shiʿr Bashshār: ikhtiyār al-Khālidiyyayn*, ed. Muḥammad Badr al-Dīn al-ʿAlawī, Cairo, 1934 [date of preface].

ʿUmar b. Abī Rabīʿa, *Dīwān*, ed. Paul Schwarz, Leipzig, 1901, 1909.

al-Ushnāndānī, Abū ʿUthmān Saʿīd b. Hārūn, *Maʿānī l-shiʿr*, ed. Ṣalāḥ al-Dīn al-Munajjid, Beirut, 1964.

Vallat, Françoise, 'Susa and Susians in Second-Millennium Iran', in Jack N. Sasson (ed.)[*q.v.*], *Civilizations of the Ancient Near East*, (ii,) 1023-33.

van der Post, Irma, 'Incest and inteelt in de Arabische wereld', undergraduate dissertation, University of Groningen, 1988.

van Ess, Josef, *Theologie und Gesellschaft im 2. und 3. Jahrhundert Hidschra. Eine Geschichte des religiösen Denkens im frühen Islam*, Berlin, 1991-1997.

van Gelder, Geert Jan, 'Beautifying the Ugly and Uglifying the Beautiful: The Paradox in Classical Arabic Literature', *Journal of Semitic Studies*, 48:2 (2003) 321-51.

———, '*Mawālī* and Arabic Poetry: Some Observations', *to appear*.

———, *Of Dishes and Discourse: Classical Arabic Literary Representations of Food*, Richmond, Surrey, 2000 (published in the USA as *God's Banquet: Food in Classical Arabic Literature*, New York, 2000).

Vrolijk, Arnoud (ed.), *De taal der engelen: 1250 jaar klassiek Arabisch proza*, Amsterdam, 2002.

Waardenburg, Jacques (ed.), *Muslim Perceptions of Other Religions: A Historical Survey*, New York & Oxford, 1999.

Wagner, Ewald, *Abū Nuwās. Eine Studie zur arabischen Literatur der frühen ʿAbbāsidenzeit*, Wiesbaden, 1965.

al-Wansharīshī, Abū l-ʿAbbās Aḥmad b. Yaḥyā, *al-Miʿyār al-muʾnis wa-l-jāmiʿ al-mughrib ʿan fatāwī ahl Ifrīqiya wa-l-Andalus wa-l-Maghrib*, ed. Muḥammad Ḥājjī, Rabat, 1981-1983.

Watt, William Montgomery, *The Formative Period of Islamic Thought*, Edinburgh, 1973.

———, *Muhammad at Medina*, Oxford, 1956.

Wehr, Hans, *A Dictionary of Modern Written Arabic (Arabic-English)*, ed. J. Milton Cowan, 4th ed., Wiesbaden, 1979.

Weisweiler, Max, *Arabesken der Liebe. Früharabische Geschichten von Liebe und Frauen*, Leiden, 1954.

Weisser, Ursula, *Zeugung, Vererbung und pränatale Entwicklung in der Medizin des arabisch-islamischen Mittelalters*, Erlangen, 1983.

Wensinck, A. J, *et al.*, *Concordance et indices de la Tradition Musulmane*, Leiden, 1936-1988.

West, E. W., (tr.), *Pahlavi Texts*, repr. Delhi, 1965 (1st ed. 1882) (Sacred Books of the East, vols. 5, 18, 24, 37, 47).

Westenholz, Joan Goodnick, 'Love Lyrics from the Ancient Near East', in Jack M. Sasson (ed.) [*q.v.*], *Civilizations of the Ancient Near East*, (iv,) 2471-84.

Westermarck, Edward A., *The History of Human Marriage*, 2nd ed., London, 1894 (1st ed. 1891).

Weststeijn, Johan, 'Abū Saᶜd al-Wāᶜiẓ al-Ḫarkūšī's *al-bišāra wa-n-niḏāra fī taᶜbīr ar-ruᵓyā*, een elfde-eeuws droomboek', unpublished MA thesis, Amsterdam, 1999.

Wilken, George Alexander, *Das Matriarchat (das Mutterrecht) bei den alten Arabern*, Leipzig, 1884.

Wilkinson, J. C., 'Bayāsirah and Bayādīr', *Arabian Studies*, 1 (1974) 74-85.

Wilson, Edward O., *Consilience: The Unity of Knowledge*, London, 1998.

———, *Sociobiology: The Abridged Edition*, Cambridge, Mass., 1980.

Wiseman, Susan J., '*'Tis Pity She's a Whore*: Presenting the Incestuous Body', in Lucy Gent and Nigel Llewellyn (eds), *Renaissance Bodies: The Human Figure in English Culture* c. *1540-1660*, London, 1990, pp. 180-97, 271-72.

Wolf, Arthur P., *Sexual Attraction and Childhood Association: A Chinese Brief for Edward Westermarck*, Stanford, CA, 1995.

Wright, J. W., 'Masculine Allusion and the Structure of Satire in Early ᶜAbbasid Poetry', in J. W. Wright and Everett Rowson (eds), *Homoeroticism in Classical Arabic Literature*, New York, 1997, pp. 1-23.

Xenophon, *Memorabilia, Oeconomicus, Symposion and Apology*, London, 1979 (The Loeb Classical Library).

al-Yaᶜqūbī, *Tārīkh*, Beirut: Dār Bayrūt, n.d.

Yāqūt, *Muᶜjam al-buldān*, ed. Ferdinand Wüstenfeld, Leipzig, 1866-1870.

———, *Muʿjam al-udabāʾ [Irshād al-arīb]*, ed. Aḥmad Farīd Rifāʿī, Cairo, 1936-1938.

Yarshater, Ehsan (ed.), *Cambridge History of Iran, 3: The Seleucid, Parthian and Sasanian Periods*, Cambridge, 1983.

Zakeri, Mohsen, 'Arabic Reports on the Fall of Hatra to the Sasanids: History or Legend?', in Stefan Leder (ed.), *Story-Telling in the Framework of Non-Fictional Arabic Literature*, Wiesbaden, 1998, pp. 158-67.

al-Zamakhsharī, *Asās al-balāgha*, Beirut, 1979.

———, *al-Mustaqṣā fī amthāl al-ʿArab*, ed. Muḥammad ʿAbd al-Muʿīd Khān, Hyderabad, 1962.

———, *Rabīʿ al-abrār*, ed. Salīm al-Nuʿaymī, Baghdad, 1976-1982.

———, *Tafsīr al-Kashshāf ʿan ḥaqāʾiq al-tanzīl*, ed. Muḥammad Mursī ʿĀmir, Cairo, 1977.

al-Zarkashī, Badr al-Dīn, *al-Burhān fī ʿulūm al-Qurʾān*, ed. Muḥammad Abū l-Faḍl Ibrāhīm, Cairo, 1972 [date of preface].

Index

ʿAbbād b. Tamīm b. Thaʿlaba 161
ʿAbd al-ʿĀṣ b. Thaʿlaba 190 n.38
ʿAbd al-Karīm al-Nahshalī 27
ʿAbd al-Malik b. Marwān 108
ʿAbd Manāf 33
ʿAbd al-Qays b. Khufāf al-Tamīmī 130
ʿAbd al-Raḥmān b. ʿAwf 80
ʿAbd al-Ṣamad b. al-Muʿadhdhal 69
ʿAbd al-ʿUzzā 81
Abel *see* Hābīl
al-Ābī 23
ʿAbīd b. al-Abraṣ 13, 130
Abimelech 65
ʿAbla 93, 171
Abraham/Ibrāhīm 60, 64-5, 80, 125, 127
ʿAbs 32
Absalom 86
Abū l-ʿAlāʾ al-Maʿarrī 45, 53, 76, 137
Abū ʿAlī b. Fatḥ 154, 158
Abū l-ʿAtāhiya 69
Abū Bakr 81
Abū l-Dhayyāl Shuways 16
Abū Dulaf Misʿar b. Muhalhil 21
Abū l-Fidāʾ 79
Abū Ḥāmid al-Marwarrūdhī 40, 43, 46-9, 59, 112
Abū Ḥanīfa 88, 90-91, 105-6, 108-9
Abū l-Ḥasan al-Anṣārī 14, 40, 42, 46, 48-50, 200-1 n.51
Abū Ḥayyān al-Gharnāṭī 90, 120
Abu-Lughod, Lila 154
Abū Muslim 51
Abū Nuwās 77, 132, 138, 184
Abū Qays b. al-Aslat 84
Abū Qurra, Theodore 38, 124
Abū Sūd 53
Abū Tammām 16, 18, 69
Abū Thawr 109-10
Abū ʿUbayda 32, 53, 85
Abū l-ʿUdhāfir Ward b. Saʿd 129
Abū Uḥayḥa Saʿīd b. al-ʿĀṣ 79
Abū Yūsuf 47-8, 105, 109
Abū Yūsuf al-Jabarī 138
Abū Zayd al-Hilālī 171
Achaemenids 38
Achmet ibn Sereim 172
ʿĀd 144
Adam/Ādam 90, 121-4, 160, 171
Ādharbayjān 45, 49
Ādhurfarnbag Farrukhzādān 205 n.144
adoption 87, 97, 119
adultery *see zinā*
Aesop 144
Aḥiqar 144
Ahithophel 86
ahl al-kitāb 'people of Scripture' 55, 72, 109; *see also* Christians, Jews
Aḥmad b. Ḥanbal *see* Ibn Ḥanbal
Ahuramazda 124
ʿĀʾisha 19-20, 115
al-ʿAjārida 75
al-Akhṭal 130-1
Albanus 102, 154
Alcibiades 38
Alexander the Great 170
ʿAlī b. Abī Ṭālib 55, 81, 102, 117
ʿAlī b. Hishām 26, 128
ʿAlqama 32
Amestris 37
al-ʿĀmilī, Bahāʾ al-Dīn 12
Āmina bt Abān b. Kulayb 79
Āmina bt ʿĀmir 79
Ammonites 64, 125
Amnon 80
ʿAmr b. ʿĀʾidh 81
ʿAmr b. Hind 130
ʿAmr b. Kulthūm 27, 36
ʿAmr b. Nufayl 79
animals 16, 41, 46, 48, 62, 95-6 116; *see also* camels, donkeys, horses, pigeons
ʿAntar 93-4, 126, 160, 169, 171
ʿAntara b. Shaddād 94, 166
Anūsharwān 45, 73-4
Apollonius of Tyre 138, 170
ʿĀqiṣa 170
Aqlīmā/Qalīmā 122-3
al-Aqraʿ b. Ḥābis 53
Arberry, A. J. 82, 96, 100, 119
Archibald, Elizabeth 153, 166, 182
Ardashīr b. Bābak 36, 73
ʿArīb 88-9

Aristotle 11, 47, 174, 183
cArjal 132
Arsacids 38, 184
Artaxerxes, son of Papak 36
Artemidorus 172, 176, 179-80
cArūs al-cArā᾽is 159-60
Asad 15, 43
Ashcab 49
al-Ashcarī 75
Ashūt 123
al-Aslat 79, 84
al-Aṣmacī 14-15, 30, 43, 187 n.10, 192 n.68
al-Aswad b. Khalaf 84
Athenaeus 38
Atossa 37
Auge 58
Avesta 36, 51
cAwāna 61
cAwf b. cAbd cAwf 80
Aws b. Ḥajar 31, 66, 79, 139
Aws b. Ḥāritha b. La᾽m 115
Aws b. Maghrā᾽ 130
Aws b. al-Ṣāmit 119
al-Awzācī 47-8
Azd 31
cAzīz b. Khālid/Khālih 171
Azraq 169
Badīc al-Zamān al-Hamadhānī 14
Baghdad 39, 112, 129, 138, 146-7, 154, 159, 164
al-Baghdādī, cAbd al-Qādir 33
al-Baghdādī, cAbd al-Qāhir 75-6
Bahā᾽ al-Dīn b. Shaddād 105
Bāhila 131-2
al-Bahīmiyya 21
Bahman b. Isfandiyādh 56-7, 169
al-Bacīth 131
Bakhtiar, Laleh 112
Balkh 73
Bandello, Matteo 154
al-Barā᾽ 104-5
Bardādas (?) 45
Bashshār b. Burd 67, 132-3, 135
Basra 129-30
al-Bāṭiniyya 76
Baybars 169-70
baysarī 33
bed-tricks 153
Beeston, A. F. L. 193 n.80
Bell, Richard 84
Benkheira, Mohammed Hocine 94-5
Bible *see* Hebrew Bible
Bih-Āfrīd b. Farwardīn 51, 58
Bilāl b. Jarīr 18
Bilha 65
Bint Abī Ṭalḥa b. cAbd al-cUzzā 84
al-Bīrūnī 51
Boswell, John 102
Bouhdiba, Abdelwahab 77-8, 93
Bousquet, G.-H. 107
al-Bukhārī 19-20, 84, 96
Bukht-naṣṣar 45, 55, 127, 204 n.204
al-Burj b. Mus'hir 53-4
Burton, Richard Francis 161, 163
Burton, Robert 10
Burton, Lady Isabel 163
Byron, Lord 164, 199 n. 26, 221 n.5
Byzantines 39, 54, 164
Cain *see* Qābīl
Cambyses 37
camels 11, 14, 29-33, 47, 139
Canaan *see* Kancān
Canova, Giovanni 171
Carmathians 45, 76
Catullus 38, 135
Chebel, Malek 3
Chelhod, J. 93
Chigil Turks 44
Chinese 20-1, 39, 78
Chosroes *see* Kisrā
Christianity, Christians 10, 25, 38, 41, 45, 54-5, 61, 63, 72, 78, 93, 100, 102-3, 109-10, 115, 122, 143, 153, 167, 169-70, 181, 183
Conte, Éduard 87, 90, 99
Cook, Michael 83
Copts 63-4, 167, 169
cousin marriage 2-3, 6, 8-9, 13, 18, 23, 25, 27-8, 32, 38, 43-5, 51, 77, 81, 87, 93
Ḍabba 130
Daghfal b. Ḥanẓala 59
Dāḥis 32

Damascus 130
al-Damīrī 47
Dārā/Darius 56-7
Ḍārāb 58
al-Dārī, al-Ḥusayn 233 n.243
Darwinism 7-8
David/Dāwūd 31, 41, 65
Davis, Dick 170
Ḍaw᾿ al-Makān 164-5
ḍawā 'stuntedness' 11-17, 21-2, 29, 34, 42-3, 48, 62, 70-1, 117
Dawkins, Richard 188 n.12
Dawood, N. J. 163
Dāwūd b. Salm 194 n.116
Dāwūd al-Iṣfahānī 90
ḍayzan 'he who marries his deceased father's wife' 79-80
al-Ḍayzan 80
al-Dhahabī 103-4
Dharīḥ b. Sunna 28
dhimma 'protection given to religious minority' 72, 109
Dhū Nuwās 55
Dhū l-Rumma 70, 132
Dhubyān 32
al-Dīnawarī, Abū Ḥanīfa 56
Dīnāzād 204 n.126
Doniger, Wendy 153
donkeys 33
dreams 172-80
drunkenness 4, 50, 53-5, 64, 131, 145
Dukhtanūs bt Laqīṭ 53
Durham, William H. 113
Durkheim, Émile 10
Egyptians, Ancient 7-8, 166, 182-3
Elamites 183
endogamy 44
Enki 38, 182
Eve *see* Ḥawwā᾿
exogamy 21; *see also gharā᾿ib, nazā᾿iᶜ*, out-marrying
Faḍl 69
al-Faḍl b. ᶜAbd al-Raḥmān 99
al-Fārābī 82, 174
al-Farazdaq 62, 67, 130-1, 135
al-Fāriᶜa bt Ṭarīf 128
al-Farrā᾿ 99
Fāṭima bt Muḥammad 114, 117, 140, 142
Fāṭima bt Yaᶜqūb b. al-Faḍl 74, 104
fatwa (*fatwā* pl. *fatāwī, fatāwā*) 'formal legal opinion' 83, 95, 101, 104-5, 136, 141, 185
fellaheen 134
Firdawsī 58
Fīrūz Shāh 58
Fitnat al-Masīḥ 170
Flaubert, Gustave 127
fornication *see zinā*
foundling 102-3
Fox, Robin 87
Freud, Sigmund 8, 10, 24, 128, 143, 168, 172, 178
Fukayha bt Qatāda 66,79
Galen 34
Gayōmart *see* Jayūmart
Gerhardt, Mia I. 162
al-Ghabrā᾿ 32
Ghanī 15
gharā᾿ib sg. *gharība* 'strange women' 11, 28, 43, 117
Ghaythā 125
al-Ghazālī 22, 115, 117
Giladi, Avner 94-5
Gondeshapur 34
Graeco-Islamic medicine 34-5
Greeks 4, 8, 11, 25, 36, 47, 80, 167, 182-3
Gregorius 102, 153
Guo, Li 134
Gurgānī, Fakhr al-Dīn 170, 184-5
Hābīl/Abel 121-3, 126, 160
ḥadd pl. *ḥudūd* 'prescribed punishment' 83, 106-9; *see also* incest, punishment of,
al-Hādī, Mūsā 74, 133
Hadith 'Tradition; the sayings and doings of the Prophet Muḥammad' 19, 93, 103
al-Ḥaḍr/Hatra 80, 170
Ḥājib b. Zurāra 52-6, 66
al-Ḥajjāj 106
Ḥammād ᶜAjrad 132
Ḥammād the Bedouin 161

Hammond, Marlé 128
Hámori, András 146
Ḥamza 169
Ḥamza b. ᶜUmāra al-Barbarī 44
Ḥamza al-Iṣfahānī 138-9
Ḥanafites 83, 86, 90, 97-8, 100, 105, 108-9
Ḥanbalites 83, 92-3, 105, 107
al-Ḥarīrī 140
al-Ḥārith b. Kalada 34-35
Ḥarrān/Carrhae 68, 72, 78, 200 n.44
al-Harrāsī, al-Kiyā 115
Hārūn/Aaron 66
Hārūt and Mārūt 55
al-Ḥasan b. ᶜAlī 81
al-Ḥasan b. al-Ḥasan b. ᶜAlī 19
al-Ḥasan al-Baṣrī 109, 111
Ḥātim al-Ṭāʾī 12
Hatra *see* al-Ḥaḍr
hawā 'passionate love' 25, 146, 161
Ḥawwāʾ/Eve 122, 124-5, 160
al-Hayfāʾ 168
Ḥāzim al-Qarṭājannī 71
Hebrew Bible 64-66, 90, 98, 103, 122-3, 125, 127, 145, 163
Héritier-Augé, Françoise 81, 88, 94, 99
Herod 126-7
Herodias 127
Herrenschmidt, Clarisse 185
Hilāl, Banū 160, 168, 171
Hilāl b. Umayya 92
Ḥimyar
Hind bt al-Mughīra 79
Hinnām b. Salama 79
homosexuality 25-6, 83, 107-8, 110, 115, 132, 176, 179, 182, 217 n.165
Hormuzd 124
horses 11, 14-15, 17, 31-3, 47-8, 62
ḥubb 'love' 25, 146, 161
Hudhayl 33
Ḥumāna/Ḥumāya/Humāy 57-8, 169
Ḥunayn b. Isḥāq 36
al-Ḥusayn b. ᶜAlī 19
al-Ḥuṣayn b. al-Ḥumām 53-4
Ḥusn bt ᶜAnīd 169
Ḥuyayy b. Hazzāl 130
Iblīs, the Devil 73, 134
Ibn ᶜAbbās 84
Ibn ᶜAbd Rabbih 47
Ibn Abī l-Ḥadīd 40
Ibn Aḥmar 4
Ibn ᶜAjarrad 75
Ibn Alghaz 130
Ibn al-ᶜAllāf 138
Ibn al-ᶜArabī, Abū Bakr 86
Ibn al-Athīr, Ḍiyāʾ al-Dīn 140
Ibn Bābawayh al-Ṣadūq 101, 121
Ibn al-Balkhī 58
Ibn Dāniyāl 134
Ibn Diḥya 39
Ibn Durayd 71
Ibn Ḥabīb 54, 79, 81, 84, 88, 145
Ibn Ḥajar 20
Ibn Ḥanbal, Aḥmad 86, 91, 101, 105, 108, 110-11
Ibn Ḥazm 24-5, 64-6, 89, 108-10, 125
Ibn Ḥuṣn 31
Ibn al-Jawzī 23, 25, 73, 99, 121, 146, 152, 154
Ibn al-Kalbī *see* al-Kalbī
Ibn Kammūna 112
Ibn Khallikān 44
Ibn Manẓūr 16, 22, 118
Ibn al-Mujāwir 21
Ibn al-Muqaffaᶜ 39
Ibn al-Muᶜtazz 207 n.174
Ibn al-Nadīm 78, 124-5
Ibn al-Naghrālī/Ibn Nagrila 65
Ibn Qayyim al-Jawziyya 65, 93, 103, 106, 108, 110-12
Ibn Qudāma 92, 105-7, 117
Ibn Qutayba 17, 40, 52-3, 60, 79
Ibn Rashīq 31
Ibn Riḍwān, ᶜAlī 36
Ibn al-Rūmī 34, 132, 136-7
Ibn Saᶜdān 39
Ibn Sahl 209 n.227
Ibn al-Ṣayqal 140-1
Ibn Sīrīn 172-4, 176-7
Ibn Taymiyya 104-5, 141
Ibn Thawāba 136
Ibn Ṭūlūn 63, 125
Ibrāhīm *see* Abraham
Ibrāhīm al-Ḥalabī 100, 119

al-Ibshīhī 117
Ikhwān al-Ṣafā᾿ *see* Sincere Brethren
ᶜImrān/Amram 65
ᶜInān 132
inbreeding
  boasting of one's, 15-17, 18, 22
  consequences of, 8, 11-19, 62-3, 117; *see also ḍawā*
  in animals 11, 13-14, 28-32, 139-40
incest
  among the Majūs *see* Zoroastrians
  among the pre-Islamic Arabs 52-5, 59-60, 78-81
  aunt—nephew, 66, 92-3, 108, 133
  double or compound, 38, 152-4
  father—daughter, 51-3, 57-8, 63, 66, 68, 74, 76-7, 90-2, 114, 121, 124-5, 130, 133, 138, 169-70, 179, 182, 232 n.226
  in dreams *see* dreams
  legislation on, 78-121
  metaphorical, 70-1, 136-8
  mother—son, 61-2, 67-8, 73-4, 114, 121, 124-5, 129-35, 148-54, 160, 167, 173, 175-80, 232 n.226
  punishment of, 83, 103-9, 162-3, 168
  rationale of — legislation 112-18
  sibling, 13, 37, 53-5, 73, 76, 92, 104, 121-5, 130-1, 133, 144-5, 150-60, 162-6, 171-2, 177, 184-5
  uncle—niece, 63, 75, 93
  unconscious, 5, 64, 102, 104, 144, 152, 164, 172-4
  universality of — taboo 8-9, 11, 78, 185
  with daughter born out of wedlock 90-2, 105
  with daughter-in-law 65, 97
  with father's concubine 65, 125, 166-8, 213 n.207
  with father's wife 4, 78-80, 84-9, 104-5, 166-8
  with foster-child 96-7
  with foundling *see* foundling
  with grandchild 75, 90, 182
  with grandparent 90, 213 n.66
  with great-nephew/great-niece 75, 93
  with half-sibling 65, 80, 92, 163-4
  with milk-relations *see raḍāᶜ*
  with mother-in-law 96
  with stepdaughter 96-7, 109
  with stepmother 65-6, 78-81, 84-9, 103-5, 107, 109, 167
  with two sisters 78-82, 98-9, 116, 125, 168, 170, 175, 215 n.113
  words for, 4, 187 n.8
India, Indians 27, 33, 39, 42, 50-1, 78
infanticide 42, 49-50, 144, 150
insults 38, 114, 129; *see also* lampoons
ᶜĪsā *see* Jesus
Isaac *see* Isḥāq
al-Iṣfahānī, Abū l-Faraj 53-4, 66
al-Isfarāyīnī, Abū l-Muẓaffar 75
Isḥāq/Isaac 65
Īshōᶜbokht 10-11
ᶜishq 'love-passion' 25, 146
Ismael/Ismāᶜīl 60
Ismāᶜīl b. Yasār 49-50
Ismāᶜīlī Shīᶜites 76
Israelites *see* Jews
al-Iṣṭakhrī, Abū Saᶜīd al-Ḥasan 44
istibḍāᶜ 'seeking a sperm donor' 19-21
istifḥāl 'procuring a stud' 21
istilḥāq 'avowal of paternity' 91
Jacob/Yaᶜqūb 98, 125
Jaᶜfar 131-2
Jaᶜfar b. Rabīᶜa 67
Jaᶜfar b. Yaḥyā l-Barmakī 89
al-jāhiliyya 'ignorance'; the pre-Islamic period' 11, 46, 52-5, 59-60, 78-81, 143-5
al-Jāḥiẓ 12-13, 15-16, 25, 27, 33, 40, 60, 62-3, 73, 96, 113, 144-5
Jamīl 194 n.116
Japheth 121-2
Jarīr 17-18, 66-7, 130-1
al-Jarīrī 144
Jaydā᾿ bt Khālid 79
al-Jayhānī 39, 50
Jayūmart/Gayōmart 124
al-Jazīrī, ᶜAbd al-Raḥmān 111
Jesus/ᶜĪsā 41, 46, 122, 127
Jews, Judaism 24, 41, 55, 57, 62-6, 72, 100, 103-4, 109-10, 121

Jihrazād *see* Shahrazād
jinn, demons 33, 121, 169
John the Baptist 41, 127
jokes, jesting 60-1, 86, 99, 134-5
Joshua/Yūsha[c] 65
Judah *see* Yahūdhā
Judaism *see* Jews
Judas 153
Justinian 8
Juwān 169
Ka[c]b al-Ashqarī 67, 129
Ka[c]b b. Zuhayr 29-32, 139
Kabul 21
Kahlān 21
Kalb 61
al-Kalbī, Hishām 31, 66
al-Kalbī, Muḥammad b. al-Sā[ɔ]ib 54, 59, 78-9
Kān Mā Kān 164
Kan[c]ān/Canaan 126
Kappler, Claude-Claire 185
al-Karābīsī 75
al-Karkhī 89
al-Kāsānī 90, 105-6, 114
Kawkab al-Ṣabāḥ 169
Khadīja 140
Khālid b. Naḍla 191 n.55
al-Khālidiyyān 17, 28
al-Khalīl b. Aḥmad 21
al-Khansā[ɔ] 128-9
Khārijites 75-6
al-Kharkūshī (Khargūshī), 233 n.243
Kharlukh Turks 21
Khawla bt Manẓūr 19
Khawla bt Tha[c]laba 119
al-Khayzurān 133
khētokdas see *khvaētvadatha*
khilāsī 'hybrid' 33
al-Khulayq 133
Khumānā/Khumānī 57
Khurāsān 75
Khurramites 58-9
Khuṭlukh Turks 44
khvaētvadatha/khwēdōdah (etc.) 'close-kin marriage' 36, 51, 63, 185
al-Khwārazmī, Abū [c]Abd Allāh 51
Kināna 18
al-Kisā[ɔ]ī 126
Kisrā (Chosroes) 52-3, 57, 67
Kubaysha bt Ma[c]n 79, 85
Kufa 44, 130
Kurds 25
Kuthayyir 194 n.116
laban al-faḥl 'stallion's milk' 95
Labūdā/Labūdhā 122
lampoons 38, 50, 66-8, 129-36
Lane, Edward W. 163
Laqīṭ b. Zurāra 53
Laylā 26
Leah/Liyā 98
Lebanon 27
Linant de Bellefonds 112
Lot 5, 51, 64-5, 125, 144-5, 171
love 24-7, 146
  between siblings 26, 128-9, 157-9, 161-6, 180
  between parent and child 24-5
  [c]Udhrite *see* [c]Udhrite love
  see also hawā, ḥubb, [c]ishq
Lubnā 28
Luqaym 144-5
Luqmān 20, 144-5, 171
Luther, Martin 154
Lyons, Malcolm C. 58, 169
al-Madā[ɔ]inī 80
Magians *see* Zoroastrians
al-Mahdī 67, 74, 132
Mahfouz, Naguib (Najīb Maḥfūẓ) 215 n.102
maḥram pl. *maḥārim* 'unmarriageable relation' 4-5, 12, 92, 107, 120, 174, 177
Majnūn Laylā 26
Majūs *see* Zoroastrians
Mālik b. Anas 92, 109, 111
Mālikites 83, 92, 101, 108
al-Ma[ɔ]mūn 61
al-Manbijī 105, 107
Manichaeans 58, 64, 74, 76, 124, 134
Manṣūr al-Ṣanādīqī 76
Manẓūr b. Zabbān 19, 79, 84
al-Maqdisī, al-Muṭahhar 58, 98
Mar[c]ash, malik al-Jinn 169
Marcionites 58

Marguerite de Navarre 154
Marvell, Andrew 163
Mary 143, 205 n.107
Marzubān b. Rustam 51
Mashyāna 124
al-Mas^c^ūdī 20-1, 56-7, 63-4, 73, 122, 125, 167
matrilineal tendencies 20, 78, 80-1, 94
al-Māwardī 18, 27, 105
Mawbad *see* Mōbad
Māwiyya (Mayya) 13
al-Maydānī 23, 145
al-Maymūniyya 75
Mazdak 73-4
Mecca, Meccans 21, 60, 80, 177
medical treatises 34-5
Medina 44, 77, 177
milk-relationship *see raḍā^c^*
Minorsky, V. 184
Mīshā/Mīshānā/Mīshī 124
Misma^c^ b. Shihāb 15
misogynism 152, 167, 170
Moabites 64, 125
Mōbad 61, 184-5
Moore, F. C. T. 172
Moses/Mūsā 41, 46, 66, 125
Mu^c^āwiya b. Abī Sufyān 61, 86
Mu^c^āwiya b. ^c^Amr 128
Mūbadh *see* Mōbad
Muḍar 21
Mughulṭāy b. Qilij 154
al-Muhallab b. al-Fatḥ 154
Muḥammad, the Prophet 10-11, 13, 19, 28-9, 34, 36, 40-1, 46, 72, 76-7, 81, 84-5, 90-2, 95, 97, 104-7, 110-11, 114-5, 117, 142
Muḥammad b. Mālik 77
Muḥammad b. Safar 70
muḥarram 'sacred, forbidden' 5, 82, 177
Muhawi, Ibrahim 171
Muḥṣin b. Abī Qays 79, 84-5
Mujāshi^c^ 67
al-Mukhtār b. Wahb 26, 194 n.116
Mulayka bt Sinān (*or* bt Khārija) 19, 79, 84
al-Muqaddasī 44-5
muqarqam 'puny, scrawny' 15-16
al-Muqtadir 44
Murra b. Sa^c^d b. Quray^c^ al-Sa^c^dī 130
muṣāhara see *ṣihr*
Muslim b. al-Walīd 16, 70
al-Mutalammis 130
al-Mutanabbī 69
al-Mutawakkil 69
al-Muṭawwaq ^c^Alī b. Fatḥ 154
Mutayyam 26, 128
Mu^c^tazilites 48, 75
Myrrha 5, 170
al-Nābigha al-Dhubyānī 130
al-Nābulusī, ^c^Abd al-Ghanī 171, 175, 178-80
al-Naḍīra 80
al-Nafzāwī 177, 182
Nāḥiya bt al-Aswad b. al-Muṭṭalib 84
Nahshal 131-2
najīb 'of noble breed; superior' 17, 20, 115
al-Namir b. Tawlab 144-5
Namrūd/Nimrod 125-6, 143, 169
nasab pl. *ansāb* 'consanguinity; pedigree, genealogy, lineage' 4, 12, 29, 31, 33, 36, 89, 94, 99-100
al-Naṣībī, Ibrāhīm b. ^c^Alī 147, 154
al-Nawbakhtī 44
*nazā'i^c^* sg. *nazī^c^a* 'women taken from outside one's group' 12, 18, 28
Nebuchadnezzar *see* Bukht-naṣṣar
Negroes 25, 39; *see also* Zanj
nikāḥ 'marriage; sexual intercourse' 19, 89-90, 114, 180
nikāḥ al-maqt 'hateful marriage (marrying one's father's wife)' 85, 88
Nimrod *see* Namrūd
Ninkhursag 182
Nufayl b. ^c^Abd al-^c^Uzzā 79
al-Nu^c^mān b. Bashīr 4
al-Nu^c^mān b. al-Mundhir 53, 130
al-Nuwayrī 152
Nuzhat al-Zamān 164-6
Oedipus 24, 88, 126, 128, 143, 183
Oman 77, 204 n.97, 209 n.225
out-marrying 11-21, 24, 27-8, 50-1, 77; *see also* exogamy

Ouyang, Wen-chin 166
Ovid 5, 170
Pahlavi texts 10, 36-7, 124, 185
Paul, St 129
Persians 7, 25, 36-77, 87, 116; *see also* Arsacid, Sasanids, Zoroastrians
Phaedra 166
pigeons 13, 33, 62
Plutarch 37
polygyny 98-9, 163, 167-8, 183
Potiphar 166
Ptolemy 36
punishment *see* incest, punishment of,
puzzles, genealogical, 29, 138-42
Qābīl/Cain 121-6, 160
Qabṭāwīl 169
Qadarites 75
al-Qāḍī Nuᶜmān 109
al-Qaffāl al-Shāshī 108
Qalīmā *see* Aqlīmā
qarāba '(close) relationship' 13, 22, 115, 117
qarāᵓib sg. *qarība* '(closely) related women' 11, 43
Qarluq Turks 21, 39
Qarmaṭians *see* Carmathians
Qays b. ᶜĀṣim 50, 52-5
Qays b. Dharīḥ 28
Qays b. Thaᶜlaba 66, 79
Qubādh 73-4
Quḍiya fa-Kān 164-5
Qur'an *passim*
  on infant burial 49-50
  on marriage impediments 3, 5, 11, 78, 81-100
  on revealing one's adornment 119-20
  on *ẓihār* 118-19
Qurayba 33
Quraysh 13
Quṣayy 81
Qusayy (Thaqīf b. Munabbih) 79
al-Qushayrī 112, 115
Rabīᶜa 21
Rachel/Rāḥīl 98
raḍāᶜ, *raḍāᶜa*, *riḍāᶜ* 'suckling; milk-relationship' 78, 83, 89, 93-6, 171, 174, 180, 184-5
al-Rāghib al-Iṣbahānī 28, 112
rahaq 'outrageousness; incest(?)' 4, 55
raḥim pl. *arḥām* 'womb; kinship' 19, 36, 98, 114, 176
Rank, Otto 1, 126, 135, 138, 153, 160, 166, 182
rape 53-5, 83, 106, 153, 160, 169-70, 185
Rayṭa bt Abī l-ᶜAbbās 74
Raythā 125
al-Rāzī, Abū Bakr 34
al-Rāzī, Fakhr al-Dīn 72, 82, 85, 88-92, 95, 97, 114-5
Raᶜziyā 125
Reuben 65
riḍāᶜ see *raḍāᶜ*
riddles 70-1, 138
Romans 1, 8, 36, 182
Ruᵓba b. al-ᶜAjjāj 12
al-Ṣābiᵓ, Hilāl 68
al-Ṣābiᵓ, al-Muḥassin b. Ibrāhīm 68
Sabians, Ṣābiᵓa 41, 68, 72, 78, 109
Ṣaddām Ḥusayn 3
Ṣafiyya bt al-Mughīra 79
Ṣafwān b. Umayya b. Khalaf 84
al-Ṣāḥib b. ᶜAbbād 50, 129
al-Sāᵓib 12
Ṣāᶜid b. Aḥmad 56
Saᶜīd b. al-Musayyab 174
Sāᶜida b. Juᵓayya 33
Ṣakhr b. ᶜAmr 128-9
Ṣakhra bt ᶜAbd b. ᶜImrān 81
Ṣāliḥ b. Maḥmūd 86
Salkhāᵓ/Sulkhāᵓ/Shalkhāᵓ 126
Salm al-Khāsir 66
Salome 127
Samuel the Nagid 65
Sanatruk 80,170
Sāqundus *see* Secundus the Silent
Sarah 64-5, 80, 127
al-Sarakhsī 94, 98, 111, 113
al-Sarūjī, Taqī al-dīn 226 n.99
Sāsān 57
Sasanids 34, 36-8, 45, 52-3, 57, 73
Satan 73, 124
Sāṭirīn 170
Sāṭirūn 80, 170

Sayf b. Dhī Yazan 169-70
Secundus the Silent 167
Serjeant, R. B. 19
Seth *see* Shīth
al-Shāfiʿī 88, 91, 98, 105, 109-11, 114, 141
Shāfiʿites 83, 86, 91-2, 97, 105, 108, 115, 117
Shahi, Ahmed Al- 172
al-Shahrastānī 51
Shahrazād, Jihrāzād 3, 57, 204 n.126
Shakespeare, William 170
Shalkhāʾ *see* Salkhāʾ
shame 22-3, 49, 58, 114-15, 134-6, 185
Shamy, Hasan El- 128, 167-8, 171
Sharīk b. Saḥmāʾ 92
Shar(r)kān 161, 164-5
Sharwīn 169
Shaybān 18
al-Shaybānī, Muḥammad 105, 109
Shelley, Percy Bysshe 129, 164, 184
al-Shifāʾ 80
shighār 'exchanging brides without payment of bridal money' 15, 191 n.56
Shīḥa 169
Shīʿites 44, 76, 104, 109, 121, 124, 142
Shihrāzād *see* Shahrazād
Shīrawayh (Shīrōye) 87
Shiraz 45
al-Shirbīnī, Muḥammad 117
al-Shirbīnī, Yūsuf 134
Shīrīn 87
Shīth/Seth 121-3
shubha 'semblance; ambiguity; *bona fides*' 92, 106
Shuʿūbites 38, 50, 56, 60
Sidler, N. 37
sifāḥ 'fornication, illegal cohabitation' 90, 141, 213 n.70
ṣihr 'affinity; relation by marriage' 4, 27, 89, 99-100
Sijistān/Sīstān 44, 75
al-Ṣimma al-Qushayrī 32
Sincere Brethren 25-6
Siyāmī 124
Smith, William Robertson 78-80, 119
Socrates 38, 189 n.20
Solomon/Sulaymān 31, 41, 65
Spooner, Brian 37
Spuler, Bertold 44
Stetkevych, Suzanne Pinckney 143
Strabo 52
Stricker, B. H. 7, 10-12, 37
stuntedness *see ḍawā*
al-Subkī 117
suckling relationship *see raḍāʿ*
Suʿdā bt al-Shamardal 128
al-Suddī 45
Sufyān al-Thawrī 109
Sufyān b. ʿUyayna 101
al-Suhaylī 30
Ṣuhr 144
Sulaymān *see* Solomon
Sulkhāʾ *see* Salkhāʾ
Sumerians 38, 129, 182-3
al-Suyūrī al-Ḥillī 218 n.181
Taʾabbaṭa Sharrā 143, 226 n.97, 227 n.123
al-Ṭabarī, ʿAlī 34
al-Ṭabarī, Muḥammad b. Jarīr 56-8, 74, 84
taboo 5, 10, 24, 78, 87-8, 182-3, 185
Taghlib 131
Tāj Nās bt Qabṭāwīl 169
Tamar 80
Tamīm 31, 50, 52-3, 130
Tamīm b. Ubayy b. Muqbil 79
al-Tanūkhī 146, 152-4, 159, 163, 166
al-Tarmānīnī, ʿAbd al-Salām 20
al-Ṭarsūsī 170
al-Tawḥīdī, Abū Ḥayyān 39-40, 44-7, 50, 52, 59-61, 67-8 ,72
Ṭayyiʾ, Taites 12,53
taʿzīr 'discretionary punishment' 105; *see also* incest, punishment of,
Telephos 58
al-Thaʿālibī 27
al-Thaʿlabī 98, 122-3, 126-7, 144
Thousand and One Nights 3, 158, 160-8, 204 n.126
al-Tibrīzī 71
al-Tīfāshī 182
al-Tijānī 22, 182

Tillion, Germaine 1
Turks 25, 44
ᶜUbayd Allāh al-Mahdī 76
ᶜUbayda b. Rabīᶜa 31
ᶜUdhrite love 24, 26
al-ᶜUfāṭa 53-4
ᶜUmar b. ᶜAbd al-ᶜAzīz 111
ᶜUmar b. Abī Rabīᶜa 32
ᶜUmar b. al-Khaṭṭāb 12-13, 79, 81, 111
ᶜUmar b. Lajaʾ 29
ᶜUmar (b.) al-Nuᶜmān 161-4
ᶜUmāra b. ᶜAqīl 30
Umayya b. ᶜAbd Shams 79
Umm ᶜUbayd bt Ḍamra 84
ᶜUrwa b. Ḥizām 194 n.116
ᶜUrwa b. Udhayna 194 n.116
al-Ushnāndānī 31
al-ᶜUtbī 192 n.75
ᶜUthmān 81
Vajda, G. 124
van der Post, Irma 3
Vikings 39
Vīs *see* Wīs
Wad el-Nimair 172
al-Wāḥidī 92
Waḥshiyya 128
al-Wakīᶜ b. Ḥassān 53
al-Walīd b. Yazīd 66
Walī Allāh, Shāh — al-Dihlāwī 116
al-Wansharīshī 216 n.128
Ward al-Masīḥ 170
Ward Shāh 58
Watt, W. M. 20, 44, 75, 94
Wēhāfrīt *see* Bih-Āfrīd
West, Edward William 36
Westermarck, Edward A. 8, 22-4, 26, 94, 113, 165
Wilde, Oscar 127
Wilken, G. A. 19,78
Wīs and Rāmīn 2, 170, 184-5
Wolf, Arthur P. 23, 27
Xenophon 189 n.20
Yahūdhā/Judah 65
Yaᶜqūb/Jacob 65
Yaᶜqūb b. al-Faḍl 74
al-Yaᶜqūbī 55-6, 121
Yāqūt 60, 80
Yazīd b. Muᶜāwiya 86
Yazīd b. al-Ṭathriyya 128
Yemen 21, 52, 76, 169
Yezdegird II 38
Yūḥābadh/Jochebed 66
al-Zabīdī, Murtaḍā 22
Zād al-Rakb (al-Rākib) 31
Ẓāhirites 90
al-Zamakhsharī 85, 97
zandaqa see *zindīq*, Manichaeans
Zanj 39, 160
al-Zanjānī 117
Zarādusht *see* Zoroaster
Zayd b. ᶜAmr b. Nufayl 79
Zayd b. Ḥāritha 97
Zaynab bt ᶜĀmir 79
Zaynab bt Aws b. Maghrāʾ 129-30
Zaynab bt Jaḥsh 97, 117
Zaynab bt al-Ṭathriyya 128
ẓihār '(formula implying abstention from intercourse with one's wife)' 118-9
zinā 'fornication' 4, 83, 103, 105-7, 109, 120, 213 n.70
zindīq pl. *zanādiqa* 'heretic; Manichaean' 73-4, 76
Ziyād al-Aᶜjam 67, 129
Zoroaster 37, 40-2, 46, 51, 56, 62, 72-3, 121, 124, 202 n.73
Zoroastrians 2, 5, 7-8, 24, 35-77, 93, 100, 105-6, 109-12, 124, 129, 134, 136, 144, 170, 175, 184-5
Zuhūr 170
Zurāra b. ᶜUdus 53, 56